WHAT FORM OF GOVERNMENT FOR THE EUROPEAN UNION AND THE EUROZONE?

What is the form of government of the European Union (EU)? And how is the institutional governance of the Eurozone evolving? These questions have become pressing during the last few years. On the one hand, the Euro-crisis and the legal and institutional responses to it have had major implications on the constitutional architecture of the EU and the Eurozone. On the other hand, the May 2014 elections for the European Parliament and the ensuing struggle to form the European Commission have brought to the fore new tensions in the EU political system. The purpose of this book—which brings together the contributions of EU lawyers, comparative constitutional lawyers and political scientists, from all over Europe and the United States—is to offer a new look at the form of government of the EU and the Eurozone and consider its potential for future development. While offering a plurality of perspectives on the form of government of the EU and the Eurozone, this book emphasises how the euro crisis represents a watershed in the process of European integration, makes the case for a more legitimate and effective form of government for the EU and the Eurozone, and identifies possible windows of opportunity for future treaty reforms. The volume will provide food for thought for scholars, policy-makers and the public at large as they continue debating the most apt form of government for the EU and the Eurozone.

Volume 54 in the Series Modern Studies in European Law

Modern Studies in European Law

Recent titles in this series:

The European Neighbourhood Policy and the Democratic Values of the EU: A Legal Analysis
Nariné Ghazaryan

EU Security and Justice Law: After Lisbon and Stockholm
Edited by Diego Acosta Arcarazo and Cian C Murphy

EU Environmental Law, Governance and Decision-Making
Maria Lee

Shaping the Single European Market in the Field of Foreign Direct Investment
Philip Strik

Nationalism and Private Law in Europe
Guido Comparato

EU Asylum Procedures and the Right to an Effective Remedy
Marcelle Reneman

The Constitutionalization of European Budgetary Constraints
Edited by Maurice Adams, Federico Fabbrini, Pierre Larouche

The EU Accession to the ECHR
Edited by Vasiliki Kosta, Nikos Skoutaris and Vassilis P Tzevelekos

The European Court of Justice and External Relations: Constitutional Challenges
Edited by Marise Cremona and Anne Thies

A Critique of Codification
Leone Niglia

Protecting Vulnerable Groups: The European Human Rights Framework
Edited by Francesca Ippolito and Sara Iglesias Sanchez

EU International Relations Law Second Edition
Panos Koutrakos

Fundamental Rights in the EU: A Matter for Two Courts
Edited by Sonia Morano-Foadi and Lucy Vickers

For the complete list of titles in this series, see 'Modern Studies in European Law' link at www.hartpub.co.uk/books/series.asp

What Form of Government for the European Union and the Eurozone?

Edited by
Federico Fabbrini
Ernst Hirsch Ballin
and
Han Somsen

•HART•
PUBLISHING
OXFORD AND PORTLAND, OREGON
2016

Hart Publishing
An imprint of Bloomsbury Publishing Plc

Hart Publishing Ltd
Kemp House
Chawley Park
Cumnor Hill
Oxford OX2 9PH
UK

Bloomsbury Publishing Plc
50 Bedford Square
London
WC1B 3DP
UK

www.hartpub.co.uk
www.bloomsbury.com

Published in North America (US and Canada) by
Hart Publishing
c/o International Specialized Book Services
920 NE 58th Avenue, Suite 300
Portland, OR 97213-3786
USA

www.isbs.com

First published in hardback, 2015
Paperback edition, 2017

British Library Cataloguing-in-Publication Data
A catalogue record for this book is available from the British Library.

ISBN: PB: 978-1-50991-656-6
HB: 978-1-84946-810-7

Typeset by Compuscript Ltd, Shannon
Printed and bound in Great Britain by by
Lightning Source UK Ltd

Foreword

De la démocratie en Europe

SYLVIE GOULARD

In the town hall of the City of Siena, there is a wonderful *affresco* from the end of the thirteenth century, *Allegoria del buono e del cattivo governo*, painted by Ambrogio Lorenzetti.

At that time, no one would talk about 'output legitimacy' but it is exactly what the paintings represent: they concretely describe the effects of a good and a bad government. On one side of the wall, one can see a prosperous city and a bucolic, fertile countryside. On another wall the painting illustrates the painful and destructive consequences of bad policies. The city is in ruins, business has vanished and the countryside has been transformed into a battlefield.

If the painter were to return to earth today, how would he paint the effects of the European Union's policies?

Peace exists, more than ever before on this continent (at least in its western part), and a certain degree of justice too. But the social environment is not as good as it should be. At the very least, Lorenzetti would have to describe deeply contrasting situations: in some Member States, unemployment remains under control; young people receive training and have individual personal perspectives for the future. Elsewhere, this is not the case for everyone. Throughout Europe growth remains limited, if compared with the United States or other parts of the world.

A certain 'Europe fatigue' is palpable almost everywhere. Anti-European, nationalist parties performed very strongly in several Member States, during the last European elections in May 2014. The turnout remained very low, although the European Parliament has been directly elected for more than 30 years now.

Naturally, the causes of populism are numerous and interlinked. The overly simplistic presentation is that all the woes of all Europeans are the fault of Europe. However, the success of these anti-European, nationalist parties actually has more to do with the weaknesses of the national democracies, as well as broader evolutions such as globalisation. But 'Europe' and 'Brussels' enable the anger to be concentrated. They are increasingly becoming the preferred scapegoat for a multitude of problems, an easy explanation for all the troubles Europe is facing currently.

In contrast, globalisation, and more specifically the rise of new global powers, should bring Europeans to the conclusion that they have to change their scale of reference and to unite quickly. If the EU did not yet exist, this would be the time to invent it: a united, democratic EU which is capable of acting on the world stage. But it is not the case. The decreasing levels of mutual trust and the lack of confidence in the common institutions should be seen as collective failures and need to be tackled seriously and urgently.

We have to ask ourselves why people are so disappointed and, when necessary, to rethink European governance. We have to come back to the '*buon governo*' which the Tuscan painter described beautifully, centuries ago.

That is the reason why this book—collecting the proceedings of a Conference organised at Tilburg Law School on 5 and 6 June 2014 by Federico Fabbrini—is very useful.

The first, obvious, reason for the evident mistrust is that the EU has not always delivered. Many promises have not been kept: Europe does not have a 'common foreign and security policy'. It only talks about it. In front of Putin or some Islamist terrorists, Europe is conceived as weak and disarmed. Europe did not provide all the welfare which was promised and eagerly awaited. In spite of the Lisbon Strategy and the EU 2020 Strategy, we are not 'the most competitive and dynamic knowledge-based economy in the world, capable of sustainable economic growth with more and better jobs and greater social cohesion', as the heads of states and government promised. We have not reduced the number of people 'in or at risk of poverty and social exclusion by at least 20 million'. The euro was meant to be an instrument of prosperity, growth and international influence. It has protected its citizens, but only to a certain extent. It has also contributed to flawed policies, such as unfair tax competition, grave policy mismanagement and easy money. The Single Market is a nice concept on paper but, on the ground, many citizens and businesses experience the lack of implementation and the holes in the level playing field on a daily basis.

The list of unkept promises shows that very often people are actually not complaining about the existence of the EU—as the Eurosceptics argue—but rather about the lack of European action. Citizens frequently blame Europe for not doing what it is actually not allowed to do: the unfinished character of the EU might well be at the core of the current crisis. This, of course, does not mean that everything has to be done at the European level. In an EU of 28 Member States and 507 million inhabitants, it would be absurd. On the other hand, the EU should have the legal and the financial means to do what it is supposed to do. The governments should remember that there is a 'principle of sincere cooperation' enshrined in the Treaties[1] and that 'Brussels' is not the enemy. Some national debates, in the UK on the increase of its contribution to the EU budget for example, or in France and Italy on the control, through the European Commission, of national budgets, show that sincere cooperation is far from being the reality. National leaders use inappropriate tones when referring to the work and responsibilities of the Commission, which acts on the basis of and within the framework of Treaties negotiated and ratified by the Member States.

[1] Art 4(3) TEU.

It is for this reason that some of the proposals currently being made to reduce actions and powers at the European level might actually be irrelevant. To have 'better regulation' is a good goal; the key question is another one however: how can we make sure that the EU can actually act, that it can be heard on the world stage with some credibility? That it can defend our interests and values? The European Central Bank (ECB) is a good example of a European success story. Within just over a decade it has established itself as a respected institution, due to clear-cut powers and a clear mandate.

In other fields action is required. And action requires a more democratic set of rules than the coordination of national governments as well as greatly increased accountability. The role taken by the European Council in the crisis was necessary, under the pressure exerted by the markets, but it is far from satisfactory. It gives announcements, made in the press room for fragmented national public opinions, more weight than necessary. Additionally, it hides the severe lack of follow-up and commitments at the national level. Without ownership in the Member States, the EU cannot be successful.

To rebuild and improve the EU is made more complicated by the fact that the EU of 28 Member States and the Eurozone (which as of January 2015 unites 19 Member States) coexist; we do not only need a multi-level governance (with the vertical integration of regions, states and the European level), we also need horizontal differentiation between the Member States which have made different sovereign choices about their currency, without putting the Union's unity in danger. In this regard, we should try to make a virtue out of necessity.

The pressure to further integrate the Eurozone is irresistible. It can be used as a tool to respond to British concerns, not to say British irrational fears. The 'ever closer union', which the UK dislikes, will take place around the euro, on the continent. The so-called 'banking union', launched in the midst of the crisis, is a good example of a federal step made in a time of rising doubts, not for the beauty of it, but as a result of necessity. The Eurozone needed cleaned up banks. The new powers of the ECB concerning the supervision of national banking sectors are those which the governments refused to give up in 2010 when the European Parliament asked for a better supervision of the banking sector. Sometimes, evolutions are even quicker than one can imagine.

Now is the time for serious reflection and action, and proposals for future action are not lacking.

In 2012, Mario Monti, Italian Prime Minister, and myself wrote a book called *De la démocratie en Europe, voir plus loin*[2] which attempts to contribute an analysis about what went wrong, how can we rebuild trust in European-level democracy and how to find the way to improve peoples' lives?

[2] S Goulard and M Monti, *De la démocratie en Europe, voir plus loin* (Paris, Flammarion, 2012), also published in Italian as *La democrazia in Europa. Guardare lontano* (Milano, Rizzoli, 2012).

Two groups from civil society, in Germany and France, the Glienicker Group and the Eiffel Group have published in 2013/2014 fully fledged proposals on the future of the Eurozone.[3]

These papers do not refrain from tackling hot issues: from the German perspective, the need to have a Eurozone budget, and some financial transfers, in order to make it an optimal currency area. For the French, the necessity of accepting supranational institutions and new, more democratic decision-making processes.

Some proposals also on the table are made by the European Commission[4] and the four Presidents of the European Council, ECB, Eurogroup, and European Commission.[5]

In this context, the arrival of a new Commission, chaired by Jean-Claude Juncker, is also good news. In his speech in the plenary of the European Parliament, in July 2014, the new President was more committed than his predecessor to the euro, stressing the positive reasons, in terms of the Single Market and world influence, why the single currency was born.

Mario Draghi, President of the ECB, also made an important speech in August 2014 in Jackson Hole,[6] stressing the need for another policy mix, combining structural reforms and sound public finances at the national level, with more proactive policies at the European level, in order to tackle low growth, unemployment and the lack of investment.

The Eiffel Group concluded that another set of institutions would be necessary for the Eurozone, not as an end in itself, but to safeguard the trust of the citizens in the political system. The North–South divide has become a source of great mistrust. Berlin is accused of 'hegemony' because it plays, *nolens volens*, a dominant role. Only strong institutions, safeguarding the rights of smaller Member States, building confidence, in the spirit of the 'méthode communautaire', are sustainable.

The Eiffel Group has proposed a working method which could be followed, in this form or an improved one, if a pan-European debate allows, of course.

— An 'optimal Europe', developed with great intellectual rigour, has a greater chance of convincing public opinion than a 'minimal Europe' which is always frustrating, as experience has shown. For approximately two decades governments have chosen to present Europe as a necessary evil whose 'damage' they try to limit, and not as a 'new frontier', to be conquered collectively. Many pro-Europeans voted no in 2005, out of disappointment. Citizens need direction, just as investors and the markets do. Why not refrain from using the term 'Eurozone', and instead use 'Euro Community'? Because the former in

[3] Available at: www.glienickergruppe.eu and www.groupe-eiffel.eu.

[4] European Commission, Communication 'A blueprint for a deep and genuine economic and monetary union, Launching a European Debate' 28 November 2012, COM (2012) 777 final available at: ec.europa.eu/commission_2010-2014/president/news/archives/2012/11/pdf/blueprint_en.pdf.

[5] H Van Rompuy in close collaboration with JM Barroso, J-C Juncker and M Draghi, 'Towards a Genuine Economic and Monetary Union', 5 December 2012 available at: ec.europa.eu/economy_finance/crisis/documents/131201_en.pdf.

[6] Available at: www.ecb.europa.eu/press/key/date/2014/html/sp140822.en.html.

no way reflects the political scope of the project. If the direction is clear and twinned with a clear and respected calendar, then that would already be progress. Each step must be taken in turn.

- Given the magnitude of reluctance, the project must be carefully prepared, firstly straight away within the confines of the current Treaties. The first priority should be to improve the economic and social situation which is causing increased tensions both in the Member States and between them. The question of debt must also be broached, as the modernisation of the 28 economies must be accelerated.
- Ultimately, the creation of a Euro Community would require a new Treaty whose ratification modalities must be decided in advance: it is possible, under international law, to foresee that ratification does not need to be unanimous (in order to avoid the possibility that a tiny minority of the population can take the whole Community hostage) and to prevent Member States who refuse to advance, from blocking others. In a democracy it must remain possible to say no but the consequences of such a rejection must be borne by the country who expressed it, not by its willing partners.
- Furthermore, the tacit consent of Europe's citizens for European integration has ceased. Thus the transition to the Community, just as the subsequent accession of new members, requires a formal democratic procedure, involving all the Europeans concerned. Europe's citizens are weary of adhesion decisions which surreptitiously alter, unbeknown to them, the boundaries of their 'shared destiny'. This is also one of the reasons why the Constitutional Treaty was rejected in 2005.
- If it proves necessary then dual negotiations must be undertaken: those concerning a Treaty for countries who wish to be part of the Euro Community and those for all 28 Member States in order to reform the EU. Two pitfalls must be avoided: any exclusion of countries who wish to progress in good faith, and blackmail by those who wish to prevent others from advancing, without nevertheless accepting the constraints of the euro themselves.

We need '*buon governo*' and *buon governo*, as Siena's *affreschi* remind us, is based on justice. As we look to the future we should remember the lesson portrayed in one of the most beautiful paintings of European culture. We should also be self-confident. This continent has a long history of great achievements and has drawn lessons from its bloody wars; it has developed unique tools with which to organise a peaceful, democratic, supranational governance. Now, it simply has to improve it.

Table of Contents

Part III: Democracy: Representation, Participation and Accountability

Part IV: The Parliamentarisation of the EU and its Critics

Part V: New Institutional Developments

List of Contributors

Carlino Antpöhler is Research Fellow at the Max Planck Institute for Comparative Public Law and International Law, Heidelberg.

Thomas Beukers is Senior Legal Advisor at the Dutch Ministry of Foreign Affairs and Visiting Fellow at the European University Institute.

Christian Calliess is Professor of Public and European Law and holds a Jean Monnet Chair Ad Personam in European Integration at the Faculty of Law, Freie Universität Berlin.

Paul Craig is Professor of English Law, St John's College, Oxford.

Deirdre Curtin is Professor of European Law at the Faculty of Law, University of Amsterdam and Director, Amsterdam Centre for European Law and Governance.

Alexandre de Streel is Professor of European Union Law at the Universities of Namur and Louvain.

Federico Fabbrini is Associate Professor of European and International Law at iCourts (Centre of Excellence on International Courts), Faculty of Law, University of Copenhagen. Previously, he was Assistant Professor of European and Comparative Constitutional Law at Tilburg Law School.

Sylvie Goulard is a Member of the European Parliament, Member of the Economic and Monetary Affairs Committee.

Ernst Hirsch Ballin is Professor of Dutch and European Constitutional Law at Tilburg Law School.

R Daniel Kelemen is Professor of Political Science and holds a Jean Monnet Chair, at the Department of Political Science, Rutgers University, New Brunswick.

Anna Kocharov is PhD candidate at the European University Institute.

Valentin Kreilinger is PhD candidate at Hertie School of Governance, Berlin, and Research Associate at Jacques Delors Institute, Berlin.

Gianni Lo Schiavo is PhD candidate at King's College, London.

Georgios Maris is Tutor in European Political Economy at the School of Economic Sciences and Business, Neapolis University Pafos.

Christian Marxsen is Senior Research Fellow at the Max Planck Institute for Comparative Public Law and International Law, Heidelberg.

Simona Piattoni is Professor of Political Science at the Department of Sociology and Social Research, University of Trento.

Uwe Puetter is Professor in Public Policy at the Central European University (CEU), Budapest and Director of the CEU Center for European Union Research.

Pantelis Sklias is Professor of International Political Economy at the Department of Political Science and International Relations, University of Peloponnese.

Han Somsen is Professor of European Law at Tilburg Law School.

Table of Cases

Court of Justice of the European Union (alphabetical listing)

Court of Justice of the European Union (chronological listing)

Germany

Table of Legislation

European Union

Treaties and Charters

Other EU Instruments

Germany

Table of International Instruments

1

Introduction: A New Look at the Form of Government of the European Union and the Eurozone

FEDERICO FABBRINI,
ERNST HIRSCH BALLIN AND HAN SOMSEN

WHAT IS THE form of government of the European Union (EU)? And how is the institutional governance of the Eurozone evolving? These questions have become pressing during the last few years, as a result of two major constitutional transformations affecting the functioning of the EU.

First, the explosion of the euro crisis has triggered a new round of legal and institutional reforms in the EU which, together with the constitutionalisation of European budgetary constraints,[1] has produced significant changes in the horizontal and vertical allocation of powers within the EU. The European Council—the EU institution congressing the heads of states and government of the EU member states, together with its semi-permanent President, and the President of the European Commission—has emerged as the agenda-setter on how to respond to the crisis.[2] The European Commission has acquired new pervasive powers to police the fiscal policy of the member states, including the authority to demand changes to draft budgetary bills if they substantially deviate from EU deficit and debt rules.[3] At the same time, a new inter-parliamentary assembly has been set up to offer a forum in which representatives from the budget committees of the European Parliament and national parliaments can meet and discuss issues of common concern.[4] And the Treaty on Stability, Coordination and Governance in the Economic and Monetary Union, the so-called Fiscal Compact, has also codified the existence of the Euro Summit—a body grouping the heads of states

[1] See M Adams, F Fabbrini and P Larouche (eds), *The Constitutionalization of European Budgetary Constraints* (Oxford, Hart Publishing, 2014).

[2] See European Parliament Research Service, 'European Council Conclusions: A Rolling Check-List of Commitments to Date', study, 7 October 2014, PE 536.359.

[3] See Art 6 Regulation (EU) 473/2013 of 21 May 2013 of the European Parliament and the Council on monitoring and assessing draft budgetary plans and ensuring the correction of excessive deficits in euro-area Member States [2013] OJ L 140/11.

[4] See Art 13 Fiscal Compact.

and government only of the Eurozone countries[5]—thus reproducing the same duplication existing at ministerial level between the Economic and Financial Affairs (ECOFIN) Council (congressing the ministers of finance of all EU member states) and the Eurogroup (bringing together the ministers of finance of the Eurozone countries) and complicating even further the institutional set-up of the 19-members Eurozone, and its constitutional relationship with the EU of 28 member states.

Second, the elections for the 8th European Parliament in May 2014, with the ensuing process of selection of the European Commission and its President, have unleashed a new dynamic in the EU institutional framework. Exploiting a provision of the Lisbon Treaty,[6] which was not yet in force in the 2009 elections, European political parties decided to bring forward lead candidates for the position of Commission President, agreeing that the political group which would win a majority at the European Parliament elections was entitled to claim the presidency of the Commission.[7] With the right-of-centre European People's Party (EPP) winning a relative majority of seats in the elections,[8] the European Council decided—albeit not without internal resistance—to appoint the EPP *Spitzenkandidat*, Jean-Claude Juncker, as President of the European Commission,[9] and the European Parliament approved him by a vote of its plenary in July 2014.[10] Nevertheless, the pressures to politicise the presidency of the European Commission were somehow tempered by the process of appointment of the College of Commissioners.[11] In common accord with the President-elect, the government of every EU member state nominated a Commissioner,[12] who was then vetted through parliamentary hearings—and the new College of Commissioners was approved as a whole

[5] See Art 12 Fiscal Compact.

[6] See Art 17(7) TEU.

[7] See European Parliament Resolution of 22 November 2012, 'On the Elections to the European Parliament in 2014', P7_TA (2012) 0462, §1 and European Commission Recommendation of 12 March 2013 'On enhancing the democratic and efficient conduct of the election to the European Parliament', (2013)1303 final.

[8] See European Parliament, *Result of the 2014 European Elections*, available at: www.results-elections2014.eu/en/election-results-2014.html.

[9] European Council Conclusions, 27 June 2014, EUCO 79/14, 11 (designating Jean-Claude Juncker as President of the European Commission with 26 heads of states and government in favour, and two against).

[10] European Parliament, Press release, 'Parliament Elects Jean-Claude Juncker as Commission President', 15 July 2014 (reporting vote to elect Jean-Claude Juncker as Commission President with 422 votes in favour, 250 against, and 47 abstentions).

[11] Within the College of Commissioners, then, President Juncker introduced a new hierarchical structure, with vice-Presidents charged to coordinate clusters of Commissioners dealing with specific themes. On this, see Editorial Comment, 'A New Commission Takes Office: On the Relevance of Union Law and the Emergence of Constitutional Conventions' (2014) 51 *Common Market Law Review* 1571.

[12] See Council of the EU, Press Release, 'Council Adopts New List of Commissioners-Candidates', 15 October 2014 (reporting the final list of Commissioners-candidates designated by the Council, in common accord with President-elect Juncker, following the resignation of one of the previous candidates in light of her negative performance during the parliamentary hearings).

in October 2014.[13] At the same time, the European Council directly appointed the High Representatives for the EU Foreign Affairs, who is also one of the Vice Presidents of the European Commission,[14] and unveiled a detailed policy plan which it tasked the new European Commission to carry through during its mandate.[15]

These recent constitutional developments have called for a new scholarly attention on the questions of the governance and institutional design of the EU and the Eurozone. Although with some noteworthy exceptions,[16] the last decade had been characterised by a remarkable dis-engagement by legal scholars from the study of the form of government of the EU. On the one hand, the majority of EU lawyers have traditionally focused their work more on the EU judicial or administrative branches, rather than on the executive and the legislature. The failure of the grand project of the Constitutional Treaty, and the return to old-style intergovernmental negotiations to pass the Lisbon Treaty, fostered this tendency to find refuge in the analysis of the case law of the European Court of Justice, or the decisions of EU administrative agencies, as evidenced by a blossoming literature on fundamental rights, citizenship and regulation.[17] On the other hand, most national constitutional lawyers have culpably omitted the analysis of the EU form of government from their research, treating the EU institutional architecture as a special type of international organisation, unworthy of comparative analysis. Political scientists have performed slightly better, since the attention on the EU institutions has remained at the heart of part of the discipline.[18] Nevertheless, save for a few comprehensive studies, most political science literature has maintained a single-institutional focus, or a self-referential methodological approach, and has been unable to reach a broader audience beyond the specific confines of its discipline.

The purpose of this book is to bring back the topic of the form of government of the EU at the centre of the scholarly analysis—and to offer a new look on the system of governance of the EU and the Eurozone. If it is true—as proclaimed in

[13] European Parliament, Press Release, 'Parliament Elects New European Commission', 22 October 2014 (reporting vote to approve the new College of Commissioners with 423 votes in favour, 209 against, and 67 abstentions).

[14] See European Council Conclusions, 30 August 2014, EUCO 163/14 (appointing Federica Mogherini as EU High Representative for Foreign Affairs).

[15] See European Council Conclusions, 27 June 2014, EUCO 79/14, Annex 1 (setting out a 'Strategic Agenda for the Union in Times of Change').

[16] See, eg P Craig, 'The Locus and Accountability of the Executive in the European Union' in P Craig and A Tomkins (eds), *The Executive and Public Law: Power and Accountability in Comparative Perspective* (Oxford, Oxford University Press, 2006) 315 and D Curtin, *Executive Power of the European Union: Law, Practices and the Living Constitution* (Oxford, Oxford University Press, 2009).

[17] See, eg F Fabbrini, *Fundamental Rights in Europe: Challenges and Transformations in Comparative Perspective* (Oxford, Oxford University Press, 2014); E Hirsch Ballin, *Citizens' Rights and the Right to be a Citizen* (Amsterdam, Brill, 2014); and F Fleurke and H Somsen, 'Precautionary Regulation of Chemical Risks' (2012) 48 *Common Market Law Review* 357.

[18] See, eg J Peterson and M Shackleton (eds), *The Institutions of the European Union*, 3rd edn (Oxford, Oxford University Press, 2012).

the 1789 French Declaration of the Rights of Man and of the Citizen[19]—that a society endowed with a constitution must ensure the protection of fundamental rights and the separation of powers, the question that this book seeks to address is: what kind of separation of power, if any, does the EU, and the Eurozone, have? That is, how does governance work in the EU? And what kind of institutional reform can make the EU institutional system more effective and legitimate to face the challenges of the twenty-first century? To answer these questions, the book has attempted to overcome long-standing cleavages, bringing together a plurality of scholars from several states within the EU and outside it. The result is a volume which combines authors with different backgrounds and competing views. To begin with, the book collects contributions of both EU lawyers and constitutional lawyers, with the aim of emphasising the increasing overlap between these two subjects. Moreover, the book joins the analyses of legal scholars with those of political scientists, on the assumption that the points of contact between these two disciplines are manifold—and that therefore a more explicit interdisciplinary approach to the study of institutional design in the EU should be adopted. Finally, the book breaks another divide, mixing works of both senior and junior scholars on the understanding that new generations of academics are less constrained by the scaffolds of the past, and can provide an enlightening contribution to understanding the new institutional reality of the EU.

The book does not endorse a specific thesis on the form of government of the EU and the Eurozone. In the comparative constitutional law literature the virtues of parliamentary versus presidential governments, and their hybrids, are a matter of constant debate.[20] And scholars of European law and governance disagree on what the EU and the Eurozone has become, and how it should evolve. While several analysts praise the efforts to politicise the presidency of the European Commission by reconnecting it to the elections for the European Parliament,[21] others doubt that this attempt to parliamentarise the EU will succeed, and some even question the wisdom of this development.[22] At the same time, while some scholars have welcomed the recent trends towards the creation of new fora for inter-parliamentary cooperation to supplement the governance of EU affairs,[23] others have raised concerns about this prospect, and rather called for a more consistent empowerment of the European Parliament as the locus of supranational

[19] See Art 16 Déclaration des droits de l'homme et du citoyen [1789] (stating that 'Toute Société dans laquelle la garantie des Droits n'est pas assurée, ni la séparation des Pouvoirs déterminée, n'a point de Constitution').

[20] See generally G Sartori, *Comparative Constitutional Engineering* (New York, New York University Press, 1994) (discussing advantages and disadvantages of alternative forms of government).

[21] See, eg M Maduro et al, 'The Euro-Crisis and the Democratic Governance of the Euro: Legal and Political Issues of a Fiscal Crisis' (Global Governance Programme Policy Report, May 2012).

[22] See, eg H Grabbe and S Lehne, 'The 2014 European Elections: Why a Partisan Commission President would be Bad for the EU' (Centre for European Reform, October 2013).

[23] See, eg B Crum and JE Fossum (eds), *Practices of Interparliamentary Coordination in International Politics: the European Union and Beyond* (Colchester, ECPR Press, 2013).

legitimacy in the European multilevel democratic system.[24] Looming behind this debate about the parliamentary, or inter-parliamentary, system of governance of the EU lays otherwise a growing awareness about the central role acquired by the European Council in EU governance,[25] with signs of a possible presidentialisation of the EU and Eurozone systems of government.[26]

Nevertheless, despite the inevitable divergences in the interpretation of the institutional trends occurring within the EU, large consensus exists on a number of points. To begin with, most observers agree about the fact that the euro crisis constitutes a turning point for the EU, which calls for brave institutional reforms. When the Lisbon Treaty entered into force in December 2009 many predicted that this would be the last attempt to redefine the institutional architecture of the EU in a generation. Yet the ink of the Lisbon Treaty was barely dried when the euro crisis began to extol its effects, opening the door to increasing calls for a redefinition of the constitutional settlement reached after the failure of the Constitutional Treaty. The European Parliament[27] and several national governments[28] have explicitly invoked a renegotiation of the Lisbon Treaty. And although so far the member states have only amended the Treaty at the margins,[29] or concluded new international agreements outside the framework of EU law,[30] the pressure to undertake a more comprehensive overhaul of the EU institutional set-up may not be resisted for much longer. In fact, the euro crisis has upset the original EU institutional balance, but also challenged the relations between the member states.[31] Addressing these problems, which strikes at the heart of the anti-hegemonic nature of the EU integration project,[32] constitutes a necessary step to put the EU back on a sustainable path.

Moreover, agreement exists on the fact that the Eurozone has acquired increasing autonomy vis-à-vis the EU as a whole. Because of the interdependencies generated by the Economic and Monetary Union (EMU), the member states that

[24] See, eg I Pernice et al, *A Democratic Solution to the Crisis: Reform Steps towards a Democratically Based Economic and Financial Constitution for Europe* (Baden-Baden, Nomos, 2012).

[25] See, eg U Puetter, *The European Council and the Council: New Intergovernmentalism and Institutional Change* (Oxford, Oxford University Press, 2014).

[26] See H De Waele and H Broeksteeg, 'The Semi-Permanent European Council Presidency: Some Reflections on the Law and Early Practice' (2012) 49 *Common Market Law Review* 1039.

[27] See also European Parliament Resolution of 2 February 2012 'On the European Council meeting of 30 January 2012', P7-TA(2012)0023, §7 (which '[i]nsists that the contracting parties fully respect their commitment to integrate, within five years at the latest, the Treaty on Stability, Coordination and Governance into the EU treaties and asks for the remaining weaknesses of the Treaty of Lisbon to be tackled on this occasion'.).

[28] See, eg A Merkel, German Chancellor, speech at the German Bundestag, 18 December 2013 (calling for a treaty change to put the Eurozone on stronger footing).

[29] See European Council Decision No. 2011/199/EU of 25 March 2011, amending Article 136 TFEU with regard to a stability mechanism for Member States whose currency is the euro, [2011] OJ L 91 1.

[30] See generally K Tuori and K Tuori, *The Eurozone Crisis: A Constitutional Analysis* (Cambridge, Cambridge University Press, 2014).

[31] See F de Witte and M Dawson, 'Constitutional Balance in the EU after the Euro-crisis' (2013) 76 *Modern Law Review* 817.

[32] See also S Bunse and K Nicolaïdis, 'Large versus Small States: Anti-Hegemony and the Politics of Shared Leadership' in E Jones et al (eds), *The Oxford Handbook of the European Union* (Oxford, Oxford University Press, 2012) 249.

adopt the euro as their currency have been pushed to integrate their policies to an unprecedented degree during the euro crisis. Institutional structures have tracked this development.[33] While the Eurogroup already worked as a coordinating body for finance ministers of the Eurozone member states,[34] the Euro Summit has been created to allow heads of states and government of the Eurozone countries to debate at highest level the future of EMU. At the same time, a new position of President of the Euro Summit has been created, along the model of the presidency of the European Council, to give continuity to the institution and steer its work.[35] And calls have also been made to establish a Eurozone assembly within the European Parliament,[36] thus reproducing also in the latter the same division *ratione monetae* existing in the European Council and the ECOFIN Council. While this last proposal is controversial, there is no doubt that the Eurozone is increasingly endowed of a system of governance which runs parallel to that of the EU. Efforts have so far been made to keep the two systems together—as evidenced by the appointment of Donald Tusk, the former Prime Minister of Poland (a non-Eurozone country) to the posts of both President of the European Council *and* President of the Euro Summit.[37] Nevertheless, the constitutional relationship between an inner, more integrated Eurozone and an outer, more devolved EU will be one of the key challenges for the coming years.[38]

Finally, widespread awareness exists on the need for the EU and the Eurozone to improve its legitimacy. Because decisions taken at EU level increasingly affect the core of national political processes, including choices about taxing, spending, and the welfare state, adequate mechanisms must be put in place so that EU citizens have a voice to choose those who decide at European level, and to hold them accountable.[39] Participatory democracy is certainly important—but it is through the channel of representation, at national and EU level, that new ways to inject the fuel of democracy into the EU engine must be explored.

[33] See JC Piris, *The Future of Europe: Towards a Two-Speed EU?* (Cambridge, Cambridge University Press, 2011).

[34] See U Puetter, *The Eurogroup: How a Secretive Circle of Finance Ministers Shape European Economic Governance* (Manchester, Manchester University Press, 2006).

[35] See Art 12(1) Fiscal Compact.

[36] See, eg Dutch Council of State, report presented upon request for information, on the embedding of democratic control in the reform of economic governance in Europe to combat the economic and financial crisis, by the President of the Senate of the States General, No. W01.12.0457/I, 18 January 2013.

[37] See European Council Conclusions, 30 August 2014, EUCO 163/14 (appointing Donald Tusk as President of the European Council) and Decision of the Heads of State and Government of the Eurozone appointing the President of the Euro Summit, 30 August 2014, Doc. 11949/14 (appointing Donald Tusk as President of the Euro Summit).

[38] See also S Fabbrini, *Which European Union? Europe After the Euro-Crisis* (Cambridge, Cambridge University Press, 2015).

[39] See generally JHH Weiler, 'The Political and Legal Culture of European Integration: An Exploratory Essay' (2011) 9 *International Journal of Constitutional Law* 678 (distinguishing between input legitimacy—ie electoral legitimacy—output legitimacy—ie legitimacy based on the results of EU integration—and Messianic legitimacy—ie the legitimacy deriving from the narrative about the good of EU integration).

The regime of 'executive federalism'[40] emerged to respond to the euro crisis, with the heads of states and governments taking decisions in the European Council and Euro Summit after night-long meetings, has produced a major problem of effectiveness and legitimacy. EU citizens have felt disempowered by a system of governance they perceive as secretive and remote;[41] and the rise of extreme, anti-system parties both in the latest national and at the European elections is a confirmation of it.[42] In this context, there is an urgent need to design strong mechanisms of decision-making which are perceived by all the EU states and citizens as leading to legitimate decision, because they allow for *ex ante* input, and *ex post* accountability. The parliamentarisation of the European Commission along a constitutional logic fusion of powers is a possible option in this regard, but it risks deepening the cleavage between large and small member states.[43] Alternatively the proposal to strengthen the power and legitimacy of the President of the European Council along a constitutional logic of separation of powers should also be considered.[44]

*****

The contributions of this volume individually address these pressing questions and collectively provide a map that can help scholars and policy-makers navigate the complexity of the evolving institutional architecture of the EU and the Eurozone. The book is opened by Sylvie Goulard's Foreword, which contextualises the challenges that the EU and the Eurozone face as far as their system of governance is concerned. In her contribution, which is informed by her experience as a member of the European Parliament—and notably its powerful Economic and Monetary Affairs Committee—but also by her expertise as a scholar—framed in the study of comparative government and European politics—Goulard examines several recent European developments and outlines a way forward for the EU. In particular, Goulard discusses the new process of appointment of the European Commission, the increasing autonomisation of the Eurozone and the growing popular disenchantment towards the EU before making the case in favour of a Euro-Community: in her view, the Eurozone governance should be put on a more solid legal basis, through a separate international treaty, and endowed with a democratic form of government, which empowers citizens to genuinely express

40 J Habermas, *The Crisis of the European Union* (Cambridge, Polity Press, 2012).

41 See D Curtin, 'Challenging Executive Dominance in European Democracy' (2014) 77 *Modern Law Review* 1.

42 See N Scicluna, 'Politicization without Democratization: How the Eurozone Crisis is Transforming EU Law and Politics' (2014) 12 *International Journal of Constitutional Law* 545.

43 See F Fabbrini, 'States' Equality v States' Power: the Euro-Crisis, Inter-State Relations and the Paradox of Domination' (2015) 17 *Cambridge Yearbook of European Legal Studies* 1, 25.

44 See F Fabbrini, 'Austerity, the European Council and the Institutional Future of the EU: A Proposal to Strengthen the President of the European Council' (2015) 22 *Indiana Journal of Global Legal Studies* 29.

their voice. As she masterfully argues with reference to Ambrogio Lorenzetti's *Allegoria del Buon Governo* in Siena's Palazzo Pubblico, Europe is at a crossroads, and decisive steps must be taken to make sure that good government is in place for the Union.

Part I of the book examines how the euro crisis has influenced the form of government of the EU and the Eurozone. The opening chapter by Paul Craig goes right to the heart of the question. It deals with two principal themes concerning the institutional concerns, triggered by the need to respond to the financial crisis: on the one hand the institutional design, on the other hand the constitutional responsibility for the choices thus made. The justification for democracy is that it allows participatory input to determine the values on which people within that polity should live. Here we are confronted with the reality of the complex distribution of power that resulted from hard-fought political battles. In the unfolding financial crisis, intergovernmental solutions came to the forefront. The European Council has taken the lead, but lacks the capacity to deal with the problems in a systematic way as the Commission and the European Central Bank (ECB) can do. Negotiation processes between the larger creditor nations and the debtor states complicate the picture further. Therefore, the focus of future considerations should include the constitutional responsibility of the member states.

In the following chapter, Christian Calliess highlights the intergovernmental nature of the economic coordination in the EU. The dominating role of the European Council in response to the financial crisis amounts to a continuing rejection of the 'Community method' with its dual legitimacy concept. The limited effectiveness of the mechanisms of prevention based on the Articles 125 and 126 Treaty of the Functioning of the European Union (TFEU) came to light when financial markets were betting on a bailout because of the systemic interdependencies between the members of the Eurozone. Calliess recommends confronting this awkward situation—a combination of democratic and technical deficits—with a direct approach: treaty reform, aimed at the establishment of a Fiscal Union, a Banking Union and a genuine Economic Union with appropriate decision-making procedures and technical rules, if necessary by a selective coalition of member states. According to the author, innovative institutional ideas, like the introduction of a Euro-Parliament consisting of members of national parliaments, might pave the way for this constitutional leap forward.

The chapter by Georgios Maris and Pentelis Sklias, instead, considers the implications of the euro crisis on EMU from a political science perspective. As Maris and Sklias maintain, the original design of EMU had been profoundly shaped by the convergence of interest between Germany and France. In their view, moreover, state interests continue to shape the framework of governance and process of reform of EMU. Nevertheless, as the authors acknowledge, the relationship between Germany and France—and between the EU member states more generally—has become increasingly unbalanced, leading to problematic developments in the governance of the Eurozone. Their contribution, which also provides a helpful overview of existing theories of European integration, endorses therefore intergovernmentalism as the key interpretative lens to explain the form of government of the EU, but raises cautionary tales on the sustainability of this mode of governance in the long term.

Part II of the book then focuses specifically on the institutional systems which have emerged during the last few years at EU level to govern *economic*, *monetary* and *banking* policies. In each of these salient areas, the euro crisis has pushed for more integration, creating however complex constellation of powers and responsibilities. Alexandre de Streel takes a highly relevant approach by analysing the decision-making process for the governance of the Eurozone. His chapter includes an overview of the surveillance, the coordination and eventually the corrective procedures including imposition of sanctions, all under the watchful eye of the national and EU courts. Given the political infeasibility of a federalisation, De Streel recommends improving the surveillance and coordination of the national economic policies based on an executive dialogue between national governments, the European Commission and the Council of Ministers. At the same time, he argues that the quality of the surveillance process should be strengthened by the introduction of an EU fiscal agency, separated from the Commission, and a network of national fiscal councils.

In his chapter, Thomas Beukers discusses the changing nature of the fragmented and plural executive power governing the euro, in relationship to the ECB. The interaction between the ECB and political executive bodies is undergoing a metamorphosis, which is illustrated by the conditionality the ECB attached to its readiness, expressed in a letter to the Italian Government in 2011, to buy Italian government bonds. The question is whether this mingling into member states' economic policies is supported by the mandate of the bank. Beukers gives an analysis of the key moments and issues of Eurozone government. As he argues, the scope of the monetary instruments has gradually widened, drawing the ECB into controversial policy considerations concerning structural economic reform. Beukers highlights the constitutional question to what extent accountability of the ECB through participation in relevant Council meetings is acceptable from the viewpoint of national, democratically elected institutions—and suggests that here the independence of the ECB is at stake.

The last chapter of part II, written by Gianni Lo Schiavo, is devoted to a recent, important renewal in the Eurozone governance: the creation of the Single Supervisory Mechanism (SSM). This is one of the elements of the European Banking Union project, next to the Single Resolution Mechanism. As Lo Schiavo explains, the ECB is thus moving into new fields of activities and acquires a full array of powers as the central bank for the Eurozone, and (if they wish) other member states through a close cooperation agreement. The ECB is vested with new powers, for example, to authorise the take up of the business of credit institutions, to require the banks to hold own funds in excess of the capital requirements, to request the divestment of activities that pose excessive risks, and to remove members from the management body. Lo Schiavo also discusses the ensuing delicate relations between the ECB's new supervisory powers and that of the national competent authorities and makes clear that the quality of their cooperation is an important condition for the success of the SSM.

After the analysis on the institutional implications of the euro crisis, part III of the book zooms back, and offers a more theoretical discussion of key concepts concerning the functioning of the EU polity. The contributions of part III, in fact, squarely address the problem of democracy in Europe, analysing its multi-faceted nature as *representation*, *participation*, and *accountability*. In her chapter Simona Piattoni identifies and elaborates the fundamental functions of representation—'voice', 'will' and 'control'—and asks where these functions are performed at national or at EU level, and whether this division of labour is a viable one. According to Piattoni, while the euro crisis has not improved the situation, it has established conditions for a step forward in representative democracy in the EU. While the measures that have been taken have obviously compromised the roles of representative institutions at EU and national levels, they have triggered a response from both national parliaments and the European Parliament to repatriate both 'voice' and 'will'. It is the fact that leaders have been concealing this interdependency from their electorates which Piattoni regards as most damaging for European democracy. Only when this veil is lifted will the European public be in a position to debate and decide about the ways in which they wish to exercise their democratic powers in an interconnected economic and political context.

In the following chapter, Christian Marxsen explores the quest for democracy and legitimacy in the EU through the lens of participatory democracy. Marxsen, in particular, considers (i) participatory measures aiming at horizontal exchange within European society; (ii) participatory measures pursuing vertical exchange between EU institutions and European society; and (iii) the European Citizens' Initiative. While acknowledging that these participatory instruments are to be viewed as supplementary to the conventional avenues of representative democracy, Marxsen undertakes a critical assessment of their current significance and future potential. The yardstick used for that endeavour is whether political actors channel the results into the political process and communicate their conclusions back to society. Marxsen's analysis, however, raises a cautionary tale, suggesting that as practised today the mechanisms of participatory democracy do not contribute to the legitimacy of the European political process. In fact, in many cases, participation is a rhetorical device used to imply that the European political process is more open than it actually is.

In the last chapter of part III, Deirdre Curtin focuses instead on the tensions and sacrifices which the euro crisis has produced in terms of multi-level democratic accountability. To this end, she first seeks to capture the reality of EU executive power in law and in practice. Subsequently, she asks whether, and how, formal and informal modes of accountability to national parliaments and the European Parliament have compensated for the rise of executive power within the EU. Curtin structures her argument by introducing 'information', 'debate' and 'consequence' as distinct stages of accountability. As she explains, working methods and secrecy of the EU executive power can seriously undermine the information stage, albeit to varying degrees and in different ways in different institutions. Limited access to information hampers the stage of debate, particularly for national parliaments, although the fact that the European Council is increasingly doing away with formal documents significantly compromises the position of the European Parliament too. And when it comes to 'consequence' (for example, sanctions), the positions of national parliaments and the European Parliament differ, but in general terms are weak. Given the limited capacity of parliamentary institutions at the national and supranational level to provide accountability, Curtin concludes by outlining a possible agenda for reform—where parliaments change their working practices and start networking to counteract the reality of executive domination.

Building on the contributions of part III, part IV focuses specifically on the trends toward the parliamentarisation of the European Commission triggered by the May 2014 European Parliament elections and the subsequent appointment of the Juncker Commission. The chapter by Daniel Kelemen, which is aptly entitled 'Towards a New Constitutional Architecture in the EU?', provides a complete summary of the events leading towards the appointment of the Juncker Commission and offers a first assessment of their pros and cons. As Kelemen explains, the pressure by the political groups in the European Parliament to advance electoral candidates for the presidency of the European Commission has unleashed a dynamic which the European Council culpably underestimated, and although some member states (such as the United Kingdom) have loudly opposed the *Spitzenkandidaten* game, the process has now succeeded and it will be impossible to revert it in the future. Nevertheless, according to Kelemen, the parliamentarisation of the European Commission is not an unproblematic development. In particular, a parliamentary form of government in the EU is at odds with the logic of separation of powers which has characterised the functioning of the EU so far. Whether the trends towards the parliamentarisation of the Commission should be seen positively or negatively remains therefore an open question.

In their contributions, Carlino Antphöler and Anna Kocharov exemplify the diametrically opposite normative readings that can be given to the process of parliamentarisation of the Commission. While Antphöler welcomes the *Sptizenkandidaten* game as a way to politicise EU decision-making, Kocharov criticises the power grab of the European Parliament as an illegitimate constitutional development. In his chapter, Antphöler draws from the principle of democracy derived from Articles 9 to 12 Treaty on European Union (TEU) to make a normative, abstract case in favour of the politicisation of the European Commission. Antphöler, in particular, posits that, as the role of the Commission has become increasingly depoliticised in the wake of the crisis, the politicisation of the choice of the President of the Commission through the *Spitzenkandidaten* procedure is only proper compensation. Kocharov, instead, reaches the opposite conclusion. In her chapter, she argues that shifting the balance from national parliaments to the European Parliament undermines, rather than enhances, the legitimacy of the process of choosing the President of the Commission. The form in which the political agreement between the Commission and the European Parliament on the

Spitzenkandidat innovation has been couched does not legally amount to an act which can be challenged by the Council before the European Court of Justice even though, substantively, Article 17(7) TEU reserves the power to propose candidates for the presidency to the European Council. In conclusion, Kocharov contends that such a twisting of the selection procedure of the Commission President imperils the impartiality of the Commission, could result in major institutional crises, and replicates at EU level the malfunctions of national democracies against which the EU is supposed to guard.

Part V, finally, focuses on a number of other recent institutional developments which have significantly affected the form of government of the EU and which must be considered as likely candidates for possible future institutional changes. Among these, first and foremost is the role of the European Council, which is at the core of the contribution by Uwe Puetter. In his chapter Puetter explains the constitutional logic for the rise of the European Council as the centre of EU politics: as he argues, since the Maastricht Treaty, the process of European integration has been characterised by a paradox since, on the one hand, member states have been willing to push integration further into new areas of state sovereignty, while, on the other, they have refused to delegate new powers to supranational authorities. In this context, the European Council has acquired a central importance in the governance of the EU, by providing the forum in which member states could coordinate their policies. While the euro crisis may have brought to the surface the growing role of the European Council, as evidenced by its almost daily management of the economic emergency and the responses to it, the institutional change is a deeper, and permanent, one: according to Puetter, the European Council will remain the main political body in the EU system of governance, and the aim to foster deliberation and consensus-building will continue to be the defining feature of the institution.

Whereas the rise of the European Council reflects a trend towards deliberative inter-governmentalism in the EU, the recent years have been characterised also by the attempts to balance this dynamic with increasing inter-parliamentarism. In his contribution Valentin Kreilinger analyses the requirement of the Fiscal Compact to establish an inter-parliamentary assembly on economic and financial affairs, and describes the (modest) steps that have been taken so far to institutionalise this body. By comparing inter-parliamentary cooperation in the field of EMU, with the pre-existing frameworks of inter-parliamentary coordination in the areas of foreign affairs and defence, and of EU policy more generally, Kreilinger provides a comprehensive account of the difficulties encountered to ensure a meaningful cooperation between the European Parliament and national parliaments. Kreilinger maintains that inter-parliamentary cooperation in EMU has a potential role to play in involving legislative branches in the management of the Eurozone. Nevertheless, as he acknowledges, the specific function of such an inter-parliamentary assembly remains somehow uncertain, and it would be unwise to put too much trust (or power) into this institutional forum.

Finally, in his chapter Federico Fabbrini seeks to map the recent calls for a more effective and legitimate form of government for the EU and the Eurozone and to identify the possible opportunities for institutional reform in the near future. As Fabbrini maintains, the euro crisis has empowered the EU heads of state and governments, congressed in the European Council and the Euro Summit. Yet this system of executive federalism has been fraught with problems—not least due to the increasing imbalances it produced in the relationship between the member states. At the same time, recent institutional developments such as the politicisation of the President of the European Commission or the incremental strengthening of the President of the European Council (and Euro Summit), while noteworthy, have not been able to change the status quo. According to Fabbrini, therefore, a revision of the EU treaties is the main road ahead to create a strong, accountable government for the EU and the Eurozone. Nevertheless, he concludes with a note of optimism, pointing out to the fact that the Fiscal Compact requires its contracting parties to incorporate the content of that treaty within the legal order of the EU by 2018, and suggesting that this provides a window of opportunity which should be used to reform the institutional architecture of the EU and the Eurozone through reflection and choice.

The systems of governance of the EU have been evolving quickly since the beginning of the euro crisis—and additional institutional changes may be expected in the future. Our hope is that this volume will provide food for thought to scholars, policy-makers and the public at large as they continue debating about the most apt form of government for the EU and the Eurozone.

Part I

The Euro-crisis and Institutional Change

2

The Financial Crisis, the EU Institutional Order and Constitutional Responsibility

PAUL CRAIG

I. INTRODUCTION

THE FINANCIAL CRISIS is arguably the most significant challenge to the European Union (EU) since the inception of the European Economic Community (EEC). It has generated an array of political, legal and institutional responses the complexity of which is daunting in itself. The current chapter considers these developments, and places them within a broader frame of institutional concerns, thereby facilitating thought about their impact on issues that have been debated more generally within the EU. The analysis has two principal themes: institutional design and constitutional responsibility for the choices thus made. These twin themes are considered in temporal perspective.

The discussion begins with the foundational institutional architecture for EU decision-making, and the debates that this has generated about democracy deficit. There has been a further resurgence of these concerns in the light of the crisis. While this is unsurprising, there is nonetheless a surprising lack of discourse as to responsibility for the status quo, and an equally surprising lack of serious discussion as to how we should think of the constitutional responsibility of Member States, and not just the EU itself, for the current institutional ordering.

The analysis then shifts to the institutional architecture of the Economic and Monetary Union (EMU) laid down in the Maastricht Treaty, with the focus once again on the relationship between the institutional attribution of power, constitutional responsibility for the shaping of these provisions, and the way in which the schema contributed to the subsequent economic malaise. The relationship between this institutional schema and subsidiarity will also be explored.

The penultimate section of this chapter considers the institutional schema that was used to deal with the financial crisis while it unfolded and the extent to which this can be properly portrayed in intergovernmental or supranational terms. The focus in the final section of the paper is on the measures that have been put in place thus far, and the institutional implications that this has had for the balance of power, both vertical and horizontal.

II. EU INSTITUTIONAL DESIGN AND CONSTITUTIONAL RESPONSIBILITY

It is unsurprising that the financial crisis should have brought back to the fore concerns about the very design of the EU's institutional structure and issues of democracy deficit,[1] on which there is already an extensive literature.[2] This is, however, matched by an equal dearth of literature concerning constitutional responsibility of Member States for the status quo. Consideration of the causal influences underpinning Treaty reform has not been matched by attendant analysis of what this should be taken to connote in terms of the constitutional responsibility of Member States for the resultant institutional architecture. This is a serious failing.

The fact that far-reaching measures were enacted pursuant to the Lisbon Treaty, and through treaties such as the Fiscal Compact and the European Stability Mechanism, to cope with the financial crisis, has led to renewed attention on the democratic credentials of the EU. There is already a very considerable body of literature dealing with such matters, and there is no intent to traverse this ground

[1] See, eg D Chalmers, 'Democratic Self-Government in Europe, Domestic Solutions to the EU Legitimacy Crisis' (Policy Network Paper, May 2013); K Nicolaïdis, 'European Demoicracy and Its Crisis' (2013) 51 *Journal of Common Market Studies* 351; S Piattoni (ed), *The European Union: Institutional Architectures and Democratic Principles in Times of Crisis* (Oxford, Oxford University Press, forthcoming); O Cramme and S Hobolt (eds), *Democratic Politics in a European Union under Stress* (Oxford, Oxford University Press, 2014).

[2] See, just in terms of books, S Garcia (ed), *European Identity and the Search for Legitimacy* (London, Pinter, 1993); J Hayward (ed), *The Crisis of Representation in Europe* (Abingdon/New York, Frank Cass, 1995); A Rosas and E Antola (eds), *A Citizens' Europe, In Search of a New Order* (London, Sage, 1995); R Bellamy, V Bufacchi and D Castiglione (eds), *Democracy and Constitutional Culture in the Union of Europe* (London, Lothian Foundation Press, 1995); S Andersen and K Eliassen (eds), *The European Union: How Democratic Is It?* (London, Sage, 1996); R Bellamy and D Castiglione (eds), *Constitutionalism in Transformation: European and Theoretical Perspectives* (Oxford, Blackwell, 1996); R Bellamy (ed), *Constitutionalism, Democracy and Sovereignty: American and European Perspectives* (Aldershot, Avebury, 1996); F Snyder (ed), *Constitutional Dimensions of European Economic Integration* (The Hague, Kluwer, 1996); R Dehousse (ed), *Europe: The Impossible Status Quo* (London, Macmillan, 1997); D Curtin, *Postnational Democracy, The European Union in Search of a Political Philosophy* (The Hague, Kluwer, 1997); P Craig and C Harlow (eds), *Lawmaking in the European Union* (The Hague, Kluwer, 1998); J Weiler, *The Constitution of Europe* (Cambridge, Cambridge University Press, 1999); C Hoskyns and M Newman (eds), *Democratizing the European Union* (Manchester, Manchester University Press, 2000); B Laffan, R O'Donnell, and M Smith, *Europe's Experimental Union: Rethinking Integration* (Abingdon/New York, Routledge, 2000); F Mancini, *Democracy and Constitutionalism in the European Union* (Oxford, Hart Publishing, 2000); K Neunreither and A Wiener (eds), *European Integration after Amsterdam, Institutional Dynamics and Prospects for Democracy* (Oxford, Oxford University Press, 2000); R Prodi, *Europe As I See It* (Cambridge, Polity Press, 2000); K Nicolaidis and R Howse (eds), *The Federal Vision, Legitimacy and Levels of Governance in the United States and the European Union* (Oxford, Oxford University Press, 2001); W van Gerven, *The European Union, A Polity of States and Peoples* (Oxford, Hart Publishing, 2005).

in detail here again. Suffice it to say that the disjunction between power and electoral accountability is the most potent aspect of the democracy deficit argument.[3]

It is axiomatic within national systems that the voters can express their dislike of the incumbent party through periodic elections. Governments can be changed if they incur electoral displeasure. In the EU, legislative power is divided between the Council, European Parliament (EP), and Commission, with the European Council playing a significant role in shaping the overall legislative agenda. The fact that different modes of representation pertain in these institutions is not itself odd, given that this is a standard feature of many federal-type polities.[4] However, in the past the voters have had no direct way of signifying their desire for change in the legislative agenda. European elections can alter the complexion of the EP, but it is only one part of the legislative process. The Council and European Council have input into the legislative agenda, but they cannot readily be voted out by the people, since the electoral accountability that exists operates at national level in relation to each national representative, and not in relation to the respective collective entities. The EP's influence over the choice of the Commission President has increased, as has the electoral accountability of the incumbent to this office, an issue to which we shall return below. Suffice it to say for the present that this alleviates, but does not cure the problem, in part because the other Commissioners remain national government appointees, and in part because the EP's power in this respect does not touch the considerable role played by the Council and European Council in the EU decision-making process.

There have been various attempts to address this concern. For some, such as Moravcsik, the response is to affirm political accountability, notwithstanding the absence of direct electoral accountability analogous to national legal regimes, the argument being that 'constitutional checks and balances, indirect democratic control via national governments, and the increasing powers of the EP are sufficient to ensure that EU policy-making is, in nearly all cases, clean, transparent, effective and politically responsive to the demands of European citizens'.[5] This in turn has been contested by others who regard electoral accountability as central to conceptions of democracy. Checks and balances are indeed part of the standard fare of democratic politics, but the justification for democracy at its most fundamental is

[3] J Weiler, U Haltern and F Mayer, 'European Democracy and its Critique' in J Hayward (ed), *The Crisis of Representation in Europe* (Abingdon/New York: Frank Cass, 1995); A Follesdal and S Hix, 'Why there is a Democratic Deficit in the EU: A Response to Majone and Moravcsik' (2006) 44 *Journal of Common Market Studies* 533; K Nicolaïdis, 'The Idea of European Demoicracy' in J Dickson and P Eleftheriadis (eds), *Philosophical Foundations of EU Law* (Oxford, Oxford University Press, 2012); K Nicolaïdis, 'Our European Demoi-cracy: Is this Constitution a Third Way for Europe?' in K Nicolaïdis and S Weatherill (eds), *Whose Europe? National Models and the Constitution of the European Union* (Oxford, Oxford University Press, 2003).

[4] D Kelemen, *The Rules of Federalism: Institutions and Regulatory Politics in the EU and Beyond* (Harvard, Harvard University Press, 2004).

[5] A Moravcsik, 'In Defence of the "Democratic Deficit": Reassessing Legitimacy in the European Union' (2002) 40 *Journal of Common Market Studies* 603, 621.

that it allows participatory input to determine the values on which people within that polity should live.[6]

It is noteworthy that the discourse concerning democracy deficit is normally presented as a critique of the EU. It is the EU qua real and reified entity that suffers from this infirmity, the corollary being that blame is cast on it. The EU is, of course, not blameless in this respect, but nor are the Member States, viewed collectively and individually. The present disposition of EU institutional power is the result of successive treaties in which the principal players have been the Member States. There may well be debate as to the relative degree of power wielded by Member States and the EU institutions in the shaping and application of EU legislation, but there is greater consensus on the fact that Member States tend to dominate at times of treaty reform.[7] The inter-institutional distribution of power is the result of hard fought battles, the results of which are embodied in Treaty amendment. Thus insofar as the present arrangements divide EU policymaking de facto and de jure between the Commission, Council, EP and European Council, this is reflective of power balances that the Member States shaped and were willing to accept. This is readily apparent when considering the initial Rome Treaty and any of the five major Treaty reforms since then. It is powerfully exemplified by the debates concerning institutional reforms in the Constitutional Treaty, which were then taken over into the Lisbon Treaty.[8] It was evident most notably in the battle as to whether the EU should have a single President who would be located in the Commission, or whether a reinforced European Council should also have a long-term President.[9] It was apparent in the debates as to Council configurations, and who would chair them. It was the frame within which the discourse took place concerning the number of Commissioners and the method of choosing them.[10]

[6] Weiler, Haltern and Mayer, 'European Democracy and its Critique' (n 3); Follesdal and Hix, 'Why there is a Democratic Deficit in the EU?' (n 3).

[7] G Marks, L Hooghe and K Blank, 'European Integration from the 1980s: State-Centric v Multiple-Level Governance' (1996) 34 *Journal of Common Market Studies* 341, 342; T Risse-Kappen, 'Exploring the Nature of the Beast: International Relations Theory and Comparative Policy Analysis Meet the European Union' (1996) 34 *Journal of Common Market Studies* 53; J Golub, 'State Power and Institutional Influence in European Integration: Lessons from the Packaging Waste Directive' (1996) 34 *Journal of Common Market Studies* 313; J Caporaso, 'The European Union and Forms of State: Westphalian, Regulatory or Post-Modern' (1996) 34 *Journal of Common Market Studies* 29, 44–48; F Scharpf, 'The Problem Solving Capacity of Multi-Level Governance' (1997) 4 *Journal of European Public Policy* 520; G Marks, F Scharpf, P Schmitter and W Streeck, *Governance in the European Union* (London, Sage, 1996); A Moravcsik, 'Preferences and Power in the European Community: A Liberal Intergovernmentalist Approach' (1993) 31 *Journal of Common Market Studies* 473; A Moravcsik, *National Preference Formation and Interstate Bargaining in the European Community, 1955–1986* (Harvard, Harvard University Press, 1992); A Moravcsik, 'Negotiating the Single European Act: National Interests and Conventional Statecraft in the European Community' (1991) 45 *International Organization* 19; M Pollack, 'International Relations Theory and European Integration' EUI Working Papers, RSC 2000/55.

[8] P Norman, *The Accidental Constitution, The Making of Europe's Constitutional Treaty*, 2nd edn (Brussels, EuroComment, 2005).

[9] P Craig, *The Lisbon Treaty, Law, Politics and Treaty Reform* (Oxford, Oxford University Press, 2010) ch 3.

[10] ibid chs 2 and 3.

This point can be reinforced by considering the reforms that would be required to alleviate the democratic deficit. The EP has been further empowered by the Lisbon Treaty through extension of what is now the ordinary legislative procedure to new areas, and it has greater control over the appointment of the Commission President than hitherto. Thus, while the European Council retains ultimate power over the choice of Commission President,[11] it will not force a candidate on the EP that is of a radically different persuasion from the dominant party or coalition. A formal linkage between the dominant party/coalition in the EP and the appointment of the Commission President serves to strengthen the connection between policy and party politics, thereby alleviating the disjunction of political power and political responsibility that has underpinned previous critiques of the EU. This link was further strengthened in the 2014 elections for the EP, in which rival candidates for the Commission Presidency campaigned openly as the chosen candidates of the two principal political groupings in the EP. The electoral success of the centre-right European People's Party led to the confirmation of Jean-Claude Juncker as the new Commission President, albeit after opposition from the UK and Hungary. The general consensus is that now that this stronger link between the EP and the Commission President has been forged it will constitute the new status quo going forward, and establish the ground rules for subsequent EP elections. The hope is that it will also increase voter interest in EU elections, since they can perceive a more proximate connection between the casting of their vote, and the policy choices carried forward after the election.

This may well be so in relative terms, but there are nonetheless obstacles that subsist to a closer link between policy and politics in the EU, even after the Lisbon Treaty reforms and changes wrought by the 2014 EP elections. The EU policy agenda is not exclusively in the hands of the EPand/or Commission. The Council and the European Council have input both de jure and de facto. Thus, even if the EP and Commission President are closely allied in terms of substantive policy for the EU, the policy that emerges will necessarily also bear the imprint of the political vision of the Council and European Council. Moreover, while the President of the Commission may well be *primus inter pares*, he or she is still only one member of the Commission team. The other Commissioners will not necessarily be of the same political persuasion as the President or the dominant party in the EP.

It would be possible in theory to have a regime in which the people voted directly for two constituent parts of the legislature, the EP and Council, and for the President of the Commission and the President of the European Council. It would be possible in theory to have the previous package, but only a single elected President for the EU as whole. The political reality is that radical change of this kind has not happened because the Member States were unwilling to accept such a disposition of power. It is certainly true that the choice between two Presidents and a single President for the EU was debated during the negotiations leading to the Constitutional Treaty. It is equally true that discourse concerning the election of

[11] Art 17(7) TEU.

the Commission President began in the 1980s. It should nonetheless be recognised that the broader reforms set out above were not on the political agenda during the extensive negotiations concerning institutional power in 2003 to 2004 during the deliberations that led to the Constitutional Treaty, nor in the subsequent discussions that culminated in the Lisbon Treaty. Even if the broader package of reforms were adopted it could not ensure that the European people would exercise electoral control over the direction of EU policy, since the European Council would still be populated by heads of state, who would continue to have a marked influence over the policy agenda, and members of the Commission, with diverse political views, would still be chosen by the Member States.

There is moreover a Catch 22 lurking here that is both constitutional and political. The constitutional manifestation flows from the realisation that the diminution of state power in the Council and European Council that would be entailed by such change would not be constitutionally tolerated in some countries and would lead to the charge that the EU was truly becoming a super-state. It would be regarded as constitutionally unacceptable in some Member States at least, which would regard such change as undermining the status of the Member States as masters of the Treaty, and instal in its place a federal state that was incompatible with the founding precepts in the constituent documents of those Member States.

The political manifestation of the Catch 22 is equally important. Changes of the kind adumbrated above would be opposed by many national parliaments, as well as national executives, which would not view with equanimity the diminution of their status that flowed from the increased legitimacy of the EU political order. This leads to the further paradox that because such changes that would alleviate the democratic deficit would not prove acceptable to national political orders, the discourse focuses on ever greater ways to involve the national parliaments in decision-making through suggestions of red cards to complement the existing colour set. I am not opposed to involvement of national parliaments in the EU decision-making process. They have a role therein, although its nature and limits are contestable. The implications of proposals for parliamentary red cards would be problematic, and this is a fortiori so for radical proposals that would give individual Member States the power to opt out of legislation that they felt to be unduly burdensome.[12] The apposite point for present purposes is, however, that the very drive for such involvement is premised on the assumption that it will thereby indirectly alleviate the EU's democratic malaise, in circumstances where other ways of attaining this end would be opposed by many national parliamentary institutions.

The political manifestation of the Catch 22 is also apparent in more subtle ways. Thus recent efforts by Martin Schulz and Jean-Claude Juncker to imbue the choice of Commission President with more electoral legitimacy, through direct campaigning combined with televised debate, proved successful in the sense that the candidate of the party that secured most seats in the EP was duly appointed

[12] Chalmers, 'Democratic Self-Government in Europe' (n 1).

as Commission President. This outcome was, however, not certain and some responded by reasserting the formal right for Member States to choose another candidate. The truth of this as a matter of formal treaty law is not open to question. It was rather the almost 'reflexive' reaction in some quarters, whereby shifts towards some greater measure of direct electoral legitimacy provoked a counter reaction reasserting Member State power as exercised through the European Council in the choice of Commission President.

I return then to the inquiry posed earlier, concerning the dearth of consideration of what the current disposition of power means in terms of Member State constitutional responsibility, connoting in this respect both their responsibility qua contracting parties to the EU and the constitutional responsibility they bear in relation to their own constitutional order. I am not referring here to this insofar as it concerns national representatives in the Council, or that of heads of state within the European Council, on which there is indeed considerable discussion. I am referring rather to the way in which we think more generally about the constitutional responsibility of Member States both as contracting parties to the EU, and in terms of their respective constitutional orders. It is the very nature of the obligations that flow from the legal maxim *pacta sunt servanda* that are of interest here. It may be helpful to contrast two perspectives in this regard.

It might be argued that there are no distinctly political obligations that can be cast in terms of Member State constitutional responsibility, and that the legal dimension of *pacta sunt servanda* exhausts the meaning of this precept. It might in this vein be contended that Member States make treaties, and legislation pursuant thereto, out of rational self-interest, maximising their personal benefit, and minimising attendant costs, with the consequence that if they can off-load responsibility for EU difficulties 'elsewhere' they will. Member State constitutional responsibility is regarded as coterminous with legal accountability narrowly construed. The state accepts the consequences of non-compliance with EU legislation, whether cast in terms of state liability in damages, Commission action for breach of EU law, or direct effect of directives. This is, however, conceived for what it is, legal accountability when one breaks the rules. It does not undermine the foundational precept that the state will act as a rational actor seeking to maximise the returns and minimise the costs of EU membership. It is integral to this approach that the state will regard it as politically 'natural' and normatively 'uncontroversial' to offload blame for failures to the EU itself, rather than accept that the states individually or collectively bear responsibility in this regard. The rational state actor as thus conceived describes not only how states behave in relation to the EU, but also sets the normative boundaries for their constitutional responsibility.

Member State constitutional responsibility might, alternatively, be conceptualised more broadly, to include, but also go beyond the limits of, legal accountability. Let us leave aside for the present the issue of how far the picture in the preceding paragraph captures the reality of state behaviour. The salient point for present purposes is that there is no a priori reason why this rationalist version of state action should translate into or dominate thought about the responsibility for state choices conceived in constitutional terms. Indeed, there are very good reasons why it should not, since it thereby denudes the concept of responsibility of almost all meaning, with detrimental consequences more generally for how we conceive of political responsibility. A richer conception of constitutional responsibility flows in part from the obligation of sincere cooperation embedded in the Treaty,[13] and in part from more general precepts of taking responsibility for one's action that should as a matter of principle pertain equally to states as to individuals as a matter of domestic constitutional principle.

The principle of sincere cooperation, whereby it is incumbent on the EU and Member States in full mutual respect to assist each other in carrying out tasks that flow from the Treaties, is central to this alternative vision.[14] So too is the remainder of this Treaty provision, which enjoins the Member States to take any appropriate measure to ensure fulfilment of the obligations arising out of the Treaties, or resulting from acts of the EU institutions, and requires Member States to facilitate achievement of the EU's tasks and refrain from any measure which could jeopardise the attainment of the EU's objectives.[15] This Treaty obligation may provide the foundation for more discrete legal obligations, as exemplified by its deployment in the jurisprudence on state liability in damages.[16] It is, however, integral to this alternative vision that Member State constitutional responsibility is not exhausted by the legal dimension to the principle of sincere cooperation.

It also has a distinctly political dimension that is expressive most fundamentally of the positive side of the maxim *pacta sunt servanda*, irrespective of whether it is capable of being embodied in a legally enforceable norm.[17] Thus the principle of sincere cooperation surely provides the basis for an obligation of political good faith engagement by Member States in ensuring that Treaty obligations are fulfilled efficaciously; the injunction on Member States to take any appropriate measure to ensure fulfilment of Treaty obligations should generate responsibility for states to be proactive in thinking about the best way to achieve Treaty imperatives; and the duty to refrain from behaviour that could jeopardise attainment of EU objectives should provide the foundation for constitutional responsibility not to offload blame onto the EU when this is unwarranted.

What this means most fundamentally is that Member States bear responsibility for the choices that they have made, individually and collectively, in shaping EU decision-making. Thus, insofar as there is a democratic deficit of the kind considered above, responsibility cannot simply be 'offloaded' by the Member States to the EU. Member States cannot carp about deficiencies of EU decision-making as if they were unconnected with the architecture thus created. They cannot moreover

[13] Art 4(3) TEU.

[14] ibid.

[15] ibid.

[16] Cases C-6 and 9/90 *Francovich and Bonifaci v Italy* [1991] ECR I-5357.

[17] What has been termed here the positive side of *pacta sunt servanda* may have legal implications. The point being made here is that even if this is not so there may still be the foundations for political obligation and constitutional responsibility.

criticise aspects of the existing decision-making process as imperfectly democratic, such as the method of representation in the EP, without at the very least being mindful of the fact that they would reject more far-reaching democratic reforms on the ground that they would thereby transform the EU into something more akin to a federal state.

It might be contended by way of response that talk of constitutional responsibility is inapt because individual Member States may disagree with the solutions embodied in the Treaty, but may be pressured to accept them by more powerful states. The legal reality is, however, that the Treaty establishes 28 veto points, given that unanimity is required for Treaty amendment. It can be accepted that in the EU, as with any other collective grouping, there is never going to be parity judged in terms of substantive influence or power, with the consequence that there may be pressure to accept a particular solution. To contend that this can be used to deny any or all constitutional responsibility for the Treaty outcome is nonetheless a non-sequitur. It would mean according states some open-ended trump to excuse them from their ratification of the Treaty amendment, without any inquiry as to the nature of the alleged pressure they were subjected to and without inquiry as to whether they should have withstood it and exercised their veto if they felt that strongly about the issue. The same applies a fortiori in relation to legislation made pursuant to the Treaty. A particular state may well disagree with some aspects of EU legislation enacted pursuant to the ordinary legislative procedure. That is inevitable in a collective entity. However, all states signed up to the rules of the game which include commitment to qualified majority decision-making, not unanimity, in the ordinary legislative procedure. It is, moreover, central to the very idea of collective action that states forego some element of individual choice for the benefit of being part of the club.

Recognition of Member State constitutional responsibility also has broader implications for discourse concerning related issues, such as social legitimacy.[18] Joseph Weiler is surely right that the EU is presently suffering a social legitimacy deficit, manifest in low voter turnout, and the rise of more anti-EU parties.[19] The causes of this deficit are complex, but the failure to articulate any developed conception of Member State constitutional responsibility for their actions, whether concerning the EU's overall decision-making architecture or individual decisions made pursuant thereto, is assuredly a factor in this regard. It should come as scant surprise that such a deficit exists if Member States are allowed to avoid constitutional responsibility for the direct effects of their own actions, and offload blame on to the 'other', even more so when they direct critical barbs at the EU, while being cognizant that they would reject most changes that could address some of the root cause of the critique. It should equally come as no surprise that

[18] See also P Lindseth, 'Power and Legitimacy in the Eurozone: Can Integration and Democracy be Reconciled?' in M Adams, F Fabbrini and P Larouche (eds), *The Constitutionalization of European Budgetary Constraints* (Oxford, Hart Publishing, 2014) ch 18.

[19] JHH Weiler, 'Europe in Crisis—on "Political Messianism", "Legitimacy" and the "Rule of Law"' [2012] *Singapore Journal of Legal Studies* 248.

more extreme parties follow the lead of mainstream parties in this respect, which should not be forgotten when engaging in the political soul-searching for causes of the recent EP election results.

The blame for failure to acknowledge such a conception of responsibility resides not just with the states themselves, but also with the broader community, including the academic community. We should, to be sure, continue to subject the EU political ordering to critical scrutiny. We should in doing so also reflect on the rationale for the current disposition of power, what alternatives are feasible and which players set the limits in this respect. The accepted critical discourse on the EU's political ordering is in reality only telling half the story, thereby ignoring conceptions of Member State constitutional responsibility that are central to a rounded understanding of the status quo and viable reform options. The nature and scope of this constitutional responsibility requires further elaboration. It is important to stress at this juncture that the preceding analysis concerns only the nature of such responsibility as it attaches to the Member States collectively and individually for the overall institutional architecture of the EU.

III. ECONOMIC AND MONETARY UNION, INSTITUTIONAL DESIGN AND CONSTITUTIONAL RESPONSIBILITY

Member State constitutional responsibility is also relevant in relation to the substantive Treaty provisions that frame economic and monetary union. There is little doubt that the EU bears some responsibility for the financial crisis, but so too do the Member States, both collectively and individually. The Treaty provisions on economic and monetary union were crafted in the Maastricht Treaty. Insofar as there was an asymmetry between EU power over monetary as opposed to economic union, this reflected what Member States were willing to accept. This is readily apparent when one considers the architecture of the EMU Treaty provisions and the Stability and Growth Pact.[20]

Monetary union was all about the single currency and the Treaty articles were powerfully influenced by German ordo-liberal economic thought, which demanded independence of the European Central Bank (ECB), governance by experts and the primacy of price stability. These foundational precepts were embodied in the primary Treaty articles.[21] It was integral to the Maastricht settlement that monetary policy was Europeanised. This was reinforced by the Lisbon Treaty provisions on competence, which stated that monetary policy for those countries that subscribed to the

[20] Council Regulation (EC) 1466/97 of 7 July 1997 on the strengthening of the surveillance of budgetary positions and the surveillance and coordination of economic policies [1997] OJ L209/1; Council Regulation (EC) 1467/97 of 7 July 1997 on speeding up and clarifying the implementation of the excessive deficit procedure [1997] OJ L209/6.

[21] Arts 127, 130, 282(3) TFEU.

euro was within the exclusive competence of the EU.[22] This was further strengthened by mandatory Treaty provisions precluding instructions or interference from any outside party, whether that was a nation state or another EU institution.[23]

The Maastricht settlement in relation to economic policy was markedly different. It was built on two related assumptions: preservation of national authority and preservation of national liability. The former was reflected in the fact that Member States retained fiscal authority for national budgets, subject to limited oversight and coordination from the EU designed to persuade Member States, with the ultimate possibility of sanctions, to balance their budgets and not run excessive deficits. The latter, preservation of national liability, was the quid pro quo for the former, which found its most powerful expression in the no bail-out provision.[24] While there was some limited qualification to this precept[25] the message was nonetheless that national governments retained authority over national economic policy, subject to the Treaty rules designed to persuade them to balance their budgets, the corollary being that if they did not do so then the consequential liabilities would remain at the door of the nation state.

Oversight of national economic policy was weakened in subsequent years through Member State unwillingness to subscribe to the rules, which led to their modification, the effect of which was to weaken centralised EU control.[26] The Maastricht 'deal' was nonetheless left largely unaltered in the Lisbon Treaty. The Member States recognised the proximate connection between economic and monetary policy. They understood that the economic health of individual Member State economies could have a marked impact on the valuation of the euro, hence the need for some oversight and coordination of national economic policy. They were, however, mindful of the policy decisions made in and through national budgets, including those of a redistributive nature, and were unwilling to accord the EU too much control over such determinations.

It was only when the financial crisis hit the EU that the Member States were willing to accept that greater control over national economic policy was a necessary condition for monetary union. This led to the plethora of measures enacted to tighten centralised control over national budgets and national banks through the six-pack, the two-pack and the Fiscal Compact. While the EU should properly be held accountable for the way in which it dealt with the financial crisis, the Member States cannot escape responsibility in this regard either. They had a major role in shaping the Maastricht architecture on EMU and determined how it was applied in the years thereafter.

[22] Arts 2(1), 3 TFEU.

[23] Art 130 TFEU.

[24] Art 125(1) TFEU.

[25] Art 122(2) TFEU.

[26] Case C-27/04 *Commission v Council* [2004] ECR I-6649; I Maher, 'Economic Policy Co-ordination and the European Court: Excessive Deficits and ECOFIN Discretion' (2004) 29 *European Law Review* 831; Council Regulation (EC) 1055/2005 of 27 June 2005 amending Regulation 1466/97 [2005] OJ L174/1; Council Regulation (EC) 1056/2005 of 27 June 2005 amending Regulation 1467/97 [2005] OJ L174/5.

There is indeed a certain gentle irony in the fact that the Maastricht Treaty contained the new provisions on EMU and on subsidiarity. The irony does not reside in the fact that the former was legally predicated on the latter. This was, of course, not so in technical legal terms. The Maastricht Treaty embodied the powers on EMU that the Member States were willing to give to the EU. These were contained in the primary Treaty provisions and thus were not themselves subject to subsidiarity, which was designed to determine whether rules would be made at EU level pursuant to the primary Treaty provisions that existed. Subsidiarity as now expressed in Article 5(3) TEU did not therefore bite on the initial choice of what power Member States should give to the EU in relation to EMU. This should not mask the reality that the choice as to what powers Member States were willing to sign over to the EU in relation to economic union was shaped substantively by subsidiarity, in the sense that it was felt right that major decisions concerning fiscal sovereignty should properly remain with the Member States, subject to limited oversight by the EU.

It is here that the irony resides for while subsidiarity may express a powerful and laudable sentiment about the locus of decision-making, the reality is that it can and often does lead to regulatory failure. The EU's financial crisis is testimony to two of the most prominent instances of such regulatory failure which played out in relation to both the sovereign debt and banking crisis. The sovereign debt crisis was causally related to the very weakness of the EU controls over economic policy, which meant that there was insufficient firepower at EU level to stem the tide of sovereign debt or deal with the problem when the dams broke.

The banking crisis was also indicative of the regulatory failure of schemes that leave too much discretion to Member States. In the case of the financial regulatory regime as it existed prior to recent reforms, this was the result of a schema shaped by subsidiarity concerns in the more technical Article 5(3) TEU sense. Subsidiarity can manifest itself in one of three ways: the area may be left to national regulation; or part of the area, such as enforcement, may be left to national regulation; the entire area may be subject to EU regulation but with subsidiarity given voice through discretion left to Member States in relation to various aspects of the policy. The Lamfalussy regime was shot through to varying degrees with subsidiarity in the second and third senses. The post-mortem as to the inadequacy of the EU response to the banking crisis was carried out in the de Larosière Report.[27] The report noted the lack of cohesiveness in EU policy, and concluded that the principal cause stemmed from the options provided to Member States in the enforcement of directives, which was itself the result of the discretion left to Member States by the primary directives that governed the area. The excessive diversity was manifest in, for example, different meanings given to 'core capital', differing degrees of sectoral supervision, diverse reporting obligations, distinct accounting provisions in areas such as pensions, and highly divergent national transposition.

[27] J de Larosière (chair), 'The High Level Group on Financial Supervision in the EU' (Brussels, 2009) paras 102–105.

IV. THE UNFOLDING CRISIS AND THE INTER-INSTITUTIONAL BALANCE OF POWER

There is unsurprisingly debate about the institutional consequences of the measures taken pursuant to the financial crisis, more especially because there is both a vertical and a horizontal dimension to this discourse. These concern respectively relations between Member States and the EU, and the inter-institutional balance of power within the EU itself, although the issue is rendered more complex by the fact that there may be inter-state tensions within the fabric of the EU institutions. It is important in approaching this issue to disaggregate between the institutional consequences as the crisis unfolded and the remedial measures that were taken, and the inter-institutional balance of power going forward, now that many of the key measures are in place. The failure to distinguish the two can lead to conclusions being made concerning the former, followed by implicit assumptions that these will inform the pattern of the latter, which is a non-sequitur.

We can begin, therefore, with the implications of the financial crisis for EU decision-making as the crisis unfolded. Sergio Fabbrini has provided an insightful analysis of this phase.[28] He contends that since the Maastricht Treaty there have been two modes of decision-making embedded in the Treaties: supranational and intergovernmental. The former was applicable to the single market and other areas, with the hallmark being the centrality of the Commission, the ordinary Community method and an important role for the ECJ. The latter was manifest not only in relation to the Second and Third Pillar, but also, albeit somewhat differently, in relation to areas such as economic union, where the hallmark was greater concentration of power in the Council and European Council, no role or a reduced role for the ECJ and substantive Treaty provisions that were couched in less hard-edged terms, as exemplified by those on economic union, where there was much talk of coordination and cooperation.

This Treaty architecture was then replicated in the response to the financial crisis, in the sense that intergovernmental solutions came to the forefront to tackle the unfolding drama. Thus Fabbrini argues that the apex of the intergovernmental moment was reached between 2009 and mid-2012, in which the French and German governments 'converged toward an intergovernmental interpretation of the integration process',[29] in which the EP, Commission and ECJ were sidelined, and decisional power concentrated in the European Council and ECOFIN. This approach was initially championed by President Sarkozy, adopted shortly thereafter by Chancellor Merkel and supported by the UK and Italy. It followed, moreover, that if operative power was to be conceived in this manner then accountability should be primarily to national parliaments, rather than the EP.

Sergio Fabbrini notes the shortcomings of the intergovernmental approach to crisis resolution. These included the 'veto dilemma', connoting in this respect the

[28] S Fabbrini, 'Intergovernmentalism and its Limits: Assessing the European Union's Answer to the Euro Crisis' (2013) 46 *Comparative Political Studies* 1.

[29] ibid 9.

need to ensure consensus before moving forward, with the consequence that European Council intervention was often too little or too late; the 'enforcement dilemma', capturing the difficulty of ensuring that voluntary agreements made outside the strict letter of the Lisbon Treaty would be applied within domestic legal orders; and the 'compliance dilemma', speaking to the difficulties of making sure that parties stick to the rules that they have made. There was moreover a 'legitimacy dilemma' that pervaded the intergovernmental approach, viz the difficulty of securing the legitimacy of decisions reached by ECOFIN and the European Council that had not been discussed or received the imprimatur of the EP. Fabbrini's analysis ends with the pulling back from the intergovernmental approach after mid-2012. There is much in this picture of the institutional response to the unfolding crisis that can be accepted. There are, however, two countervailing considerations that qualify this intergovernmental perspective.

There is the fact that a central remedial response to the financial crisis was the six-pack and the two-pack, which were enacted by the normal legislative procedures as formal regulations and directives. The ideas were generated in part by the Special Task on EU Governance, chaired by President van Rompuy,[30] but the Commission was not excluded from this process. To the contrary, it exercised the right of initiative suggesting the necessary amendments to the Stability and Growth Pact, drafting and piloting them through the legislative process. The measures became law in 2010, and the thinking behind them was already done in 2009. This was moreover a legislative process in which the EP was involved. Now to be sure there was time pressure to get the relevant measures on the statute book, which perforce limited room for EP amendment, but this did not prevent input from the EP in shaping the emergent legislation. It can be accepted that the enactment of these measures did not immediately calm the financial markets, but they were nonetheless central to the shaping of a workable economic union to accompany monetary union. The other countervailing consideration to the intergovernmental perspective is the fact that the single intervention that did more than anything else to calm the financial markets was that of the ECB President, with the statement that he would in effect do whatever it took to save the euro.

Much attention has naturally been focused on the supervisory constraints contained in the Fiscal Compact made outside the confines of the Lisbon Treaty, which exemplified the intergovernmental method. The reality is, however, that it was significantly watered down over its successive amendments, such that there is now very little difference between the supervisory rules contained in the six-pack and two-pack and those in the Fiscal Compact. It remains to be seen moving forward which provides the principal foundation for oversight of national budgets. The Commission is in the driving seat as far as enforcement goes, and its natural preference is to use norms legitimated through the ordinary Lisbon Treaty process. This is for reasons of principle, given that it dislikes 'solutions' crafted outside the formal Treaties, more especially when the results could have been achieved therein; and

[30] See U Puetter in this volume, ch 14.

for more pragmatic reasons, since the modalities of enforcement will normally be clearer in this sphere.

It should, in addition, be recognised that the intergovernmental location of certain of the remedial measures was in a real sense 'contingent' rather than 'principled', in the sense that it reflected political practicalities, rather than being reflective of a desire to proceed independently from the Lisbon Treaty. Thus the Fiscal Compact was not made outside the Lisbon Treaty because the UK had vetoed Treaty amendment. It was made in this way because both Sarkozy and Merkel, albeit for different domestic political reasons, had promised that there would be reform to the primary Treaty, the consequence being that when this was blocked political face had to be saved by making a separate Treaty, notwithstanding that the desired result could have been achieved within the confines of the Lisbon Treaty, and notwithstanding the paradoxical fact that enforcement would have been more secure if this had been done. The ESM took the form of an international treaty outside the confines of the Lisbon Treaty for rather different reasons, these being temporal, viz that it was felt necessary to establish it before the amendment to Article 136 TFEU had come into force.

V. INTER-INSTITUTIONAL BALANCE OF POWER AND NEW LEGAL MEASURES

The EU enacted a plethora of measures to address the financial crisis. They represent a secular triptych, in which the two wing panels consist of measures designed respectively to assist and oversee ailing Member States, while the middle panel is comprised of current and future initiatives that reveal the interconnection between the two wings.[31]

The EU put in place a range of measures to give *assistance* to Member States that were suffering severe economic problems as a result of the Euro-crisis. The most important common element is conditionality, connoting the basic precept that funds are given on strict conditions concerning reforms that must be put in place by the recipient state, with the ESM being the principal mechanism through which such assistance is now secured.[32] The ECB has also played a role in provision of assistance, acting pursuant to Article 127(2) TFEU, both in the form of the securities markets programme, which sanctioned ECB intervention in the Euro-area private and public debt markets,[33] and via the Outright Monetary Transactions (OMTs), which concern transactions in secondary sovereign bond markets 'that aim at safeguarding an appropriate monetary policy transmission and the

[31] P Craig, 'Economic Governance and the Euro Crisis: Constitutional Architecture and Constitutional Implications' in Adams, Fabbrini and Larouche, *The Constitutionalization of European Budgetary Constraints* (n 18) ch 2.

[32] www.esm.europa.eu.

[33] Decision 2010/281/of the European Central Bank of 14 May 2010 establishing a securities markets programme [2010] OJ L124/8.

singleness of the monetary policy'.[34] The legal status of this scheme will be determined by the CJEU in the light of the challenge raised by the German Federal Constitutional Court.

The other wing of the triptych takes the form of *increased supervision* over national financial institutions. Thus the regulatory apparatus for banking, securities, insurance and occupational pensions has been thoroughly overhauled,[35] and new measures have been introduced such as the Single Supervisory Mechanism and the Single Resolution Mechanism, which has increased EU oversight over national banking facilities. There were also major changes designed to increase oversight over national economic policy, because of the proximate connection between economic and monetary union. The driving force behind these changes was to tighten EU control over national economic policy in order to prevent the sovereign debt and banking crises that precipitated the crisis with the euro. The legislative framework for economic union was amended through the 'six-pack' of measures in 2011,[36] which were enacted pursuant to Articles 121, 126 and 136 TFEU.[37] The measures were designed to render economic union more effective by tightening the two parts of the schema, surveillance and excessive deficit, the details of which were contained in the Stability and Growth Pact.[38] Further measures, the two-pack, were enacted on May 21 2013.[39] The rules on oversight over

[34] www.ecb.int/press/pr/date/2012/html/pr120906_1.en.html.

[35] Regulation (EU) 1093/2010 of the European Parliament and of the Council of 24 November 2010 establishing a European Supervisory Authority (European Banking Authority) [2010] OJ L331/12; Regulation (EU) 1095/2010 of the European Parliament and of the Council of 24 November 2010 establishing a European Supervisory Authority (European Securities and Markets Authority) [2010] OJ L331/84; Regulation (EU) 1094/2010 of the European Parliament and of the Council of 24 November 2010 establishing a European Supervisory Authority (European Insurance and Occupational Pensions Authority) [2010] OJ L331/4.

[36] ec.europa.eu/economy_finance/economic_governance/index_en.htm.

[37] Regulation (EU) 1175/2011 of the European Parliament and of the Council of 16 November 2011 amending Regulation (EC) 1466/97 on the strengthening of the surveillance of budgetary positions and the surveillance and coordination of economic policies [2011] OJ L306/12; Council Regulation (EU) 1177/2011 of 8 November 2011 amending Regulation (EC) 1467/97 on speeding up and clarifying the implementation of the excessive deficit procedure [2011] OJ L306/33; Regulation (EU) 1173/2011 of the European Parliament and of the Council of 16 November 2011 on the effective enforcement of budgetary surveillance in the euro area [2011] OJ L306/1; Council Directive 2011/85/EU of 8 November 2011 on requirements for budgetary frameworks of the Member States [2011] OJ L306/41; Regulation (EU) 1176/2011 of the European Parliament and of the Council of 16 November 2011 on the prevention and correction of macroeconomic imbalances [2011] OJ L306/25; Regulation (EU) 1174/2011 of the European Parliament and of the Council of 16 November 2011 on enforcement measures to correct macroeconomic imbalances in the euro area [2011] OJ L306/8; Results of in-depth reviews under Regulation (EU) 1176/2011 on the prevention and correction of macroeconomic imbalances, COM (2013) 199 final.

[38] Council Regulation (EC) 1466/97 of 7 July 1997 on the strengthening of the surveillance of budgetary positions and the surveillance and coordination of economic policies [1997] OJ L209/1; Council Regulation (EC) 1467/97 of 7 July 1997 on speeding up and clarifying the implementation of the excessive deficit procedure [1997] OJ L209/6.

[39] Regulation (EU) 472/2013 of the European Parliament and of the Council of 21 May 2013 on the strengthening of economic and budgetary surveillance of Member States experiencing or threatened with serious difficulties with respect to their financial stability in the euro area [2013] OJ L140/1;

national economic policy analysis were also shaped by the Treaty on Stability, Coordination and Governance,[40] also known as the Fiscal Compact, which was signed by 25 contracting states in March 2012.[41] The provisions concerning assistance and those concerning oversight are 'joined at the hip', in the sense that grant of assistance under the ESM is conditional from 1 March 2013 on ratification by the applicant state of the Fiscal Compact.

The middle panel of the secular triptych comprises the set of measures enacted and proposed that are designed to lay the foundations for *genuine monetary and economic union*. This owes its origins to the Report produced by the President of the European Council in close collaboration with the Presidents of the Commission, ECB and Eurogroup, which may be referred to as the Four Presidents' Report.[42] It was produced at the behest of the European Council,[43] and was endorsed by it in December 2012.[44] The proposals contained a blend of assistance and supervision. Thus some proposals are principally aimed at provision of assistance that will render it less likely that Member States will need to seek help from the ESM. These proposals seek to address national economic vulnerability through 'limited, temporary, flexible and targeted financial incentives'[45] made operational through contractual arrangements between Member States and the EU, which would be mandatory for euro-area Member States and voluntary for other Member States. They also seek to endow the EU with fiscal capacity, the objective being to facilitate adjustment to economic shocks.[46] There is also an oversight/supervisory aspect to the proposals, which finds its expression principally in the proposals for an integrated financial framework, including in this respect what has become the Single Supervisory Mechanism (SSM) and the Single Resolution Mechanism (SRM).

The EU has readily embraced the new supervisory mechanisms, as attested to by the speed with which the SSM and SRM have been moved forward. Progress toward the new assistance mechanisms has been more halting. This may seem paradoxical, given the natural intuition that Member States would be more willing to accept assistance than supervision. The paradox is, however, more apparent

Regulation (EU) 473/2013 of the European Parliament and of the Council of 21 May 2013 on common provisions for monitoring and assessing draft budgetary plans and ensuring the correction of excessive deficit of the Member States in the euro area [2013] OJ L140/11.

[40] P Craig, 'The Stability, Coordination and Governance Treaty: Principle, Politics and Pragmatism' (2012) 37 *European Law Review* 231; S Peers, 'The Stability Treaty: Permanent Austerity or Gesture Politics?' (2012) 8 *European Constitutional Law Review* 404.

[41] Treaty on Stability, Coordination and Governance in the Economic and Monetary Union, 1–2 March 2012, available at: www.european-council.europa.eu/eurozone-governance/treaty-on-stability?lang=en.

[42] H Van Rompuy in close collaboration with J M Barroso, J-C Juncker and M Draghi, 'Towards a Genuine Economic and Monetary Union' 5 December 2012, available at: www.consilium.europa.eu/uedocs/cms_data/docs/pressdata/en/ec/134069.pdf. See also 'A blueprint for a deep and genuine economic and monetary union: Launching a European Debate' COM (2012) 777 final.

[43] www.consilium.europa.eu/uedocs/cms_data/docs/pressdata/en/ec/133004.pdf.

[44] European Council, 13–14 December 2012.

[45] Van Rompuy, 'Towards a Genuine Economic and Monetary Union' (n 42) 7.

[46] ibid 7.

than real. This is because of the nature of the proposed assistance and the way in which it is to be made operational. The logic behind the proposal is in many ways impeccable. If some Member States run persistent economic deficits then this must be because of deeper systemic economic problems with their economy, the response to which is limited, and targeted financial incentives designed to provide assistance, made operational through mutually agreed contracts or something akin thereto that will tailor receipt of the assistance to conditions designed to alleviate the underlying economic malaise. While the logic of the proposal may be impeccable, the effect is that the EU intervenes ever further back into Member State economies, with financial aid conditioned on tackling the economic malaise in accord with the diagnosis reached by the Commission. Member States may be reluctant to allow this degree of intrusion, since the terms will be largely dictated by the Commission. It is, therefore, not surprising that Member States have recently resisted efforts to take this type of initiative forward.

The impact on the inter-institutional balance of power of these enacted measures remains to be seen. Political reality can often belie prognostications made in the advance. We can nonetheless make certain conjectures in this respect, two of which are relatively obvious, but important notwithstanding that.

In vertical terms, the EU constraints on national political action whether in relation to fiscal policy, banking or securities regulation have been significantly increased. The imperative to clear draft national budgets with the EU before being finalised, to ensure that they are independently verified, to meet medium-term financial targets, to do so within a particular time frame and to comply with the European semester, is the direct result of the new legislative schema. The resulting macroeconomic union is unrecognisable from its Maastricht ancestor. These measures to prevent recurrence of sovereign debt crisis go hand in hand with SSM, SRM and the other features of banking union designed to render financial crisis precipitated by bank failure less likely. There is, therefore, no doubt that in vertical institutional terms the EU restraints on national political choice, whether exercised by national executives or parliaments, has increased. The very fact that Member States have been required to put in place measures to comply with their enhanced EU obligations concerning economic union has, however, also meant that national parliaments are able to scrutinise national budgets to a greater extent than hitherto, given that this area has previously been largely regarded as falling within the province of national executives.

In horizontal terms, the duty to ensure enforcement of and compliance with the new raft of measures falls primarily to the Commission and the ECB. It is, inter alia, for this reason that it is important to distinguish between the inter-institutional dimension when the measures were being forged, from the power balance now that they are in place. The European Council may well have played a central role during the former period, but viewed from the latter perspective, the Commission and ECB occupy centre stage. This is readily apparent if one stands back from the principal measures to deal with the crisis. It is the Commission that has a central role in relation to the six-pack, two-pack, ESM and Fiscal Compact, and its role will be even greater if and when other measures are enacted pursuant to the Four

Presidents' Report. The provisions concerning reverse qualified majority voting in the six-pack and the Fiscal Compact are a forceful symbolic and substantive exemplification of this power, but there are numerous other articles in both sets of measures, as well as the ESM, which accord the Commission prominence. Nor should this come as a surprise. The European Council has developed significantly since the Lisbon reforms, as has its support structure. It does not, however, have the institutional capacity of the Commission to engage in the kind of systematic and detailed scrutiny required by the new rules. It may moreover be perfectly content to let the Commission take centre stage in this respect, with the consequence that the latter takes the 'heat' for decisions that will often not be popular at national level. This is more especially so given that the ratchet-effect of increased EU economic oversight with the Commission in the driving seat carries dangers for the Commission itself. Increased power brings increased responsibility. The hard-pressed Commission will have to deliver on a whole series of fronts, which will bring it face to face with domestic political imperatives. It is one thing to write down obligations, whether in treaty provisions, legislation, other international treaties or contracts. It is quite another to enforce them. The ECB responsibilities have also been significantly enhanced in the financial sector.[47]

In intra-institutional terms, there is more room for disagreement as to the consequences of the new regime. It is tempting to think of the larger creditor nations exercising ever-greater dominance over the debtor states, and those that are smaller, within bodies such as the European Council and the Euro group. There may well be some truth in this. We should nonetheless be cautious in this regard, for two related reasons. It is not clear from a temporal perspective whether the degree of such power is really greater than it was hitherto, given that the reality was always that the larger states wielded more power within these institutions. There are equal difficulties in evaluating precisely how the power balance between creditor and debtor nations plays out. It is, of course, true that the latter will be subject to conditionality terms set in part by the former. It should, however, also be borne in mind that the creditor states have foregone for the short term at least funds to aid those states in difficulty, with the opportunity cost consequences that flow from this. The intent is that the assistance assumes the form of loans rather than outright transfers, but whether this reflects reality remains to be seen. To the extent that it does not the opportunity cost of the assistance is all the greater.

VI. CONCLUSION

The financial crisis has, as stated at the outset, shaken the very foundations of the EU and prompted renewed questions about its legitimacy, decision-making and inter-institutional disposition of power. It has, however, also revealed the EU's

[47] Council Regulation (EU) 1024/2013 of 15 October 2013 conferring specific tasks on the European Central Bank concerning policies relating to the prudential supervision of credit institutions [2013] OJ L287/63.

institutional resilience, its capacity to survive and its ability to legislate under stress, as testified by the plethora of measures enacted both within and outside the Treaty in order to meet the immediate dangers posed by the crisis and prevent its recurrence. We should, however, when reflecting on the institutional responsibility for and implications of the crisis do so in a symmetrical and balanced manner. This means thinking hard about the constitutional responsibility of Member States in this regard, rather than working on the explicit or implicit assumption that the fault resides entirely with the EU.

3

The Governance Framework of the Eurozone and the Need for a Treaty Reform

CHRISTIAN CALLIESS*

I. INTRODUCTION

CRISIS? WHAT CRISIS? an album of the pop group Supertramp asked in the seventies, showing a picture of a man enjoying The Sun amongst waste on a dump. This might remind us of the actual situation in the Eurozone: politicians and people lie back and relax in the sunbeams of the Outright Monetary Transactions (OMT) programme of the European Central Bank (ECB). But, apart from the fact that the OMT programme is challenged by a preliminary ruling of the German Federal Constitutional Court to the European Court of Justice (ECJ),[1] the crisis in the Eurozone is still far from being solved. Not least, because the current institutional framework of the Eurozone has proven to be insufficient to prevent or to resolve the financial and economic crises in a sustainable manner. The constitutional setting of the European Treaties was not capable of dealing efficiently and legitimately with the three fundamental issues of the current crisis: the banking crisis, the sovereign debt crisis and the competitiveness crisis, that led to a crisis of European democracy. All three facets of the current crisis mutually reinforced each other and are therefore closely interlinked.

II. DEFICITS IN THE GOVERNANCE FRAMEWORK OF THE EUROZONE

A. Technical Deficits

In the course of the financial and European sovereign debt crisis the weaknesses in the structure of the European Economic and Monetary Union (EMU), which had

* The author wishes to thank his assistant Christopher Schoenfleisch for his helpful support with regard to research and footnotes.

[1] Federal Constitutional Court (FCC) Case 2 BvR 2728/13 (14 January 2014), the preliminary reference is pending at the ECJ as Case C-62/14 *Gauweiler et al.* See also the contributions in the special issue of the *German Law Journal* (2014) 15(2). On the approach of the FCC towards European Integration in general, see W Heun, *The Constitution of Germany* (Oxford, Hart Publishing, 2011) 186 ff.

been repeatedly identified in theory, became apparent. The primary law framework—consisting of a 'communitarised' monetary policy (Articles 127 *et seq* Treaty on the Functioning of the European Union (TFEU)), but at the same time lacking a genuine common economic policy (Articles 120 *et seq* TFEU)—sets expectations which have been met neither by the financial markets nor by the Member States.[2]

Of course, according to Article 3(3) sentence 2 Treaty on the European Union (TEU), the European Union (EU) and its Member States are expected to achieve and to guarantee price stability. According to Article 127(1) sentence 1 TFEU, this is first of all a task of the 'communitarised' monetary policy by the European System of Central Banks; the Member States are supposed to contribute to the maintenance of price stability by avoiding excessive government deficits (Article 126(1) TFEU) within the context of their economic, financial and budgetary policy.[3]

But since the Maastricht Treaty of 1992 did not establish a supranational European economic and fiscal policy compatible with the common European monetary policy, Member States can only *coordinate* their own economic policies within the Council framework (Article 121 TFEU).[4] To bridge this institutional gap Member States agreed on two instruments to defend the stability of the euro.[5] As a first line of defence they established the excessive deficit procedure (Article 126 TFEU) and as a second line of defence they established the so-called 'no-bailout clause' in Article 125 TFEU as a signal to the financial markets.

With regard to the excessive deficit procedure as provided in Article 126 TFEU, doubts have always existed concerning the question of whether it can in fact take care of budgetary discipline in the Member States in political practice.[6] The weakening of the Stability and Growth Pact (SGP) at the instigation of Germany and France in 2005, confirmed this scepticism.[7]

Article 125(1) sentence 2 TFEU basically aims to preclude the liability of a Member State for financial commitments of another Member State. The intention of this clause—together with Articles 123 and 124 TFEU—is to ensure, in case of an increasing government debt, that Member States of the euro area are sanctioned through the financial markets by higher interest rates on their government bonds. That is why no Member State is obliged to be liable for the government debt of any other Member State. Apart from that, the interpretation of the no-bailout clause is

[2] For detail, see C Calliess, 'Finanzkrisen als Herausforderung der internationalen, europäischen und nationalen Rechtsetzung' (2012) 71 *Veröffentlichungen der Vereinigung der Deutschen Staatsrechtslehrer* 113, 129 ff. See also M Adams, F Fabbrini and P Larouche (eds), *The Constitutionalization of European Budgetary Constraints* (Oxford, Hart Publishing, 2014).

[3] M Herdegen, 'Price Stability and Budgetary Restraints in the Economic and Monetary Union: The Law as a Guardian of Economic Wisdom' (1998) 35 *Common Market Law Review* 9.

[4] F Snyder, 'EMU-Integration and Differentiation: Metaphor for European Union' in P Craig and G de Búrca (eds), *The Evolution of EU Law*, 2nd edn (Oxford, Oxford University Press, 2011) 687, 694 ff.

[5] U Häde, 'Die europäische Währungsunion in der internationalen Finanzkrise—An den Grenzen europäischer Solidarität' (2010) 45 *Europarecht* 854, 856.

[6] C Konow, *Der Stabilitäts- und Wachstumspakt* (Baden-Baden, Nomos, 2002) 32 ff.

[7] See C Tomuschat, 'The Euro—A Fortress Threatened from Within' in A Ligustro and G Sacerdoti (eds), *Problemi e Tendenze del Diritto Internazionale dell'Economia. Liber Amicorum in Onore di Paolo Picone* (Napels, Editoriale Scientifica, 2011) 275, 282 ff.

highly controversial amongst legal scholars.[8] Voluntary financial facilities and the allocation of credits in particular are often regarded as not being covered by the no-bailout clause. One may put forward that the wording of the no-bailout clause is anything but clear. But apart from a situation in which the stability of the euro as a whole is threatened, the ratio of Article 125 TFEU requires a strict interpretation. Only if financial facilities for a Member State are comprehensively prohibited can the no-bailout clause serve its purpose to incite Member States to avoid excessive government deficits through higher interest rates on their government bonds. It is also this interpretation that the ECJ gave Article 125 TFEU in its *Pringle* decision.[9]

Nevertheless, the sovereign debt crisis, as well as the competitiveness crisis in the Eurozone, showed that the financial markets' reaction in the cases of Greece and Portugal came much too late. The preventive intention of Article 125 TFEU failed because financial markets with regard to the systemic interdependencies between the members of the Eurozone were betting on a bailout. Not least, the lack of efficient banking supervision has led to a situation where Member States were forced to 'bailout' their national banks and ran into further deficits.

Against this background, it has become obvious that the incentive structures in primary law intending to safeguard the Member States' discipline in budget policy—on the one hand the disciplining through the financial markets as laid down in Article 125(1) TFEU, and on the other hand the mutual monitoring in the excessive deficit procedure (Article 126 TFEU)—were incapable of fulfilling their intended function which was to prevent a systematically relevant excess indebtedness of Eurozone Member States. Furthermore, the mere coordination of national economic policies was incapable of achieving this—due to the existing monetary and economic interdependencies—in a Monetary Union necessary policy adaptation with regard to the common monetary policy of the ECB.[10]

B. The Democratic Deficit

The European Council, and therefore the heads of state and government of the Member States, have become key players in the Eurozone's government debt crisis.

[8] For detail, see C Calliess, 'Perspektiven des Euro zwischen Solidarität und Recht—Eine rechtliche Analyse der Griechenlandhilfe und des Rettungsschirms' (2011) 14 *Zeitschrift für europarechtliche Studien* 213, 256 ff; M Selmayr, 'Die "Euro-Rettung" und das Unionsprimärrecht: Von putativen, unnötigen und bisher versäumten Vertragsänderungen zur Stabilisierung der Wirtschafts- und Währungsunion' (2013) 68 *Zeitschrift für öffentliches Recht* 259, 263 ff; A de Gregorio Merino, 'Legal Developments in the Economic and Monetary Union during the Debt Crisis: the Mechanisms of Financial Assistance' (2012) 49 *Common Market Law Review* 1613, 1625 ff.

[9] Case C-370/12 *Pringle v Government of Ireland, Ireland and The Attorney General*, judgment of 27 November 2012, not yet reported, para 129 ff; for detail, see C Calliess, 'Der ESM zwischen Luxemburg und Karlsruhe' (2013) *Neue Zeitschrift für Verwaltungsrecht* 97, 101–102; see also B de Witte and T Beukers, 'The European Court of Justice Approves the Creation of the European Stability Mechanism Outside the EU Legal Order: *Pringle*' (2013) 50 *Common Market Law Review* 805.

[10] For detail, see D Adamski, 'National Power Games and Structural Failures in the European Macroeconomic Governance' (2012) 49 *Common Market Law Review* 1319, 1320 ff.

One reason for this is the previously mentioned political decision not to establish an efficient—and with the common European monetary policy integrated—European economic and fiscal policy. As a result, Member States can only coordinate their own economic policies within the Council framework (Article 121 TFEU). This mere coordination is combined with a relatively low level of participation of the European Parliament, which does not make joint decisions—as in other areas—but is only informed of decisions made. Therefore, the institutional framework also suffers from a democratic deficit to which I will return later.

Regardless of this contractually agreed coordination, a pure intergovernmental form of coordination developed during the financial and debt crisis—for example, with the rescue packages, the European Financial Stability Facility (EFSF) and the European Stability Mechanism (ESM), and also with the Fiscal Compact.[11] This intergovernmental form of coordination stands far apart from the treaties due to the lack of European powers involved. Although it might be born pragmatically out of necessity, it is problematic in terms of democratic legitimacy if, within its framework, far-reaching decisions are made which create a quasi-liability through the heads of state and government unified under the European Council without the European Parliament having to be involved.

The domineering role of the European Council when it comes to the financial and debt crisis could be interpreted as a sign of rejecting the 'Community method' characterising European integration[12] and the specific 'institutional balance'[13] set out in the European treaties. This 'standard form' of European legislation is based on the sole right of initiative of the Commission, qualified majority voting in the Council, the joint decision-making of the European Parliament, and full judicial control by the ECJ.[14]

Based on the European principle of democracy (Article 10(2) TEU), the Community method reflects the dual legitimacy concept set out in the Treaty. According to this concept, the European Parliament as a representative of the Union and the Council as a representative of the Member States, legitimised by the national parliaments, are equally involved in adopting acts.[15] At the same time,

[11] E Chiti and PG Teixeira, 'The Constitutional Implications of the European Responses to the Financial and Public Debt Crisis' (2013) 50 *Common Market Law Review* 683, 685 ff; K Tuori and K Tuori, *The Eurozone Crisis: A Constitutional Analysis* (Cambridge, Cambridge University Press, 2014); see also generally, M Ruffert, 'Personality under EU Law: A Conceptual Answer towards the Pluralisation of the EU' (2014) 20 *European Law Journal* 346.

[12] *cf* R Dehousse (ed), *The 'Community Method' Obstinate or Obsolete?* (Houndmills, Palgrave Macmillan, 2011).

[13] For detail, see JP Jacqué, 'The Principle of Institutional Balance' (2004) 41 *Common Market Law Review* 383 ff.

[14] See the description in European Commission, 'European Governance—A White Paper' COM (2001) 428 final [2001] OJ C287/6.

[15] K Lenaerts and P van Nuffel, *European Union Law*, 3rd edn (London, Sweet & Maxwell, 2011) para 20-005; see also P Dann, 'The Political Institutions' in A von Bogdandy and J Bast (eds), *Principles of European Constitutional Law*, 2nd edn (Oxford, Hart Publishing, 2010) 237, 267 ff.

the Community method represents the difference between international law and Union law known as supranationalism, defined by primacy of application and direct effect compared with national law in the Member States.[16]

If the Union takes action based on the Community method, this fully corresponds to the concept of dual legitimacy typical of the European principle of democracy. However, insofar as the Member States coordinate their policies in the European Council, the line of legitimacy is lacking in the European Parliament because it is not involved in the decision-making process. Pursuant to the limitation on legitimacy stated in Article 10(2) of the TEU, national parliaments must then offset this and ensure a sufficient level of legitimacy.

Although the political decisions on establishing the 'rescue packages' were made in EU institutions, both the EFSF and the permanent ESM operate on formal intergovernmental agreements outside the European Treaties. As a result, the European Parliament did not contribute to establishing ESM legitimacy. Therefore, it is not only a necessity of the constitutional principle of democracy, but also one of the dual legitimacy set out in Article 10(2) TEU, that national parliaments—in Germany, the *Bundestag* and the *Bundesrat*—make the decisive contribution to legitimacy.[17]

C. Conclusions

In order to resolve the current crisis, and not least to prevent a future crisis, the economic, political and democratic integration of the Eurozone has to be deepened. Addressing all three elements of the current crisis, a renewed European Economic and Monetary Union requires a Fiscal Union, a Banking Union and a genuine Economic Union. From an institutional perspective this means that the Eurozone would need a powerful economic government which is democratically accountable to a Euro-Parliament. If the necessary Treaty amendments do not achieve consensus from all Member States of the EU, a 'Europe of Two Speeds' bringing together a 'Coalition of the Willing' should be an option. In this case, the Eurozone would need a new contractual basis of its own, a Euro-Treaty.[18] A starting point could be the Fiscal Treaty.

[16] R Dehousse, 'The "Community Method" at Sixty' in Dehousse (ed), *The 'Community Method' Obstinate or Obsolete?* (n 12) 3, 4 ff.

[17] For detail, see C Calliess, 'Finanzkrisen als Herausforderung der internationalen, europäischen und nationalen Rechtsetzung' (2012) 71 *Veröffentlichungen der Vereinigung der Deutschen Staatsrechtslehrer* 113, 160 ff.

[18] Parts of the following proposals are part of our proposals in the Glienicker Gruppe, *Towards a Euro-Union* (2013) available at: www.glienickergruppe.de/english.html.

III. FISCAL UNION

The concept of the Maastricht Treaty assumed that common debt rules as well as the no-bailout clause of Article 125 TFEU would solve the problem of irresponsible build-up of debt. Particularly the case of Greece showed this to be a delusion. Therefore, it was a first step to toughen sovereign debt rules with the 'Six-Pack', the 'Two-Pack' and the Fiscal Treaty.

A. First Steps and Deficits

1. *Secondary Legislation*

The 2011 package of secondary legislation (the so-called 'Six-Pack'),[19] consisting of five regulations and one directive reforming and amending the SGP, is intended to counter the deficits and strengthen the discipline in budgetary policy in the Member States.[20] The realignment of the SGP predominantly tries to maintain budgetary discipline through tightened supervision and sanction possibilities regarding the Member States of the Eurozone. With regard to Member States which had already infringed the SGP or which were suffering a crisis, another package of secondary legislation (the so-called 'Two-Pack') was implemented.[21]

However, those instruments, which are additionally based on Article 136 TFEU, push at the legal limits of current primary law. It is therefore crucial to consider the extent to which Article 136 TFEU permits such a deepened surveillance or

[19] Regulation (EU) 1173/2011 of the European Parliament and of the Council of 16 November 2011 on the effective enforcement of budgetary surveillance in the euro area [2011] OJ L306/1; Regulation (EU) 1174/2011 of the European Parliament and of the Council of 16 November 2011 on enforcement measures to correct excessive macroeconomic imbalances in the euro area [2011] OJ L306/8; Regulation (EU) 1175/2011 of the European Parliament and of the Council of 16 November 2011 amending Council Regulation (EC) 1466/97 on the strengthening of the surveillance of budgetary positions and the surveillance and coordination of economic policies [2011] OJ L306/12; Regulation (EU) 1176/2011 of the European Parliament and of the Council of 16 November 2011 on the prevention and correction of macroeconomic imbalances [2011] OJ L306/25; Council Regulation (EU) 1177/2011 of 8 November 2011 amending Regulation (EC) 1467/97 on speeding up and clarifying the implementation of the excessive deficit procedure [2011] OJ L306/33; Council Directive 2011/85/EU of 8 November 2011 on requirements for budgetary frameworks of the Member States [2011] OJ L306/41.

[20] See H J Blanke, 'The European Economic and Monetary Union—Between Vulnerability and Reform' (2011) 1 *International Journal of Public Law and Policy* 402, 408 ff; D Adamski, 'National Power Games and Structural Failures in the European Macroeconomic Governance' (2012) 49 *Common Market Law Review* 1319, 1336 ff.

[21] Regulation (EU) 472/2013 of the European Parliament and of the Council of 21 May 2013 on the strengthening of economic and budgetary surveillance of Member States in the euro area experiencing or threatened with serious difficulties with respect to their financial stability [2013] OJ L140/1; Regulation (EU) 473/2013 of the European Parliament and of the Council of 21 May 2013 on common provisions for monitoring and assessing draft budgetary plans and ensuring the correction of excessive deficit of the Member States in the euro area [2013] OJ L140/11.

sanctioning of the Eurozone Member States among themselves.[22] The main purpose of Article 136 TFEU is to intensify the coordination of the Economic Policy of the Member States in the Eurozone. By stating in Article 121(1) TFEU that the Member States of the Union regard their economic policy as a matter of common concern, they acknowledge the actual economical interdependencies existing between them. Hence a substantive principle of mutual consideration regarding this interdependency, reflecting the general principle of sincere cooperation (Article 4(3) TEU), is added to the procedural concept of coordination.[23] The intensified economic interdependencies between the Eurozone Member States, resulting from the common monetary policy, are reflected in Article 136 TFEU, as this Article increases the level of required consideration for the Eurozone. It thereby clarifies that the methods of cooperation, covered by the concept of coordination, such as mutually informing each other or consulting with each other,[24] are to be enhanced. However, as its wording already clearly shows, the limit of the regulatory intent of Article 136 TFEU is reached when it is used to introduce monitoring systems or sanction provisions, for which Articles 121 and 126 TFEU do not provide any legal basis.[25] As a consequence, the envisaged sanctioning of pre-emptive monitoring in Article 121 TFEU, the macroeconomical monitoring, the need to address statistical data as well as the possibilities of imposing sanctions in the excessive deficit procedure, remain in a legal 'limbo'. As a consequence, a reform of primary law (within the framework of the simplified procedure according to Article 48(6) TEU), seemed reasonable.

2. *The Fiscal Treaty*

However, after the option of a reform of the EU Treaties, which existed prior to the European Council of 9 December 2011, was politically prevented by the British veto, the Treaty on Stability, Coordination and Governance in the Economic and Monetary Union (TSCG), also known as fiscal compact, steps beside the primary law of the EU as an autonomous international treaty.[26] The contracting parties are at least the members of the Eurozone, whereas the Fiscal Treaty is open for all Members of the Union (Article 15 TSCG). This emergency solution is indeed unfortunate. However, such an option in the field of the Monetary Union has

[22] For detail, see M Ruffert, 'The European Debt Crisis and European Union Law' (2011) 48 *Common Market Law Review* 1777, 1793 ff; U Häde, 'Article 136 AEUV—eine neue Generalklausel für die Wirtschafts- und Währungsunion?' (2011) 66 *Juristenzeitung* 333 ff.

[23] *cf* M Schulze-Steinen, *Rechtsfragen zur Wirtschaftsunion* (Baden-Baden, Nomos, 1998) 137 ff.

[24] For detail, see B Braams, *Koordinierung als Kompetenzkategorie* (Tübingen, Mohr Siebeck, 2013) 105–106.

[25] C Ohler, 'Die zweite Reform des Stabilitäts- und Wachstumspaktes' (2010) 25 *Zeitschrift für Gesetzgebung* 330, 338; U Häde, 'Artikel 136 AEUV—eine neue Generalklausel für die Wirtschafts- und Währungsunion?' (2011) 66 *Juristenzeitung* 333, 334 ff.

[26] P Craig, 'The Stability, Coordination and Governance Treaty: Principle, Politics and Pragmatism' (2012) 37 *European Law Review* 231; S Peers, 'The Stability Treaty: Permanent Austerity or Gesture Politics?' (2012) 8 *European Constitutional Law Review* 404.

already been debated, even prior to the SGP.[27] Just as then,[28] the current Treaty caused controversial legal debates.

a. The New Budgetary Rule: A Debt Break?

Title III of the TSCG, which is headed 'fiscal compact', envisages in Article 3(1)(a) that the budgetary position of the general government of the contracting parties shall be balanced or in surplus.[29] In concrete terms, the annual structural budget balance has to be in accordance with the country-specific medium-term budgetary objectives, with a lower limit of a structural deficit of 0.5 per cent of the gross domestic product (GDP), as provided for in the revised SGP (Article 3(1)(b) sentence 1 TSCG). This reference to the SGP reveals that the content of the budgetary rule largely resorts to the country-specific medium-term budgetary objectives already provided in secondary legislation (see Articles 2(a) and 5 of Regulation 1175/2011). Along with this, Articles 5 *et seq.* of Directive 2011/85/EU oblige the Member States to introduce national budgetary rules which guarantee compliance with the reference levels in Article 126 TFEU. The Member States must provide for consequences in case of non-compliance, as Article 6(1)(c) of Directive 2011/85/EU determines. Now, according to Article 5 of Regulation 473/2013, Member States shall establish independent bodies for monitoring compliance with the aforementioned fiscal rules. However, with its 0.5 per cent criterion, Article 3(1)(b) sentence 1 TSCG determines a stricter target for the medium-term budgetary objective, since Article 2(a) of Regulation 1175/2011 leaves greater scope for action of the Member States concerning this matter. The medium-term budgetary objective is therefore not allowed to exceed an annual cyclically adjusted deficit of 0.5 per cent of GDP.

In the event of significant deviations from the medium-term objective or the adjustment path towards it, a correction mechanism is provided (Article 3(1)(e) TSCG). This mechanism is based on common principles proposed by the European Commission,[30] concerning the nature, size and time frame of the corrective action to be undertaken (Article 3(2) TSCG). The correction mechanism complements

[27] *cf* C Konow, *Der Stabilitäts- und Wachstumspakt* (Baden-Baden, Nomos, 2002) 36 ff; see generally, C Herrmann, *Währungshoheit, Währungsverfassung und subjektive Rechte* (Tübingen, Mohr Siebeck, 2010) 202 ff; M Selmayr, *Das Recht der Wirtschafts- und Währungsunion, Erster Band: Die Vergemeinschaftung der Währung* (Baden-Baden, Nomos, 2002) 157 ff.

[28] U Häde, 'Ein Stabilitätspakt für Europa?' (1996) 7 *Europäische Zeitschrift für Wirtschaftsrecht* 138, 140 ff; HJ Hahn, 'Der Stabilitätspakt für die Europäische Währungsunion' (1997) 52 *Juristenzeitung* 1133, 1135; U Hartmann, 'Öffentliche Finanzpolitik in der EU' (1996) 7 *Europäische Zeitschrift für Wirtschaftsrecht* 133, 136.

[29] For detail, see also F Fabbrini, 'The Fiscal Compact, the "Golden Rule" and the Paradox of European Federalism' (2013) 36 *Boston College International and Comparative Law Review* 1, 4 ff; A de Streel, 'EU Fiscal Governance and the Effectiveness of its Reform' in Adams, Fabbrini and Larouche (n 2) 85, 88 ff.

[30] European Commission 'Common principles on national fiscal correction mechanisms' COM (2012) 342 final.

the Council recommendations under the revised SGP.[31] A deviation from the rule of Article 3(1)(b) TSCG may only occur in the exceptional case of an unusual event outside the control of the contracting party or in periods of severe economic downturn (Article 3(1)(c) in conjunction with (3)(b) TSCG).

The contracting parties commit themselves in Article 3(2) TSCG to enshrine the budgetary rule, together with the correction mechanism (the so-called debt brake) in their national legal order, at the latest one year after the entry into force of the Treaty. This shall preferably take place at the constitutional level. However, with regard to referenda necessary for constitutional amendments, especially in Ireland,[32] or the complicated and lengthy constitutional revision procedure, as in the Netherlands, other provisions are sufficient, provided that their unrestricted, permanent observance and compliance is guaranteed throughout the entire national budgetary process.

b. An Automated Excessive Deficit Procedure?

Article 7 TSCG strengthens the process of the excessive deficit procedure for the Member States of the Eurozone. The 'Statement by the Euro Area Heads of State or Government' of 9 December 2011 adopted an ambitious approach, aiming to establish a fully-automated excessive deficit procedure: if the Commission assesses that a State exceeds the 3 per cent criterion the consequences shall be triggered automatically, unless a qualified majority in the Council votes to the contrary.[33] Now the contracting parties commit themselves in Article 7 TSCG only to support proposals and recommendations by the Commission, where they consider that a Eurozone Member is in breach of the deficit criterion. However, this obligation does not apply when a qualified majority of the contracting parties whose currency is the euro is opposed to the decision made by the Commission. In concrete terms, two different interpretations of this clause seem possible.[34] In view of the statement by the heads of state and government, Article 7 TSCG could be interpreted in a way that grants the Commission's recommendations legally binding effect, unless a qualified majority votes to the contrary. Such an interpretation would

[31] *cf* Art 6 Regulation (EU) 1175/2011 of the European Parliament and of the Council of 16 November 2011 amending Council Regulation (EC) 1466/97 on the strengthening of the surveillance of budgetary positions and the surveillance and coordination of economic policies [2011] OJ L306/12; Art 4(1), (2) Regulation (EU) 1173/2011 of the European Parliament and of the Council of 16 November 2011 on the effective enforcement of budgetary surveillance in the euro area [2011] OJ L306/1.

[32] For details of the Irish Implementation, see R O'Gorman, 'An Analysis of the Method and Efficacy of Ireland's Incorporation of the Fiscal Compact' in Adams, Fabbrini and Larouche (n 2) 273.

[33] See Statement by the Euro Area Heads of State or Government, Brussels 9 December 2011, 4: 'As soon as a Member State is recognised to be in breach of the 3% ceiling by the Commission, there will be automatic consequences unless a qualified majority of euro area Member States is opposed.'

[34] I Pernice, 'International Agreement on a reinforced Economic Union', Legal Opinion of 8 January 2012, 10 ff, available at: www.whi-berlin.eu/EU-Reform_2012.html. Note that the legal opinion is based on the outdated wording of Art 7 of the Treaty ('undertake to support'). The final version is 'commit to supporting'.

have a significant impact on the excessive deficit procedure in Article 126 TFEU, particularly since the Council would no longer have to constitutively declare the existence of an excessive deficit in advance (as is the case in the current legal status).[35] By contrast, the coherence clause of Article 2 TSCG expresses the will of the contracting parties to apply the provision only in accordance with the procedural steps of the contractual excessive deficit procedure. Against this background, Article 7 TSCG cannot intend more than to bind the contracting parties in respect of their voting behaviour in the Council.[36] The reverse qualified majority can then repeal this obligation.

Moreover, the scope of Article 7 TSCG is limited in two respects: First, the wording itself only concerns those votes in the Council which follow the proposal of the Commission, where a Member State of the Eurozone is held to be in breach of the *deficit criterion* and therefore to determine an excessive deficit. Thus the intention of the revised SGP, which was meant to upgrade the *debt criterion* putting it on one level with the deficit criterion, is not realised in Article 7 TSCG. Secondly, the provision does not affect the subsequent stages of the excessive deficit procedure,[37] particularly not regarding the imposition of sanctions according to Article 126(11) TFEU.

Article 7 TSCG therefore contributes to the streamlining of the excessive deficit procedure in a rather modest manner and for this reason falls far short of an automatic procedure. Nevertheless, the provision is still consistent with the realisation of the objectives of the Union and therefore does not contradict the coherence clause and the principle of sincere cooperation (Article 4(3) TEU).

c. Conclusions

Contrary to the public perception, the new TSCG does not imply a European 'Fiscal Union'. A common EU-shaped economic, financial and budgetary policy is at most rudimentary. In particular, there are no new competences established at the European level. Also the provisions on the economic policy coordination (Article 9 TSCG) have a rather limited ability to meet the existing economical interdependencies within the Monetary Union. In the end, the Fiscal Treaty predominantly operates with the same instruments as the secondary law, notably the 'Six-Pack' and the 'Two-Pack'. The TSCG also demonstrates the limits of the 'emergency solution' using international law, which—because of the non-application of Article 48 TEU and the non-participation of all EU Member

[35] ibid 11.

[36] See also A Dimopoulos, 'The Use of International Law as a Tool for Enhancing Governance in the Eurozone and its Impact an EU Institutional Integrity' in Adams, Fabbrini and Larouche (n 2) 41, 53.

[37] But here the reverse majority voting under the 'Six-Pack' does apply, for detail, see R Palmstorfer, 'The Reverse Majority Voting under the "Six Pack": A Bad Turn for the Union?' (2014) 20 *European Law Journal* 186; H Rathke, '"Umgekehrte Abstimmung" in der Fiskalunion: neue Stabilitätskultur oder halbautomatischer Vertragsbruch?' (2012) 65 *Die Öffentliche Verwaltung* 751.

States—cannot lead to a modification of primary law.[38] Consequently, the Union principle of sincere cooperation (Article 4(3) TEU) as well as the primacy and unity of Union law set necessary limits to the TSCG in the interest of EU law and the so-called Community method.[39]

The TSCG could therefore not initiate the great leap forward in the direction of a 'Fiscal Union', which removes the asymmetrical distribution of competences within the framework of the EMU. As a result, it has more of a symbolic significance than a legal one.

However, it cannot be excluded that it may become the initial point for a deepened integration of the Eurozone towards a 'Fiscal Union', because the TSCG expresses the strong will of the Member States to preserve and to strengthen the Eurozone, despite all of its deficiencies. With the Treaty, necessary attempts are made to secure the monetary stability of the Union (*Stabilitätsunion*) demanded by European and constitutional law.[40] These are, in turn, compulsory requirements for the solidarity practised in the context of the ESM within the Eurozone.[41] This solidarity cannot and may not represent a one-way street.[42] This is emphasised by the wording of Article 136(3) TFEU, which explicitly allows emergency aids as an exception to the no-bailout clause in Article 125 TFEU only on condition that reforms are implemented in the recipient country, which in return has to bring its budget back in line with the EU guidelines on stability.

B. Further Steps Towards a Fiscal Union by Treaty Reform

Against this background, it still remains doubtful whether all these measures increase the effectiveness of the surveillance of the existing budgetary commitments, especially the prevention of excessive general government deficits in a sufficient and sustainable manner. Therefore, the above reforms might not be the final answer to the financial and debt crisis,[43] since the completion of the SGP through secondary legislation, with its more severe sanctioning of the deficit-monitoring,

[38] F Schorkopf, 'Finanzkrisen als Herausforderung der internationalen, europäischen und nationalen Rechtsetzung' (2012) 71 *Veröffentlichungen der Vereinigung der Deutschen Staatsrechtslehrer* 183, 208 ff.

[39] D Thym, 'Einheit in Vielfalt: Binnendifferenzierung der EU-Integration' in A Hatje and P-C Müller-Graff (eds), *Enzyklopädie Europarecht, Band 1: Europäisches Organisations- und Verfassungsrecht* (Baden-Baden, Nomos, 2014) para 5, recital 87 ff.

[40] FCC, Case BVerfGE 89, 155 Maastricht, judgment of 12 October 1993, para 148.

[41] See generally, V Borger, 'How the Debt Crisis Exposes the Development of Solidarity in the Euro Area' (2013) 9 *European Constitutional Law Review* 7.

[42] For detail, see C Calliess, 'Perspektiven des Euro zwischen Solidarität und Recht—Eine rechtliche Analyse der Griechenlandhilfe und des Rettungsschirms' (2011) 14 *Zeitschrift für europarechtliche Studien* 213.

[43] See the proposals in President of the European Council, 'Towards a Genuine Economic and Monetary Union', 5 December 2012, www.consilium.europa.eu/uedocs/cms_data/docs/pressdata/en/ec/132069.pdf; Commission, 'A blueprint for a deep and genuine economic and monetary union: Launching a European Debate', 30 November 2012, COM (2012) 777 final/2; see also M Ruffert, 'Mehr Europa—eine rechtswissenschaftliche Perspektive' (2013) 28 *Zeitschrift für Gesetzgebung* 1.

together with the reverse majority voting procedure, lies on the outer edge of what is legally possible on the basis of current primary law, even in light of Article 136 TFEU.[44] And the Fiscal Treaty as a 'Treaty on Stability, Coordination and Governance in the Economic and Monetary Union' set expectations of which it has substantially fallen short.

Apart from the crisis mechanisms, the necessary amendment of the Monetary Union through a Fiscal Union requires a European-shaped national economic, financial and budgetary policy. In the multilevel constitutionalism of the EU this implies that the national competences will remain, but need to be vastly better interlocked with binding European guidelines combined with a more effective monitoring and surveillance resulting from this.[45] The latter especially applies with regard to those Eurozone Member States whose budgetary policy is failing the stability criteria to such an extent that financial assistance from the ESM becomes necessary.

A starting point for this reform could be the so-called 'European Semester'.[46] But, as explained above, neither the relevant secondary legislation nor the Fiscal Treaty have established the possibility of legally binding interventions in national budgets. Although the 'Two-Pack' has given the Commission the right to ask for a revision of the draft budgetary plan,[47] the review of the Commission still is not legally enforceable. Therefore, a European concept of intervention in the national budget has to be established.[48] Given the fact that such legally enforceable instruments of intervention possibly interfere with the budgetary autonomy of national parliaments,[49] they have to be arranged with view to the principle of proportionality.[50] Therefore, graduated rights of intervention in the national budgetary autonomy may be possible:

— As long as Member States comply with their obligations under the common debt rules, only legally non-binding recommendations are possible (as it is the case *de lege lata*).
— If a Member State, however, violates the stability criteria, it must be possible to make legally enforceable stipulations of how much the State has to save—but the State will keep the specific decision of where to save.

[44] *cf* C Antpöhler, 'Emergenz der europäischen Wirtschaftsregierung. Das Six Pack als Zeichen supranationaler Leistungsfähigkeit' (2012) 72 *Zeitschrift für ausländisches öffentliches Recht und Völkerrecht* 354, 369 ff; J Bast and F Rödl, 'Jenseits der Koordinierung? Zu den Grenzen der EU-Verträge für eine Europäische Wirtschaftsregierung' (2012) 39 *Europäische Grundrechte-Zeitschrift* 269.

[45] See also H Geeroms, W Moesen and S De Corte, 'The EU at a Crossroads: An Action Plan' (Centre for European Studies, Policy Brief, October 2011).

[46] KA Armstrong, 'The New Governance of EU Fiscal Discipline' (2013) 38 *European Law Review* 501.

[47] *cf* Art 7 Regulation (EU) 473/2013 of the European Parliament and of the Council of 21 May 2013 on common provisions for monitoring and assessing draft budgetary plans and ensuring the correction of excessive deficit of the Member States in the euro area [2013] OJ L140/11.

[48] *cf* Commission, 'A blueprint for a deep and genuine economic and monetary union. Launching a European Debate' 30 November 2012, COM (2012) 777 final/2, 26 f.

[49] For Germany see the case law of the FCC Case BVerfGE 123, 267 Lisbon, judgment of 30 June 2009, para 256; Case BVerfGE 129, 124 EFSF, judgment of 7 September 2011, para 125 ff.

[50] For detail, see C Calliess, 'Die Reform der Wirtschafts- und Währungsunion als Herausforderung für die Integrationsarchitektur der EU' (2013) 66 *Die Öffentliche Verwaltung* 785, 788–89.

— Only if a Member State is dependent on financial assistance from the ESM would concrete legally enforceable recommendations be possible. In a case like this it is only fair to ask to what extent a Eurozone Member State that receives money from the ESM (or a future EMF) has already lost its budget autonomy: an over-indebted Member State can ultimately only choose between a sovereign default or recourse to financial assistance of the ESM. The recipient State, therefore, autonomously agrees to a limitation of its budgetary sovereignty, when deciding to receive financial assistance from the ESM. This is even more true when the conditions serve the objective of guaranteeing compliance with the (legally binding) stability criteria. Against this background, a legally enforceable budgetary veto right on the EU level regarding the respective national draft budget can hardly be assessed as an interference with the parliament's budget sovereignty, when the only alternative is a sovereign default. In this case national budget autonomy has already been lost. Therefore, legally enforceable EU rights of intervention cannot infringe budgetary sovereignty. In such a situation, specific European provisions regarding the national draft budget, particularly on the expenditure and the revenue side, are imaginable. This approach corresponds with the conditionality established by virtue of the new Article 136(3) TFEU, enshrined in the Treaties with regard to the ESM, but also with the *Pringle* decision of the ECJ with regard to the legal conformity of EFSF and ESM in view of the no-bailout clause of Article 125 TFEU.[51]

IV. BANKING UNION: WITH OR WITHOUT TREATY REFORM?

However, it is also true that the crisis would not have been prevented by the Fiscal Treaty itself in countries like Spain and Ireland. The fiscal risks that piled up in those countries were ultimately caused by excessive private sector debt.[52] Whether the indebtedness is public or private, it becomes a problem for the monetary union only if private creditors do not write off their losses on their own account, but socialise them. But that is exactly what happened: the debts of financial institutions and of banks in particular, were socialised. The banks were able to do this, because they knew that their systemic importance would give the European taxpayer no choice but to save them.

To put a stop to this game once and for all, the Eurozone needs a robust Banking Union. A single banking supervisor must ensure that the banking sector has a solid capital base and a common bank restructuring and resolution mechanism must make creditors accountable: if banks suffer large losses, shareholders must first make good the loss, followed by subordinated bondholders, senior creditors, and

[51] On conditionality, see also, M Ioannidis, 'EU Financial Assistance Conditionality after "Two Pack"' (2014) 74 *Zeitschrift für ausländisches öffentliches Recht und Völkerrecht* 61; M Schwarz, 'A Memorandum of Misunderstanding—The Doomed Road of the European Stability Mechanism and a Possible Way Out: Enhanced Cooperation' (2014) 51 *Common Market Law Review* 389.

[52] Sachverständigenrat zur Begutachtung der gesamtwirtschaftlichen Entwicklung, 'Chancen für einen stabilen Aufschwung' (2010) Jahresgutachten 2010/2011, para 126.

lastly the bank funds financed by the banks themselves. Only when these options have been exhausted, should there be resort to the European taxpayer.

These aspects were part of a complex reform agenda beginning with the establishment of the EFSF.[53] The main task of the newly created European supervisory agencies is the coordination of the national authorities in order to ensure consistent supervisory practices. Regarding systematically relevant banks the EFSF has now been complemented by a Single Supervisory Mechanism (SSM) which is situated at the ECB.[54] The SSM was established by a Regulation based on Article 127(6) TFEU.[55] The latest political compromise was reached in December 2013 concerning the Single Resolution Mechanism (SRM) and the Single Resolution Fund (SRF).[56] The Financing of the SRF was not only politically highly controversial, it also caused serious legal doubts about whether Article 114 TFEU as the proposed legal basis is sufficient to establish the fund. In the end, the decision was reached to create an Intergovernmental Agreement (IGA) as a legal basis for the Fund complementing the SRM Regulation which is based on Article 114 TFEU. In case of the SRM—contrary to the ESM or the Fiscal Treaty—EU law is complemented by international law in an area of shared competences, the internal market (Article 4(2)(a) TFEU). The scope of the competences of the EU is therefore crucial for the legality of using international law. Only if Article 114 TFEU (perhaps in conjunction with Article 352 TFEU) does not provide a sufficient legal basis for the establishment of the SRF, are Member States free to use international law. Otherwise, the envisaged co-decision of the European Parliament could be circumvented. In the light of the previous considerations, the judiciary of the ECJ does indeed confirm the establishment and financing of independent agencies based on Article 114 TFEU.[57] But probably the intended financing of the estimated €55 billion SRF via nationally raised contributions is qualitative and quantitative beyond the scope of this judiciary. Therefore, from a legal point of view, it may have been advisable to either apply Article 114 TFEU in conjunction with Article 352 TFEU, or Article 352 TFEU alone.[58] However, this was rejected on political grounds.

[53] N Kohtamäki, *Die Reform der Bankenaufsicht in der Europäischen Union* (Tübingen, Mohr Siebeck, 2012).

[54] For detail, see E Ferran and V Babis, 'The European Single Supervisory Mechanism' (2013) 13 *Journal of Corporate Law Studies* 255; A Thiele, *Finanzaufsicht. Der Staat und die Finanzmärkte* (Tübingen, Mohr Siebeck, 2014) 519 ff; JA Kämmerer and P Starski, 'Die Europäische Zentralbank in der Bankenunion oder: Vor Risiken und Nebenwirkungen wird gewarnt' (2013) 28 *Zeitschrift für Gesetzgebung* 318.

[55] Since Art 127(6) TFEU only allows 'specific tasks' to be conferred upon the ECB this was strongly criticised. For details, see B Wolfers and T Voland, 'Europäische Zentralbank und Bankenaufsicht—Rechtsgrundlage und demokratische Kontrolle des Single Supervisory Mechanism' (2014) 14 *Zeitschrift für Bank- und Kapitalmarktrecht* 177.

[56] For the political debate, see D Howarth and L Quaglia, 'The Steep Road to European Banking Union: Constructing the Single Resolution Mechanism' (2014) 52 *Journal of Common Market Studies* 125.

[57] ECJ, Case C-217/04 *United Kingdom v Parliament and Council* [2006] ECR I-3771; Case C-270/12 *United Kingdom v Parliament and Council*, judgment of 22 January 2014, not yet reported.

[58] In legal scholarship it is controversial whether in fact Art 352 TFEU should be applied in conjunction with another competence norm, see M Rossi in C Calliess and M Ruffert (eds), *EUV/AEUV.* Das Verfassungsrecht der Union mit Europäischer Grundrechtecharta, 4th edn (Munich, CH Beck, 2011) Art 352 AEUV, para 68.

V. ECONOMIC UNION

In a renewed Eurozone national budgetary responsibility, as established by the Fiscal Union, and European solidarity should go hand in hand. Situations in which a Member State suffers an acute liquidity emergency and is forced to enact so-called 'austerity measures' on its population should remain exceptional. A genuine Economic Union should therefore aim to prevent such developments. A possible way to prevent such extremes might be to establish a Eurozone Insurance Mechanism to cushion the fiscal consequences of a dramatic economic downturn. The Eurozone could, for example, establish a common unemployment insurance system, to complement national systems.[59] All Member States which organise their labour markets in line with the needs of the Monetary Union and the Fiscal Union could be eligible for participation. This would create a mechanism to counteract deep recessions with automatic European stabilisers. Thus, the macroeconomic cohesion of the euro area could be strengthened and the integration of the European labour market accelerated.

Complementary to the no-bailout clause in Article 125 TFEU, relying only on the corrective of the financial markets by the so-called spreads,[60] more efficient precautionary measures with regard to prevent a crisis must be introduced. In view of a sovereign default with all its systemic consequences for the Eurozone and the international financial markets, it is of particular importance to provide an instrument which has a deterrent effect beforehand and at the same time a stabilising effect in the worst-case scenario. With that aim, the ESM could be developed into a European Monetary Fund (EMF),[61] which—together with the EU institutions (especially the Commission)—could be equipped with the aforementioned rights of intervention in the national budgets. Moreover, the EMF should be able to initiate the insolvency of a bankrupt Eurozone Member State. Following this, an institutionalised sovereign default should be added to the Monetary Union.[62] On that basis, an EMF could grant time-limited credits in the case of the absence of debt sustainability in order to secure, with regard to the financial stability, a structured insolvency of the Eurozone Member State concerned.

[59] See L Andor, 'Basic European Unemployment Insurance—The Best Way Forward in Strengthening the EMU's Resilience and Europe's Recovery' (2014) 49 *Intereconomics* 184; H Enderlein, 'Solidarität in der Europäischen Union—Die ökonomische Perspektive' in C Calliess (ed), *Europäische Solidarität und nationale Identität* (Tübingen, Mohr Siebeck, 2013) 83.

[60] Regarding the market failures, see C Calliess, 'Finanzkrisen als Herausforderung der internationalen, europäischen und nationalen Rechtsetzung' (2012) 71 *Veröffentlichungen der Vereinigung der Deutschen Staatsrechtslehrer* 113, 129 ff.

[61] See D Gros and T Mayer, 'How to deal with sovereign default in Europe: Create the European Monetary Fund now!' CEPS Policy Brief No 202/February 2010, updated 17 May 2010; U Häde, 'Legal Evaluation of a European Monetary Fund' (2010) 45 *Intereconomics* 69.

[62] See generally, A Krueger, *A New Approach to Sovereign Debt Restructuring* (Washington, International Monetary Fund, 2002); A von Bogdandy and M Goldmann, 'Sovereign Debt Restructurings as Exercises of International Public Authority: Towards a Decentralized Sovereign Insolvency Law' in C Espósito, Y Li and JP Bohoslavsky (eds), *Sovereign Financing and International Law* (Oxford, Oxford University Press, 2013) 39.

VI. INSTITUTIONAL REFORMS LEADING TO A NEW TREATY

In dealing with the crisis, the heads of state and government have so far played the leading role. Against this background it is not surprising, that the institutional setting of the Fiscal Treaty is arranged around the (European) Council.

A. The Fiscal Treaty as a Starting Point?

In the course of the international financial and debt crisis, a new political body, the so-called Euro Summit, emerged at the European level. Apart from the heads of state and government of the Eurozone, the President of the Commission as well as the President of the ECB are invited to attend the meetings that take place at least twice a year. This former de facto body became increasingly institutionalised, first based on political statements[63] and now formally recognised by the Fiscal Treaty (see Article 12 TSCG). The European Parliament, as well as those contracting parties whose currency is not the euro, are informed about these meetings (Article 12(5), (6) TSCG). However, the non-Eurozone Member States, which have ratified the Treaty, take part in those summits that are dedicated to fundamental issues regarding the competitiveness of the contracting parties or the global architecture of the Eurozone. Furthermore, they are invited to debates on specific issues of the implementation of the Fiscal Treaty at least once a year (Article 12(3) TSCG). Despite the fact that the Euro Summit has given itself formal Rules of Procedure,[64] it is considered by the contracting parties to be an informal meeting (Article 12(1) TSCG). Its ambivalent status resembles that of the so-called Euro Group, the meeting of the euro finance ministers, which although formally affirmed by Article 137 TFEU has likewise remained an informal meeting.[65]

Although the heads of state and government of the Eurozone are free to meet informally, the effects of these meetings on the institutional set-up of the EU are hardly predictable. In this respect, the history of the European Council serves as a vivid example of how informal bodies evolve[66] and their influence on the contractually provided decision-making procedures (Community method).[67] The participation of the President of the ECB in the meetings of the Euro Summit

[63] European Council—23 October 2011—Conclusions, EUCO 52/1/11, REV 1, CO EUR 17, CONCL 5, Brussels 30 November 2011, 5; Euro Summit Statement, Brussels, 26 October 2011, Annex 1.

[64] Available at: www.eurozone.europa.eu/summits.

[65] See U Puetter, 'Informal Circles of Ministers: A Way Out of the EU's Institutional Dilemmas?' (2003) 9 *European Law Journal* 109.

[66] *cf* C Calliess, *Die neue Europäische Union nach dem Vertrag von Lissabon* (Tübingen, Mohr Siebeck, 2010) 118 ff; P Dann, 'The Political Institutions' in A von Bogdandy and J Bast (eds), *Principles of European Constitutional Law*, 2nd edn (Oxford, Hart Publishing, 2010) 237, 261 ff.

[67] See C Calliess, 'Der Kampf um den Euro: Eine "Angelegenheit der Europäischen Union" zwischen Regierung, Parlament und Volk' (2012) 31 *Neue Zeitschrift für Verwaltungsrecht* 1; see generally, D Schwarzer, 'The euro area crisis, shifting power relations and institutional change in the EU', Paper prepared for the Dahrendorf Symposium, 9–10 November 2011 (on file with author).

could also raise problems with regard to the independence of the Central Bank (Article 130 TFEU).

The Fiscal Treaties implementation involves using the the Commission as an institution. According to previous practice, Member States can make use of EU institutions outside the legal framework of the EU provided that all Member States of the EU agree.[68] In the case of the Fiscal Treaty such consensus of all Member States was lacking due to the British veto. But with respect to the parallel 'Six-Pack' and 'Two-Pack' legislation it is questionable whether the Fiscal Treaty confers any new competences on the Commission at all. In fact, one can say that the powers provided in the Fiscal Treaty largely correspond with the Commission's role under EU primary and secondary law.[69] In addition, in its *Pringle* decision the ECJ acknowledged the use of EU institutions outside the legal framework of the EU regarding the involvement of the Commission and the ECB under the ESM Treaty.[70] The Court stated that:

> Member States are entitled, in areas which do not fall under the exclusive competence of the Union, to entrust tasks to the institutions, outside the framework of the Union … provided that those tasks do not alter the essential character of the powers conferred on those institutions by the EU and FEU Treaties'.[71]

Applying this doctrine to the Fiscal Treaty one can hardly notice an alteration of the *essential character* of the Commission's powers. The Fiscal Treaty rather confirms the role of the Commission under the 'Six-Pack' and 'Two-Pack' legislation.

The role of the ECJ, which is based on Article 273 TFEU, is also interesting. The plan to make the Luxemburg Court responsible for the compliance-control of the budgetary rules[72] would not only have been problematic with regard to Article 126(10) TFEU but also have minimal effect given the limited role of courts in such complex processes. Therefore, the ECJ was only entrusted to pass judgments on the implementation of the budgetary rule and debt brake (Article 3(2) TSCG) within the national legal orders. Article 8(1) TSCG provides that the Commission is invited to report on the provisions adopted by each of the Member States in compliance with their duties in Article 3(2) TSCG. If the European Commission, after having given the contracting party concerned the opportunity to submit its observations, concludes that an infringement has occurred, the matter will be

[68] For detail, see D Thym, *Ungleichzeitigkeit und europäisches Verfassungsrecht* (Baden-Baden, Nomos, 2004) 194 ff.

[69] For detail, see C Calliess, 'From Fiscal Compact to Fiscal Union? New Rules for the Eurozone' (2012) 14 *Cambridge Yearbook of European Legal Studies* 101.

[70] See also S Peers, 'Towards a New Form of EU Law?: The Use of EU Institutions outside the EU Legal Framework' (2013) 9 *European Constitutional Law Review* 37; P Craig, '*Pringle* and Use of EU Institutions outside the EU Legal Framework: Foundations, Procedure and Substance' (2013) 9 *European Constitutional Law Review* 263.

[71] Case C-370/12 *Pringle v Government of Ireland, Ireland and The Attorney General*, judgment of 27 November 2012, not yet reported, para 158.

[72] *cf* Statement of Chancellor Merkel prior to the European Council of 8–9 December 2011, German Federal Parliament, Pl.Prot. 17/147, 2 December 2011, 17570.

brought to the ECJ by one or more contracting parties. However, the formulation of Article 8(1) sentence 2 TSCG itself does not give an answer to the question of who has to exercise this duty in a specific case. Only a protocol to the Treaty, which was concluded on 2 March 2012 on the occasion of the signing of the contract, lays down the details. According to the protocol, the action must generally be filed by the Council Presidency (Article 16(9) TEU) within a period of three months after the submission of the Commission's report. According to Article 8(2) TSCG, if the Commission or the contracting parties are convinced that another contracting party has not complied with the judgment of the ECJ, the contracting parties may bring the case back to the ECJ and request the imposition of financial sanctions.

B. A New Institutional Design for the Eurozone by a Treaty Reform

The Fiscal Treaty made interesting steps into a special governance of the Eurozone outside the EU Treaty. It is a first step into a new institutional arrangement between a possible Euro-Treaty and the EU. Apart from the fact that it also shows the legal and practical problems of a two-speed Europe,[73] its institutional design is not up to the tasks that need to be carried out by a Fiscal and Economic Union.

The Eurozone—inside or outside the Union Treaty—needs a European executive capable of acting. An economic government should not have an intergovernmental character based on the model of the ECOFIN or the Euro-Summit. Instead, it should be established as part of the European Commission. It could be comprised of its President and five Commissioners, that deal with the relevant policy fields (for example, the Commissioners for the Monetary Union, the Internal Market, for Trade and Financial Stability). The Economic Government should have the competence to negotiate reform packages and conclude bilateral agreements with Member States undertaking structural reforms,[74] it should decide on bank closures, and it should ensure the provision of public goods by proposing legislation with regard to the Fiscal and Economic Union. Together with the above-mentioned EMF it could be equipped with the graduated instruments of intervention in national budgets described above.

Moreover, the Economic Government needs a budget to finance a growth fund with which it can support structural reform processes in those Member States that concluded a bilateral agreement. In principle, it would be possible to finance this budget through taxation. But compared to the present, rather limited, tax-raising

[73] For detail, see JC Piris, *The Future of Europe: Towards a Two-Speed EU?* (Cambridge, Cambridge University Press, 2012); D Thym, *Ungleichzeitigkeit und europäisches Verfassungsrecht* (Baden-Baden, Nomos, 2004).

[74] The Commission to the European Parliament and the Council argues in this direction, 'Towards a Deep and Genuine Economic and Monetary Union. The introduction of a Convergence and Competitiveness Instrument' COM (2013) 165 final.

competence of the EU[75] a financing via taxation would not only alter the EU's own resource system but also the political character of the EU itself. Therefore, and with regard to political and constitutional constraints in the Member States,[76] it might be preferable not to give the Economic Government extensive access to the European tax base. Instead, it makes sense to finance the budget through a membership fee, of around 0.5 per cent of GDP.

With a view to democratic accountability the Economic Government has to be elected and scrutinised by a special parliament.[77] One possibility is to staff this body with deputies from the European Parliament representing Member States of the Eurozone, since its purpose is the provision of public goods in the euro area. This approach may run counter to the normative perspective of Article 10(2) TEU according to which the European Parliament is the representative body of EU citizens and not of EU Member States.[78] Since the new parliament's responsibility would also be to pass framework legislation (together with the Council) on matters that touch such sensitive policy fields as economic, fiscal, budgetry and social policy, it might be preferable to establish a new kind of Euro-Parliament consisting of members of national parliaments. This third chamber beside the European Parliament and the Council would have special competences to ensure that control over these, from a national point of view very sensitive policy fields, remain in their hands.[79] Arguably, it is likely that such an additional institution makes European decision-making even more complex. But such a third chamber would evolve the role of the national parliaments as it is currently funded in Articles 10(2) and 12 TEU and Article 13 TSCG into a further integrated multilevel parliamentarism.[80]

Another possibility would be to establish a right to a veto (red card) for national parliaments with a view to these sensitive policy fields. In order to ensure that one national veto could not block the whole European decision-making process for an unlimited time, the veto might be of a suspending character. The European institutions would have to consider and to take into account the reasons of the national parliament. If a compromise can't be found, after a time period of six months, there could be two possibilities: either a minimum of one third of the other national parliaments supports the veto, and the proposal is taken from the agenda or, if

[75] See in detail, F Fabbrini, 'Taxing and Spending in the Euro Zone: Legal and Political Challenges Related to the Adoption of the Financial Transaction Tax' (2014) 39 *European Law Review* 155.

[76] Within German scholarship it is often assumed that the power to tax turns the EU into a Federal State, see C Waldhoff in Calliess and Ruffert (n 58) Art 311 AEUV, para 16; see also the restrictive case law of the FCC case BVerfGE 123, 267 Lisbon, judgment of 30 June 2009, para 256.

[77] See I Pernice et al, *A Democratic Solution to the Crisis. Reform Steps towards a Democratically Based Economic and Financial Constitution for Europe* (Baden-Baden, Nomos, 2012) 122–23.

[78] C Fasone, 'European Economic Governance and Parliamentary Representation. What Place for the European Parliament? (2014) 20 *European Law Journal* 164, 181 ff.

[79] For a similar approach, see S Kadelbach, 'Lehren aus der Finanzkrise—Ein Vorschlag zur Reform der Politischen Institutionen der Europäischen Union' (2013) 48 *Europarecht* 489, 500–501.

[80] For other proposals, see F Fabbrini, D Keleman and U Puetter in this volume.

this minimum is not reached, the European institutions could continue with the decision-making process. In doing so, there would need to be a unanimous decision in the Council. Such an 'emergency break' is not only a well-known approach in sensitive policy areas, just like the judicial cooperation in criminal matters (*cf* Articles 82(3) and 83(3) TFEU).[81] Its basic idea also corresponds to the right of national parliaments to raise a subsidiarity complaint (*cf* Article 12 (b) TEU).

VII. FIRST CONCLUSION

In order to avoid a general shift from the Community method to the intergovernmental method the ESM Treaty, the Fiscal Treaty and the latest IGA as part of the Banking Union have already called for a Treaty Reform. Moreover, the proper functioning of the Monetary Union supports a Europeanisation of national fiscal, economic and social policies in the framework of a real political union. This, as well as the necessary institutional changes, makes a Treaty reform inevitable. If there is no consensus between the Member States, the fiscal treaty might become the starting point for a 'Europe of Two Speeds' with some Member States going ahead and with the opportunity for other Member States to join this 'Coalition of the Willing' whenever they want.

[81] See C Calliess, *Die neue Europäische Union nach dem Vertrag von Lissabon* (Tübingen, Mohr Siebeck, 2010) 435–36.

4

Intergovernmentalism and the New Framework of EMU Governance

GEORGIOS MARIS AND PANTELIS SKLIAS

I. INTRODUCTION

THE EUROPEAN CRISIS, which manifested itself through the Greek economic crisis, is the best case study for examining both the vulnerabilities of Europe's framework for economic governance and the very process of European integration itself. That is so for various reasons. First, because the European crisis is the most serious crisis the European Union (EU) has faced to date; secondly, as a result of the crisis, the limits on the process of economic integration in Europe have been put to the test; and thirdly, because the main causes of the crisis are tied into the framework of economic governance which has been developed over the last decades, and therefore are connected to the very process of European unification itself. The primary aim of this chapter is to demonstrate whether, and to what extent, the new framework for economic governance in Europe is mainly a result of interstate bargaining, and consequently whether national preferences continue to play an important role in its general transformation.[1] Although the process of European integration is too complex to be understood from one single theoretical viewpoint, the crisis has raised old questions about European integration concerning the centrality of the state, and interstate interactions. Does intergovernmentalism triumph over supranationalism? As is clear to us, the issue of how the framework of economic governance has been transformed is no longer an issue of 'low politics' but a major issue of 'high politics' since the autonomy and sovereignty of national governments within the realm of economic policy are now at risk. That is to say, the nature of the changes being put forward in the context of economic governance in Europe today is no longer in line with a less confrontational environment. At the level of Economic and Monetary Union (EMU),

[1] For other significant contributions on the governance of the euro crisis, see S Fabbrini, 'Intergovernmentalism and its Limits: Assessing the European Union's Answer to the Euro Crisis' (2013) 46 *Comparative Political Studies* 1003, 1029; C Bickerton et al, 'The New Intergovernmentalism: European Integration in the Post-Maastricht Era' (2014) 52 *Journal of Common Market Studies* 1, 20.

the more the integration process advances, the less room there is for transferring national sovereignty to supranational bodies, and the more the importance of an intergovernmental stance is highlighted. The economic crisis showed that important issues in economic policy which had been 'swept under the carpet' over recent decades, concerning the change in economic governance and the role of the nation state, must be resolved so make the European venture viable.

This chapter also claims that intergovernmentalism has been the key factor of change the economic governance in Europe. To understand the process of change in economic governance in Europe, it is first necessary to understand the role of interstate bargaining at a European level, primarily as a result of the national preferences and interests of Member States. Moreover, it is essential to stress the role of other factors which could interfere with this change. Therefore, in addition to evaluating the new framework of economic governance in Europe, one also needs to examine the conditions under which the specific changes took place, were adopted, and have been supported at the European level. It would appear that even though a series of other factors are involved in the process of transformation of the framework of economic governance in Europe, the interests of national governments which reflect the preferences of various socio-economic actors, continue to affect the final outcome to a large degree. This chapter stresses that to a large extent, behind any decisions concerning further unification of economic policy within the EMU, lie important intergovernmental elements. Thus the process of transforming the framework of economic governance continues, to a very significant extent, to be an intergovernmental game based on the interests of Member States.

Of course, that does not mean that we should downplay the role of the political and moral arguments, which were primarily developed after the end of World War II, about the creation of the EU. Moreover, the Community method continues to affect the framework of economic governance in Europe in its own way. That is most clear in the case of the monetary aspect of EMU. In this way the supranational decision-making method plays an important role in the process of changing the framework of economic governance in Europe. However, in the economic dimension of EMU from 2010 onwards, it has been primarily Germany, and also France, that have attempted to change the framework for economic governance in Europe based on an intergovernmental approach and focused on the sovereignty of the nation state compared to supranational players; focused on the intergovernmental method over the Community method. In this regard, our aim is also to examine in depth the behaviour of France and Germany in changing the new framework for economic governance in Europe. We have taken these two countries as examples because they are the EU Member States which are decisively influencing the development and transformation of this framework. That occurs because as Heipertz and Verdun have argued, 'when Member States governments bargain with one another, the largest countries have the greater influence'.[2] Over all these years it

[2] M Heipertz and A Verdun, *Ruling Europe: The Politics of the Stability and Growth Pact* (Cambridge, Cambridge University Press, 2010) 20.

has been Franco-German relations which have driven the integration process to a significant degree.[3] Unless the views of these two countries converge, no important issue of 'high politics' can advance in the EU. To a significant degree, when it comes to transforming economic governance in Europe, the more restrictions related to the interests and sovereignty of those two countries that are introduced, the clearer the limits on the process of European unification that emerge, and the more EMU appears that it will remain in a prolonged stated of imbalance.

The chapter is structured as follows. Section II studies the theories of European integration which constitute our theoretical context. Section III describes the conditions under which the initial framework of economic governance in Europe emerged. Section IV shows not only how the EU responded to the crisis but also how Germany and France affect the transformation of the new framework of economic governance in Europe. Section V concludes.

II. THEORIES OF EUROPEAN INTEGRATION

This section of the chapter attempts to synthesise the various viewpoints about the creation of EMU into a wider theoretical framework. This is necessary because the EU and the process of European integration are too complex to be viewed from any single theoretical perspective.[4] The literature contains a series of references as the key factors that have shaped the European monetary framework. This chapter will primarily focus on the old debate between neo-functionalism and intergovernmentalism. We argue that the European crisis brought us back to old questions about European integration. In our view, what plays—and will continue to play—a dominant role is the nation state and its interests.

The reasons why EMU was set up can be classified in various different ways. The political science literature to date has mainly presented two approaches. The first refers to Amy Verdun's attempt to classify the reasons why EMU was set up by looking at a set of political theories of integration which ties together hypotheses and forecasts.[5] Verdun argues that we can group the factors that play an important role in the development of European monetary unification into three main categories: (a) the role of actors and institutions, (b) mechanisms, and (c) international structural factors. The second approach presents the framework within which monetary integration emerged by looking at four different levels of analysis: the global, the European, the national and the domestic.[6] According to Sadeh and Verdun, EMU is the result of a European reaction to global challenges which was

[3] A Cole, 'Franco-German Europe' in K Dyson and A Sepos (eds), *Which Europe? The Politics of Differentiated Integration* (New York, Palgrave Macmillan, 2010).

[4] B Rosamond, *Theories of European Integration* (Hampshire, Palgrave Macmillan, 2000).

[5] A Verdun, 'Why EMU Happened: A Survey of Theoretical Explanations' in PM Crowley (ed), *Before and Beyond EMU: Historical Lessons and Future Prospects* (London, Routledge, 2002).

[6] T Sadeh and A Verdun, 'Explaining Europe's Monetary Union: A Survey of the Literature' (2009) 11 *International Studies Review* 277, 301.

feasible because European institutions had been set up, and was primarily put forward by the Franco-German pact.[7] As a result, if we suppose that the Member States place their interests on a scale just like the theory of instrumental rationality argues that humans do, then they try to satisfy as many interests as they can, starting from what they consider to be their most important issue. In this case, the Member States prefer to remain protected in the global political and economic environment.

It is very difficult to analyse the process of economic integration of Europe from realist or neo-realist perspectives either because theorists have not given them particular importance,[8] or because they are faced with important theoretical problems.[9] The same also appears to hold true for Marxist analyses. Furthermore, although early theories of European integration significantly affected the subsequent course of developments in European studies, these theories were called into doubt because of empirical developments within the EU. In effect, almost all early attempts are theoretical constructions designed to eliminate international conflict.[10]

Under those conditions, attention must be given to theories that were developed from the 1950s onwards. First of all is neo-functionalism, which was primarily developed in the works of Haas[11] and Lindberg and Scheingold.[12] Neo-functionalism stresses that integration is the result of functional pressures exerted because of integration in low politics sectors. An important role is played in this process by higher, supranational actors which have been set up for this purpose, and which contribute a great deal to the unification process. Under these conditions, wider social groups transfer their loyalty to the new supranational institutions. Although neo-functionalism can explain to a significant degree the first attempts to unify Europe from the Treaty of Paris onwards, since integration in one economic sector (the European Coal and Steel Community (ECSC)) created functional pressures that led to the European Economic Community (EEC), it cannot explain the creation of EMU with the same degree of cogency. It is true that from 1985 to the end of 1990, following a period of extreme criticism, neo-functionalism began to be revived because of changes that were occurring at that time.[13] The key elements of this revival were, inter alia, the White Paper on Completion of the Internal Market,

[7] ibid 277, 301.

[8] A Stone, 'What is a Supranational Constitution? An Essay in International Relations Theory' (1994) 56 *The Review of Politics* 441, 474.

[9] JM Grieco, 'The Maastricht Treaty: Economic and Monetary Union and the Neo-realist Research Programme' (1995) 21 *Review of International Studies* 21, 40.

[10] Rosamond, *European Integration* (n 4).

[11] EB Haas, *The Uniting of Europe: Political, Social, and Economic Forces 1950–1957* (Stanford, Stanford University Press, 1958); EB Haas, *Beyond the Nation State: Functionalism and International Organization* (Stanford, Stanford University Press, 1964).

[12] LN Lindberg and SA Scheingold, *Europe's Would-be Polity: Patterns of Change in the European Community* (Englewood Cliffs, Prentice Hall, 1970); LN Lindberg and SA Scheingold, *Regional Integration: Theory and Research* (Cambridge MA, Harvard University Press, 1971).

[13] J Tranholm-Mikkelsen, 'Neo-functionalism: Obstinate or Obsolete? A Reappraisal in the Light of the New Dynamism of the EC' (1991) 20 *Millennium-Journal of International Studies* 1, 22.

the Single European Act and the Delors Report. Neo-functionalism seems unable to explain why EMU has today not advanced to a more integrated stage of unification. This is mainly because the supranational institutions that have already been set up do not have the appropriate jurisdiction to proceed with the economic integration of Europe on their own. This means that the transition to a supranational level is not such a reasonable dynamic, automatic and depoliticised process since political union could not be developed without taking into account the views of European citizens.[14] Despite that, there is an element of neo-functionalism which over recent years has become worthy of further attention. This is the fact that supranational decision-making would become increasingly more technocratic.[15]

The response to neo-functionalism came quickly from the intergovernmental approach. Intergovernmentalism stresses that in areas of high politics, where either the autonomy of governments or important issues of national identity are at risk, unification would be difficult to achieve.[16] Although Hoffmann's view that states are the key players in global politics reflected realistic positions, he considered that national interests were the result of domestic forces,[17] which sets his views apart from the stance taken by the realists. Therefore, one of the most important elements of the theory of intergovernmentalism was that it emphasised the supremacy of interstate bargaining in setting the pace and degree of European unification.[18] According to intergovernmentalism theory, supranational institutions, such as the European Commission and the European Court of Justice, do not play an important role in the process of European integration. The same holds true for the role and influence of international players and coalitions and the extension of functional objectives.[19]

Intergovernmentalism played an important role in the subsequent development of liberal intergovernmentalism, which is thought to be the most important example of an attempt to theorise European integration.[20] Moravcsik in effect constructed a two-level game model which consists of a liberal theory of preference formation and an intergovernmentalist analysis of strategies for Member States reaching agreement.[21] Therefore, liberal intergovernmentalism, which relies

[14] PC Schmitter, 'Ernst B Haas and the Legacy of Neofunctionalism' (2005) 12 *Journal of European Public Policy* 255, 272.

[15] Rosamond (n 4).

[16] S Hoffmann, 'Obstinate or Obsolete? The Fate of the Nation-State and the Case of Western Europe' (1966) 95 *Daedalus* 862, 915.

[17] S Hoffmann, *The European Sisyphus: Essays on Europe 1964–1994* (Boulder, Westview Press, 1995).

[18] MI Τσινισιζέλης και ΔΝ Χρυσοχόου, 'Πολιτική Θεωρία της Ευρωπαϊκής Ενοποίησης: Από τον Λειτουργισμό στο νέο Ρεπουμπλικανισμό' στο Ν Μαραβέγιας και Μ Τσινισιζέλης (επιμ), *Νέα Ευρωπαϊκή Ένωση: Οργάνωση και Πολιτικές 50 Χρόνια* (Athens, Θεμέλιο, 2007).

[19] ibid.

[20] Rosamond (n 4).

[21] A Moravcsik, 'Preferences and Power in European Community: A Liberal Intergovernmentalist Approach' (1993) 31 *Journal of Common Market Studies* 473, 524; A Moravcsik, 'Liberalism and International Relations Theory' Harvard University Center for International Affairs, Paper 1993; A Moravcsik, *The Choice for Europe: Social Purpose and State Power from Mesina to Maastricht* (Ithaca NY, Cornell University Press, 1998).

on the interaction between domestic and international politics, and attempts to explain the EU as a successful example of an intergovernmentalist regime, also includes elements from realism and from neo-liberalism.[22]

Liberal intergovernmentalism is a model comprised of three different stages that combine: (a) a liberal theory to explain how national preferences are formed; (b) an intergovernmentalist bargaining model at EU level; and (c) an 'institutional selection' model that places emphasis on the role of institutions and on the provision of reliable commitments to the governments of Member States.[23] Therefore, liberal intergovernmentalism emphasises both the role of economic interests and the importance of institutions in the process of European integration, and stresses the central role of the state, the importance of domestic economic interests, and negotiations between national governments.[24] The principles on which the theory of liberal intergovernmentalism rests argue that political integration is the result of Member States' interests, which transfer various competences and powers to the European supranational institutions only if they can take control in various policy sectors.[25] In order for integration to advance the economic or trade interests of the Member States must overlap. According to intergovernmental theory the most important, historical intergovernmental agreements, such as the Treaty of Rome or the Treaty of Maastricht, were the result of a periodic process of preference convergence among the most powerful Member States, who offered incentives to the smaller states and transferred limited powers to the European supranational institutions, which effectively remained the servants of the Member States.[26]

Both the neo-functionalist and intergovernmentalist approaches have received severe criticism over recent decades primarily because they could not explain day-to-day European politics since the EU is dominated by the actions of non-state actors. For that reason, over recent decades theorists of European Studies have shifted their focus to medium-range theories. This has happened because both neo-functionalism and intergovernmentalism cannot comprehend the full complexity and dynamism in which politics is conducted within the EU.[27] For example, one cannot ignore the fact that over recent decades supranational institutions, such as the Commission or the European Parliament, have come to play an important role in EU affairs and the European Court of Justice (ECJ) has traditionally acted as an engine of integration even in times when the consensus between states for further integration was lacking. Under these conditions, over

[22] M Cini, 'Intergovernmentalism' in M Cini (ed), *European Union Politics* (Oxford, Oxford University Press, 2007).

[23] MA Pollack, 'Theorizing EU Policy-Making' in H Wallace, W Wallace and MA Pollack (eds), *Policy-Making in the European Union* (Oxford, Oxford University Press, 2005).

[24] R Gilpin, *Global Political Economy: Understanding the International Economic Order* (Princeton, Princeton University Press, 2001).

[25] CS Jensen, 'Neo-functionalism' in M Cini (ed), *European Union Politics* (Oxford, Oxford University Press, 2007).

[26] Pollack, 'Theorizing EU Policy-Making' (n 23).

[27] Rosamond (n 4).

recent years a series of new approaches have emerged in the attempt to theorise the EU. For example, multi-level governance attaches importance to the existence of a set of super-imposed multi-level coalitions.[28] According to Marks et al, the sovereignty of nation states within the EU has been reduced because of collective decision-making and supranational institutions.[29] Alternatively, the new institutional approach treats institutions as tools for developing and shaping political behaviour, which go beyond typical governmental bodies and introduce fixed operating procedures.[30]

This chapter pushes forward the intergovernmental aspect of the factors that change the economic governance in Europe. In this regard, we analyse not only whether, and to what extent, the new framework of economic governance in the Eurozone can be understood under the prism of intergovernmentalism, but also to what extent the interstate bargaining and the national preferences are reflected and shaped.

III. THE CONDITIONS UNDER WHICH THE INITIAL FRAMEWORK OF ECONOMIC GOVERNANCE IN EUROPE EMERGED

The initial framework for economic governance in Europe was created by the Treaty of Maastricht. The Treaty of Maastricht was not the result of straightforward, unproblematic negotiations. Wyplosz argues that during the negotiations that led to the Treaty, it became clear that France's views did not match those of Germany.[31] Germany placed emphasis on the importance of economic policies and of convergence, while France stressed the creation of new institutional tools. The strategy adopted in the Treaty of Maastricht emphasised the importance of two principles: gradual transition and convergence.[32]

Due to the differing approaches taken by France and Germany, which reflected the old dispute between 'economists' and 'monetarists',[33] the Treaty of Maastricht

[28] G Marks, L Hooghe and K Blank, 'European Integration from the 1980s: State-Centric v Multi-level Governance' (1996) 34 *Journal of Common Market Studies* 341, 378.

[29] ibid 341, 378.

[30] S Bulmer, 'The Governance of the European Union: A New Institutional Approach' (1993) 13 *Journal of Public Policy* 355.

[31] C Wyplosz, 'European Monetary Union: The Dark Sides of a Major Success' (2006) 21 *Economic Policy* 207, 261.

[32] P De Grauwe, *The Economics of Monetary Union* (Oxford, Oxford University Press, 2009).

[33] 'Economists' believed that before the creation of EMU the economic and financial conditions of its long-term viability should already exist. Thus, economic convergence is a precondition for monetary integration. This view was adopted by Germany and the Netherlands. 'Monetarists' believed that the process of monetary integration could create the necessary economic conditions for EMU's long-term viability. This view was adopted mainly from France, Belgium and Luxembourg. See L Tsoukalis, *The Politics and Economics of European Monetary Integration* (London, Allen & Unwin, 1977); DC Kruse, *Monetary Integration in Western Europe: EMU, EMS, and Beyond*, (London, Butterworths, 1980). Those who designed EMU were not clear about which approach to follow in setting it up. See A Verdun, 'Economic and Monetary Union' in M Cini (ed), *European Union Politics* (Oxford, Oxford

included both supranational and intergovernmental decision-making features. The main role in the supranational approach was first played by the European Central Bank (ECB), and subsequently by the Commission, the ECJ and the European Parliament. On the other hand, the intergovernmentalist method is identified with the increased role of the European Council in the unification process.[34]

In effect, during the negotiations for the Treaty of Maastricht, the Member States agreed to transfer significant aspects of their sovereignty to the supranational level only if national governments could control decision-making capabilities.[35] This means that in addition to being technocratic in nature, economic governance in Europe is above all political since it includes political agreements that satisfy the strategic interests of the Member States and their governments.[36] Thus the convergence of interests and preferences at European level produced two heterogeneous consequences relating to the initial framework for economic governance: (a) Europe acquired an unstable form of economic and social governance;[37] and (b) a stable and differentiated context of economic policies was put in place.[38] The result was the creation of an EMU with strong elements of asymmetry under which more wide-ranging economic governance was almost impossible.[39]

What was France and Germany's stance during the negotiations for the Treaty of Maastricht and under what conditions was agreement reached? The Treaty of Maastricht was the result of a bargaining game which is best explained by the principles of liberal intergovernmentalism. For that reason, during negotiations the two European leaders of France and Germany had kept the European Commission at a distance. As Dyson pointed out: 'The French favoured this rule from arguments rooted in national sovereignty and democratic legitimation; the Germans from arguments related to preserving the independence of the ECB.'[40]

University Press, 2007). In other words, the key players were not in agreement about whether, and to what extent, the convergence of economies ought to come before the transfer of sovereignty over monetary policy to a supranational level. See A Verdun, 'A Historical Institutionalist Analysis of the Road to Economic and Monetary Union: A Journey with Many Crossroads' in S Meunier and KR McNamara (eds), *Making History: European Integration and Institutional Change at Fifty* (New York, Oxford University Press, 2007).

[34] See U Puetter, 'The European Council—The New Centre of EU Politics' Swedish Institute for European Policy Studies, October 2013.

[35] Fabbrini, 'Intergovernmentalism and its Limits' (n 1) 1029.

[36] K Dyson, 'Economic and Monetary Union in Europe: A Transformation of Governance' in B Kohler-Koch and R Eising (eds), *The Transformation of Governance in the European Union* (London, Routledge, 1999).

[37] I Begg, 'Economic and Social Governance in the Making: EU Governance in Flux' (2010) 32 *Journal of European Integration* 1, 16.

[38] K Dyson and M Marcussen, 'Transverse Integration in European Economic Governance: Between Unitary and Differentiated Integration' (2010) 32 *Journal of European Integration* 17, 39.

[39] A Verdun, 'An "Asymmetrical" Economic and Monetary Union in the EU: Perceptions of Monetary Authorities and Social Partners' (1996) 20 *Journal of European Integration* 59, 81; A Verdun, *European Responses to Globalization and Financial Market Integration: Perceptions of Economic and Monetary Union in Belgium, France and Germany* (Basingstoke, Palgrave Macmillan, 2000).

[40] K Dyson, 'The Franco–German Relationship and Economic and Monetary Union: Using Europe to "Bind Leviathan"' (1999) 22 *West European Politics* 27.

For Germany, the creation of EMU was the best way to support the country's economic growth based on the neo-liberalist principles of the open market, free trade and deflationary monetary policy.[41] Moreover, the establishment of the ECB and the subsequent Stability and Growth Pact (SGP) was a means of promoting those objectives, as established by the monetarist revolution and its domination over Keynesianism.[42] After monetarist ideas were adopted, these objectives would be best promoted through an independent central bank, price stability and fiscal discipline (today, fiscal austerity) without it being possible to coordinate fiscal policy in the medium term.[43] In doing so, Germany was favouring its business interests. German businesses would enjoy advantages from the EMU-mandated ban on the devaluation of national currencies, as an opportunity to increase exports.[44] However, at the same time this also meant that other states would lose their ability to devalue their currency and thus the chance for their businesses' products to remain competitive. In addition, even if these countries followed different policies based on a more outward-looking strategy, the expected results would not accrue because of deviations that existed in the institutional structure of the peripheral states.[45] One could argue that Germany sacrificed the German currency in order to introduce a culture of economic stability based on specific rules across the entire EMU.[46] In fact, it was clear from the outset that Germany would not accept the euro if the monetary rules were not designed on the German model of economic growth.[47]

For France on the other hand, the creation of EMU was a way of being able to compete against Germany on an economic level and also to use EMU to make it come closer to its own economic model by increasing public spending, increasing wages, and inflation, in order to stop the foreign exchange crises and debt crises of the 1970s and 1980s.[48] France was attempting to balance its relationship with

[41] Germany's negotiating position in the discussions about the Treaty of Maastricht, were influenced by the economic philosophy of *ordoliberalism.* See K Dyson and K Featherstone, *The Road to Maastricht: Negotiating Economic and Monetary Union* (Oxford, Oxford University Press, 1999) which is tied into a political approach based on the rules of *Ordnungspolitik* in which the state only lays down the legal framework within which private players can act as freely as possible. See W Mussler, 'EU Economic Governance: The German View' in JF Jamet, W Mussler and S De Corte (eds), *EU Economic Governance: The French and German View* (Brussels, Centre for European Studies, 2011). For a general overview of the main reasons for conflict between France and Germany up to the signing of the Treaty of Maastricht, see I Maes, 'On the Origins of the Franco–German EMU Controversies' (2004) 17 *European Journal of Law and Economics* 21, 39.

[42] KR McNamara, *The Currency of Ideas: Monetary Politics in the European Union* (Ithaca, Cornell University Press, 1998).

[43] PA Hall and RJ Franzese, 'Mixed Signals: Central Bank Independence, Coordinates Wage Bargaining, and European Monetary Union' (1998) 52 *International Organization* 505, 535.

[44] PA Hall, 'The Economics and Politics of the Euro Crisis' (2012) 21 *German Politics* 355, 371.

[45] ibid 355, 371.

[46] JF Jamet, 'EU Economic Governance: The French View' in Jamet, Mussler and De Corte, *EU Economic Governance* (n 41).

[47] W Mussler, 'EU Economic Governance: The German View' in Jamet, Mussler and De Corte (n 41).

[48] A Moravcsik, 'Europe after the Crisis: How to Sustain a Common Currency' (2012) 91 *Foreign Affairs* 54, 68.

Germany by reducing the credibility of the German economic model.[49] However, that required a compromise with Germany and the other countries which was never achieved, and that is considered to be EMU's greatest failure.[50] In addition to being a political plan,[51] the creation of EMU also incorporated a 'Bind Leviathan' which represented an immense challenge for French views about the sovereignty of the state and legitimacy.[52]

As the theory of liberal intergovernmentalism explained, Germany would not have set up EMU if the other European countries did not agree to adopt the German economic model at Maastricht, since it—in contrast to France—was the only country which could persuade them of the superiority of its model of economic growth. France's economic (in)effectiveness in the 1970s and 1980s left no doubt about that.[53] However, Germany overlooked the fact that the other Member States did not meet the political, economic and cultural requirements to adopt it in reality. Even if it was debated occasionally, EMU's ability to achieve real convergence was overlooked as EMU never became an Optimal Currency Area, and never acquired the necessary mechanisms for fiscal transfers and for rescuing the Member States in times of crisis.

IV. DEALING WITH THE CRISIS

Until 2008 any reactions to the global economic crisis were based on the expectations and interests of each individual state, and varied widely.[54] The size of the global economic crisis, however, increasingly prompted actions at the European and global level. However, the challenge proved to be exceptionally difficult for the Europeans, especially outside the field of monetary policy where there was already a well-organised supranational decision-making system in place, centred on the ECB.[55] For the major part of 2009, the European crisis in the eyes of EU leaders was still primarily a banking crisis. The bad thing about this, according to Pisani-Ferry and Sapir was that,

> the management of the crisis has taken place according to the assignment of competences that exists in the EU: the ECB and national central banks outside the euro area have acted as liquidity providers, national governments have dealt with financial stability, and the European Commission has enforced competition disciplines. Although some of

[49] Dyson (n 40).
[50] Moravcsik (n 48).
[51] K Dyson, *Elusive Union: The Process of Economic and Monetary Integration in Europe* (London, Longman, 1994); Dyson and Featherstone, *The Road to Maastricht* (n 41).
[52] Dyson (n 40).
[53] ibid 25, 44.
[54] SA Schirm, 'Varieties of Strategies: Societal Influences on British and German Responses to the Global Economic Crisis' (2011) 19 *Journal of Contemporary European Studies* 47, 62.
[55] L Quaglia, R Eastwood and P Holmes, 'The Financial Turmoil and EU Policy Co-operation in 2008' (2009) 47 *Journal of Common Market Studies* 63, 87.

> these players, notably the ECB, have gone beyond the pre-existing script, none has gone beyond its pre-existing role. Especially, there has been no EU-financed bail-out of ailing transnational institutions.[56]

The Greek debt crisis officially became a European problem for the first time on 8 December 2009, and from then on at the European level there was only one topic of discussion: how can the European crisis be resolved? In light of that, from early 2010 to 2013, a new, highly complex framework of economic governance was put in place.[57]

At the Euro Summit of 7–9 May 2010 European leaders announced that all European institutions were duty bound to combat the economic crisis and ensure the euro area's economic stability. As they characteristically said: 'All the institutions of the euro area (Council, Commission, ECB) as well as all Euro Area Member States agree to use the full range of means available to ensure the stability of the Euro Area.'[58] From that time on, in addition to the bailout packages for peripheral countries, important changes have been made to the framework of economic governance in Europe.

Paul Craig has examined in detail the wide range of legal and policy measures adopted to respond to the Euro-crisis in another chapter of this book. So we will not dwell on their analysis here. Instead, we want to focus on another question: under what circumstances was the new framework for economic governance in Europe set up? What factors primarily affected this transformation? In a speech in Cologne on 13 September 2011, the President of the Bundesbank, Jens Weidmann, stated that there were two paths the new economic architecture of Europe could take: either we had to return to the principles set out in the founding treaties or we had to move towards a federalist transformation of the system, with everything that entailed.[59] The second solution is quite clearly a move towards political union. Weidmann's statement hides the essence of the process of European integration, whose most important aspect affects developments in the transformation of economic governance. That element is none other than the issue of transferring national sovereignty to European supranational institutions. In other words, when the European crisis occurred, even though Member States declared they were willing to accept greater control over economic policy at national level, the majority of them were putting forward solutions which were based on the intergovernmentalist game.[60] It is no coincidence that even in the Treaty establishing the European Stability Mechanism (ESM), the European Commission only played an

[56] J Pisani-Ferry and A Sapir, 'Banking Crisis Management in the EU: An Interim Assessment' Bruegel Working Paper 07/2009, 21.

[57] F Fabbrini et al (eds), *The Constitutionalization of European Budgetary Constraints* (Oxford, Hart Publishing, 2014).

[58] See Statement of the Heads of State or Government of the Euro Area, 7 May 2010, 2.

[59] See Jens Weidenmann's speech at the Association of Family Enterprises in Cologne on 13 September 2011.

[60] Fabbrini (n 1).

advisory role, which further reduced its credibility.[61] Furthermore, the European Parliament appears to have found itself in an even worse position.[62] According to Sergio Fabbini, the 'deepening of the euro crisis has led to new treaties that do not recognize the EP as a policy-making actor'.[63] Under these conditions, the new framework for economic governance in Europe (which to some degree was imposed by the economic developments after the crisis) in effect came about more from an intergovernmental procedure than via the Community method.

These remarks may be quite significant since they indicate the limits on the potential for change in the method of economic governance in Europe. It appears that it will be very difficult to take the next steps towards fiscal and political union in Europe and that the Community method has reached its limits, as long as the interests of Europe's powerful states do not allow it to advance.[64] Having said that, it has to be acknowledged that significant new elements in the EU architecture of economic governance (such as the European Semester, the six-pack and two-pack) which were the result of the Community method, fostered the role of the Commission and bolstered the supranational aspect of EMU.[65] Nevertheless, most of the measures which were realised through the Community method were initially promoted by intergovernmental institutions, notably the European Council and its President.[66]

Almost all attempts at reform designed to improve and bolster the framework for economic governance, even the bailout plans for the Member States, fall within the same framework of analysis. However, we should remember that during the last decades one important factor has changed. France and Germany are the most powerful EU Member States, but their global and peripheral economic power and influence has not remained stable and equal. Moreover, one ought not to forget that in addition to being an imperfect economic and political framework, EMU is also a zone within which major divergent interests have emerged over recent years, especially between France and Germany.[67] These divergences appear to have created an utterly confrontational environment concerning EMU issues. As we explained in the previous section, initially, France and Germany interpreted

[61] RM Liddle et al, 'Where Next for Eurozone Governance? The Quest for Reconciling Economic Logic and Political Dilemmas' Policy Network Paper 07/2012.

[62] C Fasone, 'The Struggle of the European Parliament to Participate in the New Economic Governance' EUI Working Paper RSCAS 45/2012; P Manoli and G Maris, 'The Role of the European Parliament in Managing the International Economic and Financial Crisis' in S Stavridis and D Irrera (eds), *The European Parliament as an International Actor: Assessing the First 35 Years of a Directly-Elected "Supranational" Parliamentary Institution's External Relations* (Routledge, 2015).

[63] S Fabbrini, 'After the Euro Crisis: A New Paradigm on the Integration of Europe' ARENA Working Paper 5/2014, 9.

[64] H Kundnani, 'Europe and the Return of History' (2013) 11 *Journal of Modern European History* 279, 286.

[65] See the contribution of P Craig, ch 2 in this volume.

[66] See the contribution of U Puetter, ch 14 in this volume.

[67] S Tombazos, 'Centrifugal Tendencies in the Euro Area' (2011) 19 *Journal of Contemporary European Studies* 33, 46.

the Euro-crisis in two completely different ways. Both France and Germany saw the crisis as an opportunity to promote changes in the economic governance of Europe based on their separate interests and preferences. However, neither France nor Germany had clear-cut plans about that transformation. The views of both countries overlapped in that believing that the euro and the Eurozone had to be rescued in some way. However, there was disagreement about how to bail out Member States and the way in which the framework for economic governance ought to be transformed. Germany argued that it had to be done based on already agreed principles and rules, while France stressed that the process of economic integration in Europe had to be advanced to create economic governance.[68]

To be more specific, the Germans viewed the European crisis as the result of the fiscal condition of the Member States. At the outset, the European crisis for the Germans lacked a European dimension. What existed were separate and unique fiscal and banking crises within the Member States. To address this, Germany suggested the same tried-and-tested recipe which is based on three principles: (a) the independence of the ECB based on the monetarist approach; (b) the application of stricter rules in relation to SGP and the Excessive Deficit Procedure (EDP); and (c) fiscal consolidation of the Member States via harsh, oftentimes catastrophic, austerity and structural reforms. Why, however, did German Chancellor Merkel accept the French idea of creating economic governance for Europe? As Jamet argues, this move was purely tactical, intended to win a leadership role for herself in this debate, to mark the goalposts about rule-based governance, and to prompt France to put forward more specific, practical ideas about what economic governance would entail.[69]

One ought not to forget that since Germany is the country which reaped the most benefits from the moment EMU was created, even if it left it to the last moment it would do everything to stop the Eurozone collapsing, while keeping many peripheral Member States in a 'coma' due to its unwavering and intransigent policy. Germany only makes compromises when it knows that this will not have a negative impact on the interests of German businesses or if in practical terms disaster is just one step away. It is the country which stands to lose the most from the collapse of the Eurozone and its export sector would be irreparably hit. According to a Bertelsmann Stiftung report,[70] default on Greece's part and its exit from EMU might not have major impacts on the Member States since Greece only represents a very small part of the European economy overall, but because of the domino effect that would very likely occur, it could provoke the collapse of the money markets in Spain, Portugal and Italy and reduce the overall GDP in the world's 42 largest countries by a figure of around €17.2 trillion. On the other hand, to be fair, it is essential to stress that Germany is the country which has contributed the most to

[68] Mussler (n 47).

[69] Jamet (n 46).

[70] Bertelsmann Stiftung, 'Economic Impact of Southern European Member States Exiting the Eurozone' Bertelsmann Stiftung Policy Brief 06/2012.

financing bailout packages for Greece, Ireland, Portugal, Spain and Cyprus given its participation in the programmes and the country's simultaneous exposure to European Financial Stability Facility (EFSF) and ESM solidarity obligations of 27 per cent,[71] while the initial potential cost is around €79.4 billion.[72]

At the same time, from the onset of the crisis Germany has been in the most advantageous position compared to other Member States. EMU not only generates immense economic benefits for it but also gives it (as the theory of liberal intergovernmentalism states) a very major comparative advantage in negotiations at European level. Even though, for example, it initially disagreed with the bailout plans for the peripheral states or the establishment of the EFSF or ESM because they violated the Treaty of Maastricht, or with ECB policy on the purchase of bonds from deeply indebted states from the secondary market, it did in the end make certain concessions which, in a very smart way, did not undermine German interests. Among other things, Germany did not want to pay the bill alone. Germany refused for a long time to rescue Greece, so that the issue of the Greek crisis was left hanging by a thread. In doing so, Germany reduced the negotiating power of the other European players and limited the ability to present alternative forms of bailout to a minimum. Clearly, Germany appears to have adopted this strategy so that it could lay down its own terms and conditions in the new framework for economic governance and so as to safeguard German economic interests in the best possible way. The bailout plans of deeply indebted Member States resulted in the EU offering

> the most cost-effective and politically expedient way for Berlin to ensure that German banks and bondholders get paid back for their imprudent international loans. It is no surprise then, that strong support from German business has been decisive in ensuring a multiparty majority in the Bundestag behind committing resources to defend the euro.[73]

From 2010 onwards Germany stressed the need for changes in the framework of economic governance; changes that needed to be based on robust legal foundations. The alibi of the German Constitutional Court was always very credible. For example, during the Euro Summit of 9–10 May 2010, Germany reacted to a much more ambitious attempt at bailout put forward by the European Commission and in particular to its proposal to set up a bailout fund to purchase the bonds of indebted Member States.[74] The German delegation argued that if such a proposal were to be adopted there would be problems with the Constitutional Court.[75] According

[71] J Bibow, 'Germany and the Euroland Crisis: The Making of a Vulnerable Have' Levy Economics Institute Working Paper 767/2013.

[72] C Broyer et al, 'Impact of the Euro Crisis on the German Economy' Allianz Working Paper 154/2012.

[73] Moravcsik (n 48) 61.

[74] L Gocaj and S Meunier, 'Time Will Tell: The EFSF, the ESM and the Euro Crisis' (2013) 35 *Journal of European Integration* 239, 253.

[75] T Barber, 'Saving the Euro: Dinner on the Edge of the Abyss' *Financial Times* (London, 22 April 2010).

to the German Chancellor, the main changes ought to be made in three areas: (a) better fiscal discipline via the SGP; (b) improved coordination of economic policy; and (c) the setting up of a crisis management mechanism. For the German authorities, change in sector one was based on very clear-cut views, whereas the framework for changes in the other two areas was not quite so clear-cut. When it came to setting up a framework to encourage competitiveness and growth, Germany stressed that any changes ought to be made so as not to affect the German export sector. Moreover, the German government did everything it could to avoid setting up a 'European transfer union', along the lines proposed by the French approach. In September 2010 a German non-paper stated the need to accelerate fiscal consolidation procedures by putting in place automatic sanctions on states which violated the SGP. In this way, the German approach stressed the need to set up a much more de-politicised fiscal sanctions procedure. Any sanctions ought not to be a matter of the European Council's discretion but ought to be imposed automatically. In effect, all these developments brought the Franco–German dispute about rule compliance and the governance policy to the fore.[76] In fact, Germany wanted not just to make the sanctions under the SGP automatic and in that way depoliticise the Excessive Deficit Procedure, but also via the European Semester to make European fiscal supervision more compact.[77] At the same time, it introduced multilateral supervision based on specific metrics and sanctions on non-compliant states via the new Excessive Imbalance Procedure. In addition, Gocaj and Meunier have argued that the way the EFSF operated reflects the German attempt to control the new institution and to segregate it from the European technocratic management approach, since EFSF is a company based in Luxembourg and does not belong to either the Commission or the Council.[78] The same argument can be made for the creation of ESM. It is thus clear that even with the setting up and running of the EFSF and the ESM, there were political reasons at play which affected the final outcome. Germany also appears to have supported the French proposal concerning the Euro Plus Pact because it was in effect based on the intergovernmental process and not on the Community method. In effect, most European Councils from 2010 to 2012 entailed an asymmetric bargaining game between Germany and the other Member States. All the measures put forward do not appear to have negatively impacted on German economic interests despite being condemned numerous times by various interest groups within Germany.

Did France react in any way to all this? Back when EMU was being designed and planned, France supported the idea of creating a so-called '*gouvernement economique*', albeit one based on an intergovernmental mode. The idea of economic governance had been raised by Mitterrand during the negotiations for the Treaty of Maastricht. Moreover, while France supported the idea of creating the

[76] Mussler (n 47).

[77] J Schild, 'Leadership in Hard Times: Germany, France, and the Management of the Eurozone Crisis' (2013) 31 *German Politics & Society* 24, 47.

[78] Gocaj and Meunier, 'Time Will Tell' (n 74).

ECB and the SGP primarily to prevent French governments recklessly increasing public debt and public deficit, it refused to accept the blind nature of the economic governance rules which Germany imposed since it also wanted to ensure that it was possible for French governments to intervene in times of crisis.[79] From the French perspective, the establishment of a framework for economic governance in Europe ought to be based on four principles: (a) suitable coordination of EU economic policy and the development of a suitable economic policy mix by the ECB; (b) a more active role for the EU in stimulating economic growth and job creation; (c) more reliability and legitimation for EMU; and (d) challenging the objectives and independence of the ECB.[80] Of course, that did not mean that the French had taken a clear-cut, firm line about how the new framework for economic governance ought to look. The French had for a long time been stuck on the questions of whether and to what extent aspects of national sovereignty ought to be surrendered.[81] Howarth stresses that, 'the most common feature of French communicative discourse on economic governance has been the absence of any concrete proposal of transferring real economic policy competences from the national to the European level'.[82] That is perhaps why even today France has not fully clarified what the concept of economic governance in Europe means.

Over recent years France's approach to the creation of economic governance in Europe has not radically altered since it always appears to be closer to an intergovernmental rather than a supranational approach.[83] Although the current French approach to dealing with the debt crisis initially differed considerably from the German approach because of the fear that France would remain unprotected on the global markets, France came to accept Germany's stance on implementing a restrictive economic policy.[84] Of course, that does not mean that the French authorities stopped attaching importance to issues of economic growth and to fiscal stimulus and wider coordination and a degree of latitude when it comes to fiscal and monetary policy.[85] It is clear that today France prefers a 'weaker' euro so as to bolster the competitiveness of French businesses, while Germany wants a 'stronger' euro so it does not acquire European competitors in the global economy. That is why the French focused their attention on macroeconomic imbalances and the problems of competitiveness faced by the Member States.

In particular, in contrast to the German insistence on stability, France took the view that the focus should be on growth. The proposals to bolster European

[79] D Howarth, 'Making and Breaking the Rules: French Policy on EU "Government Economique"' (2007) 11 *Journal of European Public Policy* 1061, 1078.

[80] ibid 1061, 1078.

[81] JL Arnaud, 'France and Europe: The Debate in France at the Start of the French Presidency' Notre Europe Research and Policy Papers 10/2000; H Drake, 'France on Trial? The Challenge of Change Posed by the French Council Presidency of the European Union' (2001) 94 *Modern and Contemporary France* 453, 466.

[82] Howarth (n 79) 1075.

[83] Jamet (n 46).

[84] Fabbrini (n 1).

[85] See J Pisani-Ferry et al, 'A European Recovery Programme' Bruegel Policy Brief 2008.

economic policy, to revitalise the European single market and to develop a single European investment strategy are all focused in this direction. France proposed that a Eurobond be created—a proposal Germany rejected based on moral hazard. France also supported the plans of the Commission's president for joint European borrowing to finance investment plans. In relation to the financial framework, France stressed the need to increase financial supervision and promoted the creation of the European Systemic Risk Boards as well as three other European authorities.[86]

On the issue of setting up a crisis mechanism, France initially agreed with Germany to the establishment of a permanent crisis resolution mechanism. However, it did not put forward detailed proposals about how such a mechanism would operate. In March 2010 Germany proposed that a European Monetary Fund be set up, to provide direct cash injections to Member States and to eliminate the risk of default. But France blocked such a development. There were two main reasons for this. First, France did not want the European Monetary Fund to be considered to be a regional competitor of the International Monetary Fund (IMF) in the context of the presidency of the G-20. And secondly, given a potential default, the markets would be looking for higher returns on sovereign bonds and the European banks would be weakened.[87] That is why France turned its attentions towards supporting the creation of the ESM which was promoted by Germany. It should be stressed that the French President, Sarkozy, had also proposed that the EFSF should have unlimited access to ECB funds. The ECB should also intervene (as it did) by buying up the bonds of deeply indebted Member States from the secondary markets. This provoked major reactions from German officials at the ECB. On the issue of the Greek bailout package, France was initially in favour of providing direct assistance to Greece and rejected any IMF involvement. In contrast, Germany examined the prospects of a 'Grexit', refused any bailout plan, and stressed that any bailout of Greece would have to be decided on with the active involvement of the IMF. The results are now known to all.

As far as the fiscal supervision framework is concerned, in October 2010 France reached agreement with Germany on supporting the imposition of strict sanctions on any Member States that violated the SGP. They even went so far as to agree on banning Member States that violated the fiscal framework from taking part in votes at European Councils, but this proposal was not accepted in the end.[88] France also promoted the strengthening of multilateral fiscal supervision via the adoption of the Euro Plus Pact on 25 March 2011. It added the idea of coordinated action being taken against countries with excessive surpluses to the debate, so as to support the effective demand of national economies. However, as one might have expected, that proposal was rejected by Germany which stressed the need for structural reforms.

[86] Jamet (n 46).

[87] ibid.

[88] W Kösters, 'Credible Rules, Not Discretion, Will Make the Euro Sustainable' (2010) 45 *Intereconomics* 340, 343.

V. CONCLUSION

The EMU is a 'major political issue' which touches upon the very 'heart of the issue of national sovereignty'.[89] The economic crisis showed that important issues in economic policy, which were 'swept under the carpet' over recent decades concerning the change in economic governance and the role of the nation state, must be resolved in order to make the European venture viable.

Since 2010, immense changes have occurred in relation to the economic and monetary aspects of EMU creating a new, complex system of economic governance. At the same time, the Euro-crisis brought up old questions about European integration concerning the centrality of the state, and transnational interactions. As this chapter has argued, the new framework of economic governance in Europe is largely the result of an intergovernmental approach. This shift towards the intergovernmental method undoubtedly shows us that the process of economic unification in Europe is not only moving forward one step at a time but that it can be affected by the interests of the Member States. In fact, as the process of integration continues, the issues of 'low politics' are substituted by the significant issues of 'high politics'. Yet, in this way the possibility of the transformation of economic governance in Europe becomes weaker. The more the process of integration moves forward, the more the margins for transferring national sovereignty to supranational institutions are narrowing, and the more the importance of the intergovernmentalist stance is highlighted. Of course, today Europe appears to have the will to overcome barriers and to surpass itself; however the end result of this process is not predictable.

As this chapter has suggested, from the institutional point of view, the crisis is the result of the structural choices made at Maastricht, as a corollary of the convergence of the interests and preferences of the powerful Member States. Even today the creation of a new framework for economic governance appears to continue to be a bargaining game. Although supranational actors have played or continue to play an important role in developments concerning changes in the framework for economic governance in Europe, especially in relation to the economic dimension of EMU, the intergovernmental approach has remained prominent. Sovereignty and the centrality of the nation states appear to be unchallenged, although in some cases they could be contested. Under these circumstances, any future changes in the framework for economic governance are not expected to significantly affect the centrality and importance of the nation state to such a degree that one could talk about the importance of intergovernmentalism diminishing. Therefore, the process of European unification and of transforming the new framework of economic governance can only advance to the extent that the interests of the strong Member States permit it.

[89] Λ Τσούκαλης, *Η Νέα Ευρωπαϊκή Οικονομία: Στο Κατώφλι του 21ου Αιώνα* (Athens, Παπαζήση, 1998) 247.

Without any doubt, the international and European bargaining game over economic relations is much more complex today than it was in the past.[90] However, the key factor affecting both negotiations and the outcome of negotiations on the new framework for economic governance is none other than the interests of the Member States. Both Germany and France turned to the intergovernmentalist approach to find solutions to the crisis. The basis of that approach is the sovereignty of the nation state over supranational players; the intergovernmental method over the Community method. Therefore, the changes and necessary adjustments required at EMU level, such as changes in the labour market or the setting up of fiscal transfer mechanisms or the introduction of Eurobonds or the promotion of banking union, will not be the result of some automatic or depoliticised process. Critical changes are not put forward unless there is convergence between the economic interests of the strongest Member States, namely France and Germany. This conclusion is consistent with the core of the theory of liberal intergovernmentalism. However, in a globalised world 'state interests' are no longer only determined by the domestic context. One could argue that the Member States place their interests on a scale just like the theory of instrumental rationality argues that humans do. From there they try to satisfy as many interests as they can, starting from what they consider to be their most important interests. So even within such a diverse union, integration can be promoted because all Member States recognise that in all events it is not in their interests to be isolated and to face the globalised environment on their own. However, that would not appear to change our basic conclusion that as long as restrictions relating to interests and sovereignty are included in the context of transforming economic governance, the clearer the limits on the transformation and on the general process of economic integration are, and the more EMU will, it seems, remain imbalanced for a long time to come. In this regard, it appears that the EMU will remain in a prolonged state of imbalance.

[90] B Eichengreen, 'European Monetary Integration with Benefit of Hindsight' (2012) 50 *Journal of Common Market Studies* 123, 136.

Part II

The Governance of Economic, Monetary and Financial Affairs

5

The Confusion of Tasks in the Decision-Making Process of the European Economic Governance

ALEXANDRE DE STREEL

I. INTRODUCTION

SINCE THE START of the Euro-crisis in 2010, the governance of the Eurozone has been substantially revised to an extent unthinkable before the crisis. The governance is now based on four main pillars whose objectives, scope and European oversight vary.[1] The first pillar relates to *surveillance of national fiscal imbalances.* It aims to prevent and, if necessary, correct fiscal imbalances having spill-over effects between Member States and threatening the stability of the Eurozone; it applies to all Member States of the European Union (EU) with the possibility of more sanctions against the states of the euro area. The second pillar relates to the *surveillance of national macroeconomic imbalances.* As for fiscal imbalances, it aims to prevent and correct macro-economic imbalances having spill-over effects. The third pillar relates to the *coordination of national economic and social policies.* It aims to achieve economic convergence within the EU; it applies to all Member States; and it does not provide for sanctions against defaulting Member States. The fourth pillar relates to *conditional solidarity between Member States*. It aims to alleviate the bankruptcy of a Member State and ensure the stability of the Eurozone; it is limited to the Member States of the euro area.

This paper focuses on the first two pillars of the reformed economic governance applied to the Member States of the euro area. Section II describes the new decision-making process to ensure surveillance and coordination of the national economic policies as well as to sanction the violation of the rules by the Member States. Section III explains how the functioning of the national governments, the

[1] For a description of the evolution of the different pillars of the economic governance, see J-P Keppenne, 'Institutional Report' in *The Economic and Monetary Union*, XXVI FIDE Congress in Copenhagen (2014) 179–257; A de Streel, 'The Evolution of the EU Economic Governance since the Treaty of Maastricht: An Unfinished Task' (2013) 20 *Maastricht Journal of European and Comparative Law 20th Anniversary Issue* 336.

European Commission and the Council of Ministers has been improved for a better compliance with the rules. Section IV claims that the new process does not sufficiently distinguish between the technical assessment and the discretionary choices made by each institution, and does not sufficiently subject each of those tasks to effectiveness and legitimacy requirements. Section V shows that a different allocation of competences could make the decision-making process more effective and legitimate.[2] Finally, Section VI concludes with proposals for policy reforms.

II. THE DECISION-MAKING PROCESS FOR THE GOVERNANCE OF THE EURO AREA

The decision-making process for the first two pillars of the reformed economic governance is based on: (a) a dialogue between the national governments, the European Commission and the Council of Ministers for the surveillance and the coordination of national economic and social policies; which (b) may lead to financial sanctions decided by the Council; and which (c) takes place in the shadow the EU and national courts.

A. The Annual Cycle of Surveillance of Imbalances and Coordination of Economic Policies: An Executive Dialogue

1. *The Surveillance of National Fiscal Imbalances*

The surveillance of national fiscal imbalances takes place as follows.[3] In April, each Member State submits to the Commission its *Stability Programme (SP)* which describes its fiscal policy for the next three years.[4] Such stability programme should be based on macroeconomic forecasts produced or endorsed by a national independent fiscal council.[5] At the same time, each Member State adopts

[2] The effectiveness and the legitimacy of the EU budgetary constrain are analysed in several contributions published in M Adams, F Fabbrini and P Larouche (eds), *The Constitutionalization of European Budgetary Constraints: Comparative and Interdisciplinary Perspectives* (Oxford, Hart Publishing, 2014).

[3] For an overview of the revised Stability and Growth Pact, see European Commission, 'Building a Strengthened Fiscal Framework in the European Union: A Guide to the Stability and Growth Pact' (2013) European Economy: Occasional Paper 150; European Commission, 'Vade mecum on the Stability and Growth Pact' European Economy: Occasional Paper (2013) 151.

[4] Art 4 Council Regulation (EC) 1466/97 of 7 July 1997 on the strengthening of the surveillance of budgetary positions and the surveillance and coordination of economic policies [1997] OJ L209/1, amended by Council Regulation (EC) 1055/2005 of 27 June 2005 [2005] OJ L174/1 and by Regulation (EU) 1175/2011 of the European Parliament and of the Council of 16 November 2011 [2011] OJ L306/12; Specifications of 3 September 2012 on the implementation of the Stability and Growth Pact and Guidelines on the format and content of Stability and Convergence Programmes.

[5] Art 2(1b) Regulation (EU) 473/2013 of the European Parliament and of the Council of 21 May 2013 on common provisions for monitoring and assessing draft budgetary plans and ensuring the correction of excessive deficit of the Member States in the euro area [2013] OJ L140/11.

a *medium-term fiscal plan* compatible with the fiscal country-specific recommendation addressed previously by the Council to the Member State.[6]

In May, the Economic Department of the European Commission (the Directorate-General for Economic and Financial Affairs, DG ECFIN) produces the Spring Economic Forecast, which projects the macroeconomic and budgetary indicators for each Member State. On that basis, the DG ECFIN assesses whether each stability programme complies with the EU deficit rules (the 3 per cent of the GDP ceiling set for the nominal public deficit and the Medium Term Objective set for the structural public balance) and debt rule (the 60 per cent of the GDP ceiling).[7] On the basis of this analysis, and within the discretion provided by the EU fiscal rules, the Commission College recommends to the Council of Ministers the adoption for each Member State of *one fiscal country-specific recommendation (CSR)* which sets fiscal targets and/or means to achieve those targets.

In June, the Economic and Financial Committee, which is composed of senior officials of the national finance ministries and of the European Commission,[8] analyses the economic assessment made by the Commission services and negotiates the fiscal country-specific recommendations proposed by the Commission's College. Then, the Council of Finance Ministers (ECOFIN) adopts by qualified majority the fiscal CSRs[9] and can only amend the Commission proposal by explaining the reasons for the changes ('comply or explain' rule).[10] As was the case for the Commission, the Ministers decide within the discretion provided by the EU fiscal rules.

Note that if a Member State does not comply with its fiscal country-specific recommendation, the Commission addresses a warning and proposes a new and more prescriptive recommendation. The Council adopts this recommendation by qualified majority and following the 'comply or explain' rule.[11] The Commission may also propose a deposit bearing interest of 0.2 per cent GDP. This sanction is automatically adopted by the Council unless a qualified majority opposes, that is, under a reverse qualified majority voting system.[12]

Then in October, each Member State submits to its national parliament its *draft budget*[13] and submits to the European Commission a *draft budgetary plan*, which summarises the draft budget.[14]

[6] Art 4 Regulation 473/2013.

[7] Those rules are provided by primary EU law (Art 126 TFEU and Protocol 12), secondary EU law (Art 2(a) Regulation 1466/97) and international treaties (Arts 3–4 TSCG).

[8] The Economic and Financial Committee is established by Art 134 TFEU and the Council Decision 2012/245 of 26 April 2012 on a revision of the Statutes of the Economic and Financial Committee [2012] OJ L121/22.

[9] Such recommendation is adopted on the basis of Art 121(2) TFEU.

[10] Art 2-ab(2) Regulation 1466/97 amended.

[11] Such recommendation is adopted on the basis of Art 121(4) TFEU.

[12] Art 4 Regulation (EU) 1173/2011 of the European Parliament and of the Council of 16 November 2011 on the effective enforcement of budgetary surveillance in the euro area [2011] OJ L306/1.

[13] Art 4(2) Regulation 473/2013.

[14] Art 6 Regulation 473/2013, Section II of the Specifications of 1 July 2013 on the implementation of the Two Pack and Guidelines on the format and content of draft budgetary plans, economic partnership programmes and debt issuance reports.

In November, the Economic Department of the European Commission produces the Autumn Economic Forecast. On that basis, the DG ECFIN assesses whether each draft budgetary plan complies with the EU fiscal rules, respects the Stability Programme and takes into account the fiscal country-specific recommendation. On the basis of this analysis, the Commission College adopts an *opinion* on each draft budgetary plan, and if it does not comply with EU rules, it may request a revision of the plan.[15] Here again, the College decides within the discretion left by EU fiscal rules.

2. *The Surveillance of Macroeconomic Imbalances and the Coordination of National Economic and Social Policies*

The surveillance of macroeconomic imbalances and the coordination of national economic and social policies runs as follows. In November, the Commission adopts the *Annual Growth Survey* which summarises the economic situation of the EU and proposes priorities for economic reforms at European and national levels to stimulate growth and jobs. The Commission also reviews the *macroeconomic evolution* of the Member States on the basis of a scoreboard of 11 indicators and indicates the States which justify an in-depth review.[16]

In the spring, the priorities of the Annual Growth Survey are discussed by several Council configurations (in particular, the Council of Finance Ministers, the Council of Employment and Social Affairs Ministers and the Council of Competitiveness Ministers), the European Council (composed of the heads of state or government) and the European Parliament. The Commission also concludes the macroeconomic in-depth review indicating the Member States which present imbalances to be corrected.[17]

Then in April, each Member State submits its *National Reform Programme (NRP)*, which describes their past and future reforms for economic, employment and social policies.[18] Such national reform programme should be based on national macroeconomic forecast produced or endorsed by a national independent fiscal council and be consistent with the stability programme.

In May, a core group of the Commission departments (mainly Economic and Financial Affairs, Employment and Social Affairs and the Secretariat General) assesses whether each national reform programme takes into account the Council integrated economic policies guidelines,[19] the Commission Annual Growth Survey and the country-specific recommendations previously addressed by the Council

[15] Art 7 Regulation 473/2013.

[16] Arts 3 and 4 Regulation (EU) 1176/2011 of the European Parliament and of the Council of 16 November 2011 on the prevention and correction of macroeconomic imbalances [2011] OJ L306/25.

[17] Art 5 Regulation 1176/2011.

[18] Art 2-a (2d) Regulation 1466/97 amended.

[19] Council Recommendation (EU) 2010/410 of 13 July 2010 on broad guidelines for the economic policies of the Member States and of the Union [2010] OJ L291/28 and Council Decision (EU) No 2010/707 of 21 October 2010 on guidelines for the employment policies of the Member States [2010] OJ L308/46.

Table 1: Annual Cycle of Surveillance and Coordination Procedures[20]

<table>
<tr><th></th><th></th><th></th><th>Fiscal Surveillance</th><th>Macroeconomic Surveillance</th><th>Socio-economic Coordination</th></tr>
<tr><td>April</td><td>National Government</td><td>T: Independent Fiscal Councils</td><td>— Budgetary statistics
— Macroeconomic forecasts</td><td></td><td></td></tr>
<tr><td></td><td></td><td>C: National Ministers</td><td>Stability Programme (SP)</td><td colspan="2">National Reform Programme</td></tr>
<tr><td>May</td><td>European Commission</td><td>T: Economic and Employment Departments</td><td colspan="3">— Macroeconomic and budgetary forecasts
— Technical assessment
— Macroeconomic imbalance review</td></tr>
<tr><td></td><td></td><td>C: College of Commissioners</td><td>Fiscal draft country-specific recommendation (CSR)</td><td>Other draft country-specific recommendations (CSR)</td><td>Other draft country-specific recommendations (CSR)</td></tr>
<tr><td>June–July</td><td>Council of Ministers</td><td>T: Expert Committees</td><td>Economic and Financial Committee
Negotiate fiscal CSR</td><td>Economic Policy Committee:
Negotiate other CSRs</td><td>Economic Policy Committee, Employment Committee, Social Protection Committee:
Negotiate other CSRs</td></tr>
<tr><td></td><td></td><td>C: Ministers</td><td>Council of Finance Ministers
Adopt CSR</td><td colspan="2">Council of Finance and of Employment Ministers
Adopt other CSRs</td></tr>
<tr><td>October</td><td>National Government</td><td>T: Independent Fiscal Council</td><td>— Budgetary statistics
— Macroeconomic and budgetary forecasts</td><td></td><td></td></tr>
<tr><td></td><td></td><td>C: National Ministers</td><td>Draft Budgetary Plans</td><td></td><td></td></tr>
<tr><td>November</td><td>European Commission</td><td>T: Economic Department</td><td>— Macroeconomic and budgetary forecasts
— Technical assessment</td><td></td><td></td></tr>
<tr><td></td><td></td><td>C: College of Commissioners</td><td>Opinion (pos. revision request)</td><td></td><td></td></tr>
</table>

[20] T refers to technical analysis and assessments while C refers to discretionary choices.

to the Member State concerned. It also assesses the evolution of macroeconomic imbalances. On the basis of those analyses, the Commission College recommends to the Council the adoption of several *country-specific recommendations (CSR)* to be combined with the fiscal recommendation. Such recommendations may set objectives to be met and/or socio-economic policies to achieve those targets. In doing so, the College enjoys a broad political discretion.

In June, four Council committees composed of senior national officials (the Economic and Financial Committee, the Economic Policy Committee, the Employment Committee and the Social Protection Committee) analyse the Commission services economic assessment and discuss the recommendations proposed by the College. Then, Council of Finance Ministers and the Council of Employment Ministers negotiate the draft CSRs. Then, the Summer European Council endorses the texts of the Councils and, finally, the Council of Finance Ministers formally adopts the country-specific recommendations by qualified majority and following the 'comply or explain' rule. Like the Commission, the Council enjoys political discretion in the negotiation of the CSRs.

B. Sanctions when Rules are Violated

If a Member State violates the EU fiscal rules or presents excessive macroeconomic imbalances, it faces corrective procedures leading to the imposition of financial sanctions by the Council.

In case of violation of the EU deficit or debt rules, a Member State may be subject to the *excessive deficit procedure (EDP)* with the following steps: (i) On the basis of a thorough economic analysis by Economic Department of the European Commission, the College of Commissioners may propose to the Council of Finance Ministers to place a Member State under an excessive deficit procedure and to set up a fiscal trajectory to comply with EU rules.[21] In proposing this trajectory, the Commission enjoys some political discretion. (ii) After an opinion of the Economic and Financial Committee, the ECOFIN Council adopts a decision opening the excessive deficit procedure by reverse qualified majority of the Member States of the euro area[22] and the State concerned cannot vote to alleviate an obvious conflict of interest.[23] The Council also adopts a recommendation setting a deadline to reduce the deficit to below 3 per cent of the GDP with a fiscal trajectory to reach such deadline.[24] Here again, the Council enjoys some political discretion. (iii) In this case, the Member State is subject to extensive reporting requirements

[21] Art 126(3) TFEU.
[22] Art 126(6) TFEU, Art 139(4b) TFEU and Art 7 TSCG.
[23] Art 126(13) TFEU.
[24] Art 126(7) TFEU.

with the regular submission of economic partnership programmes which allow the DG ECFIN and then the College of Commissioners to closely monitor the implementation of the budgetary trajectory imposed by the Council.[25] In case of non-compliance, the College of Commissioners proposes a graduation of financial sanctions. The ECOFIN Council decides those sanctions by reverse qualified majority.[26]

This EU corrective procedure is now complemented by a *national correction procedure.* If the national independent fiscal council observes a significant deviation from the Medium Term Objective set for the structural public balance, a national correction procedure proportionate to the deviation should be triggered.[27]

In case of excessive macroeconomic imbalances, a Member State may be subject to an *excessive imbalance procedure (EIP)* with the following steps: (i) After a thorough economic analysis by Economic Department of the European Commission, the College of Commissioners may propose to the Council of Finance Ministers to place a Member State under excessive imbalance procedure.[28] Here also, the Commission enjoys some political discretion in making this choice. (ii) After discussion in the Economic and Financial Committee, the ECOFIN Council adopts, by qualified majority and following the 'comply or explain' rule, a decision opening an excessive imbalance procedure. It also adopts a recommendation[29] on the socio-economic policies to be adopted to correct the imbalances. (iii) In this case, the Member State submits a corrective action plan, which should be endorsed by the Council of Finance Ministers.[30] (iv) The DG ECFIN monitors the implementation of the plan and, in case of violation, the College of Commissioners proposes financial sanction (up to 0.1 per cent of GDP). After discussion in the Economic and Financial Committee, the ECOFIN Council decides the sanction by reverse qualified majority.[31]

[25] Arts 9–10 Regulation 473/2013 and Section IV of the Specifications of 1 July 2013 on the implementation of the Two Pack and Guidelines on the format and content of draft budgetary plans, economic partnership programmes and debt issuance reports.

[26] Art 126 (11) TFEU, Art 7 TSCG, Arts 5–6 Regulation 1173/2011.

[27] Art 6 Council Directive EU 2011/85 of 8 November 2011 on requirements for budgetary frameworks of the Member States [2011] OJ L306/41, Art 5 Regulation 473/2013, Art 3(1e) TSCG and Communication of the Commission, 'Common principles on national fiscal correction mechanisms' COM (2012) 342.

[28] Art 7 Regulation (EU) 1176/2011 of the European Parliament and of the Council of 16 November 2011 on the prevention and correction of macroeconomic imbalances [2011] OJ L306/25.

[29] This recommendation is adopted on the basis of Art 121(4) TFEU.

[30] Art 8 Regulation 1176/2011.

[31] Art 10(4) Regulation 1176/2011 and Art 3(2a) Regulation (EU) No 1174/2011 of the European Parliament and of the Council of 16 November 2011 on enforcement measures to correct excessive macroeconomic imbalances in the euro area [2011] OJ L306/8.

Table 2: EU Corrective Procedures[32]

			Excessive Deficit Procedure (EDP)	**Excessive Imbalance Procedures (EIP)**
Decision to require correction	European Commission	*T: Economic Department*	— Macroeconomic and budgetary forecasts — Technical assessment	Macroeconomic in-depth review
		C: College of Commissioners	— Report — Proposal to place in EDP	Proposal to place in EIP
	Council of Ministers	*T: Experts Committee*	Economic and Financial Committee Opinion	
		C: Council of Finance Ministers	— Decision EDP — Recommendation: deadline and fiscal trajectory	— Decision EIP — Recommendation: policy actions
Implementation of the correction	National Government	*T: Independent Fiscal Councils*	— Budgetary statistics — Macroeconomic forecasts	
		C: National Ministers	Economic Partnership Programmes	— Corrective Action Plan — Progress Reports
	European Commission	*T: Economic Department*	— Macroeconomic and budgetary forecasts — Technical assessment	— Macroeconomic and budgetary forecasts — Technical assessment
		C: College of Commissioners	— Pos. Proposal for non-compliance — Pos. Proposal for sanctions (up to 0.5% GDP)	— Pos. Proposal for non-compliance — Pos. Proposal for sanctions (up to 0.1% GDP)
	Council of Ministers	*T: Experts Committee*	Negotiation in the Economic and Financial Committee	Negotiation
		C: Ministers	Pos. Decision on sanctions	Pos. Decision on sanctions

[32] T refers to technical analysis and assessments while C refers to discretionary choices.

C. The Shadow of the Courts

As several authors have observed, the reformed economic governance increases substantially the role of the national and EU courts in budgetary and economic choices and policies.[33] Although Article 126(10) TFEU excludes an infringement procedure against a Member State violating the EU fiscal rules, EU courts have other means to control the budgetary compliance of the Member States. First, the Court of Justice of the European Union controls the transposition (but not the implementation) of the golden rule and the national automatic correction mechanism provided by the Treaty on Stability, Coordination and Governance in the Economic and Monetary Union (TSCG).[34] Secondly, when the Council imposes a financial sanction against a defaulting Member State, that State may request an annulment of the Council decision by the EU Court. In adjudicating such a case, the Court has to review the compliance by the State concerned of the EU budgetary rules. In addition, at the national level, the automatic correction may allow national courts to annul or suspend a budget violating the Medium Term Objective (MTO) rule.

III. BETTER INSTITUTIONS FOR BETTER RULES COMPLIANCE

As the reformed economic governance is mainly based on an interaction between national governments, the European Commission and the Council of Ministers, it is essential that each of those institutions performs their tasks properly. That is why EU law, and sometimes international law such as the TSCG, impose minimum requirements on national executives and improve the functioning of the Commission and the Council.

Regarding national institutions, EU law requirements mainly focus on the production of statistical data and economic forecasts as well as on the implementation of the national correction mechanism. First, public accounting systems should be subject to national internal control and independent audits[35] as well as to the control of Eurostat, the statistics department of the Commission.[36] Secondly, macroeconomic forecasts should be realistic, produced or endorsed by an independent fiscal council, and significant divergences with the Commission forecasts should be explained.[37] Moreover, budgetary forecasts should be realistic

[33] For instance, F Fabbrini, 'The Euro-Crisis and the Courts: Judicial Review and the Political Process in Comparative Perspective' (2014) 32 *Berkeley Journal of International Law* 64.

[34] Art 8 TSCG.

[35] Art 3 Directive 2011/85.

[36] Arts 11–11b Council Regulation (EC) 479/2009 of 25 May 2009 on the application of the Protocol on the excessive deficit procedure annexed to the Treaty establishing the European Community [2009] OJ L145/1, amended by Council Regulation (EC) 679/2010 of 26 July 2010 [2010] OJ L198/1.

[37] Art 4 Directive 2011/85 and Art 2(1) Regulation 473/2013.

and may, but should not necessarily, be produced or endorsed by an independent fiscal council. Thirdly, the implementation of the national correction mechanism in case of violation of the fiscal rules should be monitored by the independent fiscal council.[38] Thus, EU requirements mainly relate to the technical tasks of the national executives and the main innovation is the obligation to set up a national fiscal authority whose independence and resources are guaranteed.[39]

Regarding the European Commission, improvements were achieved at the technical as well as the political levels. At the technical level, the DG ECFIN has been reinforced notably with more staff. At the political level, the Commissioner for Economic and Monetary Affairs and the Euro received extensive empowerment in order to increase the independence of its decision-making process.[40]

Regarding the Council of Ministers, improvements have also been achieved at the technical and the political levels.[41] At the technical level, the Economic and Financial Committee, and its Eurogroup sub-committee (the Eurogroup Working Group (EWG)) have a full-time and Brussels-based President. At the political level, it is envisaged that the Eurogroup will also have a full-time and Brussels-based President.[42] Moreover, the decision-making process has been made more automatic as the majority of the recommendations and the decisions are adopted following a 'comply or explain' rule and under reverse qualified majority voting.

IV. CONFUSION OF ROLES IN THE DECISION-MAKING PROCESS

The recent reforms of the EU economic governance gives important new tasks to each of its three main actors (national governments, European Commission and Council of Ministers) but it does not sufficiently distinguish between technical assessment and discretionary choices and, more critically, it does not sufficiently ensure the effectiveness and the legitimacy of each task.

A. Technical Analysis and Assessments

Before taking budgetary and economic decisions in economic governance, each of the three main institutions involved has to undertake complex technical macroeconomic assessments. At the national level, government departments and independent fiscal councils produce statistical data as well as macroeconomic and

[38] Art 5(2) Regulation 473/2013, Art 3(1e) TSCG and Communication of the Commission, 'Common principles on national fiscal correction mechanisms' COM (2012) 342, Principle 7.

[39] On the usefulness of the independent fiscal council in correcting the short-term bias of the budgetary authority, see X Debrun, D Hauner and M Kumar, 'Independent Fiscal Agencies' (2009) 23 *Journal of Economic Surveys* 44.

[40] See European Commission Press Release, 27 October 2011, IP/11/1284.

[41] Points 7 and 8 of Annex I to the Euro Summit Statement of 26 October 2011: Ten measures to improve the governance of the euro area.

[42] ibid point 5.

budgetary forecasts and, when necessary, implement a national correction mechanism. At the European Commission level, Eurostat controls the statistical data sent by the Member States and the DG ECFIN produces macroeconomic and budgetary forecasts. At the Council level, the expert committees (Economic and Financial Committee, Eurogroup Working Group, Economic Policy Committee, Employment Committee and Social Protection Committee) analyse implicitly in their discussions the validity and the robustness of the Commission technical analysis.

To be legitimate and reliable, those technical macroeconomic analyses should comply with good governance principles.[43] (i) They should be based on methodologies that are transparent, non-discriminatory between Member States and consistent over time, and reflect mainstream economic theories. (ii) Those methodologies should be periodically assessed and, when needed, corrected or adapted. (iii) They should be produced by departments or agencies that are sufficiently independent from the political and budgetary authority to alleviate capture and time inconsistency, and that have sufficient financial and human resources to deliver quality work. (iv) Those departments or agencies should cooperate in a vertical way (between the national and the European levels) as well in a horizontal way (between national authorities) to exchange best practices as well as to develop common methodologies.

Unfortunately, those principles are not sufficiently met today. At the national level, the most important analysis and forecasts are produced or endorsed by fiscal agencies whose independence and resources are guaranteed.[44] However, a vertical cooperation between those independent fiscal councils and the European Commission as well as a horizontal cooperation among independent fiscal councils have not yet been formally organised. The creation of a European network composed of the national independent fiscal councils and the European Commission could improve the quality of each member of the network, reinforce their independence vis-à-vis their national budgetary authorities and contribute to the development of European methodologies.[45]

At the Commission level, the DG ECFIN depends on the political orientation given by the College of Commissioners. It is true that the Commissioners are independent from the Member States[46] but they are not independent from political tendencies. On the contrary, the new President of the Commission, Juncker, made clear that he wants a more political Commission. In this context, it is more difficult to guarantee the independence of the DG ECFIN's analysis. If the

[43] On those principles see, eg R Baldwin, M Cave and M Lodge, *Understanding Regulation: Theory, Strategy and Practice*, 2nd edn (Oxford, Oxford University Press, 2012).

[44] Art 2(1a) Regulation 473/2013.

[45] Such networks of authorities have been set up for the regulation of network industries: Regulation (EC) 1211/2009 of the European Parliament and of the Council of 25 November 2009 establishing the Body of European Regulators for Electronic Communications (BEREC) and the Office [2009] OJ L337/1, and Regulation (EC) 713/2009 of the European Parliament and of the Council of 13 July 2009 establishing an Agency for the Cooperation of Energy Regulators [2009] OJ L211/1.

[46] Art 17(3) TEU.

Commission becomes a fully-fledged political government of the EU, then the DG ECFIN should be removed from the Commission and made an EU fiscal agency with similar independence and resource requirements to those imposed by EU law for national fiscal councils.[47]

At the Council level, the functioning and the methodologies used by the technical committees, in particular the Economic and Financial Committee, remain very secretive. For instance, the implementation of methodologies used to determine the medium-term objective set for the structural public balance of each Member State is not public although this objective is now one of the key rules of the economic governance.[48] In addition, the methodologies used to propose the budgetary trajectory in case of excessive deficit procedure are not clear. Therefore, the functioning and the methodologies of those technical committees should be more transparent.[49]

B. Discretionary Choices

On the basis of those technical assessments, each of the three main institutions involved in economic governance enjoys some political discretion in making choices about fiscal and economic policies. At the national level, the governments decide their budgetary trajectories as well as the level of public expenses and revenues to meet those trajectories. At the Commission level, the College of Commissioners proposes recommendations and decisions on compliance with EU hard and soft law by the Member States. In case of corrective procedures, the College also proposes the imposition of financial sanctions against defaulting Member States. At the Council level, the Ministers decide, often by reverse qualified majority voting, on all the proposals made by the College of Commissioners.

To be legitimate in a parliamentary democracy, those discretionary fiscal and economic choices should be made by a parliamentary assembly or, at least, by an institution directly accountable to a parliamentary assembly. However, the parliamentary oversight needed for economic governance recommendations and decisions is complex because, on the one hand, it relates budgets and policies adopted at the national level which calls for national oversight but, on the other hand, it relates to decisions having spill-over effects between Member States which calls

[47] A similar argument can be made for the other quasi-judicial or technical tasks done by the Commission and requiring independence, such as the enforcement of competition rules.

[48] The methodological principles to calculate the Medium Term Objective are described in the Specifications of the Council of 3 September 2012 on the implementation of the Stability and Growth Pact and in European Commission, 'Vade mecum on the Stability and Growth Pact' (2013) (n 3) 151. However, the implementation of those principles to calculate the MTO of each Member State is not made public.

[49] J-V Louis, *L'union européenne et sa monnaie*, Commentaire Mégret, 3rd edn (Brussels, Université de Bruxelles, 2009).

for European oversight. Because of this inherent complexity, the parliamentary involvement in the economic governance remains weak to date.[50]

Recommendations and decisions, and the political choice they imply, are proposed by the Commission and adopted by the Council. The European or national parliaments are only indirectly involved as the Commission is accountable before the European Parliament and each Minister, member of the Council, is accountable before his or her own national parliament. Moreover, a soft economic dialogue has been set up between, on the one hand, the European Parliament and, on the other hand, representatives of EU executive institutions (Commission, Council and European Council) or the Member State concerned.[51]

The question is whether this mere indirect parliamentary involvement is adequate to give democratic legitimacy to budgetary and economic choices having far-reaching consequences for the citizens. I think it is not adequate for several reasons. First, it involves mainly the European Parliament and not sufficiently the national parliaments whose core competences in fiscal, economic and social policies are at stake. Secondly, it leads merely to a bilateral relationship between the European Parliament and EU or national institutions and not to a multilateral relationship between national national parliaments. Thirdly, it merely leads to a dialogue and not to recommendations or decisions.

Thus the next question is how to ensure a more important involvement of parliamentary assemblies without impeding effectiveness. I think this involvement should be based on national parliaments (because economic governance relates to national budget decisions), having a horizontal dialogue (because those national budget decisions have spill-over effects between Member States). Such horizontal parliamentary dialogue would parallel the horizontal executive dialogue in the Council. To be efficient, the horizontal dialogue could be organised within a permanent Conference of representatives of national parliaments[52] adopting non-binding opinion before the Council of Ministers takes decisions and recommendations on economic governance.

In summary, to improve the effectiveness and the legitimacy of the current decision-making process of the European economic governance, I call for a clearer distinction between the technical assessment and the discretionary choices made by the national governments, the European Commission and the Council of Ministers. I also suggest subjecting the technical assessments to more transparency,

[50] On that point, see also F Amtenbrink, 'General Report' *The Economic and Monetary Union*, XXVI FIDE Congress in Copenhagen (2014) 107 and the references to the national reports.

[51] Art 2-ab Regulation 1466/97 amended; Art 2a Regulation 1467/97 amended; Art 3 Regulation 1173/2011; Art 14 Regulation 1176/2011; and Art 15 Regulation 473/2013.

[52] This is not the same as the inter-parliamentary conference set up by Art 13 TSCG which comprises representatives of the national parliaments but also the EU Parliament. I think the representatives of the EU Parliament should not be part of the Conference because it creates a confusion between the EU and the national levels of legitimacy and because economic governance relates to purely national decisions. On the difficulties of the functioning of the Art 13 Inter-parliamentary Conference, see V Kreilinger, 'The new Inter-Parliamentary Conference for Economic and Financial Governance' (Notre Europe—Jacques Delors Institute, 2013).

consistency, non-discrimination and independence and submitting political choices to more democratic parliamentary control. However, such reforms are hard to implement for several reasons. Technical assessments and discretionary choices are closely related and may be difficult to separate. Moreover, the additional control by parliamentary bodies, in particular national parliaments, is difficult to set up in an efficient manner.

V. THE ALTERNATIVE ROUTE: INTEGRATION INSTEAD OF SURVEILLANCE

Thus a more radical reform may be required to achieve effectiveness and legitimacy more easily. Instead of leaving economic policies entirely in the hands of the Member States and increasing their surveillance and coordination, federalising part of the economic policies with an increase of the EU budget and/or the creation of a fiscal capacity for the euro area (and ideally with the granting of taxation power to the EU) is the alternative route. This route could be more effective and raise fewer legitimacy concerns.

Regarding effectiveness, many economists[53] and the Four Presidents Report[54] claim that a federal budget and partial federal economic policies are needed to balance a federal monetary policy. In particular, the creation of a euro area fiscal capacity to absorb asymmetric macroeconomic shocks may be necessary to guarantee the sustainability of a monetary zone.[55] Regarding legitimacy, the increased EU budget or a newly created euro area fiscal capacity could be adopted by the European Parliament (or a euro area Parliament) to achieve the double legitimacy on which the European integration is now based.

VI. CONCLUSION

Ideally, a policy reform should meet three conditions: political feasibility, maximisation of its effectiveness and maximisation of its legitimacy. A reform of the EMU

[53] P De Grauwe, *Economics of Monetary Union*, 9th edn (Oxford, Oxford University Press, 2012).

[54] H Van Rompuy in close collaboration with JM Barroso, J-C Juncker and M Draghi, 'Towards a Genuine Economic and Monetary Union' 5 December 2012.

[55] See also, F Fabbrini, 'From Fiscal Constraints to Fiscal Capacity: The Future of EMU and its Challenges' in M Adams, F Fabbrini and P Larouche (eds), *Constitutionalization of European Budgetary Constraints: Comparative and Interdisciplinary Perspectives* (Oxford, Hart Publishing, 2014) 399–418. However, the leaders refused at this stage to create such fiscal capacity. It is striking to observe that the European Council discussed at the same time the reform of the economic governance and the future of the EU budget (the Multiannual Financial Framework 2014–2020) and both issues were never linked politically, although they are clearly related economically. Since then, a single resolution fund for the banking sector has been agreed and may be the first step of a euro area fiscal capacity: Regulation (EU) 806/2014 of the European Parliament and of the Council of 15 July 2014 establishing uniform rules and a uniform procedure for the resolution of credit institutions and certain investment firms in the framework of a Single Resolution Mechanism and a Single Resolution Fund and amending Regulation (EU) 1093/2010 [2014] OJ L225/1 and International Agreement of 21 May 2014 on the transfer and mutualisation of contributions to the Single Resolution Fund.

ensuring effectiveness and legitimacy is the partial federalisation of the economic policies to balance the full federalisation of the monetary policy and the establishment of a fiscal capacity for the euro area. However, this reform is at present not politically acceptable although the recently established single resolution fund for the banks is an encouraging step in this direction.

As the only politically feasible option today is the surveillance and coordination of the national economic policies based on an executive dialogue between national governments, the European Commission and the Council of Ministers in the shadow of the Courts, improvements are needed to increase effectiveness and legitimacy. First, the technical assessment and the discretionary political choices made by each institution should be better distinguished. Secondly, each of those tasks should be subjected to additional effectiveness and legitimacy requirements.

Regarding the technical analysis and assessments, the newly created national fiscal councils should have sufficient resources and expertise and be truly independent from their budgetary authorities, the independence of the DG ECFIN should be guaranteed especially as the European Commission becomes more politicised and the dialogue among national fiscal councils as well as with the Commission should be strengthened, possibly by establishing a formal European network of fiscal councils. Moreover, the functioning of Council committees, in particular the Economic and Financial Committee and their use of economic methodologies, should be more transparent.

Regarding discretionary choices, these need to be explicitly recognised instead of remaining hidden behind complex economic analysis and EU rules. Once recognised, they should be better legitimised. One way to do that is to require that economic governance recommendations and decisions adopted by the Council of Ministers take into account an opinion of a newly created conference of representatives of national parliaments.

6

Constitutional Changes in Euro Government and the Relationship Between the ECB and the Executive Power in the Union

THOMAS BEUKERS*

I. INTRODUCTION

ON 5 AUGUST 2011 the Italian government received a letter from the European Central Bank (ECB). It was meant as a clear signal. The ECB was willing to buy Italian government bonds, which had the effect of lowering the interest rate and enabling the country to refinance its debt. But help from the ECB was not unconditional. The letter contained a very detailed agenda for reform, which Italy was expected to carry out.[1]

This ECB intervention in Italian politics is illustrative of the changing relationship between the ECB and executive power in the Union as a consequence of the crisis. It can also be said to be problematic in several ways. First of all, it was (initially) secret and thereby illustrative of the obscurity surrounding many of Frankfurt's interactions with other executive institutions during the crisis. Secondly, it raises the question of the desirability of ECB intervention in Member State policy-making. How exactly should the ECB relate to Member State economic policies?[2] Do the

* The opinions expressed are the author's own and do not reflect the view of the Dutch Ministry of Foreign Affairs.

[1] The full text of the letter is available on the website of Italian newspaper *Corriere della Sera* available at: www.corriere.it/economia/11_settembre_29/trichet_draghi_inglese_304a5f1e-ea59-11e0-ae06-4da866778017.shtml?fr=correlate.

[2] The EU Treaties define neither monetary nor economic policy, and the exact scope of both policy areas has become the subject of much controversy during the Eurozone crisis, eg in the *Pringle* case ECJ, Case C-370/12 *Pringle v Government of Ireland, Ireland and The Attorney General*, judgment of 27 November 2012, not yet reported on the ESM Treaty, and in the *Gauweiler* case ECJ, Case C-62/14 *Peter Gauweiler and Others v Germun Bundestag* (pending) on the ECB's OMT programme. On the distinction between monetary and economic policy see, eg K Tuori and K Tuori, *The Eurozone Crisis. A Constitutional Analysis* (Cambridge, Cambridge University Press, 2014) 30–31.

letter and the accompanying bond purchase by the ECB undermine Member State independence? Can the ECB be held sufficiently accountable for such intervention in national politics?

Moreover, the ECB letter to the Italian government illustrates a number of relevant issues. It signals the emergence from the crisis of a new balance of power between executive bodies in the euro area. The relationship between the ECB and executive power in the euro area is key to understanding the government of the single currency. The crisis is changing the nature of the fragmented and plural executive power governing the euro, including the ECB, Euro summits, Eurogroup, European Commission, European Stability Mechanism (ESM) Governing Council, and Member State governments. Importantly, the interaction between the ECB—which has proven to be a fundamental player—and other executive bodies—often representing the Member States—is undergoing a metamorphosis.

The letter is also illustrative of the complex mix of instruments used by executive bodies during the crisis. Parallel to the informal conditionality attached to ECB action, bailout instruments such as Memoranda of Understanding and Council Decisions formally impose (similar) conditionality on—sometimes the same—Member States. These instruments are of a varying legal nature, taken either within the European Union (EU) legal order or outside of it, being either legally binding or not.[3] What implications does this have for legal accountability—the possibility to challenge them before the court—and political accountability?[4]

It is clear that the Eurozone crisis raises a great number of constitutional questions concerning euro government.[5] It is not within the scope of this paper to discuss all these questions exhaustively. Rather, the objective of this paper is (1) to illustrate their relevance by highlighting and analysing the rapidly changing government structures of the euro, including the relationship between the ECB and executive power as a consequence of the crisis; and (2) to discuss the implications of these changes for how we study the government of the euro in two ways. First, it will be argued that conceptual innovations are needed to understand government of the euro today. Secondly, it will be argued that the accountability framework for euro government needs to be reassessed.

To this end, several substantive key issues of euro government will first be identified, which have gained new or renewed importance during the crisis (Section II).

[3] For a detailed analysis of the nature of the bailout instruments and the possibilities of challenging them, see C Kilpatrick, 'Are the Bailouts Immune to EU Social Challenge because they are not EU Law?' (2014) 9 *European Constitutional Law Review* 393.

[4] Another example is the ECB's 'announcement' of the OMT programme in a press release, which has not been activated, nor even taken the form of a legal decision, but has nonetheless been challenged before the Bundesverfassungsgericht and is the subject of a preliminary reference to the European Court of Justice; see European Central Bank, Press Release, 'Technical features of Outright Monetary Transactions', 6 September 2012 available at: www.ecb.europa.eu/press/pr/date/2012/html/pr120906_1.en.html.

[5] The concept of government is preferred here over the concept of governance, since the analysis is not focused on eg networks and non-public actors, but on substantive tasks and institutional issues traditionally associated with government.

Then a further illustration of the changing government functions concerning the euro will be given through an analysis of the responsibility for financial stability (Section III). After that, a case will be made for the use of innovative concepts in the analysis of euro government (Section IV). Finally, it will be argued that the changing government of the euro requires a critical assessment of existing accountability structures (Section V).

II. KEY MOMENTS AND ISSUES OF EURO GOVERNMENT

The Euro-crisis has put several issues of euro government high on the political agenda. Many of the recent developments and tensions in government of the euro concern the relationship between the ECB and executive power. The different political views about what constitutes the *appropriate* relationship have caused many political showdowns over recent years. Below I illustrate this by highlighting a few of the many key moments relating to a number of substantive issues where this relationship was central to heated debate, either internally within the ECB, among political leaders, between the ECB and political leaders, by academic scholars, or in all these places. The events illustrate not only the (potential) role for the ECB in the post-crisis Economic and Monetary Union (EMU), but also its position at the centre of the executive powers taking responsibility for the management of the crisis.

A. Financial Stability of Member States (1) Financing Assistance/ESM Firepower

A central part of the crisis management is the various emergency funds that are intended to safeguard the stability of the euro area. The credibility of these emergency funds, or their ability to provide financial assistance not only to relatively small economies like that of Greece and Portugal, but also to Spain and Italy if necessary, has been a main concern. Several controversial options have been advocated, in one way or another involving the ECB.

On the eve of the G20 meeting in Cannes on 2 November 2011, in an informal meeting of Merkel, Sarkozy, Obama, Van Rompuy, Barroso, Berlusconi and Papandreaou to discuss the cases of Italy and Greece, chair of the session Obama (!) turned to the role of the ECB in increasing the firepower of the ESM. The very technical option of filling the ESM fund with special drawing rights (so-called SDRs, not real money, but foreign reserves held by the central bank) was discussed, and was rejected by Germany because of a lack of support from the Bundesbank for this idea as SDRs are 'the exclusive responsibility of the independent central bank to manage—not for politicians to commit willy-nilly to rescue programmes'.[6]

[6] P Spiegel, 'How the euro was saved' *Financial Times* (London, 11 May 2014).

In the summer of 2012, when the markets turned their attention to Spain (which on 24 June made a formal application for financial assistance) the firepower of the ESM was again the subject of fierce debate. This time another option was put on the table: Italian Prime Minister Monti and French President Hollande pushed hard for the possibility of the ESM to borrow from the ECB, though without success.[7]

These debates touch upon central political questions relating to the government of the euro: who helps out Member States when they are at the verge of bankruptcy? And who is responsible for the financial stability of the euro area? The EMU has been designed in a way that should stimulate budgetary discipline of Member States (see, for example, the excessive deficit procedure of Article 126 TFEU) and avoid help from other Member States (see the so-called 'no-bailout clause' of Article 125 TFEU) or from the ECB (see the so-called monetary financing prohibition of Article 123 TFEU). The crisis has, however, illustrated that financial assistance in certain circumstances may be unavoidable, and responsibility for this has been taken by the Member States (mostly of the euro area) collectively.

B. Financial Stability of Member States (2) Government Bond Buying

Responsibility for the financial stability of the (Member States of the) euro area has also been taken by the ECB. In fact, the role of the ECB in safeguarding the financial stability of Member States has come up not only in relation to the firepower of the ESM, but also with regard to the sovereign bond market.

In May 2010 the French President exerted strong pressure on the ECB to start buying government bonds.[8] The ECB, however, did not move before the political decision to institute emergency funds (European Financial Stability Facility/ European Financial Stability Mechanism (EFSF/EFSM)) was taken. Still, the ECB Governing Council had to deviate from standard practice and decide by majority, as the German members of the Governing Council in particular could not agree to bond buying, thereby illustrating the different visions within the ECB about the appropriate relationship between the ECB and Member State debt. When the ECB decided to buy (also) Italian and Spanish bonds in August 2011, it did so only after the euro area Member States had politically decided on 21 July to upgrade the EFSF to be able to buy bonds on the secondary market (so

[7] 'Rescue Fund Controversy: France and Italy Seek Ultimate Firepower for ESM' available at: www.spiegel.de/international/europe/euro-zone-states-discuss-plan-to-give-esm-unlimited-funding-from-ecb-a-847415.html.

[8] As evidenced by the explicit demands by the then French President Sarkozy for an active ECB role in the crisis, eg on 7 May 2010—shortly before the ECB started its first bond-buying programme—when Sarkozy during a meeting with heads of state and government in Brussels pressured ECB President Trichet to start buying sovereign bonds by shouting: 'Come on, come on, stop hesitating!' T Barber, 'Saving the euro: Dinner on the edge of the abyss' *Financial Times* (London, 10 October 2010).

to potentially take over this role from the ECB).[9] Also, the announcement on 26 July 2012 by ECB President Draghi that his institution would 'do whatever it takes to preserve the euro',[10] came after strong pressure from Italian Prime Minister Monti on German Chancellor Merkel, and after an alleged threat that Italy would simply oppose everything unless it would be given some relief. Moreover, it came after an important European Council and Eurosummit meeting at the end of June 2012, where further decisions were taken on the application of the ESM funds.

The main question here is again who should help out Member States and whether the ECB should act as Lender of Last Resort (LOLR) only for banks, or for sovereigns as well. The latter is extremely controversial for its relation to the monetary financing prohibition of Article 123 TFEU.

Importantly, the examples given illustrate that the government of the euro is rapidly changing as a consequence of the substantive necessity to safeguard the financial stability of Member States in the euro area. They also illustrate the complex web of links between the ECB and political actors in this process, and that actions from both sides are not unrelated.

C. Financial Stability of Banks: Liquidity Provision (eg LTRO) and Banking Union

The necessity of stability in the banking sector has also led to important changes in euro government, including the adoption by the ECB of unconventional policy measures and the development of a European banking union.

Although it is less controversial than the ECB's role in safeguarding the stability of Member States, the role of the ECB in safeguarding the stability of the financial system has also raised concerns. Thus, it has been argued that the ECB's increased direct exposure to banks could threaten its operational independence,[11] and that its practically replacing interbank markets is at tension with the principle of an open market economy with free competition.[12] Moreover, injecting liquidity in the banking system has not been without effect on the fiscal position of Member States and therefore illustrates a politically sensitive link between ECB policy and Member States. Massive liquidity injections like the ECB's long-term refinancing operations (LTRO), decided at the end of 2011, enable so-called carry trade, where banks borrow money from the ECB at a low interest rate to then lend it to

[9] Statement by the Heads of State or Government of the Euro Area and EU Institutions, 21 July 2011, point 8, available at: www.consilium.europa.eu/uedocs/cms_data/docs/pressdata/en/ec/123978.pdf.

[10] Speech by M Draghi, President of the European Central Bank at the Global Investment Conference in London, 26 July 2012, available at: www.ecb.europa.eu/press/key/date/2012/html/sp120726.en.html 'Within our mandate, the ECB is ready to do whatever it takes to preserve the euro. And believe me, it will be enough.'

[11] Tuori and Tuori, *The Eurozone Crisis* (n 2) 167.

[12] ibid 164.

Member States—by buying government bonds—at a higher rate. This has raised concerns about the ECB actually helping Member States refinance through the LTRO programme. Finally, the ECB's expanding powers of supervision of banks lead to concerns over tensions between a supervisory mandate and the traditional ECB monetary mandate.

At Trichet's end of term party of 19 October 2011, Sarkozy—in front of Juncker, Van Rompuy, Barroso and Lagarde—clashed with both Merkel and Trichet over the ECB's role in the Eurozone crisis.[13] Sarkozy wanted a more active and political ECB. At the Euro Summit held a week later on 26 October 2011 the following sentence was among the most fiercely debated: 'We fully support the ECB in its action to maintain price stability in the euro area.'[14] In fact, a call on the ECB to continue with its unconventional measures was deleted from an earlier draft version of the summit conclusions. Nonetheless, in early December the ECB announced that it would provide cheap loans to credit institutions with long maturity (the abovementioned LTRO), a decision that was closely related to the agreement by most EU Member States on the Fiscal Compact. The Bundesbank was against the decision on LTRO, as it was against sovereign bond buying.[15]

The main question these events raise is how to manage the link between sovereigns and banks. Who is responsible for the stability of the financial system? How can a central bank be prevented from lending to insolvent banks or ensure that it safeguards the stability of Member States through cheap credit for banks (who use it to buy government debt)?

D. Structural, Economic Reform

Fundamental changes are taking place in euro government in relation to decision-making on (structural) economic reform, a policy area in which the Union has a limited competence. The economic policy conditionality attached to the financial assistance provided by emergency funds constitutes an unprecedented intervention by the collectivity of Eurozone Member States in the economic policy of single Eurozone Member States (with a role for the ECB in the Troika as well). Parallel to this type of intervention are ECB interventions in Member State economic policy-making. On several occasions during the crisis, the ECB has intervened, in a more or less direct way, in Member State policy-making by exercising pressure to adopt very detailed fiscal and structural reforms. Both developments raise the question about the appropriate division of responsibilities between European executive powers and national governments over Member State economic policy, and about the appropriate role of the ECB in relation to Member State economic policy.

[13] M Visser, 'Euroredding in tien aktes' *Het Financieele Dagblad* (Amsterdam, 29 October 2011); H Carnegy, 'Draghi signals support of bond buying' *Financial Times* (London, 27 October 2011); G Moes, 'Frankfurtgroep regeert eurolanden in barre tijden' *Trouw* (Amsterdam, 15 November 2011).

[14] Euro Summit Statement, 26 October 2011, para 2.

[15] J Wilson, 'Bundesbank squares up to ECB's Draghi' *Financial Times* (London, 1 March 2012).

The ECB letter of 5 August 2011 to the Italian government—mentioned in the introduction—is only one example of this ECB intervention. On this occasion, the ECB exercised pressure on Italy to implement reform in exchange for sovereign bond buying. On other occasions the ECB has exercised pressure on Member States through its decisions about the collateral that banks could use to borrow from the ECB,[16] or the possibility for national central banks to engage in emergency lending (emergency liquidity assistance (ELA)) to credit institutions. For example, on 21 March 2013 the ECB decided it would reject ELA provision by the Central Bank of Cyprus in four days (25 March) if by that time a programme were not in place in Cyprus. The programme had to ensure the solvency of the banks concerned. This put pressure on Cyprus to accept a programme nine months after its request for financial assistance on 25 June 2012.[17]

Finally, the new macroeconomic imbalances procedure should also be mentioned here. This new procedure, introduced as part of the 'six-pack' of rules on economic governance, which entered into force in December 2011, is part of a more general attempt to increase the influence of European institutions over national economic policy-making, and to induce Member States to adopt structural reforms.

Who decides, and should decide, on Member State economic policy? Formally, the EU only had a coordinating role in this policy area. How should we understand the ECB's active role during the crisis with regard to individual Member States and the conditionality attached to financial assistance? What implications do these centralising elements of economic policy-making have for Member State sovereignty and for accountability structures?

E. Bearing the Losses: Debt Restructuring

Interestingly, euro area government since the crisis also includes decision-making over debt restructuring. Executive bodies have taken different views on the right approach to restructuring debt of Member States. Because of the importance of debt sustainability in its lending policies, the International Monetary Fund (IMF) has also actively taken part in this discussion.

In their Deauville meeting of October 2010 German Chancellor Merkel managed to secure the support of French President Sarkozy for the idea of private sector involvement (PSI). This private sector involvement in sovereign debt restructuring was, however, fiercely opposed by the ECB because of the impact this would have on investor confidence and financial stability.[18] In fact, in the restructuring/bail-in negotiations on both Greece and Cyprus the ECB has taken clear substantive positions.[19]

[16] For examples, see T Beukers, 'The New ECB and its Relationship with the Eurozone Member States' (2013) 50 *Common Market Law Review* 1579, 1595.

[17] ibid 1593.

[18] See, eg R Atkins, 'ECB warns against private role in bail-outs' *Financial Times* (London, 13 October 2011).

[19] *cf* Tuori and Tuori, (n 2) 104.

The negotiations on debt restructuring also illustrate the changed interaction between the ECB and political actors from an institutional perspective. On Wednesday 20 July 2011, on the eve of an important 'Euro Summit', Sarkozy invited Trichet to join him on his visit to Berlin to prepare a deal on Greece. Trichet initially rejected the invitation, but when he was again invited later that night while attending an anticipated Governing Council meeting, he noticed that the idea of him joining the political leaders found wide support among his colleagues.[20] In fact, participation of the ECB President in ad hoc informal mini-summits, and also at European Council meetings, has become regular practice.[21]

The main political question of euro area government here is: who decides when and how losses are to be taken? This raises a number of further relevant questions: how do and should these decisions relate to Member State sovereignty? How are those deciding on losses held accountable? What is the role of the ECB both in deciding on losses and in bearing losses (public sector involvement)?

III. CHANGING GOVERNMENT FUNCTIONS: FINANCIAL STABILITY

As evidenced above, governing the euro today is not only an issue of the monetary policy of an independent ECB combined with weak fiscal rules.[22] It is also a matter of safeguarding the financial stability of Member States and banks, of providing financial assistance in exchange for credible economic reform, and of addressing economic imbalances. Moreover, it is about the fundamental decision on who is to bear losses if things go wrong. In other words, it is a matter of deciding on (the costs of) restructuring—or not—of sovereign debt, of resolving failing banks and deciding who should pay the bill.

An illustration of the changing government functions (and their allocation) can be given by the responsibility for financial stability. The concept is not easy to define, either in its generic sense,[23] nor in its recent Euro-crisis use of 'financial stability of the euro area as a whole'.[24] Neither is it easy to exactly determine the division of responsibilities between the EU and the Member States in this area. The ECB has been assigned modest tasks in the area of prudential supervision of

[20] F Lemaître and P Ricard, 'La folle nuit de Berlin' *Le Monde* (Paris, 26 July 2011). Confirmed by an ECB Executive Board member involved in a private conversation with this author.

[21] In his meeting with Merkel and Sarkozy, Trichet expressed the ECB's strong opposition to a Greek default, but one day later the heads of state and government of the Eurozone nonetheless reached political agreement on the modalities of involvement of the private sector in the Greek crisis. See the Statement by the Heads of State or Government of the Euro Area and EU Institutions, 21 July 2011, available at: www.consilium.europa.eu/uedocs/cms_data/docs/pressdata/en/ec/123978.pdf.

[22] One can add to this exchange rate decision-making.

[23] V Borger, 'The ESM and the European Court's Predicament in Pringle' (2013) 14 *German Law Journal* 113, 135.

[24] Tuori and Tuori, (n 2) 57.

credit institutions and the stability of the financial system.[25] But responsibilities in this area are clearly shifting as a consequence of the crisis.

For instance, the provision of financial assistance to Member States to safeguard the financial stability of the euro area has been elevated to the level of the euro area Member States collectively (notably outside the EU treaty framework through the ESM Treaty). Several controversial issues exist here relating to the role of the ECB. A number of Member States have—in order to increase the firepower of the ESM emergency fund—advocated the possibility for the ESM to become counterparty to the ECB, enabling it to borrow from this institution (see above). The ECB has always opposed this, and in fact it has not happened. In addition, the ECB is given an institutional role in the application of the ESM treaty, since the Commission negotiates conditionality and monitors Member State compliance in liaison with the ECB. Chiara Zilioli, Director General Legal Services at the ECB, emphasises that the ECB 'is not the decision-maker (the main actor on the EU side is the Commission) but a technical adviser'.[26] In fact, this role has raised some concerns within the ECB about the impact on its independence.[27]

Responsibilities are also shifting in relation to the stability of banks and of the financial system. Without amendment of the treaties, a banking union is being developed in which the ECB has an important role in the supervision of banks. Responsibility is therefore—at least partly—elevated from the national to the European level. In particular, the relationship between new supervisory tasks and its monetary policy mandate has raised concerns in light of independence.[28] The ECB moreover faces a challenge of credibility in its relation to the banking system.

Also related to stability is the safeguarding of the composition of the euro area or the prevention of a breakup. The Treaties contain a number of elements to safeguard the sustainability of the single currency, such as rules on budgetary discipline and the coordination of economic policy. First, as is well known, the treaties do

[25] See Article 127(6) TFEU. See also, eg 'Financial Stability' available at: www.ecb.europa.eu/ecb/tasks/stability/html/index.en.html.

[26] Presentation by Zilioli on 22 November 2012 at the European University Institute (EUI), 'The European Central Bank: a fiscal policy-making institution?'. With regard to ECB participation in missions, Zilioli argues that the ECB is under no obligation to act when invited by the Commission.

[27] *cf* W Münchau, eurointelligence.com, 5 March 2012: 'Frankfurter Allgemeine reports that some senior central bankers close to the ECB (aka the Bundesbank) are concerned about the role of the ECB in the troika. The article appears to point to political interference in two directions. Being part of the troika makes the ECB vulnerable to pressure from the IMF and the European Commission. And it also gives the ECB political power for which there is no political legitimacy. Claus Hulverscheidt, writing in Süddeutsche Zeitung, does a good job to put the story into context. He says there is a debate in the context of the ECB's position in the Irish case, and this debate might get louder when it comes to the inevitable debt write off for Greece. He said the Bundesbank has sympathies for an ECB exit from the troika, but nothing is not going to change.'

[28] The Commission in its proposal for a Single Supervisory Mechanism has reacted to these concerns by suggesting a strict separation of the monetary policy tasks of the ECB from supervisory tools 'to eliminate potential conflicts of interest between the objectives of monetary policy and prudential supervision'. Commission, 'Proposal for a Council regulation conferring specific tasks on the European Central Bank concerning policies relating to the prudential supervision of credit institutions' COM (2012) 511 final, 12 September 2012, 7.

not go as far as to create a power for the Union to decide on the economic policy of the Union and its Member States. Many economists have argued that (historically) such an imbalance is unsustainable,[29] and some movement towards formal and informal supranationalisation of economic policy-making is in fact taking place. An example is provided by the conditionality attached to financial assistance,[30] and here the ECB has played a both interesting and controversial role through its interventions in economic policy-making of Member States by way of 'informal' conditionality of sovereign bond buying under Securities Markets Programme (SMP) (for example, the above-mentioned letter to Italy).

Secondly, the Treaties do not assign the responsibility for the survival of the currency to any (single) institution. But the actions of different institutional actors to safeguard the financial stability of the euro area can be interpreted in exactly this light, for example, some actions of the ECB have been explicitly justified in this light. But the evolving relationship between the ECB and the sustainability of the single currency is not uncontroversial. The ECB has defended its Outright Monetary Transactions (OMT) programme with reference to preventing the breakup of the single currency (redenomination risk). But the Bundesverfassungsgericht in its decision on OMT of January 2014 has simply denied the ECB responsibility for a stable composition of the euro area.[31] Interestingly, the ECB has defended its responsibility by referring to the consequences of the risk of a break-up for another issue related to financial stability, namely price stability.[32]

In the area of price stability, responsibility is clearly in the hands of the ECB (European System of Central Banks (ESCB)).[33] Here too, important changes are taking place and tensions about the relationship between the ECB and broader executive power are illustrated. One of these relates to the above-mentioned—very controversial—broad interpretation of the ECB of its mandate concerning government bond buying, which is intended to restore the proper functioning of the monetary policy transmission mechanism. The ECB bond-buying programmes, which ultimately intend to safeguard price stability, clearly affect Member States' fiscal position, and thus the relationship between the ECB and the Member States.

How should the ECB relate to Member States when it comes to sovereign debt?[34] Can the monetary policy function of the OMT programme be separated from the

[29] *cf* P de Grauwe, *Economics of Monetary Union*, 9th edn (Oxford, Oxford University Press, 2012) 119.

[30] Or through the new macroeconomic imbalances procedure introduced by the six-pack.

[31] Bundesverfassungsgericht [BVerfG—Federal Constitutional Court (FCC)] 2 BvR 2728/13, (14 January 2014) available at: www.bundesverfassungsgericht.de/SharedDocs/Entscheidungen/EN/2014/01/rs20140114_2bvr272813en.html, para 73.

[32] Introductory statement by Mr J Asmussen, Member of the Executive Board of the European Central Bank, in the proceedings before the Federal Constitutional Court, Karlsruhe, 11 June 2013: 'I am firmly convinced that introducing the OMT programme was the right thing to do to ensure price stability in the euro area. After all, a currency can only be stable if its continued existence is not in doubt.'

[33] Art 127 TFEU.

[34] Even though many economists argue that the ECB is the only credible option for a lender of last resort function (see, eg de Grauwe, *Economics of Monetary Union* (n 29) 124), such a role remains extremely controversial (as evidenced by the recent Bundesverfassungsgericht decision on

LOLR message that the ECB gives when it promises (conditional) unlimited purchases? Is and should price stability still be the ECB's main concern?[35] And who should decide on the appropriate balance?

Financial stability is an area in which we witness both a new responsibility emerging at supranational level (stability of Member States and of the euro area collectively) and existing responsibilities shifting from Member States individually to the EU level (stability of the financial system through the banking union). At the same time, new responsibilities are emerging (debt restructuring) and shifting (structural economic reform) in other areas. This rapidly changing context leads to important, often controversial, new roles for, and relationships between, various executive bodies, for example in the Troika of the European Commission, ECB and (external) IMF. They raise important empirical and normative questions about the relationships between executive bodies governing the euro.

IV. RETHINKING THE CONCEPTUAL FRAMEWORK OF THE RELATIONSHIP BETWEEN CENTRAL BANKS AND GOVERNMENTS

Traditionally, concepts such as independence and accountability are used to characterise the relationship between central banks and governments. The examples given above illustrate that there is a need to rethink and refine the conceptual framework used to characterise the (changed) interaction between the ECB and (other) executive bodies in the Union, and thus to characterise an important part of euro government. This can increase our understanding of the changed interaction between executive powers governing the euro.

In doing so, it is useful to keep building on the existing theoretical framework on the constitutional relationship between central banks and governments, which as explained focuses on independence and accountability.[36] Independence has often been used as an analytical tool to understand the nature of the government of a currency through the relationship between expert bodies such as central banks

the OMT programme, see Bundesverfassungsgericht [BVerfG—FCC] 2 BvR 2728/13, (14 January 2014) available at: www.bundesverfassungsgericht.de/SharedDocs/Entscheidungen/EN/2014/01/rs20140114_2bvr272813en.html. See the second issue of (2014) 15 *German Law Journal* for several different analyses of this case, available at: www.germanlawjournal.com/index.php?pageID=2&vol=15&no=2.

[35] M Hellwig has, for example, recently argued at the ECB research conference that financial stability should be elevated to a target of the same weight as price stability, see eurointelligence.com, 27 May 2014.

[36] eg F Amtenbrink, *The Democratic Accountability of Central Banks. A Comparative Study of the European Central Bank* (Oxford, Hart Publishing, 1999); B Laurens, M Arnone and J-F Segalotto, *Central Bank Independence, Accountability, and Transparency* (New York, Palgrave Macmillan, 2009). More recently and related to the crisis, S Baroncelli, 'The Independence of the ECB after the Economic Crisis' in M Adams, F Fabbrini and P Larouche (eds), *The Constitutionalization of European Budgetary Constraints* (Oxford, Hart Publishing, 2014) 125. See also M van der Sluis, 'Maastricht Revisited: Economic Constitutionalism, the ECB and the Bundesbank' in M Adams, F Fabbrini and P Larouche (eds), *The Constitutionalization of European Budgetary Constraints* (Oxford, Hart Publishing, 2014) 105.

and political bodies such as governments. A common distinction is made between personal, institutional, functional and financial independence, for example by lawyers interested in the nature of the relationship between institutions governing a currency,[37] but also by economists analysing the optimal relationship between independence and output/price stability.[38]

It is, however, also necessary to go beyond existing research and to refine the conceptual framework by including innovative constitutional concepts for the characterisation and understanding of the interaction between the ECB and executive powers, such as the nature of executive power in the context of the EU and central bank intervention.

A. Central Bank Intervention

The crisis has caused an important shift in the ECB approach to the economic policy of Member States. In the past it restricted itself to (simply) critically assessing policy, and making suggestions and recommendations; now it (also) strongly pressures a specific course of action. The ECB is keen to emphasise that it is not negotiating with Member States,[39] nor imposing any measures,[40] and that instead it is only sending messages to Member States collectively and individually. In reality, it combines these messages with significant pressure through the use of its powers in an unconventional manner and reinforced by its role in the Troika. The combination of three important characteristics of the 'messages' given by the ECB to Member States in relation to their fiscal policy and structural reforms—they are (1) directed at individual Member States, (2) detailed, and (3) combined with strong and effective pressure—is unprecedented, and justifies speaking of central bank intervention in the area of economic policy-making.[41] The nature of these interventions needs to be studied in more detail, and its implications for other aspects of the relationship between the ECB and executive powers, for example, in terms of accountability, need to be assessed (see also Section V below).

B. The Pluralist Nature of EU Executive Power Governing the Euro

The nature of the euro government can be said to be unique, because of the specific federal division of powers concerning monetary policy on the one hand, and

[37] *cf* Amtenbrink, *The Democratic Accountability of Central Banks* (n 12).

[38] eg A Cukierman, S Webb and B Neyapti, 'Measuring the Independence of Central Banks and its Effect on Policy Outcomes' (1992) *World Bank Economic Review* 358.

[39] J-C Trichet, ECB Press Conference, 6 October 2011: 'As regards the letter; we are not negotiating with anybody.'

[40] *cf* Trichet, ECB Press Conference, 8 September 2011: 'As regards Italy, as I said, these are messages: we are not dictating or imposing anything.'

[41] See also Beukers, 'The New ECB and its Relationship with the Eurozone Member States' (n 16) 1604.

economic policy on the other hand. As mentioned, monetary policy is an exclusive power of the Union, but economic policy is certainly not. Member States traditionally only coordinate economic policy and the lack of a political union is considered to undermine the sustainability of EMU (although above we have seen that relevant developments, for example, related to conditionality, are taking place in this area). In general, a distinction has been made between political executive power (European Council, Council and Commission), administrative executive power (Commission) and satellite executive power (ECB, agencies) in the Union.[42]

This unique constitutional settlement also has institutional consequences for the relationship between executive bodies governing the euro. In particular, it means that the ECB does not engage with a single government, but with many different executive bodies at Union, and most importantly national, level. The unique design of European economic and monetary union means that one cannot simply speak of a traditional relationship between the central bank and the 'government'. In the EU there is no single government or authority with which the ECB interacts.[43]

Also, the crisis is changing the nature of the fragmented and plural executive power governing the euro, including the ECB, Euro summits, Eurogroup, European Commission, ESM Governing Council, and Member State governments. Several developments stand out here that need to be further analysed and critically assessed. First, there is a further proliferation and fragmentation of executive bodies governing the euro,[44] with a role for external parallel bodies such as the ESM Board of Governors/Directors and even for the external IMF. Secondly, there are modest developments in the establishment of political authority at the level of the Eurozone, for example, the convening of Euro Summits and the further development of the Eurogroup.[45] Thirdly, and more specifically, the ECB is forced to fill the gap left by the lack of effective action by a single political authority and to take a more prominent role than envisaged by the treaties, most notably in relation to the stability of the euro area (in a broad sense).[46]

Several questions follow from these developments. What new balance of powers is emerging from the crisis? What formal and informal relations are developing

[42] See D Curtin, *Executive Power of the European Union: Law, Practices, and the Living Constitution* (Oxford, Oxford University Press, 2009).

[43] In understanding the changing relationship between the ECB and executive power, it is arguably useful to engage in comparative constitutional analysis, eg by looking at relevant elements of the US Government. A study of the relationship between the US Government and the Federal Reserve would, considering the federal character of this system, be useful to understand the nature of euro government (*cf* J Mélitz, 'How to save the euro? Lessons from the US' in M Beblavy et al (eds), *The Euro Area and the Financial Crisi* s (Cambridge, Cambridge University Press, 2011) 340–43).

[44] For example, through the involvement of the Troika of European Commission, ECB and IMF in negotiating and monitoring financial assistance.

[45] D Hodson, *Governing the Euro Area in Good Times and Bad* (Oxford, Oxford University Press, 2011).

[46] Further developments are the shift to the Union level of powers in the area of banking union, and the significantly increased involvement of the European Commission in national budgetary affairs.

between the various executive bodies governing the euro? And to what extent are these developments desirable? For example, what price does the ECB pay for its prominent role in terms of its primary objective and independence, for instance through open internal conflict in decision-making,[47] or through the combination of monetary and supervisory tasks?

V. WHAT GOVERNMENT FOR THE EURO? RETHINKING THE ACCOUNTABILITY FRAMEWORK

The rapidly changing government of the euro not only warrants new studies using conceptual innovations. It also asks for critical assessment. In particular, there is a need to rethink normatively the role of the ECB and its relationship with executive, but also representative, institutions in the euro area.[48]

In this exercise, it is useful to apply traditional concepts such as independence and accountability not only in analysing and explaining the relationships between institutions (see Section IV above), but also to take into account their normative assumptions and implications. And again, the role of innovative concepts should be considered. For example, the greater centralisation of economic policy raises pressing questions about the appropriate involvement of the ECB in Member State economic policy-making. To what extent is it desirable that the ECB goes beyond signalling and suggesting, and complements this with interventions in Member State economic policy?

In this paragraph I will focus on the issue of accountability and argue that, together with the shifting balance of powers between executive bodies governing the euro, relevant changes are also taking place in the existing accountability structures.[49] These changes may not be sufficient however.

Several changes can already be identified in the accountability structures governing the ECB, both in the form of legal rules and institutional practices. First, the prominent role of the ECB in the Eurozone crisis has led to debate within (and also outside) the ECB Governing Council about the desirability of publishing minutes of Council meetings. On 3 July 2014 the ECB announced its commitment to publish regular accounts of the Governing Council's monetary policy meetings as of January 2015.[50] This represents a revolutionary break with past tradition. Secondly, the European Parliament has insisted on increased accountability of the ECB for the latter's supervisory tasks in the banking union, and in fact it secured

[47] J-V Louis, Guest Editorial: 'The no-bailout clause and rescue packages' (2010) 47 *Common Market Law Review* 971.

[48] And, one can add that there is a need to rethink the relationship between the ECB and the banking sector.

[49] See also the contribution by D Curtin, ch 10 in this volume.

[50] ECB Press Conference, 3 July 2014, 'ECB to adjust schedule of meetings and to publish regular accounts of monetary policy discussions in 2015', available at: www.ecb.europa.eu/press/pr/date/2014/html/pr140703_1.en.html.

new accountability requirements in an Interinstitutional Agreement between the two institutions on cooperation on the Single Supervisory Mechanism.[51] Thirdly, the announcement of unconventional ECB action through government bond purchases on the secondary market (the so-called OMT programme) has led to an unprecedented preliminary referral by the German Bundesverfassungsgericht to the European Court of Justice.[52] This is an important new case of legal accountability for ECB action. Fourthly, the Eurozone crisis has led to a historical visit by ECB President Draghi to the German Bundestag. On 24 October, shortly after the ECB announcement on the OMT programme, Draghi defended the programme in the German parliament. In contrast, former ECB President Trichet has recently refused to appear before the Irish Parliament (Oireachtas).[53]

Do these developments provide sufficient accountability of the ECB? It seems that at least one important development, namely the ECB interventions in Member State economic policy-making (see Section II above),[54] has not been matched with further accountability structures. Is ECB accountability through participation in relevant Council meetings and through its monetary dialogue with the European Parliament sufficient? Should the ECB President not (have) appear(ed) before the Italian Parliament to explain the timing, reason and substance of the letter of 5 August 2011, in which it asked the Italian government for structural reform in exchange for its Italian bond purchases? In 1999 Amtenbrink has argued that accountability of the ECB before national parliaments should not take the form of a requirement to appear at hearings before them.[55] That thesis should be reconsidered in light of recent events. A case can be made for institutionalising the possibility for national parliaments to hear the ECB president with regard to the specific policy recommendations the ECB makes to their government, in particular when these recommendations are accompanied by strong and effective pressure.

VI. CONCLUSION

The Eurozone crisis has led to substantive changes in government of the euro with relevant institutional implications. For example, collective decision-making among representatives of the euro area Member States now takes place regarding financial stability, economic and structural reform, and the taking of losses. In many cases

[51] Available at: www.ecb.europa.eu/ecb/legal/pdf/celex_32013q113001_en_txt.pdf.

[52] See extensively on this referral *German Law Journal* (2014) 15 special issue no 2, including T Beukers, 'The Bundesverfassungsgericht Preliminary Reference on the OMT Program: "In the ECB We Do Not Trust. What About You?"' (2014) 15 *German Law Journal* available at: www.germanlawjournal.com/index.php?pageID=11&artID=1624.

[53] S Collins, 'Trichet's attitude to planned inquiry "arrogant"' *The Irish Times* (8 May 2014) available at: www.irishtimes.com/business/financial-services/trichet-s-attitude-to-planned-inquiry-arrogant-1.1787117.

[54] See also Beukers, (n 16) 1579.

[55] Amtenbrink, (n 36) 366.

the ECB has taken a prominent role, creating new dynamics between the ECB and other executive bodies governing the euro. Among the institutional implications are significant shifts in the balance of powers between the Member States of the euro area, EU institutions and new supranational institutions. Although these shifts are accompanied by new developments in the area of accountability, it is argued that in some cases, notably ECB involvement in Member State structural economic reform, these developments are not yet sufficient.

7

The Single Supervisory Mechanism: Building the New Top-Down Cooperative Supervisory Governance in Europe

GIANNI Lo SCHIAVO*

I. INTRODUCTION

THE CREATION OF a single currency (the euro) and the conferral of exclusive monetary powers to the European Central Bank (ECB) did not provide for the creation of a centralised level of supervision over credit institutions in the euro area.

Prior to the outbreak of the financial crisis, prudential supervision in Europe remained a national competence. The lack of a European level of prudential supervision has been considered as a major pitfall in the structure of the Economic and Monetary Union (EMU). The recent financial and sovereign debt crisis has shown that the European banking system is still vulnerable and that the liquidity or the solvability of credit institutions can easily spread towards other banks and to the real economy in Europe.

As from the second half of 2012, a new institutional structure for the governance of prudential supervision has taken place, the Single Supervisory Mechanism (SSM).[1] This is part of the wider 'European Banking Union' (EBU) project, which consists of a new institutional reform for prudential regulation, supervision and resolution of credit institutions in the European Union (EU). The set-up of the EBU consists of two pillars: the Single Supervisory Mechanism and the Single Resolution Mechanism (SRM). The former confers prudential supervisory tasks to the ECB and establishes a system of dual-tier prudential supervisory governance shared between the ECB and the national supervisory authorities (hereafter

* Part of the analysis has benefited from my working experience at the SSM Secretariat of the European Central Bank. The opinions expressed are the author's own and do not reflect the view of the European Central Bank.

[1] See, generally, R Lastra, 'Banking Union and Single Market: Conflict or Companionship?' (2013) *Fordham International Law Journal* 1190; N Moloney, 'European Banking Union: assessing its risks and resilience' (2014) *Common Market Law Review* 1609.

NCAs or national competent authorities). The latter establishes a dual-tier supranational level for banking resolution by creating the Single Resolution Board, a common procedure for supranational banking resolutions and a phased-in Single Bank Resolution Fund.[2] While the SRM is an important crisis-related reform to avoid systemic banking crises and public expenses to bailout credit institutions, the SSM is a critical institutional reform as it empowers the ECB—an EU institution—with direct supervisory tasks and powers over credit institutions in Europe. For this reason, this contribution intends to assess the SSM from an institutional perspective.

The process of adoption of the SSM officially began in September 2012. Together with the 'A Roadmap towards the Banking Union',[3] the Commission tabled two proposals of Regulation in September 2012. These aimed at establishing the SSM by conferring new supervisory tasks to the ECB and by revising the European Banking Authority (EBA) decision-making procedures. The main SSM proposal aimed at conferring prudential tasks on the ECB for the prudential supervision of credit institutions.[4] In the words of Barroso, the proposals intended to establish a 'new system, with the European Central Bank at the core and involving national supervisors … [to] restore confidence in the supervision of all banks in the Euro area'.[5] During the process of adoption of the SSM proposal, the European Council conclusions of 14 December 2012 substantially modified the content of the proposal especially as regards the scope of the ECB supervision. The process of adoption of the main SSM Regulation was completed in October 2013.[6] On 4 November 2014 the EBU reached a major milestone when the SSM became operational and the ECB acquired its new and unprecedented supervisory competences.

At present, many challenges are open to debate and it remains to be seen how a 'genuine' EBU will work. In March 2015, the ECB has published the first Annual Report on the ECB supervisory activities that shows the role and importance of the SSM for a 'genuine' EMU.[7] Surely, the setup of the EBU will give rise to many new topics for analysis and discussion in future. In light of the SSM governance framework, this chapter suggests that both the ECB and the national competent authorities will play an essential role in conducting prudential supervision in a new governance framework. In this sense, the SSM shows that the European model of prudential supervision has moved from coordination to cooperation of administrative supervisory functions. This is because the SSM is structured as

[2] For a first comment on the SRM, see G Lo Schiavo, 'The Development of a New Bank Resolution Regime in Europe: Fit for Purpose?' (2014) *Journal of International Banking Law and Regulation* 689.

[3] Commission, 'A Roadmap towards a Banking Union' COM (2012) 510 final.

[4] Commission, 'Proposal for a Council Regulation conferring specific tasks on the European Central Bank concerning policies relating to the prudential supervision of credit institutions' COM (2012) 511 final.

[5] European Commission, Press Release, 'Commission proposes new ECB powers for banking supervision as part of a banking union' 12 September 2012, IP/12/953.

[6] Council Regulation (EU) 1024/2013 of 15 October 2013 conferring specific tasks on the European Central Bank concerning policies relating to the prudential supervision of credit institutions [2013] OJ L287/63 (hereafter 'SSM Regulation').

[7] ECB, Annual Report on supervisory activities, March 2015, available at: www.bankingsupervision.europa.eu/ecb/pub/pdf/ssmar2014.en.pdf?a88c90797b71eea2e8c133ef20a370d1.

a 'top-down cooperative' institutional arrangement shared between the ECB and the NCAs.

The chapter is structured as follows. The first section will briefly identify who exercised prudential supervision in Europe before the SSM reform and why the pre-SSM arrangements have been unsuccessful. In this sense, an analysis on the use of Article 127(6) TFEU will be made. The second part appraises the most critical elements of the SSM from a governance perspective with regard to the role of the ECB and that of the NCAs. The chapter concludes by arguing that the SSM is structured as a single *top-down cooperative* supervisory mechanism where both the ECB and NCAs play an essential role.

II. SHAPING A NEW INSTITUTIONAL REFORM FOR THE EMU: THE FINANCIAL CRISIS AND THE ESTABLISHMENT OF THE SINGLE SUPERVISORY MECHANISM

A. Taking Stock of Prudential Supervision in Europe: From the National to the Supranational Level

From a general perspective, it is important to distinguish between prudential regulation and supervision. Many studies have provided analysis on the distinction between regulation and supervision.[8] Whilst regulation refers to the creation of rules for the conduct of prudential activities, supervision consists in the oversight on regulated market players.[9] Before the outbreak of the crisis, it was well established that central banks or other supervisory entities at national level exercised the mandate for supervision of credit institutions in Europe.[10]

Even after the creation of the European System of Central Banks (ESCB) and the conferral of exclusive monetary policy to the ECB, prudential supervision remained at national level.[11] Hence, while the ECB could be consulted for prudential supervision matters,[12] only NCAs supervised directly credit institutions in Europe. The establishment of a system of bank supervision at ECB level was not conceived as the leading model of supervision in Europe.[13] Authors were divided between those supporting a coordinated level of decentralisation and those favourable to centralisation at European level of supervisory functions.[14]

[8] See E Wymeersch, 'The future of financial regulation and supervision in Europe' (2005) 42 *Common Market Law Review* 987, 988.

[9] ibid.

[10] L Dragomir, *European Prudential Banking Regulation and Supervision: The Legal Dimension* (Abingdon/New York, Routledge, 2010) 238.

[11] See J Pisani-Ferry et al, 'What Kind of European Banking Union?' (2012) *Bruegel Policy Contribution* 6.

[12] Art 127(5) TFEU.

[13] C Goodhart, 'The Political Economy of Financial Harmonisation in Europe' in J Kremers et al (eds), *Financial Supervision in Europe* (Cheltenham, Edward Elgar, 2003) 132.

[14] See R Lastra, 'The Governance Structure for Financial Regulation and Supervision in Europe' (2003) 10 *Columbia Journal of European Law* 55.

The use of the 'enabling clause' under Article 127(6) TFEU remained unexplored. Rather, scholarship promoted the creation of a new system of financial supervision through reinforced coordination and cooperation between national authorities in network-based or agency structures at the European level.[15]

When in February 2009 the de Larosière report was published,[16] the need to put forward a reform of the system of financial—and thus banking—supervision was envisaged. The findings of this document were an important step that prompted a change in the approach to be taken at supervisory level.[17] However, the de Larosière report did not suggest the use of the 'enabling clause' under Article 127(6) TFEU in order to confer supervisory tasks to the ECB.[18] This was mainly because there were concerns over conflicts of interest, supervisory competences and procedural difficulties.[19] In sum, there was not a sufficiently strong momentum to reinforce micro-prudential supervision in the first phase of the financial crisis by conferring direct prudential functions to the ECB.

In 2010 the Commission proposed the creation of three new European agencies in the financial sector: the European Supervisory Authorities (ESAs) in charge of the banking (EBA), the securities (European Securities and Markets Authority (ESMA)) and the insurance and pensions (European Insurance and Occupational Pensions Authority (EIOPA)) sectors. The creation of ESAs has been a significant step forward towards regulatory and prudential convergence.[20] In particular, the EBA has as acted as 'an integrated network of national and Union supervisory authorities, leaving day-to-day supervision to the national level'.[21]

Nonetheless, the degree of EBA's prudential supervisory powers, and generally of European micro-prudential supervision, has remained constrained for a number of reasons and the ESA structure did not prove to be a successful reform to boost the supranational dimension of micro-prudential supervision. First, the EBA lacks real-teeth powers to supervise market players and to enforce decisions, as the *Meroni* doctrine does not allow a European agency to enjoy full discretionary powers.[22] Secondly, the EBA's operational functioning is national-centric as national supervisors have extensive powers in the Board of Governors. Thirdly, the EBA is based on cooperation and consultation between national supervisory

[15] R Smits, *The European Central Bank, Institutional Aspects* (Alphen aan den Rijn, Kluwer, 1997) 76–77.

[16] J de Larosière, 'Report of the High-Level Group on Financial Supervision in the EU' (Brussels, 2009) (hereafter 'de Larosière Report').

[17] For a general picture on the regulatory and supervisory response to the financial crisis, see E Wymeersch, KJ Hopt and G Ferrarini (eds), *Financial Regulation and Supervision. A Post-Crisis Analysis* (Oxford, Oxford University Press, 2012).

[18] de Larosière Report, 42–43.

[19] ibid 43.

[20] See M Chamon, 'EU Agencies between Meroni and Romano or the Devil and the Deep Blue Sea' (2011) 48 *Common Market Law Review* 1055; M Busuioc, 'Rule-making by the European Financial Supervisory Authorities: Walking a Tight Rope' (2013) 19 *European Law Journal* 111.

[21] Regulation (EU) 1093/2010 of the European Parliament and of the Council of 24 November 2010 establishing a European Supervisory Authority (European Banking Authority), amending Decision 716/2009/EC and repealing Commission Decision 2009/78/EC [2010] OJ L331/12 Recital 9.

[22] Case C-9/56 and 10/56 *Meroni v High Authority* [1957/1958] ECR 133.

authorities and is not a central authority for the conduct of micro-prudential supervision. In sum, the EBA has acted as an integrated network of supervisors and not a new independent and strong decision-making European authority.

The new supervisory structure on credit institutions based on the de Larosière report and implemented in the EBA has not been as evolutionary as expected. While national supervision, ring-fencing policies and market fragmentation continued to exacerbate financial markets, the new—and unprecedented—reform to establish the EBU was launched in summer 2012.

B. The Conferral of Supervisory Competences to the ECB Through Article 127(6) TFEU

Both the Treaty and the Statute of the ESCB refer to the possibility of enabling the ECB with supervisory functions for credit institutions.[23] Article 127(6) TFEU is the explicit legal basis that envisages the possibility to centralise supervisory functions within the ECB.

Article 127(6) TFEU reads as follows:

> The Council, acting by means of regulations in accordance with a special legislative procedure, may unanimously, and after consulting the European Parliament and the European Central Bank, confer specific tasks upon the European Central Bank concerning policies relating to the prudential supervision of credit institutions and other financial institutions with the exception of insurance undertakings.

The wording of the enabling clause shows the divergences of opinions at the time of the drafting of the Treaty of Maastricht. The Draft ESCB Statute included 'prudential supervision' among the basic tasks of the ESCB. However, at that time, there was strong opposition on the part of some Member States to qualify prudential supervision and the stability of the financial system as a basic task of the ESCB.[24] The outcome of the negotiation process ended up framing prudential supervision and stability of the financial system as non-basic ESCB tasks. This led political negotiators to agree on the introduction of an enabling legal basis to confer prudential supervision to the ECB at a later stage.

Against this background, in 2012 the European Council mandate to explore fully Article 127(6) TFEU allowed the Commission to make appropriate use of this article with a view to creating the SSM. Scholarship argued that conferring an extensive mandate to the ECB to exercise prudential powers for credit institutions would be possible under this legal basis.[25] The interpretation of the expression 'confer specific tasks upon the European Central Bank' in Article 127(6) TFEU

[23] See, inter alia, R Lastra, *International Financial and Monetary Law* (Oxford, Oxford University Press, 2015) 357–58.

[24] ibid.

[25] E Wymeersch, 'The Single Supervisory Mechanism or "SSM", Part One of the Banking Union' (2014) *ECGI Working Paper Series in Law* 18–19.

provides for extensive grounds to centralise supervisory functions.[26] Other legal bases, such as Article 352 TFEU, the flexibility clause,[27] or Article 114 TFEU, would not have been sufficient to provide for such conferral. Similarly, the centralisation of supervisory functions by the implied powers doctrine[28] through an extensive reading of Article 127(5) TFEU does not appear feasible.

From an institutional perspective, Article 127(6) TFEU is the most appropriate legal basis to structure the new supervisory mechanism with the ECB at its centre. Firstly, the addressee of the 'tasks' is the ECB, an EU institution that is not limited in its decision-making powers by the restrictive judicial interpretations held in *Meroni*.[29] According to this (in)famous ruling, European agencies cannot fully exercise their functions as they cannot be delegated pure discretionary powers.[30] The EBA Regulation shows that the Commission exerts some limits on EBA decision-making and enforcement powers. These have been restated in a recent case before the ECJ on ESMA. The Court has somehow stressed that the conferral of functions to European agencies cannot be fully discretionary, but need to be circumscribed by conditions and criteria imposed by the delegator.[31] On the contrary, the ECB is an EU institution that can exercise full decision-making powers. No limitations on the scope of supervisory powers are contained in Article 127(6) TFEU, with the notable exception of supervision on insurance undertakings. Hence, the expression 'specific tasks' does not pose *ex ante* limits to the Council in conferring prudential competences to the ECB.

Secondly, Article 127(6) TFEU places the ECB as the best-placed institution to exercise the appropriate degree of supervision without concerns on the problem of delegation of powers.[32] Three arguments support this. First, according to Article 25(1) of the ESCB Statute, the ECB enjoys wide advisory competence in prudential matters.[33] Second, the ECB plays an important role in contributing to regulatory activities in financial markets in Europe. In particular, the ECB exercises consultative powers when banking regulation is adopted. Third, the ECB has explicit regulatory powers as stated in Article 132(1) TFEU which do not include prudential functions of supervision, but do not exclude them either. This serves

[26] Another open legal problem is whether the use of Art 127(6) TFEU could be extended to non-euro area Member States. Art 139(3)(c) TFEU extends Art 127 TFEU to Member States with a derogation. However, Art 139(2)(e) excludes that acts of the European Central Bank apply to non-euro area Member States.

[27] Smits, *The European Central Bank* (n 15) 356.

[28] L Panourgias, *Banking Regulation and World Trade Law: GATS, EU and Prudential Institution Building* (Oxford, Hart Publishing, 2006) 173–77.

[29] Case C-9/56 and 10/56 *Meroni v High Authority* (n 22).

[30] See very recently, Case C-270/12 *United Kingdom v European Parliament and Council of the European Union*, judgment of the Court of 22 January 2014, not yet reported, on the powers to ban financial products by the ESMA in financial markets. In this case, the ECJ held that the power to impose a ban on financial products by the ESMA is compatible under EU law.

[31] ibid paras 42 and 53. See also the AG conclusions on the EBA case, Case C–507/13 *United Kingdom v European Parliament and Council*, 20 November 2014, paras 56 *et seq*.

[32] See Pisani-Ferry et al, 'What Kind of European Banking Union?' (n 11) 11.

[33] See more extensively, Dragomir, *European Prudential Banking* (n 10) 226–30.

to sustain the view that the ECB is well placed to exercise regulatory and supervisory powers under EU primary law.[34] While these arguments suggest that the ECB has been given some regulatory powers through the Treaty and the ESCB Statute, there is nothing to prevent the ECB from enjoying direct or indirect supervisory powers.

To put this into perspective, the (re-)use of such legal basis will exclude Treaty changes that would insert new legal bases. The faster and more efficient solution of using legal bases avoids the opening of lengthy and burdensome revisions procedures to the Treaty. In other words, the use of this legal basis does not require a burdensome Treaty change to extend supervisory powers further. Article 127(6) TFEU is already very wide in this sense.

In sum, a number of arguments support the use of Article 127(6) TFEU to establish the SSM. Such legal basis provides for the required legal certainty on the conferral of prudential functions to the ECB within the SSM. Article 127(6) TFEU remedies the constitutional difficulties in conferring limited prudential tasks to 'established' or new European agencies or authorities.[35]

III. THE SSM INSTITUTIONAL GOVERNANCE: A TOP-DOWN SUPERVISORY STRUCTURE SHARED BETWEEN THE ECB AND THE NCAS

Having examined the *ex ante* grounds on the conferral of supervisory tasks and powers to the ECB, this section explores the new supranational governance framework.

A. The SSM and the ECB

The ECB is one of the EU institutions as indicated in the Treaty. As part of the ESCB, the ECB's primary function is to conduct monetary policy for the Member States whose currency is the euro, together with the National Central Banks.

The SSM Regulation confers a new competence to the ECB for the supervision of credit institutions in participating Member States. This results in a profound change for the governance structure of the ECB.

1. *The Supervisory Role of the ECB within the SSM*

Chapter II of the SSM Regulation is at the centre of this examination as it elucidates the degree of supervisory tasks and powers of the ECB and of NCAs. In particular, Articles 4 and 6 are the key provisions on the supervisory tasks and

[34] See ibid 226.

[35] However, at the time of writing a legal challenge against the SSM and the use of its legal basis has been put forward in Germany. See S Wagstyl, 'Europe's Banking Union Faces Legal Challenge in Germany' *Financial Times* (London, 27 June 2014).

powers of the ECB. These show that the ECB exercises prudential tasks together with the NCAs.

The ECB and the NCAs are both competent to carry out supervisory tasks in relation to credit institutions established in participating Member States.[36] The title of Article 6—'Cooperation within the SSM'—shows that the SSM is not based on a strict hierarchy where the ECB conducts most or all the operations while NCAs simply implement or enforce the ECB's decisions. Rather, the ECB and the NCAs cooperate with each other. In other words, the responsibility for banking supervision in participating Member States is not fully denationalised.

The Commission proposal gave full supervisory tasks to all euro area banks.[37] Its explanatory memorandum emphasised that the ECB would have been responsible for carrying out key supervisory functions tasks 'for all credit institutions … regardless of their business model or size'.[38] On the contrary, after the December 2012 Council conclusions, the scope of ECB supervision has been considerably reduced.

Pursuant to Article 6 of the SSM Regulation the ECB and the national authorities share SSM supervisory activities based on a distinction between 'significant' and 'less significant' credit institutions. The SSM sets a 'significance' threshold where the ECB directly supervises the significant ones. This is the essential paradigm for the exercise of the powers of the ECB and national authorities over credit institutions in participating Member States.[39] Conversely, pursuant to Article 6(4) NCAs exercise the powers of supervision for less 'significant credit institutions'.

The credit institution is not 'less significant' when:

(i) the total value of its assets exceeds EUR 30 billion;

(ii) the ratio of its total assets over the GDP of the participating Member State of establishment exceeds 20%, unless the total value of its assets is below EUR 5 billion;

(iii) following a notification by its national competent authority that it considers such an institution of significant relevance with regard to the domestic economy, the ECB takes a decision confirming such significance following a comprehensive assessment by the ECB, including a balance-sheet assessment, of that credit institution.[40]

These three criteria of 'significance' are not exclusive. Three other cases justify exclusive ECB supervision.

Firstly, the ECB can also consider an institution of 'significant relevance' if it has 'established banking subsidiaries in more than one participating Member States and its cross-border assets or liabilities represent a significant part of its total assets

[36] See Art 4 SSM Regulation.

[37] Commission, 'Proposal for a Council regulation conferring specific tasks on the European Central Bank concerning policies relating to the prudential supervision of credit institutions' COM (2012) 511 final, Art 4.

[38] ibid explanatory memorandum 4.

[39] Art 6(4) SSM Regulation.

[40] ibid.

or liabilities'.[41] This means that the ECB can evaluate the possibility of a bank being of significant relevance by referring to the corporate structure of the specific credit institution.

Secondly, the ECB exclusive supervision also includes the banks that have requested and received financial assistance directly from European and/or international assistance programmes.[42]

Thirdly, the last subparagraph contains an all-encompassing condition for supervision that is that the ECB is competent to exercise its supervisory tasks for the three most significant credit institutions in each of the participating Member States, unless justified by particular circumstances.[43] Finally, the ECB may also decide to exercise directly itself all the relevant powers for one or more credit institutions regardless of their significance but based on high supervisory standards.

In September 2014 the ECB has adopted the decisions defining 120 credit institutions as significant under the SSM framework.[44] These comprise 85 per cent of the banking assets in participating Member States.

From the SSM framework, it emerges that only banks that are considered as 'significant' or are covered by the three circumstances indicated above are directly supervised by the ECB. The others continue to be supervised by NCAs. As put by Ferran and Babis, the question that remains open is 'whether the allocation of supervision of less significant banks to national authorities may not afford the ECB with sufficient visibility'.[45] Nonetheless, it appears that the ECB is also fully committed to aim for uniformity in the application of the SSM rules as regards less significant banks.[46]

The possibility of conferring supervision to the ECB without a distinction between 'significant' and 'less-significant' credit institutions would have been more in line with the idea to create an effective top-down governance model. Such structure would have established a new administrative structure with the ECB as the exclusive supervisor of all credit institutions in participating Member States. Such a solution would have made clear that the ECB exercises prudential supervision over all credit institutions in participating Member States while national supervisors would be executors or ancillary bodies to the ECB similarly to monetary policy in the euro area. Political negotiations, procedural intricacies and the need for a national oversight of medium or small credit institutions (for example, on the Spanish *cajas* or the German *Landesbanken*) prevailed over the initial Commission proposal and led to the adoption of a dual-tier system of supervision.

[41] ibid.

[42] ibid.

[43] ibid.

[44] The ECB list of significant credit institutions is available at: www.bankingsupervision.europa.eu/ecb/pub/pdf/ssm-listofsupervisedentities1502en.pdf?f09030f0fef8ac51447a9046f45e882d. The list has been updated to reflect in particular the inclusion of the three new significant institutions established in Lithuania, as from 1 January 2015 Lithuania has become the 19th euro-area Member State.

[45] E Ferran and V Babis, 'The Single Supervisory Mechanism' University of Cambridge Faculty of Law Research Paper No 10/2013, 11.

[46] 'Transcript of interview with Danièle Nouy' *Financial Times* (London, 9 February 2014). Danièle Nouy is the SSM Supervisory Board Chair.

In perspective, it is expected that the ECB will carry out the most important functions of supervision only as regards 'significant' credit institutions and, over time, be ready to supervise indirectly 'less significant' institutions, especially when these may be problematic from a European or national systemic risk point of view.

2. *The SSM Governance Structure: The Supervisory Board and the Governing Council*

The SSM provides for a new organisational structure inside the ECB with the establishment of a new body, the Supervisory Board, in charge of prudential supervision as well as the conferral of decision-making functions on supervision to the Governing Council. These institutional changes attempt to solve the problems of a 'national imprinting' in the decision-making for bank supervision that were not solved when the EBA was set up.[47]

The SSM Regulation provides for a critical change in the structure of the ECB as it establishes the Supervisory Board, an independent and autonomous internal body that undertakes the ECB supervisory functions.[48] This body is a new internal organ of the ECB composed of a Chair, a Vice-Chair, four representatives of the ECB and one representative from the NCAs in each participating Member State.[49] The main role of the Supervisory Board is to plan and execute the supervisory tasks conferred on the ECB. The decision-making procedure requires that the Supervisory Board adopts draft decisions by simple majority[50] or by qualified majority in case of regulations,[51] which are then submitted to the Governing Council for final approval. The draft decision is deemed to be adopted if the Governing Council does not object within a maximum of 10 working days.[52]

The current structural arrangements could be criticized. Ferran and Babis submit that the Supervisory Board is not fully independent in conducting supervisory functions within the governing structure of the ECB.[53] However, the governance safeguards in the decision-making procedure (the Supervisory Board decisions need to be adopted by the Governing Council under non-objection) and the strong links with the Governing Council do not undermine the required level of independence to carry out supervisory functions. Furthermore, the requirement to have the approval of the Governing Council for all supervisory acts might make the decision-making procedure burdensome and inefficient especially when fast supervisory decisions need to be taken. In order to solve this problem, the unofficial consolidated Rules of Procedure of the ECB introduce a non-objection procedure according to which, for supervisory decisions,

[47] Recital 52 EBA Regulation, affirms that the Board of Supervisors, the main decision-making EBA body is composed of national supervisor from each Member State.

[48] Art 26 SSM Regulation.

[49] ibid.

[50] ibid.

[51] ibid.

[52] ibid.

[53] See Ferran and Babis, 'The Single Supervisory Mechanism' (n 45) 14.

the Governing Council may only express an objection to the draft decision of the Supervisory Board within ten working days.[54] To simplify the procedure further, the Rules of Procedure of the ECB have been recently amended to shorten the timeframe for written procedures by allowing Governing Council's members to consider supervisory acts only within a maximum of five working days, or within a maximum of two working days in the case of macro-prudential action.[55]

An alternative solution would have been to create a completely independent status for the Supervisory Board or a separation of tasks in the Governing Council structure provided in the ESCB Statute. An interesting proposal was to establish a new body with an Executive Board and the presidents of national supervisory bodies.[56] However, these proposals would not have been simple or quick to realise. The former option would have left the Supervisory Board in a 'non-Treaty limbo'. The latter would have required an ESCB Statute amendment pursuant to Article 48 TEU.[57]

The separation of supervisory and monetary policy functions is another critical aspect in the conduct of a sound monetary policy in order to achieve an effectively independent prudential supervision. While pursuant to Article 127(1) TFEU monetary policy functions are aimed at maintaining price stability as the overarching objective of the ECB, the exercise of supervision has a different objective that is to 'protect the safety and the soundness of credit institutions and the stability of the financial system'.[58] Article 25 SSM Regulation provides that the ECB separates the monetary and the supervision functions.[59] There are arguments in favour and against this. The main argument for separation is justified by the need to avoid conflicts of interest, policy conflicts and procedural difficulties. Goodhart and Schoenmaker argued that separation mainly aims to avoid conflicts of interest in conducting different functions.[60]

The main argument for non-separation is the convergence of policy-making functions, economies of scope and procedural simplification. Moreover, national experience shows that some Member States confer to the same authority monetary and supervisory powers.[61]

[54] See Art 13g of the Decision ECB/2004/2, unofficial consolidated text produced by the Publications Office of the European Union, 24 January 2014 available at: www.ecb.europa.eu/ecb/legal/pdf/http___eur-lex.europa.eu_legal-content_en_txt_pdf__uricelex_02004d0002-20140124fromen.pdf.

[55] See www.ecb.europa.eu/ecb/legal/pdf/en_ecb_2015_8_f_sign_.pdf.

[56] See J Carmassi, C Di Noia and S Micossi, 'Banking Union: A Federal Model for the European Union with Prompt Corrective Action' (2012) *CEPS* Policy Brief 282.

[57] The ESCB Statute provides for simplified amendments to the Statute. These are limited only to a number of procedural provisions and not to the true separation of monetary and supervisory functions.

[58] Recital 65 SSM Regulation.

[59] See also the Decision of the ECB of 17 September 2014 on the implementation of separation between the monetary policy and supervision functions of the ECB (ECB/2014/39) OJ L300, 18 October 2014.

[60] C Goodhart and D Schoenmaker, 'Should the Functions of Monetary Policy and Banking Supervision be Separated?' (1995) *Oxford Economic Papers* 539–60.

[61] For instance, this is the case of Italy, Spain and France.

In practice, the transfer of the Supervisory Board preparatory work to the Governing Council questions the real effectiveness of the regulatory arrangements to separate monetary and supervisory functions in particular. The SSM Regulation mandates that the meetings and agendas are separated when the Governing Council exercises the two functions. This suggests that there is a relative separation of monetary and supervisory functions.

3. *The Powers of the ECB in the SSM*

While the SSM does not aim to create an exclusively ECB-centred structure for prudential supervision, the conferral of ECB direct supervisory powers towards credit institutions is one of the most remarkable aspects of the SSM.

Before the SSM, the ESAs had not been vested with extensive supervisory powers and their decision-making powers were restrained by procedural constraints. These limitations gave leeway to national supervisors to adopt their own supervisory powers that eventually led to fragmentation and ring-fencing in the internal market.[62]

The ECB acquires an essential role in the SSM with respect to the exercise of supervisory powers on credit institutions, and in particular on significant credit institutions. It is argued that the ECB exercises powers that have a top-down governance impact on credit institutions in participating Member States. Four cases show the extent of ECB direct supervisory powers: the authorisation procedure, supervisory powers, investigatory powers and sanctioning powers.

Firstly, the SSM Regulation involves NCAs in the exercise of ECB powers for authorisation (and withdrawal of authorisation) as it provides for a bottom-up system where the NCAs are the entry point for the authorisation or the withdrawal of authorisation of banking activities and the ECB is the final decision maker on authorisation.[63] The NCAs issue a draft decision for the ECB to assess. Only when the draft decision does not comply with the conditions for authorisation, may the ECB object the authorisation. National competent authorities have a significant role on the grounds of authorisation. This is shown by the procedure according to which where the ECB does not object the draft decision, this is deemed to be adopted.[64] However, the ECB has the final say on the authorisation matter in all participating Member States and it is the ultimate arbiter on the authorisation or withdrawal of authorisation for all credit institutions.

[62] See Commission, 'Proposal for a Council regulation conferring specific tasks on the European Central Bank concerning policies relating to the prudential supervision of credit institutions' COM (2012) 511 final, explanatory memorandum, Section I.

[63] See Art 14 SSM Regulation.

[64] ibid.

Secondly, the ECB exercises essential supervisory powers on significant supervised entities under Article 16 SSM Regulation. These are critical powers allowing the effective supervision of significant supervised entities in order to respect high supervisory standards. In particular, the ECB is empowered to require institutions, among others things: to hold own funds in excess of the capital requirements (Article 16(2)(a)); or to request the divestment of activities that pose excessive risks to the soundness of an institution (Article 16(2)(e)); or to restrict or limit the business, operations or network of institutions or to request the divestment of activities that pose excessive risks to the soundness of an institution (Article 16(2)(e)); or to require institutions to limit variable remuneration as a percentage of net revenues (Article 16(2)(g)); or to remove members at any time from the management body of credit institutions (Article 16(2)(i)). These are complemented by supervisory powers provided in the Capital Requirement Regulation[65] and Capital Requirement Directive[66] as the 'single rulebook' for supervised institutions. The correct exercise of supervisory powers is critical to allow the ECB to exercise real teeth towards significant supervised entities. For instance, the Supervisory Review and Evaluation Process (SREP), which the ECB conducted at the end of 2014, has shown to what extent the ECB has been ready to impose additional supervisory requirements on significant supervised entities.[67]

Thirdly, the ECB possesses investigatory powers on significant supervised entities as it is able to request information, conduct general investigations and on-site inspections.[68] The scope of ECB intervention is quite wide as the ECB requests extend from credit institutions established in the participating Member States to third parties to whom credit institutions in participating Member States, financial holding companies in participating Member States, mixed-activity holding companies in participating Member States and persons belonging to them have outsourced functions or activities. In particular, pursuant to Article 12 SSM Regulation, the ECB can conduct on-site inspections. The ECB investigatory powers are very similar to European competition enforcement and, arguably, future practice will be similar to the exercise of the Commission's powers.

Fourthly, Article 18 SSM Regulation provides for the 'administrative penalties' that the ECB can impose in cases of breach on the part of significant supervised entities. The SSM Regulation states that the ECB can impose administrative pecuniary sanctions of up to twice the amount of the profits gained or losses avoided, or up to 10 per cent of the total annual turnover. The scope of sanctioning powers is

[65] Regulation (EU) No 575/2013 of the European Parliament and of the Council of 26 June 2013 on prudential requirements for credit institutions and investment firms and amending Regulation (EU) No 648/2012 [2013] OJ L 176.

[66] Directive 2013/36/EU of the European Parliament and of the Council of 26 June 2013 on access to the activity of credit institutions and the prudential supervision of credit institutions and investment firms, amending Directive 2002/87/EC and repealing Directives 2006/48/EC and 2006/49/EC [2013] OJ L 176.

[67] See ECB, Annual Report on supervisory activities 36–37.

[68] ibid Arts 10 and 12.

limited to credit institutions, financial holding companies, or mixed financial holding companies within the SSM scope. Accordingly, and similarly to antitrust law, Recital 53 stresses that the ECB cannot impose penalties on natural or legal persons other than credit institutions, financial holding companies or mixed financial holding companies. In this sense, the ECB has amended the ECB Sanction Regulation of 1998 to include the sanctioning powers in supervision.[69]

In general terms, the ECB is vested with new and extensive investigatory, supervisory and sanctioning powers. While the ECB exercises these powers, the SSM Regulation provides that the NCAs cooperate and use their own powers where the Regulation does not confer such powers on the ECB.[70] It is expected that direct ECB supervisory powers will be exercised in an exclusive way (that is, implemented only by ECB officials and staff) as regards significant supervised entities, even if the ECB may be ready to cooperate actively with NCAs. Therefore, it is argued that the SSM is structured as a top-down supervisory mechanism with the national authorities being involved in the exercise of ECB supervisory powers.

B. The SSM and the NCAs

The NCAs play an essential role within the SSM for the conduct of supervisory activities.

As indicated above, the SSM is based on a division of supervisory competences between the ECB and the NCAs. National competent authorities continue to play an essential role in the SSM governance structure for banking supervision. The SSM does not 'denationalise' the supervision of credit institutions in Europe but 'captures' the ECB in the supervisory realm.

Ratione materiae, the SSM deals with prudential supervision of credit institutions. Thus, as clearly indicated in Recital 28, the SSM in no way impinges on other competences attributed to the national authorities. For instance, national authorities remain competent for the oversight exercise of the right of establishment or the provision of services for entities not qualified as 'credit institutions' as well as for issues regarding consumer protection and money laundering.[71] Hence, NCAs remain fully competent outside the scope of application of the SSM.

As regards prudential supervision of the SSM supervised entities, national supervisors retain full supervisory powers for 'less significant' institutions by exercising full supervision of credit institutions that are qualified as 'less significant'. According to Article 6 SSM Regulation, national competent authorities conduct full supervision over 'less significant' credit institutions. However, this does not

[69] See Recommendation for a Council Regulation amending Regulation (EC) 2532/98 concerning the powers of the ECB to impose sanctions (ECB/2014/19), OJ C144 available at: www.ecb.europa.eu/ecb/legal/pdf/celex_52014hb0019_en_txt.pdf.

[70] Recital 35 SSM Regulation.

[71] See Recital 26 SSM Regulation.

prevent the ECB from adopting guidelines or instructions for the exercise of supervisory functions common to the two levels of supervision.[72]

Furthermore, the role of NCAs is noteworthy as regards significant credit institutions in some cases. Firstly, national supervisors are part of the Joint Supervisory Teams (JSTs). The presence of national supervisors is essential for reasons of language and culture as well as to build on the pre-existing expertise and knowledge of the previous national supervisors. Secondly, national supervisors have a major role in the implementation and enforcement phases when ECB decisions shall be acted upon and there is a need to conduct the day-to-day supervision of the institutions. Thirdly, from a governance perspective, the structure of the Supervisory Board shows that the national competent authorities still have a role inside the ECB decision-making process as a supervisor. As required by the SSM Regulation, the Supervisory Board comprises one representative of each participating Member State. This means that the Supervisory Board includes national supervisory members who may influence the SSM decision-making process and may contest the ECB's competence to adopt supervisory decisions.

Overall, the NCAs have an essential role within the SSM. It is hoped that the dual-tier SSM arrangement will not fragment supervision of credit institutions in participating Member States between the ECB and NCAs.

IV. PUTTING TOGETHER THE THREADS OF THE DUAL-TIER SSM GOVERNANCE: THE SSM AS A SINGLE *TOP-DOWN COOPERATIVE* SYSTEM

From the analysis conducted above, it appears that the SSM is a new institutional framework for the governance of supervision of credit institutions in participating Member States. While the SSM confers an unprecedented supervisory competence to the ECB, the NCAs remain essential components under the SSM framework.

Both the scope and functioning of the SSM reveal that the SSM, as it currently stands, acts as a de facto *cooperative* supervisory mechanism. The ECB conducts primary supervisory functions, especially on significant credit institutions, while the NCAs are attributed considerable powers both as regards less significant credit institutions and in the execution and implementation of the supervision on 'significant' institution. This makes clear that the NCAs—differently from what was envisaged in the Commission proposal—are not 'ancillary' to the ECB mandate on prudential supervision. Rather, they play a leading role together with the ECB to shape prudential supervision in participating Member States.

While the SSM looks as a hybrid governance framework for prudential supervision, it remains clear that it creates a system of top-down supervision. This is because the ECB is the central player in directing prudential supervision of the banking systems in participating Member States. In this sense, it is expected that

[72] ibid Art 6(3).

both the ECB and the NCAs will contribute to the setting up of a prudential model where prudential functions are shared between the two levels. In particular, the ECB and the NCAs will cooperate over time in order to achieve a sound level of supervision in compliance with the principle of loyal cooperation as enshrined in the Treaties.[73] With that said, two cases show that the ECB nonetheless plays a pivotal role shaping a top-down supervisory governance model.

A. The Possible 'Supervision' of the ECB over NCAs

The 'supervision' of the ECB on NCAs is an important governance function in the SSM. The ECB is given certain coordination tools that make it possible to maintain the ECB as being effectively at the centre of the SSM without prejudice to the role and powers of NCAs.

Firstly, the ECB keeps overall oversight of the system especially within the SSM Framework Regulation[74] that provides for the essential relationship between the ECB and the national authorities.

Secondly, the ECB has the power to issue regulations, guidelines and general instructions for the performance of supervisory tasks by national supervisors.[75] This means that the ECB is ready to indicate what the national supervisor shall do in order to conduct an adequate national supervision. However, the dividing line between what powers the ECB can exercise in a supervisory decision and what powers require an instruction to NCAs is still unclear.

Thirdly, the NCAs shall follow the instructions of the ECB for the exercise of supervisory duties and tasks common to the two levels of supervision[76] and the ECB may request them to exercise their supervisory and investigatory powers under national law for the benefit of the SSM.[77]

Fourthly, the ECB may request reports from the national supervisors on the way in which they have performed their task. This means that the national competent authorities may be accountable before the ECB for their activities.

Fifthly, the ECB may call for information from the national supervisors and from the less significant banks directly as well as undertake investigations. However, the ECB is not allowed to undertake policy or disciplinary actions against national supervisors, but only as regards one or more credit institutions.

In sum, the role of the ECB as the main entity within the SSM shows that there is ground for the ECB to 'supervise' NCAs without prejudice to the SSM repartition of supervisory functions.

[73] See Art 4 SSM Regulation.

[74] See Art 6(7) SSM Regulation. See Regulation (EU) No 468/2014 of the ECB of 16 April 2014 establishing the framework for cooperation within the Single Supervisory Mechanism between the ECB and national competent authorities and with national designated authorities (SSM Framework Regulation) (ECB/2014/17) [2014] OJ L141/1.

[75] Art 6(5)(a) SSM Regulation.

[76] ibid Art 6(3).

[77] ibid Art 9(2) subpara 2.

B. The Degree of Cooperation of Supervisory Tasks

The ECB/NCA allocation of responsibilities is an essential aspect of the SSM. This relationship creates a cooperative and integrated supervisory framework.

First, the SSM Regulation is designed to create an integrated framework of activities between the ECB and the NCAs. The SSM Framework Regulation clearly indicates the topicality of the duty to cooperate in good faith and to provide for exchanges of information between the ECB and NCAs.[78] This is achieved in three ways: 'joint supervisory teams' composed of ECB and national officials to conduct day-to-day supervision of significant institutions;[79] staff information exchanges between the ECB and NCAs;[80] the ECB right to instruct national authorities to use their powers and to take action if the ECB has a supervisory power but no related power.[81] These suggest that the ECB seeks information and cooperation from national authorities as well as gives instructions to NCAs. In sum, the SSM establishes a top-down *cooperative* centralisation of prudential supervision.

Secondly, the SSM Regulation provides extensive ECB powers for the purpose of conduct of direct supervision going beyond the application of EU law. In fact, as Article 4(3) of the SSM Regulation states:

> [T]he ECB shall apply all relevant Union law, and where this Union law is composed of Directives, the national legislation transposing those Directives. Where the relevant Union law is composed of Regulations and where currently those Regulations explicitly grant options for Member States, the ECB shall apply also the national legislation exercising those options.

This provision indicates that the ECB has a wide array of sources to use in conducting supervision. Interestingly, the ECB also has the power to apply national law implementing European Directives or in those cases where EU Regulations give some discretion to Member States these national provisions.[82] This is a critical aspect of the SSM as the ECB can apply national law provisions implementing EU law. Such application may create some divergences as to the role of the ECB and that of the NCAs in applying and interpreting national law provisions and on who effectively shall take decisions to that effect.

Thirdly, national competent authorities are required to provide all the information necessary as well as assist the preparation and implementation of ECB direct supervision. The ECB exercises some key functions such as authorisation, licensing, withdrawal of authorisation, assessment of qualifying holdings, fit and

[78] Art 20 SSM Framework Regulation.

[79] ibid Art 3. The JSTs are the day-to-day supervisory bodies for significant institutions. These are composed of both ECB and NCA staff members and a JST coordinator; an ECB staff member, manages the JSTs' activities on a day-to-day basis.

[80] ibid Art 21.

[81] ibid Art 22.

[82] For discussions on the ECB use of national supervisory powers, see A Witte, 'The Application of National Banking Supervision by the ECB: Three Parallel Models of Executing EU Law?' (2014) *Maastricht Journal of European and Comparative Law* 89.

proper assessment and the general direction of supervision on significant credit institutions. Nonetheless, the SSM Regulation provides that the NCAs prepare and implement the ECB supervision guidance, especially in supervising less significant institutions. Hence, these arguments show that the SSM is a top-down supervisory system where the ECB seeks to provide executive cooperation and provide guidance on supervisory tasks to the NCAs.

In sum, the SSM framework shows that the ECB has an important margin of manoeuvre to establish a top-down supervisory system, but the NCAs still exercise considerable powers within such framework.

C. The SSM as a Single *Top-Down Cooperative* Supervisory Mechanism

From the analysis conducted above it emerges that the SSM works in a top-down 'supranational cooperative fashion'.[83] The SSM is not simply a *Single* Supervisory Mechanism, but also a Single *top-down cooperative* Supervisory Mechanism where both the ECB and NCAs conduct supervision over credit institutions in participating Member States in line with the principle of loyal cooperation and separation of competences enshrined in the Treaty.[84] The system is *top-down* as the supervision is conducted from the European level, the ECB, to the national level, the NCAs and *cooperative* as the ECB and the NCAs exercise shared supervision over credit institutions. To that extent, the ECB tasks and powers mark a new stage in supervision of banks in participating Member States as banking supervision has become a shared competence in the Union via the ECB and the NCAs.

V. CONCLUSION: THE SSM AND BEYOND

This chapter has shown that the SSM is a new institutional structure for the governance of credit institutions in Europe. The SSM is part of the EBU reform which—to date—constitutes 'the more important and far reaching reform in the European Union since the creation of the euro'.[85] Among other aspects, this contribution has examined the yet-to-be tested relationship between the ECB and the national competent authorities within the SSM as a new governance model.

Even with limits and uncertainties as to its functioning, the SSM is a critical reform for the future development of the Eurozone governance with a view to reach further economic integration. The analysis of the SSM governance structure has not shown grounds to point against the ineffectiveness of the system. Rather, the fortunate presence of Article 127(6) TFEU as well as the established role of

[83] See in other fields, R Schütze, 'From Rome to Lisbon: "Executive Federalism" in the (New) European Union' (2010) 47 *Common Market Law Review* 1385.

[84] Art 4(3) TEU.

[85] Speech by V Constâncio, Vice-President of the ECB, 'Banking Union and European Integration', 12 May 2014.

central bank involvement in prudential supervision reveals that the SSM can be a success from its beginning.[86]

In this context, it was argued that the SSM would work as a top-down cooperative supervisory mechanism where both the ECB and the NCAs play key roles in the correct functioning of the supervisory system. This appears a far more appealing solution than a European network structure where national supervisors would gather and decide on supervision in European fora.

The tasks and powers conferred on the ECB in the SSM for the supervision of credit institutions established in participating Member States are unprecedented and will—hopefully—contribute to establish a better framework for top-down supervisory governance in participating Member States and lead to a strengthened model of bank supervision. However, other areas of financial regulation and supervision in Europe remain nationally centred without supranational governance frameworks. For instance, this is the case of the competences in the matters of consumer protection and money laundering as well as the supervision of financial institutions other than credit institutions. In future, the ECB or the ESMA may be given direct supervisory powers for systemically important financial institutions other than entities qualified as significant supervised institutions under the SSM framework.

The SSM reform is not the only one to improve the governance of the banking system in Europe. The SSM is a necessary but not a sufficient institutional reform for the governance of credit institutions in the Eurozone. Three other reforms have been, or should be, put forward to shape a new Eurozone governance to boost financial integration and financial stability.[87]

Firstly, the Single Resolution Mechanism constitutes the other 'limb' of the EBU project. The SRM aims to create a system of common institutional and substantive resolution for credit institutions in participating Member States. At present, the legislative framework of the SRM is well in place for the establishment of the new governance structures throughout 2015 and 2016. Banking resolution will soon be centred with the Single Resolution Board, a new European agency at the centre of the system that will draft the resolution decisions to be adopted by the European Commission (and the Council).

Secondly, another important reform will come from the progressive harmonisation of Deposit Guarantee Schemes (DGSs) in Europe. The Banking Union Roadmap in 2012 envisaged the creation of a common deposit guarantee scheme for the Eurozone.[88] This proposal was watered down and no political consensus was found among institutional players on a new governance model for the management of a Single Deposit Guarantee Scheme in Europe. The 2014 DGS directive

[86] See E Ferran, 'European Banking Union: Imperfect, But It Can Work' (2014) Cambridge Legal Studies Research Paper Series 11.

[87] See H Van Rompuy in close collaboration with J M Barroso, J-C Juncker and M Draghi, 'Towards a Genuine Economic and Monetary Union', 5 December 2012, 5, available at: www.consilium.europa.eu/uedocs/cms_data/docs/pressdata/en/ec/134069.pdf.

[88] See Commission, 'A Roadmap towards a Banking Union' COM (2012) 510 final.

improves harmonisation of the rules on the functioning of deposit guarantees.[89] However, it does not create a new governance framework on DGSs in Europe.

Finally, there is still the need to establish a clear and widely accepted supranational governance framework on Lender of last resort functions and on a common fiscal backstop for financial institutions and sovereign in the EMU (and Europe).

In the words of Mario Draghi, the 'SSM offers a tremendous opportunity to move from different national approaches to the treatment of banks to a genuinely European perspective'.[90] In that sense, it is critical that, firstly, the ECB carries out the appropriate level of supervision, and that, secondly, both the ECB and the NCAs closely cooperate for a truly single supervision at the highest level. These will not be simple tasks. However, it is undisputed that, to date, the SSM is a critical evolutionary governance reform in Europe, 'probably the most ambitious and encompassing reform of the EU architecture since the institution of the single currency'.[91]

[89] Directive 2014/49/EU of the European Parliament and of the Council of 16 April 2014 on deposit guarantee schemes [2014] OJ L173/149. The new DGS Directive does not establish a new DGS governance framework in Europe.

[90] Opening Speech by M Draghi at the European Banking Congress 'The Future of Europe' Frankfurt am Main, 22 November 2013.

[91] Speech by P Praet, Member of the Executive Board of the ECB, Panel intervention 'Fixing finance', The Economist's Lisbon Summit, Lisbon, 18 February 2014, available at: www.ecb.europa.eu/press/key/date/2014/html/sp140218.en.html.

Part III

Democracy: Representation, Participation and Accountability

8

Is the EU a Representative Democracy? The Normative Debate and the Impact of the Euro-crisis

SIMONA PIATTONI*

I. INTRODUCTION

THIS CHAPTER LOOKS at the problems that emerge in multilevel political systems, like the European Union (EU), when the three fundamental functions of representative assemblies—the organisation of political preferences (voice), the making of policy decisions (will), and the oversight over the executive branches (control)—are assigned to different assemblies positioned at different levels of the political system. What may be compromised through the peculiar division of labour among parliamentary assemblies that attains in the EU is *full democratic representation*, which must secure simultaneously the delegation of authority to elected representatives, the articulation of preferences, and the control of the representatives by the represented. It will be argued that this peculiar division of labour stifles the dialogue between represented and representatives, which is the hallmark of full democratic representation since both sets of actors are likely to talk about the 'wrong' questions in the 'wrong' assemblies. Such dialogue takes also place outside parliamentary chambers—within political parties, functional associations, interest and pressure groups, the public sphere and governance forums—but it is ultimately within parliamentary chambers that the result of these exchanges must make an impact.

Normally, analyses of EU democracy try to trace the chains of delegation and accountability that flow from the European *demoi* to EU institutions and backwards, and discover that they are broken or weakened at given junctures.[1]

* Parts of this chapter also appear in S Piattoni, 'Elections in Multilevel Political Systems: Implications for Representative Democracy' in L Bardi, H Kriesi and AH Trechsel (eds), *Elections in Europe in Times of Crisis* (San Domenico di Fiesole, European University Institute, 2014) 186.

[1] D Curtin, 'Holding (Quasi-)Autonomous EU Administrative Actors to Public Account' (2007) 4 *European Law Journal* 523; F Scharpf, 'Legitimacy in the Multilevel European Polity' (2009) 2 *European Political Science Review* 173.

They conclude that democracy requires the restoration of these chains of delegation and accountability. I will argue that trying to restore the integrity of these chains is only part of the problem—and not even the most important one—for it is more important to assess which types of subjectivities are represented,[2] and which representational functions are performed at each level. Moreover, studies of the multilevel representative space have analysed each of these functions in isolation, investigating the institutions which have secured one or the other, without assessing the overall impact that this state of affairs has on *the quality of democratic representation, understood as advocacy and dialogue.*

In this chapter, I will start from the theory of representation as elaborated by Hanna Pitkin, Nadia Urbinati and Michael Saward in order to identify the fundamental functions of representation and to inquire where these functions are performed, whether at national or EU level.[3] I will also analyse whether the current crisis has helped EU citizens understand at what level these various functions are being performed and decide whether the division of labour between European and national parliaments is a viable and sustainable one. In what follows, I will first introduce the notion of full democratic representation; I will then highlight the peculiar division of labour among parliamentary assemblies situated at different governmental levels; I will further elaborate on the fragmented nature of the representation thus provided and draw the implications for the meaning of elections at each of these levels; and I will conclude by discussing whether the Euro-crisis has aggravated this disconnect, has left it unchanged, or promises to improve the situation.

II. THE ROLE OF ELECTIONS IN REPRESENTATIVE DEMOCRACIES

In parliamentary democracies elections are the means through which representatives are chosen and parliaments—the embodiments of the sovereign people—are formed. In presidential democracies elections also serve the purpose of selecting the chief executive, the president. Most European democracies, however, are parliamentary democracies: European citizens are therefore used to electing their parliamentary representatives and expect that these will form a parliamentary majority which will express an executive. There are many different ways to establish these linkages, ranging from the attainment of more or less 'constructed' parliamentary majorities and the implicit designation of the majority party leader as chief executive, as in the United Kingdom (UK), to systems in which parliamentary majorities are built with great difficulty through inter-party

[2] S Kröger and D Friedrich, 'Democratic Representation in the EU: Two Kinds of Subjectivity' (2013) 2 *Journal of European Public Policy* (special issue) 171.

[3] H Pitkin, *The Concept of Representation* (Berkeley, University of California Press, 1967); N Urbinati, *Representative Democracy. Principles & Genealogy* (Chicago, The University of Chicago Press, 2006); M Saward, 'The Representative Claim' (2006) 5 *Contemporary Political Thought* 297.

negotiations and the executive and its leader are chosen after excruciating bargaining, as in Belgium—and everything in between. True, in Europe there is a handful of political systems in which the President of the Republic has particularly strong powers (Finland, Poland, Portugal), and at least one semi-presidential system in which it is the President who exerts direct decision-making powers particularly in matters of foreign and macroeconomic policy (France).

Representation, therefore, is the distinctive trait of contemporary European democracies. As a response to the practical impossibility of having direct democracy in large political systems, representative democracy is normally presented as an expedient, but inferior, form of democracy. For some

> it is paradoxical to call it [representative democracy] *democratic*, for the only moment the citizens decide directly is when they delegate legislative powers. Elections mean that popular sovereignty appears 'at fixed and rare intervals' much like a comet; citizens exercise it 'always only to renounce it'.[4]

Urbinati, who traces the genealogy of representative democracy and also discusses the citicisms levied against it (such as the one reported above), thinks that it is in fact not a second-best form to direct democracy but arguably a superior form or, in any event, an apt form of democracy in times of full democratisation.[5]

In national political systems, through elections, citizens do not only appoint legislators or express policy preferences, they also express their sovereignty. The existence of a *demos*, capable of delegating its authority to elected representatives, is normally considered a precondition for the formation of a sovereign parliament legitimated to legislate on behalf of the people. The distinctive problem of the EU, therefore, seems to be that no such single *demos* exists,[6] rather several *demoi* which supposedly can delegate their authority *legitimately* only to their elected representatives and, through them, to their governmental representatives. The EU *demoi* also directly elect EU representatives to the European Parliament (EP); however, this parliament is considered as a weaker, defective version of a sovereign parliament for several reasons which I will review below.

Before addressing the distinctive aspects of EU representative democracy, it is worth recalling that, even in national political systems, elections are the necessary but not sufficient condition for representative democracy. Following Hanna Pitkin's magisterial discussion of the concept,[7] representation is not exhausted by elections, but requires ongoing exchanges between represented and representatives to be obtained also through direct participation of the former in politics. Far from being antithetical or inimical to it, as some elitist political theorists argue (first and foremost Schumpeter),[8] representation does not rule out participation.

[4] Urbinati, *Representative Democracy* (n 3) 3 (emphasis added).

[5] ibid, Introduction.

[6] J Weiler, U Haltern and F Mayer, 'European Democracy and its Critique: Five Uneasy Pieces' EUI Working Paper RESC 95/11, Florence.

[7] Pitkin, *Representation* (n 3).

[8] A Schumpeter, *Capitalism, Socialism and Democracy* (New York, Harper & Row, 1942).

Direct and continuous participation of citizens in public discussions and in interaction with their representatives are for Pitkin necessary complements to elections in any truly democratic representative democracy.

> … representing here means acting in the interest of the represented in a manner responsive to them. The representative must act independently; his actions must involve discretion and judgment; he must be the one who acts. The represented must also be (conceived as) capable of independent action and judgment, not merely being taken care of. And, despite the resulting potential for conflict between representative and represented about what is to be done, that conflict must not normally take place. The representative must act in such a way that there is no conflict, or if it occurs an explanation is called for. He must not be found persistently at odds with the wishes of the represented without good reason in terms of their interests, without a good explanation of why their wishes are not in accord with their interests.[9]

According to Urbinati,[10] representative democracy is about the expression of *judgement* and the activation of *will*. The essence of democracy entails, according to Urbinati, the equal right of all citizens to participate in the formation of *judgement* (*isegoria*) and the equal right of all citizens to participate in the expression of *will* (*isonomia*). Judgement in turn has two aspects: an *ex-ante* (Urbinati calls it 'positive') doing as *proposing* and *activating* and an *ex-post* (Urbinati calls it 'negative') doing as *receiving* and *surveillance*. Judgement, therefore, does not merely signal *ex-post* evaluation of someone else's activity or inactivity, as if the only reactions could be 'consent or rebuff', but also an *ex-ante* activity of prodding and activating. I will indicate as 'voice' the active *ex-ante* activating and proposing and as 'control' the *ex-post* receiving and surveillance.[11]

While both judgement and will are essential elements of democratic representation, contrary to the current tendency to consider the right to decide on one's own destiny all that matters in democracy, Urbinati underscores the importance of judgement. Hence *delegation* does not exhaust the essence of democratic representation, but offers only a partial hence limited form of representation.[12] Pitkin's notion of *full* (as opposed to partial) *political representation* coincides with Urbinati's notion of *democratic representation* and implies that 'the representative must pursue his constituents' interests in a manner at least potentially responsive to their wishes, and that conflict between them must be justifiable in terms of those interests'.[13] Responsiveness to the constituents' interests is therefore central to her notion of representation. Mere authorisation will not do: the relationship between represented and representative must be ongoing and entail 'discretion and judgment' both on the part of the representative and on the part of the

[9] Pitkin (n 3) 209–10.

[10] Urbinati (n 3) Introduction.

[11] I slightly modify Urbinati's vocabulary. She uses 'voice' to indicate both the active and the passive components of judgement, while I find it clearer to indicate with 'voice' the active component and with 'control' the passive one. Urbinati (n 3) 5.

[12] Pitkin (n 3).

[13] ibid 213.

represented. The represented, therefore, do not divest themselves of their capacity for independent judgement, and even direct action, after the mere act of voting.

If elections are not a sufficient condition for representative democracy, they still are a necessary condition. They are a fundamental component of democracy because, through the act of voting and selecting representatives, citizens set in motion a process of democratic representation that unfolds well beyond elections. Judgement requires 'presence through ideas and speech',[14] activities which cannot be delegated once and for all exclusively to elected representatives. 'Focus on the presence through ideas and speech reveals participation and representation not as alternative forms of democracy but as related forms constituting a continuum of political judgement and action in modern democracy'.[15]

In electoral studies, instead, the emphasis on the expression of will has driven an almost exclusive attention to the role of political parties in the formation of governmental majorities: the emphasis has been on 'democratic *government*' rather than on 'democratic *representation*'.[16] 'The very notion that we can have representation as such, or representation without an intimate connection to government, is quite alien to a European tradition of political representation in which representation and government are combined through the aegis of party'.[17] More generally, in EU studies the distinction is often made between the institutional 'power' to decide and mere 'influence' on decision-making, clearly suggesting that the one is more important than the other, perhaps because the former is more easily observed and formalised than the latter. I have argued elsewhere[18] that exclusive attention to the expression of will leads to an understanding of representation as a mere act of authorisation and, ultimately, to an impoverishment of the notion of democratic representation. It also leads to a general downgrading of the formation of judgement (both active and passive) as channelled also by the consultative bodies of the EU, such as the Committee of the Regions,[19] or as expressed in governance arrangements which oversee over the implementation of the broad policy frameworks legislated by Council and Parliament.[20]

Urbinati's theorisation allows for a fuller appreciation of *representation as advocacy*, that is as the formation of judgement in both its active and passive aspects.[21]

[14] Urbinati (n 3) 3.

[15] ibid.

[16] P Mair and J Thomassen, 'Political Representation and Government in the European Union' (2010) 17 *Journal of European Public Policy* 20.

[17] ibid 23.

[18] S Piattoni, 'Representation as Delegation: A Basis for EU Democracy?' (2013) 20 *Journal of European Public Policy* (special issue) 224.

[19] S Piattoni and J Schönlau, *Shaping EU Policy from Below. EU Democracy and the Committee of the Regions* (Cheltenham, Edward Elgar, forthcoming).

[20] C Sabel and J Zeitlin (eds), *Experimentalist Governance in the European Union. Towards a New Architecture* (Oxford, Oxford University Press, 2010); S Piattoni, 'The Committee of the Regions and the Upgrading of Subnational Territorial Representation' in S Kröger and D Friedrich (eds), *The Challenge of Democratic Representation in the European Union* (Basingstoke, Palgrave-Macmillan, 2011) 59.

[21] N Urbinati, 'Representation as Advocacy: A Study of Democratic Deliberation' (2000) 6 *Political Theory* 758.

'*Representation highlights the idealizing and judgmental nature of politics*, an art by which individuals transcend the immediacy of their biographical experience and social and cultural belongings and interests, and educate and enlarge their political judgment on their own and other's opinions'.[22] In this respect, representative democracy is *superior* to direct democracy in that it forces citizens to elevate themselves from their specific socio-economic conditions while obviously departing from their biographical details when expressing their views and interests. 'Political representation … entails a complex political process that activates the "sovereign people" well beyond the formal act of electoral authorisation. Representative politics has the power of unifying and connecting … the "fluctuating units" of civil society *by projecting citizens into a future-oriented perspective*'.[23] Through democratic representation, then, the subject—the *demos*—is created: disparate individuals, entrapped in their own particularities, discover that they have common values and interests and become a collective subject. In the EU, this notion of full democratic representation helps us see how the 'no demos' problem may be overcome.

In this respect, Nadia Urbinati's position is not so distant from Michael Saward's understanding of representation as 'claim-making': 'A *maker* of representation (M) puts forward a *subject* (S) which stands for an *object* (O) which is related to a *referent* (R) and is offered to an *audience* (A)'.[24] Representative claims succeed if the audience accepts them. 'A representative claim is a double claim: about an aptitude or capacity of a would-be representative, and also about relevant characteristics of a would-be audience (nee constituency)'.[25] Representation as judgement accomplishes what representation as will cannot: while the expression of will presupposes the existence of a subject (a demos, a constituency, a forum), representation as judgement is capable of creating one.

> Makers of representative claims attempt to evoke an audience that will receive the claim, and (hopefully, from the maker's point of view) receive it in a certain, desired way. Makers of representative claims suggest to the potential audience: (1) you are/are part of this audience, (2) you should accept this view, this construction—this representation—of yourself, and (3) you should accept me as speaking and acting for you. The aim of the maker of the claim in such cases can be said to be to avoid disputatious 'reading back', or contestation of their claims, by would-be audience members.[26]

Clearly, representation as claim-making implies that there must be a dialogue between the object/referent, the audience, and the claim-maker/subject. The audience is constituted through the claim-making activity of the representative. Obviously, the claim will be all the more successful the more it resonates with

[22] Urbinati (n 3) 5 (emphasis added).
[23] ibid.
[24] Saward, 'The Representative Claim' (n 3) 302.
[25] ibid 303.
[26] ibid.

'ready-mades, existing terms and understandings which the would-be audience will recognize'.[27] While this may appear as a fleeting and ethereal notion of representation, it describes particularly well a situation—like that which obtains at EU level—in which the represented are somehow still undefined or are still in the process of being constituted into a *demos*. This vision of representation as an ongoing dialogue between a claim-maker and an audience rhymes well (in my opinion) with Urbinati's view of representation as advocacy, as a process through which what is common among disparate individuals becomes apparent as it gets distilled and defined during the very process of representation. To conclude,

> Representation is a comprehensive filtering, refining and mediating process of political will formation and expression. It models the object, style and procedures of political competition and action. It helps to depersonalize the claims and opinions, which in turn allows citizens to mingle and associate without erasing the partisan spirit essential to free political competition or obscuring the majority/minority divide ... Representation can never be truly descriptive and mimetic of social segmentation and identities because of its unavoidable inclination to transcend the 'here' and 'now' and to project instead a 'would-be' or 'ought-to-be' perspective that translates almost naturally into advocacy.[28]

III. EU MULTILEVEL REPRESENTATIVE DEMOCRACY

The coexistence, within the EU multi-level political system, of two levels (and in fact more if we count the sub-state levels) of political representation complicates the activity of democratic representation. Conventional (and Lisbon Treaty) wisdom has it that EU citizens enjoy two types of electoral representation: *direct electoral representation* in their national parliaments and the EP, and *indirect electoral representation* in the Council of the European Union and the European Council through their national governmental representatives and heads of state and government. *National parliaments* serve a double function: they contribute to the formation of political will at EU level through the authorisation that they give to their governmental representatives to decide in the Council of the European Union and the European Council, and control EU legislation through the early warning mechanism (EWM) in defence of the subsidiarity and proportionality principles. The *European Parliament* directly contributes to legislating at EU level and exerts a certain degree of control on the EU executives (the Commission and the other EU agencies). The *Council of the European Union* and the *European Council* are only indirectly representative of their national constituencies, but they are democratically legitimated to make decisions on their behalf. What more could an EU citizen ever wish for?[29]

[27] ibid.

[28] Urbinati (n 3) 6.

[29] A Moravcsik, 'In Defence of the "Democratic Deficit": Reassessing Legitimacy in the European Union' (2002) 40 *Journal of Common Market Studies* 603.

For a long time, the literature has highlighted a number of problems with this inter-parliamentary 'division of labor'[30] which are well known and will be rehearsed here only in order to focus on their effect on representation and their impact on elections. I will focus exclusively on *directly representative institutions*, ignoring the problems connected with indirectly representative ones.

First, conventional wisdom assumes that EP elections are 'second order national elections',[31] meaning that they are fought on national issues and not on issues of direct pertinence to the EU. As a consequence, national electoral cycles will affect the outcome of EP elections, giving an advantage to governmental parties if EP elections are held close to national elections, or to opposition parties if they happen to take place in the middle of the electoral cycle.[32] Generally speaking, turnout at EP elections is lower than at national elections, and small and opposition parties tend to do better at EP than at national elections, as voters often take this chance to express their dissent vis-à-vis their current governments. The EP is therefore composed of a rather disparate set of representatives selected for the 'wrong' reasons, that is, without any sort of 'mandate'[33] to form judgement and express will on EU issues but rather with a potentially overwhelming mandate to oppose and criticise the Union. Compounding factors are the absence of true pan-European electoral campaigns, the absence of a pan-European public sphere and the lack of a pre-existing European *demos*.[34]

Secondly, as a consequence of this state of affairs, the obvious roles of the European and the national parliaments, particularly in the formation of judgement, are inverted:

> [I]t is argued that the national electoral arena is best suited to the contestation of key European issues, whereas the European arena is best suited to debate about more everyday policy questions. More often than not, however, the debates are actually pursued the other way around, with the result that elections in each arena fail to prove decisive. The voters have a voice, of course, but it tends to be on matters that sometimes cannot be decided in the particular arena in question.[35]

Even though later Mair acknowledged that Euro-parties in fact behave pretty much as most national parties and that the political space in the EP does not differ substantially from that of most national parliaments, stretching along a left–right dimension,[36] the disconnect between the types of issues debated in national

[30] P Mair, 'The Limited Impact of Europe on National Party Systems' (2010) 4 *West European Politics* 28.

[31] K Reif and H Schmitt, 'Nine Second-Order National Elections—A Conceptual Framework for the Analysis of European Elections Results' (1980) 8 *European Journal of Political Research* 3.

[32] S Hix and C Lord, *Political Parties in the European Union* (London, Palgrave Macmillan, 1997).

[33] To be understood in a weak, common language sense rather than in the strong sense of 'imperative mandate' normally attributed to it by political philosophers.

[34] H-J Trenz, 'Uniting and Dividing: The European Public Sphere as an Unfinished Project' in J Grisprud et al (eds), *The Public Sphere, Volume IV: The Future of the Public Sphere* (London, Sage Publications, 2011) 363; Weiler, Haltern and Mayer, 'European Democracy and its Critique' (n 5).

[35] Mair, 'The Limited Impact of Europe' (n 30) 28.

[36] Mair and Thomassen, 'Political Representation and Government in the EU' (n 16).

parliaments and in the EP, and therefore the different motivations with which national and EU representatives are elected, still have an impact on the type of representation being offered in each of them.

Thirdly, despite the momentous institutionalisation of the EP and the 'normalisation' of EP political dynamics, other authors have argued that rather than a conventional left–right political space, the EP presents a green, alternative, libertarian (GAL) versus traditional, authoritarian, nationalistic (TAN) political dichotomy.[37] They start by observing that extremist left and right parties oppose European integration, while centrist (social democratic, Christian democratic, liberal, conservative) parties favour it. They explain this phenomenon as opportunism:

> Parties that are successful in the existing structure of contestation have little incentive to rock the boat, while unsuccessful parties, that is, parties with weak electoral support or those that are locked out of government, have an interest in restructuring contestation. The same strategic logic that leads mainstream parties to assimilate the issues raised by European integration into the Left/Right dimension of party competition leads peripheral parties to exploit European integration in an effort to shake up the party system.[38]

The fourth fundamental element that affects the type of representation expressed by both types of representative assemblies is their different collocation in the democratic chain of delegation and their different institutional powers.[39] National parliaments, while *politically* relatively disempowered by the process of European integration, are nevertheless still the central formal *institutional* link in the chain of representation that flows from the several peoples of Europe to their executives and their bureaucracies and are normally also perceived to be the crucial *institutional* link in the chain of accountability that flows in the opposite direction. National parliaments are therefore formally at the centre of those institutional chains of delegation and accountability that are normally identified with representative democracy.[40]

The EP has acquired greater co-decision powers and increased control functions. Still this does not compensate for the fact that a European 'government' does not germinate from within the EP and does not respond directly to it nor that the formation of judgement at EU level is still only in its infancy. The attempt in 2014 to link at least the selection of the President of the Commission to the political orientation of the EP and its increased powers to approve or reject the candidate President and the College of Commissioners does not compensate for the fact that the EU executive does not express a EU-wide parliamentary majority—and this confirms the distinctiveness of the EP vis-à-vis national parliaments. Likewise, the protracted tug of war between Council and Parliament over the control powers of

[37] L Hooghe, G Marks and C Wilson, 'Does Left/Right Structure Party Positions on European Integration?' 8 (2002) 35 *Comparative Political Studies* 965.

[38] ibid 968–69.

[39] K Strøm, W Müller and T Bergman (eds), *Delegation and Accountability in Parliamentary Democracies* (Oxford, Oxford University Press, 2003).

[40] Curtin, '(Quasi-)Autonomous EU Administrative Actors' (n 1).

the latter over comitology committees, demonstrates how the surveillance function of the EP has also been hampered by its peculiar institutional position. However, Urbinati's criteria for democratic representation are both more nuanced and more demanding and cannot be exhausted simply by checking where parliaments are institutionally positioned along the chains of delegation and accountability. Therefore, the fact that the EP does not constitute the central link of both chains of delegation and accountability at EU level does not weaken its democratic centrality.

A fifth, more political aspect of the distinctiveness of the EP is the fact that, unlike all other parliaments, it is partially excluded from a number of highly relevant policy areas, be they old community policies (such as agriculture) or newer intergovernmental policies (such as taxation).[41] Even in federal systems (to which the EU system is sometimes assimilated), it is the federal chamber that may be excluded from some decisions, never the house of representatives! Moreover, the fact that most of the EP's decisions 'must' be politically supported by super-majorities clearly shows that this chamber lacks a conventional majority-opposition dynamic, which is the hallmark of a working parliament. This too tends to muzzle electoral competition and to encourage the vote for extremist, anti-systemic parties given the impossibility of perceiving with any accuracy the political difference that casting the vote for one or the other centrist parties would really make. In their turn, national parliaments, while institutionally stronger than the EP, are not capable of capitalising on their formally stronger institutional position.

With exceptions, national parliaments are perceived to be the big losers of European integration.[42] The process of integration has caused a 'verticalisation' of politics, meaning that national executives and their representatives are in the driving seat of most decisions, both political and technical. Only extraordinarily well-organised national parliaments—the Danish Folketing is a myth in this respect—can attempt to keep abreast of EU decision-making and make their voice heard with any consistency. With the Treaty of Lisbon, national parliaments have acquired greater powers, particularly the possibility of inducing a revision of legislative proposals when issuing a yellow or an orange card in the EWM. Moreover, the horizontal relations among European Affairs Committees (COSAC), and more generally among parliamentary chambers, has created what Crum and Fossum call a 'multilevel parliamentary field'[43] which could, in theory, allow sustained exchanges of judgement and voice among national parliaments. Unfortunately, it would seem that the Euro-crisis has distorted this field in favour of some national parliaments—such as the Bundestag and the Assemblée Nationale—at the

[41] F Fabbrini, 'From Fiscal Constraint to Fiscal Capacity: The Future of EMU and Its Challenges' in M Adams, F Fabbrini and P Larouche (eds), *The Constitutionalization of European Budgetary Constraints* (Oxford, Hart Publishing, 2014).

[42] T Raunio, 'National Parliaments and European Integration: What we Know and Agenda for Future Research' (2009) 15(4) *Journal of Legislative Studies* 317.

[43] B Crum and JE Fossum, 'The Multilevel Parliamentary Field: A Framework for Theorizing Representative Democracy in the EU' (2009) 1 *European Political Science Review* 249.

expense of others—such as the parliaments of the southern, debt-burdened states—and has therefore injected a new type of 'democratic deficit' into the Union.[44]

The provisions of the Treaty of Lisbon and in particular the EWM, while formally giving substance to the control powers of national parliaments, have so far had a minimal impact (and will probably continue to do so). However, the EWM contains a certain potential for the upgrading of the common interests of several national constituencies which should not be underestimated, although scepticism and contrary opinions remain.[45] In this respect the experience of an even weaker EU body, like the Committee of the Regions (CoR), is instructive. It is precisely because it *cannot* count on any constitutionally enshrined decision-making powers, that the CoR has learnt how to upgrade the territorial interests of its members and to make its voice heard by seeking to influence more subtly the community's decision-making process.[46]

IV. FRAGMENTED DEMOCRATIC REPRESENTATION

Under these circumstances, which aspects of representation are offered, respectively, by national and European parliaments? From Urbinati (2006) we know that the three functions of representation are the articulation of *voice*, the production of *will*, and the exercise of *control*. Does the mutual co-existence of national and European parliaments stifle the fulfilment of their democratic roles?

Let us look first at the EP. Does the EP allow for the articulation and expression of voice? Does it exercise control over the executive(s)? Does it contribute to the formation of will? Finally, are voters induced to vote at EP elections in order to select those representatives that will best perform these functions? Since the Single European Act (1988), the EP has managed to raise the volume of its voice and strengthen the expression of its will. With the help of the European Court of Justice,[47] it has gained co-decision powers in an increasing number of policy areas. However, if we want to analyse separately the expression of voice and the exercise of will, we need to focus on the activating and proposing powers of the EP separately from its decision-making powers. With regard to policy initiation, we notice that the Commission still enjoys, at least formally and in most policy areas, the exclusive right of legislative proposal.

Alliances between members of the EP, Commission functionaries and civil society activists have been observed to have led to important chapters of EU legislation: gender equality legislation has been stimulated precisely by the formation of

[44] A Benz, 'An Asymmetric Two-Level Game: Parliaments in the Euro Crisis' in B Crum and JE Fossum (eds), *Practices of Interparliamentary Coordination in International Politics* (Colchester, ECPR Press, 2013) 125–42.

[45] Fabbrini, 'From Fiscal Constraint to Fiscal Capacity' (n 41) 18.

[46] Piattoni and Schönlau, *Shaping EU Policy from Below* (n 20).

[47] M Pollack, 'Control Mechanism or Deliberative Democracy? Two Images of Comitology' (2003) 36 *Comparative Political Studies* 125.

such a 'velvet triangle'.[48] Similarly, environment-friendly MEPs have succeeded in stimulating environment-conscientious Commissioners who have then promoted environmental legislation which responded to diffuse citizens' concerns.[49] To the extent that EP elections have returned a significant number of environment-friendly MEPs, we may say that citizens can indeed exert (the positive aspect of) judgement through the EP. However, one cannot fail to notice how circuitous this activity necessarily is. How many MEPs have been actually elected *because* of their EU-level green agenda? How many of them have campaigned on a green agenda that explicitly mentioned the EU as an important level at which to act? Has the green vote rewarded EP candidates for what they promised to do at EU level or for their past, present and future activities at national level? Have not in fact transnational NGOs been much more effective in proposing and activating the Commission than environment-friendly MEPs? The literature confirms that the GAL wing of the EP occupies an entire extreme of the EP political space, but the extent to which it has been elected to the EP specifically to that end is still unclear.[50]

How about the passive side of judgement, that is, *receiving* and *surveillance*? As we know, the EP cannot dismiss the Commission President or his commissioners unless they are accused of misconduct or wrongdoing—and even then the solution may be a political resignation rather than a vote of censure (*cf* the Santer affaire). However, surveillance is also a menial and day-to-day activity, and concerns the extent to which the 'government' of the EU (the Commission, comitology committees, and other agencies) is kept on its toes as regards the translation of legislative decisions into outputs and the implementation (or supervision of implementation) of those decisions. This is particularly important to the extent that these agencies and committees are often called to complete the legislative process by translating general principles into actionable criteria and standards. The EP has fought tooth and nail to protect its right/duty to be kept informed of committees' activity and to control agencies' and comitology committees' decisions,[51] but its relative success has not depended on the pressure of the electorate. In other words, when trying to defend its prerogatives and strengthen its institutional position, the EP is not so much responsive to its electorate as it is driven by an inter-institutional jockeying for power. We must conclude with Schimmelfennig that the democratisation of the EU is driven not so much by societal pressures as by inter-institutional dynamics.[52]

[48] A Woodward, 'Building Velvet Triangles: Gender and Informal Governance' in T Christiansen and S Piattoni (eds), *Informal Governance in the European Union* (Cheltenham, Edward Elgar, 2014).

[49] A Lenschow, 'Environmental Policy. Contending Dynamics of Policy Change' in H Wallace, W Wallace and M Pollack (eds), *Policy-Making in the European Union* 4th edn (Oxford, Oxford University Press, 2005).

[50] Hooghe, Marks and Wilson, 'Left/Right Structure' (n 37).

[51] Pollack, 'Control Mechanism or Deliberative Democracy?' (n 47); Curtin (n 2).

[52] F Schimmelfennig, 'The Normative Origins of Democracy in the European Union: Towards a Transformationalist Theory of Democratization' (2010) 2 *European Political Science Review* 211.

As is known, the EP has made its greatest strides in the exercise of *will*, the second fundamental component of democratic representation and that to which most EU scholars have directed their attention. The EP now has co-decision powers in most areas of EU competence. Does this guarantee political equality to all EU citizens? The resounding answer has been 'no' and, according to some scholars, this is a fundamental problem. Strict proportionality and an essentialist notion of *demos* induce Kröger and Friedrich[53] and apparently also the German Constitutional Court to conclude that only an EP that proportionally represents the several peoples of the Union can be entitled to democratically express the will of the Union. However, nowhere in Europe (with the only possible exception of Germany, in fact) has the existence of the national *demos* been the precondition for state- and democracy-building. Rather, the construction of the national *demos* has been the (often incomplete and contested) outcome of those processes.[54] Strict proportionality, therefore, does not seem the solution to granting 'political equality' to the citizens of the Union.[55]

If Mair's 'reversal of roles' thesis is still valid,[56] then MEPs' legislative activity is not what drives the European vote, and this is a much more damning circumstance than the absence of strict proportionality. In order to make the vote for the EP politically consequential, the vote for the EP has been linked to an indication for the preferred partisan candidate for President of the Commission.[57] Right now, MEPs are elected on the basis of how much or how little they claim the EU should legislate, not on how they actually (co-)legislate, that is, on whether they promote a coherent political agenda. High doses of potentially lethal de-institutionalising pathogens are thus inoculated into the parliamentary body. The expression of will is consequently diverted onto a different agenda, one that has to do with the scope and reach of the EU rather than with concrete policy-making. The EP's will has been strengthened, but its voice is still partially muffled and control remains weak.

National parliaments find themselves in the opposite situation. They debate extensively over policy decisions whose content has often been decided at EU level. Parliamentary fights concern the short-term implementation of decisions taken elsewhere, rather than long-term strategies. The crisis has only accentuated this situation. Many authors have denounced the apparent 'suspension of democracy' particularly in those euro-area Members States subjected to special surveillance because of their shaky national accounts.[58] Extraordinary elections or new governmental majorities have been necessary in some of these countries (Greece,

[53] Kröger and Friedrich, *The Challenge of Democratic Representation* (n 20).

[54] S Bartolini, *Restructuring Europe: Centre Formation, System Building, and Political Structuring between the Nation State and the European Union* (Oxford, Oxford University Press, 2005).

[55] C Lord and J Pollak, 'Unequal but Democratic? Equality According to Karlsruhe' (2013) 20 *Journal of European Public Policy* (special issue) 190.

[56] Mair (n 30), but see Mair and Thomassen (n 16).

[57] On the potential pros and cons of this strategy see the contributions of Kelemen, Antpöhler and Koncharov, chs 11, 12 and 13 in this volume.

[58] B Crum, 'Saving the Euro at the Cost of Democracy' (2013) 51 *Journal of Common Market Studies* 616.

Spain, Italy) to face the emergency caused by the risk of default, but nowhere has democracy been actually suspended. Oversized majorities or grand coalition governments, in fact, are also becoming more common in euro-area Member States which for the moment do not appear to suffer from the crisis, such as Germany. Generally speaking, times of crisis suggest the expansion of majorities to include normal-times opposition parties. Is this general decline in majoritarian politics a consequence of the crisis, the effect of the reversal of roles between European and national parliaments, or just a trend common to all democracies?

Still, at national level, there is ample space for *activating* and *proposing* measures that complement EU legislation. The better organised national parliaments manage to direct their governmental representatives' activity in the Council and the European Council even before decisions are made.[59] Moreover, national parliaments can still exert control. This activity is premised on national parliaments *receiving* EU legislative proposals early on from the Commission and *surveilling* the extent to which it meets criteria of subsidiarity and proportionality. Unfortunately, these important functions—formation of voice, expression of will and exertion of control—are often obliterated by emptier, although noisier, activities such as complaining against decisions already made in Brussels by national representatives (at least in some EU Member States). Raunio convincingly argues that such a distorted expression of judgement is due to the actual lack of interest on the part of the main governmental and opposition parties to debate publicly the issues that really matter in plenary sessions (accessible to the wider public).[60] They share an interest in carrying out these discussions in closed (or less publicised) parliamentary committee debates, in which the distance between their factual support of EU policies and their public disavowal of the same would become apparent. While this behaviour serves the immediate purposes of 'mainstream' parties and the cause of 'integration by stealth', it does undermine the role of national parliaments as forums for the articulation and expression of judgement on EU issues.

National parliaments have always had the opportunity—in fact the right and duty—to oversee the activity of European institutions, but with the Treaty of Lisbon they have also acquired the formal capacity to defend the principle of subsidiarity through the EWM. One third of the votes allocated to national parliaments (two each, for a total of 56 votes) can issue a reasoned opinion requesting the Commission to revise a legislative proposal which is deemed to breach the principles of subsidiarity and proportionality, to which the Commission can react by maintaining, amending or withdrawing the proposal (yellow card). If reasoned opinions are submitted by at least a simple majority of the votes allocated to the national parliaments, the proposal must be reviewed. After such review, it is the Commission that may decide to maintain, amend or withdraw it. If the Commission decides to maintain the proposal, a majority in the EP, or 55 per cent of

[59] T Raunio, 'The Gatekeepers of European Integration? The Functions of National Parliaments in the EU Political System' (2011) 33 *Journal of European Integration* 303.

[60] ibid.

the Member States in the Council, may oppose it, but this is very unlikely. Some commentators think that this alone is sufficient to conclude that the Treaty of Lisbon has not contributed to filling the democratic deficit of the Union.[61] Raunio concurs and concludes that national parliaments have increasingly become the 'gatekeepers' of integration since it is their receiving and surveiling functions that have been increasingly strengthened.[62] I too believe that it is the misallocation of judgement and will at the national versus the European level that is responsible for much of the democratic deficit we experience today in Europe.

To conclude, the EU cannot be formally considered a parliamentary democracy, nor a separation-of-powers (presidential) system. Although different scholars have compared it to either model, the EU stubbornly remains *sui generis*, with traits that draw from a number of formats without reproducing any of them. New and old terms have been used to describe it and make sense of its institutional architecture, from 'condominium'[63] to 'regional state',[64] from 'compound democracy'[65] to 'empire'.[66] Scholars have also offered different methods of closing this democratic deficit, mainly suggesting prodding its development towards one or the other existing models.[67] I believe that trying to replicate at EU level existing models is the wrong way to go and that the value added of the EU lies in its revealing beyond dispute the transformations that democracy is currently undergoing. We are at the cusp of another momentous transformation of democracy, similar to that from direct to representative democracy which is still so differently assessed. While the contours of this new democracy are still blurry, some of its apparent shortcomings (according to the currently predominant notions of democracy) are glaringly apparent. However, there is no other solution than to start from these apparent defects to elaborate the notion of a 'new' type of democracy—some would call it transnational[68]—for an interdependent world.

The strange division of labour between parliamentary assemblies situated at different levels of government is the most evident trait of the novel situation. Understandably, national citizens and national representatives are at a loss as to how to use their powers and where to make their contribution. To the extent that

[61] eg P De Wilde, 'Why the Early Warning Mechanism does not Alleviate the Democratic Deficit' OPAL Online P Paper 6/2012 available at: www.opal-europe.org.

[62] Raunio, 'The Gatekeepers of European Integration?' (n 59).

[63] P Schmitter, *How to Democratize the European Union—and Why Bother?* (Lanham, Rowman & Littlefield, 2000).

[64] V Schmidt, *Democracy in Europe: The EU and National Polities* (Oxford, Oxford University Press, 2006).

[65] S Fabbrini, *Compound Democracies. Why the United States and Europe are Becoming Similar* (Oxford, Oxford University Press, 2007).

[66] J Zielonka, *Europe as Empire. The Nature of the Enlarged European Union* (Oxford, Oxford University Press, 2006); U Beck and E Grande, 'Empire Europe: Statehood and Political Authority in the Process of Regional Integration' in A Wiener and J Neyer (eds), *Political Theory of the European Union* (Oxford, Oxford University Press, 2011).

[67] eg S Hix, *What's Wrong with the European Union and How to Fix It* (Cambridge, Polity Press, 2008).

[68] J Bohman, *Democracy Across Borders. From Demos to Demoi* (Cambridge, MIT Press, 2007).

they express judgement and exercise will in the 'wrong' representative assembly on the 'wrong' issues, national candidates and voters prevent themselves from engaging in that meaningful dialogical exchange which makes for full democratic representation. Unless the multi-level institutional context in which representation takes place in today's Europe is fully factored in, and voters and representatives behave accordingly, the distance between European candidates and voters cannot be closed. Has the crisis affected this situation? In the concluding section I will argue that, while the crisis has not improved the situation, it has created the possibility of its improvement.

V. CONCLUSION

As we have seen, the crisis has triggered exceptional measures taken via exceptional means (international law, treaty amendments) and creating exceptional procedures which exceptionally sideline representative institutions at both EU and national level (but see Craig, chapter two in this volume). Yet, representative assemblies at both EU and national level have fought back and have claimed the opportunity to contribute both voice (national parliaments) and will (the EP) in the area of macroeconomic and crisis management. How can we interpret the current situation? Are the two constitutional perspectives—the supranational and the intergovernmental—that govern, respectively, the Single Market and the EMU creating tensions that jeopardise EU legitimacy, as Sergio Fabbrini argues,[69] or can they be accommodated within a federalist or federalising perspective as the Presidents' document *Towards a Genuine Economic and Monetary Union* foreshadows?[70] Is the European semester procedure fundamentally disempowering national parliaments of one of their primary tasks, that is, fashioning the budget and steering macroeconomic management or do these practices conform to a necessarily modified notion of 'shared and responsible self-determination' in the increasingly interconnected context of the EU? Must we seek to restore democratic decision-making by strengthening voice, will or control—or all three?

The economic crisis that besets the EU has had the merit of exposing the reversed division of labour that had been established between the EP and national parliaments and of prompting these chambers to rectify it. National parliaments have started to debate not so much the details of the macroeconomic policies enacted by their governments—which have been mostly dictated by commitments made in Maastricht and repeated during the crisis (think of the reinforced Stability and Growth Pact and the provisions contained in the Treaty on Stability,

[69] S Fabbrini, 'Intergovernmentalism and its Limits: Assessing the European Union's Answer to the Euro Crisis' (2013) 46 *Comparative Political Studies* 1003.

[70] H Van Rompuy in close collaboration with JM Barroso, J-C Juncker and M Draghi, 'Towards a Genuine Economic and Monetary Union' 5 December 2012, available at www.consilium.europa.eu/uedocs/cms_data/docs/pressdata/en/ec/134069.pdf.

Coordination and Governance)—but they have begun to address the wisdom of remaining within the current Union and the possibility of reforming it. In other words, they have re-appropriated their constitutional role—while complaining of their dispossession of the conventional powers of setting the budget and deciding on deficit spending. The European Semester, in particular, has raised complaints about the marginalisation of national representative assemblies in the determination of the national budget until very late in the game, but it has also driven home the importance of keeping the promises that the Member States have made to one another and to fully consider the repercussions that 'sovereign' decisions may have on the partner countries. This is problematic only if we cling to a conventional notion of democracy as 'unencumbered self-determination', therefore as 'sovereignty'. As we saw, representative democracy is less about the delegation and retrieval of will than about judgement as activating and proposing and as receiving and surveiling. When delegated, will cannot be completely retrieved,[71] while judgement cannot ever be completely delegated.

The existence of the above institutional mechanisms reveals a level of interdependence that defies any conventional notion of democracy as self-determination. Sovereignty in the EU, and even more in the euro area, must be understood as 'shared and responsible sovereignty'. Euro-area executives must be not just responsive and accountable to their own parliaments and citizens, but must also be responsible vis-à-vis the commitments that they have made with the other euro-area partners. The costs and benefits for the citizens of the euro-area partners must be fully factored in the fiscal and budgetary decisions made by each euro-area government. It is no longer sufficient to seek authorisation from national parliaments and be willing to be held accountable for decisions made at EU level as if the delegation of will were all that is implied by democratic representation. European citizens must be fully involved in the formation of voice, the expression of will and the exertion of control at *both* EU *and* national level, and for this to happen, elections must be aimed at establishing that dialogical relationship of representation. Only then will representatives be truly accountable to those they represent and only then will the represented supersede their particularities and forge new subjectivities. This new kind of accountability requires no formal overhaul of European political systems, but full reckoning with the 'changed circumstances of politics'.[72]

What kind of democracy does the Euro-crisis bring about? Sergio Fabbrini[73] argues that several democratic models are simultaneously being pursued at EU level since Maastricht—an economic community, a parliamentary union and an intergovernmental union—which clash with one another creating confusion and tensions

[71] H Agné, 'The Myth of International Delegation: Limits to and Suggestions for Democratic Theory in the Context of the European Union' (2007) 42 *Government and Opposition* 18.

[72] Bohman, *Democracy Across Borders* (n 68).

[73] S Fabbrini, 'Alternative Views of the European Union: Which Institutional Architecture for a Political Union?' in S Piattoni (ed), *The European Union. Democratic Principles and Institutional Architectures in Times of Crisis* (Oxford, Oxford University Press, 2015) 184.

in various area of EU activity, particularly macroeconomic management and foreign policy (see also Craig, chapter two in this volume). Ben Crum borrows from Rodrik's trilemma[74] to illustrate three possible 'solutions'—executive federalism, democratic federalisation or EMU dissolution—which can reconcile any two items of the trilemma but never all three of them, and concludes that the solution currently adopted (executive federalism) is still the most plausible.[75] Fritz Scharpf continues with his critique of EU governance which pits law against politics and negative against positive integration and prevents a social Europe from being sustained by the current institutional architecture of EMU.[76] In all three cases, representative democracy is hampered or constrained. It is only if we embrace a new notion of democracy as 'responsible and shared self-determination' that we begin to see the role that European and national representative assemblies can play in it. The EP must also be allowed to co-decide in the realm of macroeconomic policy while national parliaments must supervise and control breaches of not just formal subsidiarity aspects, but also the political substance of macroeconomic decisions.

What is most damaging EU and European democracy right now is the fact that facing up to this challenge has not yet entered the public debate in EU Member States. European citizens are still kept in the dark by their leaders on the extent to which EU Member States—and particularly Euro-area Member States—are already interdependent.[77] The European public should be allowed to first, 'get the full story' and then, debate the ways in which they wish to exert their democratic powers of judgement within this dramatically altered economic and political context. Unless citizens are fully informed by their own representatives of 'the changed circumstances of politics', populist appeals aimed at regaining an illusionary full sovereignty will carry the day.

[74] D Rodrik, *The Globalization Paradox: Democracy and the Future of the World Economy* (New York, Norton & Company, 2011).

[75] Crum, 'Saving the Euro' (n 58).

[76] F Scharpf, 'Monetary Union, Fiscal Crisis and the Pre-emption of Democracy' in JJ Hesse (ed), (2011) 2 *Zeitschrift für Staats- und Europawissenschaften* 163.

[77] L Schucknecht, P Moutot, P Rother and J Stark, *The Stability and Growth Pact. Crisis and Reform*, European Central Bank Occasional Paper Series, 129/11 available at: www.ecb.europa.eu; Van Rompuy et al, 'Towards a Genuine Economic and Monetary Union' (n 70).

9

Participatory Democracy in Europe: Article 11 TEU and the Legitimacy of the European Union

CHRISTIAN MARXSEN

I. INTRODUCTION

PARTICIPATION OF SOCIETAL groups in the development of policies has played a crucial role throughout the history of European integration. With the Lisbon Treaty, participatory democracy has been declared a constitutional principle of the European Union (EU), aiming at improving its democratic legitimacy. In this chapter I provide a review of the developing practice of participatory democracy and raise the question whether in fact these practices promote democracy at the European level. I start by situating the principle of participatory democracy in the current legal framework of the EU (Section II). I will then review the major dimensions of participatory democracy, namely mechanisms that aim to set up and promote a horizontal exchange within the European society (Section III), mechanisms that shall foster a dialogue between European institutions and societal organisations (Section IV), and the European Citizens' Initiative (ECI) (Section V). I will discuss these mechanisms with reference to the institutional claims and to their actual functioning. The chapter concludes with a critical assessment of the state of participatory democracy in Europe (Section VI).

II. PARTICIPATION AS A CONSTITUTIONAL PRINCIPLE OF THE EU

Participation of societal actors forms an essential part of European politics and law-making, and it has been important for European law-making since the early days of the European integration. Participation also has many facets. A first form that dates back to the very beginning of European institutions is the participation of societal actors through consultative bodies, such as the Economic and Social Committee in which delegates from employer, employee and other organisations are represented. A second dimension of participation lies in targeted contacts between European institutions and societal actors. The intensity of such contacts often varies depending on the policy field and reaches from sporadic targeted consultations to a more continuous partnership in specific areas.[1]

While such traditional mechanisms of exchange between the Commission and society as well as various informal ways of communication continue to play an important role,[2] a third—much more generalised—dimension of participatory mechanisms has emerged in light of the legitimacy crisis, which has threatened European integration since the 1990s. The Danish Maastricht Treaty referendum made clear that the 'ever closer union' would soon stagnate if the European Community (EC) were not able to change the public perception of European institutions. In the words of the European Commission: 'Many people are losing confidence in a poorly understood and complex system to deliver the policies that they want. The Union is often seen as remote and at the same time too intrusive.'[3] European institutions became aware that if citizens could not be won for the European project, integration would find its certain limits at the next referendum.

Participatory mechanisms were increasingly seen as a promising way to overcome the remoteness and perceived hierarchic character of European institutions and, as a consequence, participatory mechanisms were deepened, generalised and intensified. The so-called 'governance turn in EU-studies'[4] expressed the belief that participation could provide European institutions, above all the Commission, with more legitimacy,[5] without actually requiring radical and unrealistic institutional reforms. The aim of the promotion of participatory mechanisms is—in that line of thought—to put forward a new design of transnational legitimacy. Most notably, the Commission's 2001 'White Paper on European Governance' proposed overall changes of the Unions political structure: 'The White Paper proposes opening up the policy-making process to get more people and organisations involved in shaping and delivering EU policy. It promotes greater openness, accountability and responsibility for all those involved.'[6] These ideas have since also affected the understanding of the concept of democracy at the European level.

The 1997 Treaty of Amsterdam had for the first time established an obligation of European institutions to adhere to the principle of democracy.[7] However, not until the Draft Treaty establishing a Constitution for Europe was the understanding of democracy further elaborated. This draft treaty acknowledged the principle of representative democracy as foundational,[8] but also established the principle

[1] B Kohler-Koch and B Finke, 'The Institutional Shaping of EU–Society Relations: A Contribution to Democracy via Participation?' (2007) 3 *Journal of Civil Society* 205, 209–10.

[2] See, eg on informal ways of NGO advocacy, I de Jesús Butler, 'Non-governmental Organisation Participation in the EU Law-making Process' (2008) 14 *European Law Journal* 558.

[3] European Commission, 'European Governance—A White Paper', 25 July 2001 (Communication) COM (2001) 428 final 3.

[4] S Smismans, 'New Modes of Governance and the Participatory Myth' (2008) 31 *West European Politics* 874.

[5] See B Kohler Koch, 'Governing with the European Civil Society' in B Kohler-Koch et al (eds), *De-Mystification of Participatory Democracy* (Oxford, Oxford University Press, 2013) 21.

[6] European Commission, 'European Governance' (n 3) 3.

[7] Art 6(1) of the TEU as amended by the Amsterdam Treaty.

[8] Art I-45 Draft Treaty Establishing a Constitution for Europe.

of participatory democracy.[9] With slight amendments, both provisions have been incorporated into the Lisbon Treaty. Article 10 Treaty on European Union (TEU) now prescribes, for the first time, a certain model of democracy for the EU.[10] This provision makes clear that the general functioning of the Union shall be based on the principle of representative democracy. Citizens shall be represented by the European Parliament as well as by the governments of their states. Mechanisms of participatory democracy are then referred to in Article 11 TEU. The article's pendant in the constitutional draft treaty made this reference more explicit through the headline 'participatory democracy', which has been removed in the Lisbon Treaty.

The provisions of Article 11 TEU now form the core of the European concept of participatory democracy. We can distinguish three groups of participatory mechanisms: those aiming at a horizontal exchange within the European society, those aiming at a vertical exchange between EU institutions and the European society, and the European Citizens' Initiative. The element of a *horizontal exchange* is provided for in Article 11(1):

1. The institutions shall, by appropriate means, give citizens and representative associations the opportunity to make known and publicly exchange their views in all areas of Union action.

This paragraph constitutes an obligation for European institutions to enable an exchange between citizens and organisations among each other. This constitutes the obligation for European institutions to create forums of exchange and provide support for their functioning, but does not necessarily also require the institutions to actively participate herein.[11]

Mechanisms of *vertical exchange* are contained in paragraphs (2) and (3):

2. The institutions shall maintain an open, transparent and regular dialogue with representative associations and civil society.
3. The European Commission shall carry out broad consultations with parties concerned in order to ensure that the Union's actions are coherent and transparent.

Both provisions address the vertical exchange between European institutions on the one hand and representative organisations as well as civil society on the one hand. Citizens as such are not addressed here. While the second paragraph applies to all European institutions, the third is narrower by specifically referring to the European Commission. It provides a constitutional foundation to the Commission's practice of open consultations that has been developed since the late 1990s.

[9] See ibid Art I-46.

[10] See E Grabitz, M Hilf and M Nettesheim, *Das Recht der Europäischen Union* Vol I (September 2013) Art 11, margin number 8.

[11] R Bieber, 'The Citizens' Initiative—A Source of Additional Legitimacy for the European Union?' in JM Beneyto and I Pernice (eds), *Europe's Constitutional Challenges in the Light of the Recent Case Law of National Constitutional Courts* (Baden-Baden, Nomos, 2011) 232.

The *European Citizens' Initiative* is referred to in the fourth paragraph:

4. Not less than one million citizens who are nationals of a significant number of Member States may take the initiative of inviting the European Commission, within the framework of its powers, to submit any appropriate proposal on matters where citizens consider that a legal act of the Union is required for the purpose of implementing the Treaties.

The wording as well as the systematic relation between Articles 10 and 11 TEU make clear that participation is not supposed to account for an overall legitimacy of the Union. It is conceptualised as a complement to, or—as some put it—-enrichment of, the system of representative democracy.[12] This complementary function may nevertheless be seen as crucial; since the representative system at the European level remains chronically underdeveloped, the question whether and to what extent participatory mechanisms can be substitutes for the existing deficiencies is pressing.

Participatory democracy therefore forms a constitutional principle of the EU. Not any form of participation of societal actors in law-making or implementation can be seen as an expression of such participatory democracy however. The legitimating potential of participatory mechanisms is rooted in the sub-principles of openness, inclusiveness and responsiveness. These sub-principles are underpinned by democratic theory but can also be reconstructed from a number of policy documents in which the Commission has substantiated its participatory practices. *Openness* requires that participatory mechanisms are functioning in a transparent manner that enables the public to assess the input and the process, as well as the outcome.[13] For this reason, the Commission's regime of targeted involvement of certain pre-selected stakeholders has raised the suspicion to promote an undemocratic and corporatist arrangement in which only established influential societal players have a say.[14] The principle of *inclusiveness* demands that participatory mechanisms are open to a general participation and that societal interests are included as widely as possible.[15] Participatory mechanisms can only produce a balanced account of societal interest, when they are based on a roughly representative societal participation. The principle of *responsiveness* ultimately requires policy-makers to provide an adequate feedback about what they intend to do with the input they have received.[16] Although participation is about having

[12] Grabitz, Hilf and Nettesheim, *Das Recht der Europäischen Union* (n 10) margin number 6.

[13] See for the commitment to openness, European Commission, 'European Governance' (n 3) 10; European Commission, 'Towards a Reinforced Culture of Consultation and Dialogue—General Principles and Minimum Standards for Consultation of Interested Parties by the Commission' 11 December 2002, COM (2002) 704 final, 17; European Commission, 'Plan-D for Democracy, Dialogue and Debate' 13 October 2005, COM (2005) 494 final, 9.

[14] See Grabitz, Hilf and Nettesheim (n 10) margin number 21.

[15] See European Commission, 'European Governance' (n 3) 17; European Commission, 'General Principles' (n 13) 16.

[16] See European Commission, 'Plan-D' (n 13) 9; European Commission, 'General Principles' (n 13) 21.

a 'voice' and not a 'vote', its meaningfulness depends on whether political actors channel the results into the political process and communicate their conclusions back to society.

By providing normative criteria, these yardsticks do not function in dichotomies. They are not either fulfilled or not, but the extent to which they are and should be applied in regard to concrete participatory mechanisms, depends on the mechanism's aim and character. Having outlined the general role of participation within the EU, it is now time to take a closer look at the three dimensions of participation envisioned by Article 11 TEU.

III. DIMENSIONS OF PARTICIPATION I: HORIZONTAL EXCHANGE

The quest to increase a horizontal exchange between citizens and organisations is rooted in the perceived lack of a specifically European public and political sphere, which mark important preconditions for every polity. The need to involve citizens and to set up a transnational exchange over the Union's course received increased attention after the failure of the constitutional treaty. The limits of European integration had been reached and further integration would require a change in the public perception of the EU. The Commission announced a 'period of reflection' and that 'any vision of the future Europe needs to build on a clear view on citizen's needs and expectations'.[17] In order to win the hearts and minds of the people, the Commission developed a comprehensive programme for a societal exchange. In particular, the Commission's 2005 'Plan D for Democracy, Dialogue and Debate' created a framework and funding opportunities for a structured dialogue on European politics. Though these mechanisms were largely set up before the current provision of Article 11 TEU entered into force, they still provide us with insight into how EU institutions tackle the quest to set up a transnational debate.

The Commission has articulated two principal aims here. First, the participatory mechanisms are supposed to be a 'listening exercise'.[18] That means that the Commission claims to be learning from those debates in order to develop policies that suit the interests of the people. A second declared aim is to 'set out a long-term plan to reinvigorate European democracy and help the emergence of a European public sphere, where citizens are given the information and the tools to actively participate in the decision making process and gain ownership of the European project'.[19] The Commission tackles a problem here that has been discussed at length: the lack of an integrated European political and public sphere.[20] The Commission's diagnosis points out that European integration depends on the

[17] European Commission, 'Plan-D' (n 13) 2.

[18] ibid 4.

[19] ibid 3.

[20] See for a review of the literature on that issue, C Bärenreuter et al, 'An Overview of Research on the European Public Sphere (updated version)' (2009) Eurosphere Working Paper Series 3/2009.

existence or at least emergence of such a sphere while at the same time it sees that its programmes cannot realise that. The desired 'pan-European political culture'[21] cannot be created in Brussels but needs to emerge from the basis.[22] The Commission can, therefore, only try to provide impulses in the hope of fostering a transnational political exchange at the level of citizens and associations.

The range of mechanisms that have been established to further debate and deliberation is broad and has mostly involved citizens, but sometimes also representatives of organisations. It involves online tools and events of face-to-face communication. The online mechanisms include rather simple exchange and communication tools such as online debate forums.[23] Mechanisms of face-to-face communication often rely on a certain methodology and partly preselect participants according to specific criteria. 'Citizens consensus conferences', for example, are based on the idea of educating a group of laypersons that then enters into a debate with experts.[24] The aim is to establish consensual recommendations that take expert knowledge into account. Thus the outcome should be the expression of an informed citizen's perspective. A similar approach is taken by the Citizens' Agoras that the European Parliament has conducted regularly since 2007. Other models include the 'consultation of citizens' in a conference-like setting without prior education.[25]

The most sophisticated methodology is applied within deliberative polls.[26] Based on this methodology, a representative random sample of the population debates a policy issue. Initially, deliberative polls conduct a survey of the participants' opinions. The next step is to provide the participants with balanced briefings on the topic as well as expert input. Based on that input the participants enter into a debate. The following second survey is the most important step. The assumption is that the positions of the participants will often have changed and that the post-deliberation measurement could give an indication of what the public would think if it had engaged with the issue more deeply and on a more informed basis.[27]

[21] European Commission, 'White Paper on a European Communication Policy' 1 February 2006 (Communication) COM (2006) 35 final 5.

[22] See ibid 11.

[23] See for more details on those projects, A Fischer-Hotzel, 'Democratic Participation? The Involvement of Citizens in Policy-Making at the European Commission' (2010) 6 *Journal of Contemporary European Research* 335, 343–44).

[24] See L Boussaguet and R Dehousse, 'Too Big to Fly? A Review of the First EU Citizens' Conferences' in (2009) 36 *Science and Public Policy* 777.

[25] L Boussaguet, *Listening to the Views of European Public—An Assessment of the First Participatory Experiments to be Organized across the Community* (Paris, Notre Europe Jacques Delors Institute, 2011) 12.

[26] A concise introduction into the methodology can be found in R Luskin et al, 'Considered Opinions: Deliberative Polling in Britain' (2002) 32 *British Journal of Political Science* 455, 456–61; see also JS Fishkin, *Democracy and Deliberation: New Directions for Democratic Reform* (New Haven, Yale University Press, 1991) 81–104.

[27] See JS Fishkin, *When the People Speak—Deliberative Democracy and Public Consultation* (Oxford, Oxford University Press, 2009) 135 ff for empirical examples of the changes of the opinions of participants.

Deliberative polls thus aim for the considered and potentially revised judgements of citizens, not their initial and actual ones.[28]

This list is by no means exhaustive. Other participatory models have been conducted without following a prescribed scientific method.[29]

What is, ultimately, the impact of such forms of horizontal exchange? First, can they be regarded as elements initialising and promoting a pan-European political debate? Secondly, do the results of these participatory practices articulate anything more than the isolated views of those particular participants? In other words: how inclusive and representative are they? Thirdly, how are European institutions relating to the results of these mechanisms?

A. Promoting the Emergence of a European Political Sphere

Evaluating whether these mechanisms in fact promote the emergence of a European political sphere is difficult. The reason is that the emergence of a political or public sphere can hardly be satisfactorily validated by robust empirical criteria. It requires societal change and the relevant variables are too complex to calculate scientifically. The mechanisms might therefore make a contribution that plays out indirectly and in the long run, but are not be measurable today. However, based on the accessible facts, the results of the participatory mechanisms look rather sobering. The online participation tools have only attracted a rather limited number of participants. The 'Debate Europe' project that has been established under the framework of 'Plan D' was the most successful in that regard. It attracted 6,620 participants that engaged in 171,373 posts on matters of climate change, the future of Europe, and other issues.[30] In view of around 500 million citizens, this number nevertheless still is quite marginal. Other projects had even significantly fewer participants. The 'RadioWeb' project on enlargement and mobility received just 21 responses. Other projects also lacked any significant participation.[31]

As regards the face-to-face events, the limited number of participants is even more striking. Citizen conferences and deliberative polls have involved a varying number of citizens, which ranged from around 20 to 400, which in any event remains insignificant compared to the size of the Union. Media coverage has been suggested as a way of broadening the reception of these events,[32] but in practice that has rarely happened. The lack of media attention is unsurprising, since there

[28] D Espen, H Olsen and HJ Trenz, 'From Citizens' Deliberation to Popular Will Formation? Generating Democratic Legitimacy in Transnational Deliberative Polling' (2014) 62 *Political Studies* 117, 118.

[29] The most comprehensive lists of participatory projects that have been conducted so far can be found in: Fischer-Hotzel, 'Democratic Participation' (n 23) 343; S Boucher, 'If Citizens have a Voice, Who's Listening? Lessons from Recent Citizen Consultation Experiments for the European Union' (2009) EPIN Working Paper No 24/2009, 6–7.

[30] Fischer-Hotzel (n 23) 344.

[31] See for more statistical data ibid 344 ff.

[32] See JS Fishkin and RC Luskin, 'Broadcasts of Deliberative Polls: Aspirations and Effects' (2006) 36 *British Journal of Political Science* 184, 184–88.

appears little point in following the debates of randomly selected citizens, compared to the debates of the actual decision-makers. All in all, there is no evidence that exchanges between citizens who have an interest in European affairs in any event (as they otherwise would not participate in the matter), does have an overarching societal effect.

B. Inclusiveness

The second question concerns the inclusiveness of the mechanisms and raises the issue whether they can provide indications as regards the interests of EU citizens more generally. The models that simply assemble an arbitrary group of people can certainly not give rise to a strong claim of any form of representativeness since their sample is simply too narrow.[33] Deliberative polls, on the other hand, try to assure representativeness by selecting the participants based on scientific criteria: they aim to assemble a representative image of the population. The founder of the methodology of deliberative polls, James S Fishkin, claims that it 'does not make any appreciable statistical difference whether the same size sample is representing a town, a city, a small nation, or the entire European Union. The precision of the estimates with which that sample can represent a population will be essentially the same.'[34] The underlying claim of deliberative polls is that the constituted 'mini-public' of the deliberating sample can stand for the positions that a wider, that is, European population would take after informed deliberation.[35]

There are two central problems with that claim. Suspicion is warranted as regards the assumption that some hundred individuals can represent the complexity of views and interests that would enter into a debate of a constituency of 500 million people. The linkages between the micro-public of this 'de-contextualized form of lab participation'[36] and the actual macro-public are far from evident, especially since the results of the deliberation experiments are rarely reflected in the media.[37]

Furthermore, the processes of a limited deliberation on a certain issue do not necessarily correspond to the processes that characterise the political deliberation and decision-making of an entire society.[38] Does it make sense to tell people based

[33] See Boucher, 'If Citizens have a Voice, Who's Listening?' (n 29) 8 ff.

[34] Fishkin, *When the People Speak* (n 27) 96.

[35] Olsen and Trenz (n 28) 121 ff.

[36] A Bogner, 'The Paradox of Participation Experiments' (2012) 37 *Science Technology Human Values* 506, 521.

[37] Olsen and Trenz, 'From Citizens' Deliberation' (n 35) 130 ff.

[38] It is not even clear what makes people change their positions in deliberative polls. David Sander explores different explanatory models which all turn out to be unsatisfactory. His eventual consideration is that the change in attitudes might not even be rooted in the deliberation, but in the deliberative poll event and the liberal atmosphere created by those organising the event. See D Sander, 'The Effects of Deliberative Polling in an EU-wide Experiment: Five Mechanisms in Search of an Explanation' (2012) 42 *British Journal of Political Science* 617, 640.

on the results of a deliberative poll that a certain policy is justified because it is the conclusion that people would arrive at when they were only sufficiently informed about the matter and engaged in deliberation? Such a view is certainly paternalistic and actually at odds with democratic ideas. The significance of the results of deliberative polls for an evaluation of public opinion is therefore rather limited.

C. Institutional Follow-Up

The last question raised is, whether and how European institutions relate to the results of the events, that is, how responsive they are. As stated above, from its wording Article 11(1) TEU does not require the institutions to do more than provide the forums but it is a common and legitimate expectation that institutions will somehow take the results into account. The Commission did in fact profess to do so when it announced the need for a 'listening exercise'. The participatory mechanisms are supposed to have some sort of influence on policy-makers and provide them with information regarding the needs and concerns of society.[39] However, evidence that such listening actually takes place is thin. Stephen Boucher has reviewed the impact of a number of participatory mechanisms and concluded that there is a lack of mechanisms through which these results could be channelled into the political process:

> One would expect at least to find traces of the debates indicating some measure of 'listening', i.e. noticing and commenting. For instance, one could expect MEPs, commissioners, ministers or national parliamentarians to refer to the debates in public statements. While more detailed research might unveil a greater level of interest, we find little evidence of this.[40]

One reason for this is surely that many of the participatory events have not been linked to concrete policy projects so that the results could not enter into a specific consideration of choices.[41] Moreover, based on the described lack of representativeness, institutions do not even have a strong reason to pay too much attention to these results.

In conclusion, the mechanisms of horizontal exchange in many cases constitute a very low-threshold form of participation. Their justification as specifically democratic tools, however, remains questionable. Not only is the actual number of people participating marginal compared to the overall European population, but the external effects on the general public or on political officials are also insignificant. These mechanisms' primary role may be seen in the political education for

[39] eg James S Fishkin and Robert C Luskin—the fathers of deliberative polls—state that deliberative polls are 'intended to have some policy impact—not to determine policy but to be something policy makers can take into account'. (Fishkin and Luskin (n 32) 188).

[40] Boucher, (n 29) 12.

[41] Fischer-Hotzel (n 23) 346.

the few participants who are actually involved. They might very well change participants' attitudes and promote a more generalised perspective on political issues. The external evaluation of one project, for example, concluded that citizens were fascinated by the European dimension and felt 'more like Europeans' afterwards.[42] The societal dimension, however, remains peripheral.

IV. DIMENSION OF PARTICIPATION II: VERTICAL EXCHANGE

A vertical exchange between European institutions and society constitutes the second group of participatory mechanisms. Article 11(2) TEU envisions an 'open, transparent and regular dialogue with representative associations and civil society'. An authoritative framework for the functioning of such a generalised dialogue has not yet been established. Despite calls to set standards and provide for a more structured dialogue,[43] the EU has not come up with a proposal so far. However, there is an established practice of continuous dialogue between a number of Directorates General (DG) or Agencies and societal associations. The DG Trade, for example, has established the 'Trade Civil Society Dialogue' which usually consists of around 20 meetings a year and attracts a couple of hundreds of representatives, particularly from professional organisations and business associations, per year. The EU Agency for Fundamental Rights has established the Fundamental Rights Platform, a network of over 300 mostly public-interest civil society organisations, and other similar models can be found elsewhere.

The most advanced scheme of vertical exchange that will be focused on here is the Commission's practice of stakeholder consultations (Article 11(3) TEU). The Commission defines consultations as the 'processes through which [it] wishes to trigger input from outside interested parties for the shaping of policy prior to a decision by the Commission'.[44] It conducts targeted consultations of specific actors whose input is expected to be relevant and has established a comprehensive system of open consultations using the online consultation platform 'Your Voice in Europe'.[45] This online consultation mechanism forms the core of the Commission's approach to participatory democracy: with around 100 consultations per year, this mechanism is the most comprehensive scheme of generally accessible societal participation in EU policy-making.[46]

The Commission developed the main characteristics and procedures of the open consultative scheme at the beginning of the new millennium.[47] Policy-makers

[42] P Sellke et al, *European Citizens' Panel—Final Report of the External Evaluation* (Stuttgart, University of Stuttgart, 2007) 51.

[43] See, eg European Economic and Social Committee, 'Principles Procedures and Action for the Implementation of Articles 11(1) and 11(2) of the Lisbon Treaty' 6 February 2012 SOC/423.

[44] European Commission, General Principles (n 13) 15–16.

[45] ec.europa.eu/yourvoice/.

[46] 2010: 96 consultations; 2011: 130 consultations; 2012: 112 consultations; 2013: 99 consultations.

[47] C Quittkat, 'New Instruments Serving Democracy—Do Online Consultations Benefit Civil Society?' in B Kohler-Koch et al, *De-Mystification of Participatory Democracy* (Oxford, Oxford University Press, 2013) 89.

have essentially two expectations of these open consultations. The first aim is to increase the effectiveness of the political process by generating better outcomes.[48] Consultations are meant to improve the quality of the political process by mobilising external knowledge[49] and by ensuring that—as Article 11(3) TEU states—the 'Union's actions are coherent and transparent'. The second aim is to increase legitimacy by allowing citizens to raise their voice within the decision-making process. Open consultations are meant to provide equal access to all groups with an interest in a certain issue and shall be held on 'major policy initiatives'.[50] The intention is to 'reduce the risk of the policy-makers just listening to one side of the argument or of particular groups getting privileged access'.[51]

The consultations are not primarily designed as a means of citizen participation, although citizens are not explicitly excluded. They involve all kinds of stakeholders, including civil society organisations, private companies, business associations and public authorities. The procedure for the consultations is not regulated by law, but by non-binding practice regulations, established by the Commission in its 'General Principles and Minimum Standards for Consultation of Interested Parties'.[52]

The consultative mechanisms are expected to render the EU more democratic as they allow diverse societal interests to have a voice within the political process. Recent empirical studies have, however, presented a more critical evaluation of the Commission's practice and the possible legitimating effects of the consultations in general. Three points, all related to openness, inclusiveness and representativeness, are particularly worth pointing out: first, an unsatisfying approach of the Commission in regard to the coherence and transparency of consultations; secondly, a lack of representativeness of the actual participants; and thirdly, ambiguity about the overall effect of the consultations.

A. Coherence and Transparency of the Consultations

The first set of problems regards the coherence and transparency of the consultations. The problems are often of a seemingly trivial technical nature but undermine public access to the consultation results. The documentation of past consultations is not generally stored at the Commission's 'single access point', but are partly scattered around the different websites of the Directorates General. In a significant number of cases the consultation documents and results are not accessible, partly since they are not provided at all, and partly because the internet pages are outdated and links to the actual results are broken.[53] Another hurdle for transparency

48 See European Commission, 'Impact Assessment Guidelines' 15 January 2009 SEC (2009) 92 19.

49 European Commission, General Principles (n 13) 5.

50 ibid 15.

51 European Commission, European Governance (n 2) 17.

52 European Commission, General Principles (n 13).

53 C Marxsen, 'Open Stakeholder Consultations at the European Level—Voice of the Citizens?' (2015) 21 *European Law Journal* 257, 272.

is that the Commission often does not publish an evaluation report so that it is hard to tell what the Commission actually makes of the submissions.

B. Representativeness of the Consultations

The crucial problem, however, is the lack of representativeness of the consultations. The field of participants is strongly biased,[54] and generally does not reflect the diversity of existing societal perspectives and interests. A first remarkable fact is that—with the exception of a few cases—citizens rarely participate in the consultations. This is not a problem as such, since the design of open consultations is not suitable for a broad participation of citizens. The process would indeed collapse if thousands or millions of citizens actually decided to participate. The consultations primarily aim at organisations that represent a certain aggregated group interest.

One major problem is that mainly economic interest groups, such as business associations or private companies, manage to be represented in the consultations. Other societal spheres, for example, representing social or cultural interests, have not established a comparable organisational density. One reason for this imbalance is that establishing a presence at the European level is resource intensive. Therefore, only organisations that are backed with significant economic power can establish a recognisable presence at the European level. In 2011, for example, in over 70 per cent of all consultations, organisations with a business background formed the largest group of participants.[55] For non-profit organisations, a recognisable and continuous presence in the consultations has only been established by a few trade unions and consumer protection organisations. Other than that, citizen interests or general public interests are fundamentally under-represented. The reality of open consultations hardly measures up to the idea that organisations could mobilise societal support and express the interests of those suffering from exclusion and marginalisation, the suggested core feature of participatory mechanisms.[56]

In addition, there is a strong geographical bias in favour of the 'old' Member States while organisations from new Member States rarely participate.[57] Especially due to a lack of resources of groups without a business background, and the often underdeveloped system of civil society organisations particularly in new Member States, the consultative scheme generally lacks inclusiveness.

[54] Quittkat (n 47) 95–100; Marxsen (n 53) 573 ff.

[55] Marxsen (n 53) 268–69.

[56] The Commission had pointed to the importance of that aspect in its White Paper on Governance (n 2) 14: 'Civil society plays an important role in giving voice to the concerns of citizens and delivering services that meet people's needs. Churches and religious communities have a particular contribution to make. The organisations which make up civil society mobilise people and support, for instance, those suffering from exclusion or discrimination.'

[57] Quittkat (n 47) 106–108.

C. The Impact of Consultations on Decision-Making

The third problem concerns the question as to how the contributions to consultations are taken into account by policy-makers. The nature of consultations obviously does not warrant the expectation that everything that is submitted will have an effect on final outcomes. Consultations are not about deciding on any particular matter, but about providing an entry point for input during the decision-making process. They are, as mentioned before, about having a voice, not a vote. At the same time, consultations are not ends in themselves, but should have some form of impact.

Research on the ways in which the Commission deals with the submissions received and on how the open consultations actually affect and shape policy outcomes is rather scarce. The principle of transparency would require the Commission to give some sort of indication as to its evaluation of the submissions. By contrast, as the Commission often does not provide sufficiently detailed evaluation reports, it remains unknown whether and how the Commission takes heed of the submissions. However, the limited existing research suggests that the contributions and policy recommendations of well-established organisations are considered much more thoroughly than proposals by representatives of smaller public-interest organisations are.[58]

An overall evaluation of the current consultative mechanism therefore shows a strong structural bias in favour of established organisations. Consultations are mechanisms that lead to involvement of a well-organised and often economic European elite. To a certain extent, this fact is beyond the Commission's control as it simply mirrors the power relations within society. In fact, the Commission even tries to counter this bias by funding certain civil society initiatives. Simultaneously, the Commission also plays a role in furthering this structural bias. First, some highly controversial issues are simply not made the subject of online consultations at all, or the questions raised do not engage the core of the problem. The DG Agriculture and Development, for example, for years has rarely conducted consultations at all, especially not on its Common Agricultural Policy.[59] This is possible because there is no obligation, but merely a self-commitment to conduct consultations.

Another recent example is the highly controversial EU–US free trade agreement, Transatlantic Trade and Investment Partnership (TTIP), on which meaningful consultations have long been avoided. The DG Trade conducted a first consultation in 2012.[60] That consultation, however, was entirely phrased in the language

[58] T Hüller, 'Gut beraten? Die Online-Konsultationen der EU Kommission' (2008) 1 *Zeitschrift für Politikberatung* 359, 378.

[59] C Quittkat and B Kohler-Koch, 'Involving Civil Society in EU Governance—The Consultation Regime of the European Commission' in C Quittkat and B Kohler-Koch (eds), *De-Mystification of Participatory Governance* (Oxford, Oxford University Press, 2013) 52.

[60] European Commission, 'Initial General Public Consultation on EU–US High Level Working Group on Jobs and Growth' available at: trade.ec.europa.eu/consultations/?consul_id=160.

of economic growth and international competitiveness and did not address the potential ecological and social dimensions of the agreement. The participants in the consultations were almost exclusively transnational business associations and companies.[61] Based on such an unrepresentative set of perspectives, it is not surprising that the Commission could conclude that stakeholders were 'generally highly supportive of a transatlantic initiative that would boost trade and generate growth and jobs across the Atlantic'.[62] A similarly narrow perspective and a comparable field of participants characterise the second consultation on a potential trade agreement.[63] Despite societal controversies, a third consultation on specificities of investment protection as part of the EU–US agreement closed in July 2014, avoiding the 'if' question, and instead concentrating on detailed 'how' questions. Reflecting the public debate on TTIP, this consultation has now attracted an overwhelming participation of almost 150,000 replies.

Another limiting factor is that consultations often raise highly specific questions that cannot be answered without expert knowledge. While the specificities of policy proposals certainly need to be addressed, there is rarely an element that would acknowledge the political character of the issues. Most consultations are not phrased in the language of political choice but operate *based on political choices* and then provide a very narrow and often highly specific framework for input. The Commission uses an administrative terminology that implies that the problem under consideration is one of scientific accuracy and not at least as much one of political choices. In doing so, the Commission covers the underlying political choices and strictly directs the input into a certain direction and henceforth creates a structural bias in favour of the established political course. In too few cases, the Commission actually explicitly raises political issues and puts them up for discussion. In the face of the financial crisis, for example, it raised the issue of taxations for the financial sector and asked whether that would be a desirable political aim.[64] The consultation raised principal issues of the direction of EU policies and attracted quite significant participation by citizens, the private sector and also NGOs and public authorities.[65]

In most cases, however, the open mechanism does not actually lead to more inclusive participation, but provides the already powerful with an additional tool to influence the policy-making process or to voice their interests.

[61] Overall participants: 48; business associations: 44; public authorities: 2; citizens: 2.

[62] European Commission, 'Results of the initial public consultation on the EU-US High-Level Working Group on growth and jobs' undated document available at http://trade.ec.europa.eu/consultations/documents/consul_148.pdf.

[63] European Commission, 'Public Consultation on the Future of EU–US Trade and Economic Relations' available at: trade.ec.europa.eu/consultations/?consul_id=169.

[64] European Commission, 'Consultation on financial sector taxation' available at: ec.europa.eu/taxation_customs/common/consultations/tax/2011_02_financial_sector_taxation_en.htm.

[65] Total submissions: 3,624; citizens: 3,432 (of which 21 were individual contributions, the rest petitions); organisations with a business background: 91; not-for-profit organisations: 79; public authorities: 17; political parties/parliamentary groups: 5.

V. DIMENSIONS OF PARTICIPATION III: THE EUROPEAN CITIZENS' INITIATIVE

The third type of mechanism—the European Citizens' Initiative (ECI)—was introduced by the Lisbon Treaty and is the first manifestation of direct democracy at the European level. It allows EU citizens to 'take the initiative of inviting the European Commission, within the framework of its powers, to submit any appropriate proposal on matters where citizens consider that a legal act of the Union is required for the purpose of implementing the Treaties'.[66] The initiative is limited to fields in which the Commission has competencies to act.

The details and the procedure of the ECI are provided for in Regulation (EU) 211/2011.[67] The main requirements for a successful ECI are the following. First, citizens have to form a citizens' committee that consists of members from at least seven Member States. Secondly, the ECI has to be registered with the Commission which reviews formalities: it checks whether the proposal falls manifestly outside of its powers to initiate legislation, and whether the proposal is manifestly abusive or contrary to the values of the Union. Thirdly, after registration, the citizens' committee has one year to collect statements of support. Fourthly, the ECI is successful if it manages to collect at least one million signatures from at least one quarter of the Member States, whereby specific country quotas have to be met.[68] Fifthly, a successful ECI is submitted to the Commission, which then has three months to submit its answer.

Since its establishment, a number of citizens' initiatives have been launched. The main inputs are of a political or ethical nature: They are often linked to a quest for more solidarity and in many cases related to the protection of animals. Anti-EU positions have also been expressed by some initiatives.[69] As of August 2014, 43 ECIs have been filed with the Commission. The Commission rejected the registration of 18 initiatives on the grounds of a lack of competencies in the respective fields.[70] A significant number of ECIs (13) ended without having gathered sufficient support, or have been withdrawn. As of January 2015, the Commission has answered two initiatives, namely the 'Right2Water' campaign that aimed at stopping the privatisation of water management, and the 'One of Us' campaign that aimed at promoting the protection of human embryos.

[66] Art 11(4) TEU.

[67] Regulation (EU) 211/2011 of 16 February 2011 of the European Parliament and of the Council, [2011] OJ L65/1.

[68] These quotas correspond to the number of members of the European Parliaments elected in each country multiplied by 750. Accordingly, the range lies between 4,500 (Luxembourg) and 74,250 (Germany) required statements of support.

[69] See the citizens' initiatives on: 'A new EU legal norm, self-abolition of the European Parliament and its structures, must be immediately adopted' and 'To hold an immediate EU Referendum on public confidence in European Government's (EG) competence'.

[70] See ec.europa.eu/citizens-initiative/public/initiatives/non-registered, for a list of refused requests for registration.

When measured against the yardsticks of openness, inclusiveness and responsiveness, an evaluation of the Commission's practice leads to mixed results. In terms of openness, the practice appears favourable. Regulation (EU) 211/2011 provides clear rules and each of an initiative's steps is made transparent on the Internet.

As regards inclusiveness, some criticism has been raised. ECIs do not offer ordinary citizens easy access to the Commission. The high number of ECIs whose registration was refused, as well as those that did not win a sufficient number of supporters, illustrate that the ECI demands a rather high organisational capacity of its initiators in order to be successful. Significant resources, a transnational network, and access to a (quasi)professional infrastructure for public relations are necessary. Initiatives that have been successful in gaining sufficient support accordingly built on a strong organisational basis. They were backed by powerful international associations with a large membership base,[71] or by a broad network of smaller supporting organisations,[72] and above all by substantial financial resources.[73] It is therefore important to notice that the ECI is in fact not primarily a mechanism for the involvement of individual citizens as it requires transnationally organised European groups focusing public opinion on certain issues and mobilising support for their claims.

Of crucial concern is the aspect of responsiveness. During the initial debate on the citizens' initiative, the question of what kind of obligations a successful ECI should be able to impose on the Commission was contested. Maximalists demanded that the Commission should be obliged to present a legislative proposal,[74] even if it did not necessarily follow the exact proposal of the initiative. Such an interpretation, however, is neither implied by the wording of Article 11(4) TEU ('inviting the European Commission ... to submit any appropriate proposal') nor is it plausible to force the Commission to adopt legislation at any cost. The text of the TEU makes clear that the Commission is not bound by the concrete proposal of the initiative. If it can adopt legislation on the matter different from that proposed by the ECI, then preventing the Commission from refraining from adopting any legislation would—*a maiore ad minus*—not make sense.[75]

[71] The Right2Water initiative was carried by a number of organisations, most importantly by the European Trade Union Confederation (ETUC) and the European Federation of Public Service Unions (EPSU).

[72] The campaign 'Stop Vivisection' gained the support of more than 200 animal rights/animal protection groups.

[73] The Right2Water initiative was granted around €140.000 by EPSU; the 'One of us' initiative gained donations of more than €150.000.

[74] Grabitz, Hilf and Nettesheim (n 10) margin number 27; KH Fischer, *Der Europäische Verfassungsvertrag* (Baden-Baden, Nomos, 2005) 202; A Epiney, 'Europäische Verfassung und Legitimation durch die Unionsbürger' in S Kadelbach (ed), *Europäische Verfassung und direkte Demokratie* (Baden-Baden, Nomos, 2006) 49.

[75] See HP Folz, 'Art I-47' in C Vedder and WH von Heinegg (eds), *Europäischer Verfassungsvertrag* (Baden-Baden, Nomos, 2007) 221.

The actual approach implemented by Regulation (EU) 211/2011 follows the latter approach. The regulation makes clear that the Commission, after receiving the citizens' initiative, shall 'within three months, set out in a communication its legal and political conclusions on the citizen initiative, the action it intends to take, if any, and its reasons for taking or not taking that action'.[76]

Regarding the two successful ECIs, no action has been taken and both initiatives have strongly criticised what they perceived as a lack of responsiveness. The Right-2Water initiative criticised a lack of ambition in the response,[77] whereas 'One of Us' expressed its 'strongest indignation' against the Commission's response which were 'contrary to the principle of "participatory Democracy" promoted by the Treaty of Lisbon'.[78]

These remain isolated cases for now, but depending on how the Commission will deal with the issue of responsiveness in the future civil society organisations will or will not make use of it. Specific political aims were, of course, campaigned for at the European level in the past long before the citizens' initiative,[79] and it remains an open question whether the ECI has anything additional to offer. The risk of failing to achieve anything because the quorum is not met is substantial, and it only makes sense to take such a risk if the gains of a successful initiative are equally substantial.

Striking a balance here is not going to be easy, because there is an inherent tension associated with the ECI. On the one hand, as shown, it sets a relatively high threshold for societal participation and is therefore fairly exclusive. At the same time, however, this high threshold appears low compared to the overall European population. A successful initiative only requires the support of around 0.2 per cent of the European citizens, and therefore does not express an established pan-European public opinion on an issue. It is even possible that a controversial topic could provoke two initiatives with contradictory aims that eventually turn out to be formally successful. This makes clear that the Commission cannot be evaluated in terms of whether and how it implements a successful ECI, but in terms of how it introduces the proposal into the overall political process and further deals with it. The Commission will have to strike a delicate balance between acknowledging the democratic character of successful initiatives and their aforementioned limited scope. In a case where the Commission does not implement a proposal, the reasonable expectation will be that it takes the proposal seriously and honours

[76] Regulation 211/2011 (n 67) Art 10(1)(c).

[77] Press Release 'Commission Lacks Ambition in Replying to first European Citizens' Initiative', 19 March 2014, available at: www.right2water.eu/news/press-release-commission-lacks-ambition-replying-first-european-citizens%E2%80%99-initiative.

[78] Press Release from the Executive Board of the European Citizens Initiative 'One of Us', 5 June 2014, available at: www.oneofus.eu/press-release-from-the-executive-board-of-the-european-citizens-initiative-one-of-us.

[79] A prominent example in that regard is the successful campaign of the 'Starting Line Group' to establish anti-discrimination rules at the EU level. See generally Butler, 'Non-governmental Organisation Participation' (n 2) 572 ff.

successful initiatives by, inter alia, putting the issue on the agenda, conducting more research, promoting more debate and channelling the proposal into the forums that are dealing with the issue politically. In doing so, the Commission might in fact discover that an ECI proposal has broader Member State and societal support, or would at least give it the chance of triggering a change in political attitudes. In any case, even if the proposal were eventually not implemented, such a process would establish a substantiated reasoning for such omission.

So far, the Commission has rejected both successful ECIs and provided a response in papers numbering some 15 pages. Unless the Commission finds ways to take the proposals more seriously, it is highly unlikely that the ECI will play any significant role in the future. Organisations might then find ECIs too resource- and time-consuming compared to a summary response by the Commission.

VI. THE STATE OF PARTICIPATORY DEMOCRACY

In summary, this paper argues that all of the mechanisms designed to enhance participatory democracy suffer from a common failing, in that they do not have a significant effect on the legitimacy of the political process. They have been implemented as an answer to the critique against the EU's legitimacy deficit, but have failed to make the political process more transparent, accessible and representative. In brief, they have not led to a more inclusive system of governance. The mechanisms that aim at establishing and promoting platforms for horizontal exchange (Article 11(1) TEU) from the outset are rather weak democratic tools. They are, as has been shown, primarily a tool for the political education of the actual participants, and therefore promote democracy, if at all, only indirectly.

The other provisions of Article 11 grant a greater degree of influence on the political process for societal groups. However, they turn out to be problematic when measured against the yardsticks of openness, inclusiveness and responsiveness. The mechanisms of vertical exchange (Article 11(2) and (3) TEU) lack inclusiveness and thus do not establish a more representative image of the existing societal perspectives. Caution is therefore warranted: policy-makers should not mistake the positions expressed in the consultations for actual articulations of the will of European society. In most cases, structural discrepancies in the distribution of participation in terms of north and south, west and east, as well as rich and poor, are too profound.

Finally there is the ECI, the only mechanism of Article 11 TEU that is subject to further legal articulation by means of a regulation. Although there is little practical experience with the regulation yet, so far it appears that the Commission does not take the proposals sufficiently seriously.

Thus, as practised today, the mechanisms of participatory democracy do not contribute to the legitimacy of the European political process. In many cases, participation is a rhetorical device used to imply that the European political process is more open than it actually is. This becomes evident, for example, when the

Commission claims to say 'yes to the first successful European Citizens' Initiative'[80] while, in fact, rejecting its core demands.

The crucial remaining question is what the prospects for participatory democracy at the European level are and if the deficits can be remedied. At least some can. The ECI is a tool that can mobilise citizens for a certain aim and channel their input into the political process. Whether that turns out to be meaningful will depend, as I have argued, on whether the Commission will be able to strike a balance between an ECI's demands and other legitimate aims.

The situation seems much more complicated regarding open consultations, and dialogues with civil society and representative organisations. Some aspects could easily be improved. The Commission could, for example, promote openness and transparency of participatory mechanisms if it pushed for legally binding rules on when and how such participation should take place. That could limit the Commission's ability to refrain from consultations in policy areas in which it does not favour broad public debate, such as in regard to the TTIP agreement for example, touched upon above. Also, clear rules should be provided regarding publication of the results of participatory input, and on how the Commission deals with the input it has received. However, there is no indication that the problems in regard to the inclusiveness of the process could be overcome soon. The legitimating potential of participatory tools at EU level remains, for the time being, precarious.

[80] European Commission, Press Release, 'Commission says yes to the first successful European Citizens' Initiative', 19 March 2014.

10

Democratic Accountability of EU Executive Power: A Reform Agenda for Parliaments

DEIRDRE CURTIN

I. INTRODUCTION

EUROPEAN 'GOVERNMENT' HAS evolved considerably in reach and in intensity over the course of the past few years, especially since the Treaty of Lisbon (2009). Government-like activity by European Union (EU) level executive actors embraces the Treaty-based powers and practices of three key political actors (the European Council, the Commission and the Council), in particular, their role in law making and execution.[1] The European Council sets the agenda and directs the law-making institutions; the Commission proposes the content of far-reaching legislation, ensures its implementation and negotiates international agreements; and the Council is co-legislator, main decision-maker and executive actor depending on the policy area. European governance in the broader sense of non-core executive actors, such as European level agencies and 'comitology' committees, is included within the embrace of executive power in the EU.[2] Their decisions matter, also ultimately for the European citizen, even if they are only sporadically or invisibly affected. In between is the European Central Bank (ECB), a supranational actor with an increasingly wide remit and ever more salient tasks in terms of supervision over national banks.

In terms of power, *executive* power has long been the 'residual', hard-to-define and rarely attempted category, and as exercised within the EU political system, it is clearly not unitary.[3] It consists of supranational institutions *and* the governments

[1] The term 'government', when used in this chapter for the EU, connotes the key EU executive actors—the European Council, the Council and the Commission. It is not implied that it is government in the broader sense, which includes all three branches in a tripartite national political system. Rather, it is used as a synonym for EU executive power—a specific and fragmented phenomenon.

[2] See further, D Curtin, H Hofmann and J Mendes, 'Constitutionalising EU Executive Rule-Making Procedures: A Research Agenda' (2013) 19 *European Law Journal* 1.

[3] N Barber, 'Prelude to the Separation of Powers' (2001) 60 *Cambridge Law Journal* 59.

and civil servants of the Member States (with the input of 'experts'). The two most important institutions in this context are the European Council, 'the alpha and omega of executive power in the EU',[4] and the Council of Ministers. The Councils of the EU are, in fact, the institutions in the EU political system where the most powerful actors—the Member State governments—reside.[5] National executives are involved both at the level of ministers and prime ministers in the Council and the European Council, and also at the lower levels of institutions (working parties, committees) where civil servants operate in largely invisible supporting roles.[6]

Executive actors and administrative constellations transgress levels of government and national borders in a manner that challenges the coherence of national governments in an unprecedented way. The result is an increasingly compound and accumulated 'order' of executive power in contemporary Europe.[7] The chameleonic and variegated nature and function of the executive at the European level, with the supranational intertwined with the national, has a habit of popping up often in an unpredictable and novel manner in evolving legal and institutional practices.[8] It also evolves and changes—unpredictably—over time. Thus, executive power within the Council of Ministers has migrated away from it in recent years as a result of the shift of some sensitive and operational policy areas either to the Commission, in the case of police and judicial cooperation,[9] or to the new High Representative of the Union for Foreign Affairs and Security Policy and the European External Action Service (EEAS) in terms, generally, of foreign affairs.[10] Yet the Council still retains executive powers of a more operational kind, for example, over areas such as the imposition of sanctions and the blacklisting of terrorists.

The economic crisis has reinforced certain government-like powers of other actors such as the Commission, and also of the more 'autonomous' and technical ECB. The phenomenon of strong executive power sidelining the institutions of representative or liberal democracy often consolidates and intensifies in times

[4] D Curtin, *Executive Power of the European Union: Law, Practices and the Living Constitution* (Oxford, Oxford University Press, 2009) 70.

[5] H Wallace and F Hayes-Renshaw, *The Council of Ministers* (Basingstoke, Palgrave MacMillan, 2006). See also, D Naurin, 'Representation in the Councils of the EU' in S Kroger (ed), *Political Representation in the European Union: Still Democratic in Times of Crisis?* (London, Routledge, 2014).

[6] K Juncos and A Pomorska, 'Invisible and Unaccountable? National Representatives and Council Officials in EU Foreign Policy' (2011) 18 *Journal of European Public Policy* 1096.

[7] See further, D Curtin and M Egeberg, 'Tradition and Innovation: Europe's Accumulated Executive Order' (2008) 31 *West European Politics* 639.

[8] See further, D Curtin and I Dekker, 'The European Union from Maastricht to Lisbon: Institutional and Legal Unity out of the Shadow' in P Craig and G de Búrca (eds), *The Evolution of EU Law* (Oxford, Oxford University Press, 2011).

[9] See in general, S Peers, *EU Justice and Home Affairs Law* (Oxford, Oxford University Press, 2011).

[10] See Council Decision 2010/427/EU of 26 July 2010 establishing the organisation and functioning of the European External Action Service, [2010] OJ L201/30; S Vanhoonacker and N Reslow, 'The European External Action Service: Living Forwards by Understanding Backwards' (2010) 15 *European Foreign Affairs Review* 1; and S Blockmans et al, *EEAS 2.0: A Legal Commentary on Council Decision 2010/427/EU Establishing the Organisation and Functioning of the European External Action Service* (Brussels, CEPS, 2013).

of emergency or crisis.[11] The US security emergency had repercussions worldwide including in Europe, and continues to be felt today.[12] The fight against terrorism has spawned a variety of disputed legal acts and legislation in Europe with fundamental implications for the privacy and civil liberties of citizens and non-citizens.[13] Unilateral control over information and decision-making at the expense of parliaments is a long-standing feature of more 'inter-governmental' arenas of decision-making including the EU's Common Foreign and Security Policy (CFSP).[14] The most recent emergency or crisis, the economic crisis, resulted in an acceleration of decision-taking by supranational and national executives at the European level, often with a very profound and wide-reaching national impact.[15] The new role of the EU in the adoption process of national budgets is obviously of direct consequence to the financial well-being of citizens across Europe.[16] The implementation of a single supervisory mechanism for banks,[17] and of a banking resolution authority,[18] touch on very sensitive areas of national policy. Executive dominance by EU institutions and by (some) national actors at the European level has now reached into such sensitive policy fields as national budgets and macroeconomic decisions (for example, with regard to Cyprus).[19]

[11] See D Curtin, 'Challenging Executive Dominance in European Democracy' (2014) 77 *Modern Law Review* 1, 2–3, where the argument is developed more extensively.

[12] See for a long-standing challenge to the blacklisting of terrorists by the EU, Joined Cases C-584/10 P, C-593/10 P and C-595/10 P *Commission and Others v Kadi*, judgment of 18 July 2013, not yet reported.

[13] See, eg the Proposal for a Directive of the European Parliament and of the Council on the use of Passenger Name Record data for the prevention, detection, investigation and prosecution of terrorist offences and serious crime, 2 February 2011 COM (2011) 32 final. The EP was set to vote on this proposal on 10 June 2013, but the vote has been delayed.

[14] See further, the special issue of the *Journal of European Public Policy* edited by H Sjursen, 'The EU's Common Foreign and Security Policy: The Quest for Democracy' (2011) 18 *Journal of European Public Policy*.

[15] See in general, F Scharpf, 'Monetary Union, Fiscal Crisis and the Pre-emption of Democracy' (2011) MPIfG Discussion Paper 11/11; J Habermas, *The Crisis of the European Union: A Response* (Cambridge, Polity Press, 2012); J Weiler, 'In the Face of Crisis: Input Legitimacy, Output Legitimacy, and the Political Messianism of European Integration' (2012) 34 *Journal of European Integration* 825; M Maduro, 'A New Governance for the European Union and the Euro: Democracy and Justice' (2012) RSCAS Policy Papers, PP, 2012/11; K Nicolaïdis, 'European Democracy and Its Crisis' (2013) 51 *Journal of Common Market Studies* 351; B Crum, 'Saving the Euro at the Cost of Democracy?' (2013) 51 *Journal of Common Market Studies* 614.

[16] See, eg D Chalmers, 'The European Redistributive State and a European Law of Struggle' (2012) 18 *European Law Journal* 667.

[17] See Council Regulation (EU) 1024/2013 of 15 October 2013 conferring specific tasks on the European Central Bank concerning policies relating to the prudential supervision of credit institutions, [2013] OJ L287/63; Regulation (EU) 1022/2013 of the European Parliament and of the Council of 22 October 2013 amending Regulation (EU) 1093/2010 establishing a European Supervisory Authority (European Banking Authority) as regards the conferral of specific tasks on the European Central Bank pursuant to Council Regulation (EU) 1024/2013, [2013] OJ L287/5.

[18] See Regulation (EU) 806/2014 of the European Parliament and of the Council of 15 July 2014 establishing uniform rules and a uniform procedure for the resolution of credit institutions and certain investment firms in the framework of a Single Resolution Mechanism and a Single Resolution Fund and amending Regulation (EU) 1093/2010, [2014] OJ L225/1.

[19] See too, J Fossum, 'The Structure of EU Representation and the Crisis' in S Kroger (ed), *Political Representation in the European Union* (n 5).

The phenomenon of executive dominance in the EU context should not be seen as particularly exceptional or *sui generis* in comparative terms.[20] Rather, it can be understood as part of a much wider phenomenon of the migration of executive power towards types of decision-making that eschew forms of electoral accountability and popular democratic control in a context where there is less party on the ground [21] Peter Mair's work shows how the very rationale behind the EU, long before the economic crisis, conforms closely to more general thinking about the role and the drawbacks of popular democracy. He analysed the EU as a deliberate construction by national executives as 'a protected sphere' in which policy-making can evade the constraints imposed by representative democracy at the national level.[22] This may also be the case at the European level of governance (the European Parliament (EP)). This democratic gap is fed by far-reaching secrecy arrangements and practices exercised in a concerted fashion by the various executive actors at different levels of governance and resulting in the 'blacking out' of crucial information and documents—even for parliaments.[23] Unilateral executive control over whatever information the executive chooses to consider sensitive disconnects part of the essential machinery of representative democracy.[24] The limited perspective of this chapter is on the role of parliaments (national, European) in giving flesh to notions of democratic accountability of EU executive power. It is beyond its scope to include other ways in which notions of direct popular accountability could possibly take shape in the EU context (direct elections of EU Presidents and so on).[25]

This chapter will analyse the existing reality of executive power at the EU level in law and in practice (Section II) as well as the existing manner in which this fragmented 'government' is embedded in practices of multi-level democratic accountability (Section III). On the basis of these findings, a number of issues will be highlighted as part of an agenda for reform in a manner that challenges existing executive dominance.

[20] See too, Curtin, 'Challenging Executive Dominance in European Democracy' (n 11) 3.

[21] R Katz and P Mair, *How Parties Organize: Change and Adaptation in Party Organization in Western Democracies* (London, Sage, 1994).

[22] See further, P Mair, *Ruling the Void: The Hollowing of Western Democracy* (London, Verso, 2013) in particular ch 4, 99. See too, P Lindseth, *Power and Legitimacy: Reconciling Europe and the Nation-State* (Oxford, Oxford University Press, 2010).

[23] See further, D Curtin, 'Overseeing Secrets in the EU: A Democratic Perspective' (2014) 52 *Journal of Common Market Studies* 684.

[24] Curtin (n 11) 4.

[25] For arguments in favour of direct election of the Commission President, see S Hix, 'Elections, Parties and Institutional Design: A Comparative Perspective on European Union Democracy' (1998) 21 *West European Politics* 19, 45–47. See also, F Decker and J Sonnicksen, 'An Alternative Approach to European Union Democratization: Re-Examining the Direct Election of the Commission President' (2011) 46 *Government and Opposition* 168. For a view advocating the direct election of the European Council President, see W van Gerven, *The European Union: A Polity of States and Peoples* (Stanford, Stanford University Press, 2005) 367.

II. EUROPEAN EXECUTIVE POWER: AN ONWARD MARCH?

A. Introduction

One of the key characteristics of the practice of executive-type power by various institutions and actors, as it has emerged over the past decades, is its fragmentation.[26] To state the obvious: there is no single, comprehensive and unitary European executive institution or body that can, in any meaningful way, be described as an EU government in the sense that we know it from the national domain. The fragmentation is both at the political level of executive power and also in terms of the administrative apparatus.[27] At the same time, if one shift is reinforced by the EU's reaction to the economic crisis, it is the shift that has taken place from a more normative or rule-making type of governance to one clearly and explicitly exercising hands-on governmental-type power even in such sensitive policy fields as national budgets and macroeconomic decisions. Crisis management by the European Council in particular, has shifted from 'economic governance' in the sense of a rules-based normative system to 'economic government' entailing discretionary executive decisions.[28]

All the 'governance' literature and analysis of recent years notwithstanding,[29] 'government' in a non-unitary sense is also part of what must be studied and understood in the context of the evolving political system of the EU. In this line, two main actors are the focus of more detailed attention: the European Council in the lead and the Council where the (national) executive power legislates and supranational executive power is also exercised. The Commission too can be described in these terms, especially in view of its new powers in the European Semester and its 'power' in that context over national governments and their budgets (together with other institutions). As a result of the financial and economic crises, the ECB has also become an important actor, wielding significant powers over the economies and the banking system of the Eurozone states (and beyond).

B. The European Council: 'Leading' Executive Power

The 'ever mighty' European Council is the top-level 'leader' of the EU as such. It has seen its executive powers consolidated and even expanded in processes of

[26] See B Crum, 'Executive Accountability in the European Union' (2013) paper presented at the EUSA Thirteenth Biennial Conference, Baltimore, USA, 9–11 May 2013. This section draws on my earlier work, *Executive Power of the European Union* (n 4) and 'Challenging Executive Dominance in European Democracy' (n 11).

[27] H Sjursen, 'Not so Intergovernmental After All? On Democracy and Integration in European Foreign and Security Policy' (2011) 18 *Journal of European Public Policy* 1078, 1082.

[28] See P de Schoutheete and S Micossi, 'On Political Union in Europe. The Changing Landscape of Decision-making and Political Accountability' (2013) CEPS Essay No 4, 21 February, 5.

[29] For an overview, see J Zeitlin and C Sabel (eds), *Experimentalist Governance in the European Union: Towards a New Architecture* (Oxford, Oxford University Press, 2010).

incremental institutionalisation, first, in layers of legal and institutional practices and, after the entry into force of the Lisbon Treaty, in formal Treaty provisions.[30] It has been for a long time the motor behind many important steps in the European integration process, particularly those at its outer edges, such as initially, justice and home affairs, and foreign and defence policy and most recently, the EU reactions to the economic and financial crises.[31] With the Lisbon Treaty, the European Council formally became an institution of the Union subject to its rules, rather than floating outside it, and in Article 15(1) of the Treaty on European Union (TEU), its powers are explicitly stated to be non-legislative, defining the 'general political directions and priorities'.

The European Council has gradually developed into a very significant agenda-setter of the larger developments of the EU, in spite of the Commission's monopoly of legislative initiative.[32] Empirical evidence points to a 'progressive erosion' of the Commission's power of initiative and a much more pronounced role of the European Council in setting the legislative agenda.[33] An example of this shift in the balance of legislative power is the strongly worded resolution of the EP, which stressed 'that any further initiative … must imperatively be established in accordance with the Community method' and which called upon the European Council 'to stop instructing the Commission on the form and/or content of any further legislative initiative', emphasising in this respect that '[the European Council] does not have any Treaty-based prerogative of legislative initiative'.[34]

The European Council is, in addition, a type of default 'crisis manager' of the EU, handling successive events such as the constitutional crisis of 2005, the banking crisis of 2008, and the euro and economic crises that followed from it.[35] Given that the EU has found itself in a more or less perpetual crisis in recent years, this key role accentuates a strong—even dominant—executive power. The European Council also plays a role within the European Semester for economic policy coordination (annual policy guidance and endorsement of the Country Specific Recommendations).

The European Council President, with his own Cabinet and supported by the Council, plays a fundamental role in enabling the European Council to be the agenda-setter and effective coordinator and power broker of Union institutions and the Member States.[36] These tasks belonged in the past to the Commission,

[30] See too, D Curtin (n 4) 73–81.

[31] See, in general, L van Middelaar, *The Passage to Europe* (New Haven, Yale University Press, 2013).

[32] P Bocquillon and M Dobbels, 'An Elephant on the 13th Floor of the Berlaymont? European Council and Commission Relations in Legislative Agenda Setting' (2014) 21 *Journal of European Public Policy* 20.

[33] P Ponzano et al, *The Power of Initiative of the European Commission: A Progressive Erosion?* Studies and Research No 89 (Notre Europe—Jacques Delors Institute, 2012).

[34] EP Resolution of 1 June 2013 on strengthening European democracy in the future EMU (2013/2672 (RSP)) points 2–4.

[35] Naurin, 'Representation in the Councils of the EU' (n 5) 69.

[36] See, special issue of *West European Politics* edited by D Naurin and A Rasmussen, 'Linking Inter- and Intra-institutional Change in the European Union' (2011) 34(1) *West European Politics*.

but the latter has seen its position to some extent weakened over the years as bit-by-bit the European Council has progressively assumed steering and supervision roles.[37] The European Council calls the shots in general terms and largely tells the Commission (and the Council) what to do if formal legislation needs to be adopted. For example, the European Council (pushed arguably by certain Member States within it) took the lead and called on the Commission to present a legislative proposal on a pan-European supervision of banks, the Single Supervisory Mechanism (SSM).

In addition, the European Council is prepared to lead more generally in the context of socio-economic governance.[38] Its former President Herman van Rompuy directly participated on two occasions in the deliberations of the Employment, Social Policy, Health and Consumer Affairs Council (EPSCO) formation.[39] Van Rompuy's decision to directly talk to EPSCO ministers 'was unprecedented and reflected the fundamentally changed relationship between the European Council and the Council in the new areas of EU activity'.[40] Van Rompuy seemingly referred to his visit as 'historic'[41] because of this (new) possibility of direct discussions between the President of the European Council and the ministers in Council.

The professionalisation of the support of the European Council has meant that it has been able to increase greatly the frequency with which it meets, over and above the four times a year prescribed in Article 15(3) of the Treaty on the Functioning of the European Union (TFEU). The Euro Summits emerged as a potential rival to European Council summits from the end of 2011. In current practice, these Euro Summits are often held in the full European Council format and supported by the General Secretariat of the Council. The European Council President is the Chair of these Summits as well. The centrality and sheer leading power of both types of summit meetings are now very visible as a result of the debt crisis measures in particular, and this contributes to their empowerment. In addition, the political salience of what is being discussed has led to repercussions at the national level, especially in debtor states, in the shape of governmental crises and political downfalls.[42]

The use of informal working methods has become much more extensive in recent years. This includes the routine of regular informal coordination meetings

[37] M Dawson and F de Witte, 'Constitutional Balance in the EU after the Euro-crisis' (2013) 76 *Modern Law Review* 817, 830.

[38] I draw on the work of Uwe Puetter in this context and am grateful for our ongoing dialogue.

[39] U Puetter, *European Council and the Council: New Intergovernmentalism and Institutional Change* (Oxford, Oxford University Press, 2014) 120–121.

[40] ibid 121.

[41] *Agence Europe*, 28 February 2013, quoted by Puetter, *European Council* (n 39) at 121.

[42] W Wessels et al, 'Democratic Control in the Member States of the European Council and the Euro Zone Summits' (2013) study requested by the Constitutional Affairs Committee of the European Parliament, DG for Internal Policies study, Annex II: In-depth reports on 12 Member States, the reports on Greece and Italy regarding the resignation of Greek PM Papandreou over the bailout packages in 2011 and the fall of the Berlusconi III government (2008–2011) over Berlusconi's increased isolation at European Council summits.

between the European Council President, the President of the Eurogroup, the Euro Commissioner and the ECB President ahead of Eurogroup meetings.[43] The European Council President thus plays a decisive role in inter-institutional coordination. At the same time, the President has exercised leadership internally with regard to the working methods of the European Council itself. In one of his first statements as new President, Herman van Rompuy defined the adjustment of working methods as one of his main priorities: He called for sessions with fewer officials; a distinction between formal and informal meetings; and fewer written documents tabled for discussion, thus allowing more room for *open debates* between participants.[44] This means that 'all important policy debates, for which a frank exchange of views is essential, and difficult negotiations take place under a further tightened confidential scheme, which ensures that nobody except the heads has access to the discussion'.[45] The emphasis on secrecy in the working methods of the European Council, steered by its President, may make it easier for the heads of state and government to reach agreement on important and controversial issues, but it also means that no (public) documents are available in advance or even after the meetings have taken place (see further below).

It is no longer just the European Council as a formal EU institution that is taking the significant leading decisions. Within the European Council, Member States may change hats and convert themselves into another entity with fewer participants because of a looming veto or otherwise and adopt decisions outside the EU framework altogether. This is done largely *en marge* of a (European) Council meeting. As far as the Council is concerned, the non-euro area Member States cannot vote on euro area issues anyway. For example, the votes of the ESM Board of Governors are cast on the margins of the Eurogroup, not on the margins of the subsequent Council of Finance Ministers (ECOFIN) Council meetings. A variety of clever legal constructions are used that are tailor-made for each situation—the view seemingly being that there is no alternative.[46] In such circumstances, there is no 'President' or other entity to be held politically accountable for the decisions taken at any level of governance.

C. The Commission: 'Normal' Executive Power

Executive power was in fact never meant to reside at the European level in its original design. To the extent it did, only the *Commission* was originally given tasks

[43] Puetter (n 39) 117.

[44] U Puetter, 'Europe's Deliberative Intergovernmentalism: The Role of the Council and European Council in EU Economic Governance' (2012) 19 *Journal of European Public Policy* 161, 174.

[45] U Puetter, 'The European Council—the New Centre of EU Politics' (2013) Swedish Institute for European Policy Studies, 2013:16 European Policy Analysis, at 8.

[46] See B de Witte, 'Using International Law in the Euro Crisis: Causes and Consequences' (2013) Arena Working Paper 4 available at: www.sv.uio.no/arena/english/research/publications/arena-publications/workingpapers/working-papers2013/wp4-13.pdf.

of an actual executive nature. Most prominently, the Commission exercised supranational executive power in imposing sanctions on companies for infringement of the Treaty competition rules. However, this situation has evolved considerably and there are now over 40 agencies at the EU level that exercise a more *expert-driven*, or technocratic, executive power. At the same time, the Commission has 'normalised' in the sense that it acquired many of the organisational features and behavioural patterns that are highly typical of the 'normal' executives in national settings.[47] This normalisation process was taken a step further in various measures that were adopted in the context of crisis management. In particular, the role and power of the Commission regarding the content of national budgets in the context of the so-called European Semester has enhanced its executive powers vis-à-vis the Member States.

'The function of the European semester is to draw together and synchronise … distinct *co-ordination processes* within a single governance framework'.[48] The origins of the European Semester lie in the Lisbon Strategy for the coordination of the economic and employment policies of the Member States. Within the framework of the Strategy, the Member States produced National Reform Programmes (NPRs) which were subject to EU-level evaluation. Fiscal coordination under the Stability and Growth Pact (SGP) also entails 'multilateral surveillance' in the form of the production of stability and convergence reports by the Member States—subject to assessment by the Commission and the Council. The 'six-pack' and the 'two-pack' measures further extend this policy coordination through the development of procedures for monitoring the national economies and budgets of Eurozone states.[49]

'That EU legislative action can give rise to policy coordination as an output is not itself novel and was a feature of the SGP prior to the crisis. What is noteworthy is both the intensification of the coordination effort and its relationship to rules-based governance'.[50] In the first half of the semester, the required national reports are drafted, taking into account the Commission's Annual Growth Survey, the conclusions adopted by the Council of Ministers, and the conclusions adopted by the spring European Council. The second half of the semester focuses on the discussion of the national reports with the Commission and the adoption of the Country-Specific Recommendations (CSRs) by the Council. 'This, "meta-OMC",[51] or the "coordination of coordination",[52] was an early response to the economic crisis

[47] A Wille, *The Normalization of the European Commission. Politics and Bureaucracy in the EU Executive* (Oxford, Oxford University Press, 2013).

[48] K Armstrong, 'The New Governance of EU Fiscal Discipline' (2013) 38 *European Law Review* 601, 609.

[49] ibid.

[50] Armstrong, 'The New Governance of EU Fiscal Discipline' (n 48) 609.

[51] L Tholoniat, 'The Career of the Open Method of Coordination: Lessons from a "Soft" EU Instrument' (2010) 33 *West European Politics* 93.

[52] K Armstrong, 'The Lisbon Agenda and Europe 2020: From the Governance of Coordination to the Coordination of Governance' in P Copeland and D Papadimitriou (eds), *The EU's Lisbon Strategy* (Basingstoke, Palgrave Macmillan, 2012). Also K Armstrong, 'EU Social Policy and the Governance Architecture of Europe 2020' (2012) 18 *Transfer: European Review of Labour and Research* 285.

and, while initially developed through practice, is institutionalized in legislation adopted as part of the "six-pack" reforms to the SGP.'[53] Hard new rules allow for easier sanctions against Member States with excessive deficits. In addition to hard executive power being exercised by the Vice-President of the Commission vis-à-vis individual Member States, there is also a 'softer' and less visible part of the governance framework. This relates to the central role built into the Semester framework for the more experimental mechanism of *peer review*.

A new monitoring mechanism was introduced and enforceability of the pact was improved in order to avoid the lenient implementation of the past. Yet the Commission's Country-specific reports show that there is some room for discretion in the implementation of hard and fast rules. The role of the Euro Commissioner is crucial in this context, and he is in fact the one who determines in first instance the rules to be respected and their breach or otherwise by individual Member States. In so doing, his role has developed autonomously from the power of the Commission as a whole, and he (and his Directorate General) has his own structures of economic analysis—the 'independent' *Chief Economic Analyst*. The Euro Commissioner (and the Commission President) can request from him opinions on the economic situation in the different countries. The service that is responsible for producing the analytical data is part of the Directorate General of Economic and Financial Affairs (DG ECFIN) that also works on the CSRs and exercises control over implementation. The actual decisions on coordination of economic and budgetary policy and the CSRs are not taken by the Commission as a whole according to its normal internal decision-making procedure but are part of an 'accelerated written procedure'. This is a written procedure initiated by the Euro Commissioner and managed by the Secretariat General of the Commission.[54] This kind of authorisation procedure, in principle, even applies to quasi-automatic recommendations for sanctions.[55] These powers and structures within the European Semester system reinforce the 'autonomous' decision-making powers of the Euro Commissioner over and above the normal role of other Commissioners within the *collegium*.

D. The European Central Bank: 'Intervening' Executive Power

As a result of the financial and economic crises, the ECB has significantly changed, both in law and in fact, through unprecedented actions, new responsibilities, competences and tasks. Instead of ECB *independence* as the standard constitutional *leitmotif* we are now witnessing ECB *intervention* into the economic policies of

[53] Armstrong (n 48) 609.

[54] See Advisory Council on International Affairs (AIV), *Public Support for the European Union: Building Trust*, Advisory Report 88, April 2014, 28.

[55] ibid.

the Member States.[56] This major shift has taken place due to a number of cumulative factors. First, the financial crisis has led to the multiplication and the intensification of forums dealing with economic policy of which the ECB has formal or informal membership—for instance, the Eurogroup, the Macroeconomic Dialogue, the Euro Summit, ad hoc summits of political leaders, and the Task Force on Economic Governance.[57] Secondly, the crisis has led to the expansion of ECB powers through its membership in the Troika (of the ECB, Commission and IMF) and in 'enhanced surveillance and review missions' and through its use of unconventional measures to deal with the effects of the crisis.[58] The latter include long-term refinancing operations (LTROs) to provide ample liquidity to credit institutions; bond-buying programmes such as the Securities Markets Programme (SMP) and the Outright Monetary Transactions programme (OMT);[59] and an unprecedented use of ECB's collateral framework.[60] These factors have led to an increased leverage of the ECB vis-à-vis the Member States of the EU. As Wilsher points out:

> [T]he ECB has been emerging as the most important creditor and, therefore, the actor with most *de facto* political power. Even though it has not directly provided funds to Member States, the ECB has become heavily involved in approving and monitoring the fiscal and socio-economic restructuring of debtor countries.[61]

The powers of the ECB have also expanded due to more concrete steps by the Union leaders towards the realisation of the Banking Union. This was again prompted by the financial and economic crisis. The legislative negotiations on the Banking Union are still in progress, but it is clear that the real 'winner' at the supranational level is the ECB that is now being given a leading and unprecedented role in the day-to-day management of credit institutions. The Regulation on the Single Supervisory Mechanism (SSM Regulation) came into force on 3 November 2013.[62] This regulation confers new functions on the ECB: on 4 November 2014, 12 months after the entry into force of the Regulation, the ECB fully assumed its responsibilities as the supervisor of nearly 130 of the largest banks in the Eurozone (with the possibility that this supervision will extend beyond the euro area if any non-euro Member States decide to join the SSM). Additional steps towards a fully-fledged banking union include a single resolution

[56] T Beukers, 'The New ECB and its Relationship with the Eurozone Member States: Between Central Bank Independence and Central Bank Intervention' (2013) 50 *Common Market Law Review* 1579.

[57] ibid 1584–86

[58] ibid 1588.

[59] The legality of the OMT has been challenged by the German Federal Constitutional Court which has made an unprecedented referral to the ECJ on this matter: See Case C-62/14 *Peter Gauweiler and Others v German Bundestag* (pending).

[60] Beukers, 'The New ECB' (n 56) 1591–92.

[61] D Wilsher, 'Law and the Financial Crisis: Searching for Europe's New Gold Standard' (2014) 20 *European Law Journal* 241, 273.

[62] Council Regulation (EU) 1024/2013 (n 17).

mechanism[63] for failing banks and a common deposit guarantee scheme.[64] The visible and new non-monetary powers of the ECB raise novel issues of delegation of powers to non-majoritarian institutions in the supranational context and in particular the legitimacy of epistocracy.[65]

As a result of the post-crisis changes to the Union's economic governance framework, the President of the ECB has gained significant new powers. Among these de jure powers are the following. First, the financial supervision regime established in January 2011 and known as the European System of Financial Supervision (ESFS) includes the European Systematic Risk Board (ESRB) 'responsible for the macro-prudential oversight of the financial system within the Union in order to contribute to the prevention or mitigation of systemic risks to financial stability in the Union'.[66] Pursuant to the ESRB Regulation, the President of the ECB is the ESRB chair for five years following the entry into force of that Regulation (as of 16 December 2010).[67] The President of the ECB (along with the Vice-President) is also a Member—with voting rights—of the ESRB General Board.[68] Secondly, the Treaty on Stability, Coordination and Governance (TSCG or Fiscal Compact) provides that the ECB President 'shall' be invited to take part in Euro Summit meetings.[69] Thirdly, according to the Treaty on the European Stability Mechanism (ESM), the ECB President 'may' participate in the meetings of the ESM Board of Governors and 'may' appoint an observer to the ESM Board of Directors.[70] Lastly, he participates in Eurogroup meetings. The cumulative effect of the latter two developments is that 'Draghi has a seat at the table where important decisions are taken by the Ministers of Finance of the Eurozone Member States on financial aid and the (economic policy reform) conditions attached'.[71]

III. DEMOCRATIC ACCOUNTABILITY: INFORMATION, DEBATE AND CONSEQUENCE

A. Introduction

The rise of EU executive power after the various crises raises important issues of executive accountability. Has the rise been accompanied by an equal increase in formal

[63] Regulation (EU) 806/2014 (n 18).

[64] Directive 2014/49/EU of the European Parliament and of the Council of 16 April 2014 on deposit guarantee schemes (recast) [2014] OJ L173/149.

[65] E Eriksen, 'Governance Between Expertise and Democracy: The Case of European Security' (2011) 18 *Journal of European Public Policy* 1169.

[66] Art 3(1) of Regulation (EU) No 1092/2010 of the European Parliament and of the Council of 24 November 2010 on European Union macro-prudential oversight of the financial system and establishing a European Systemic Risk Board [2010] OJ L331/1.

[67] Art 5(1) Regulation (EU) 1092/2010.

[68] Art 6(1)(a) Regulation (EU) 1092/2010.

[69] Art 12(1) Treaty on Stability, Coordination and Governance in the Economic and Monetary Union.

[70] Arts 5(3) and 6(2), respectively, of Treaty Establishing the European Stability Mechanism.

[71] Beukers (n 56) 1586.

and informal accountability relations? Accountability is conceptualised as an institutional relation in which an actor can be held to account by a forum.[72] Accountability is 'a relationship between an actor and a forum, in which the actor has an obligation to explain and to justify his or her conduct, the forum can pose questions and pass judgement, and the actor may face consequences'.[73] The locus of analysis is the way that these institutional relations operate; and the focus is whether actors are or can be held accountable *ex post facto* by accountability forums.

In this chapter, I only concentrate on political accountability, on accountability to political forums—parliaments. This is justified by the fact that there is no system of direct elections by the citizens in the EU of executive actors but only of the directly elected EP and there are various accountability mechanisms that apply in law and in practice. My analysis is limited to two types of political forums: the EP (and its various committees) and the national parliaments. Three different elements or stages of accountability are distinguished—information, debate and consequence. These three inter-related elements will now be examined closer in the remainder of this paragraph.

B. Information Provision: National Parliaments and the European Parliament

The first stage is to know to what extent the actor is obliged to *inform the forum about his or her conduct*, by providing various sorts of data about the performance of tasks, about outcomes, or about procedures. Often, and particularly in the case of failures or incidents, this also involves the provision of explanations and justifications.[74] Informing can be done in a general way, directed at the general public, or only as part of specific accountability relations, for example, by providing explicit information to parliamentary committees. The extent of the

[72] See P Day and R Klein, *Accountabilities: Five Public Services* (London, Tavistock, 1987); C Scott, 'Accountability in the Regulatory State' (2000) 27 *Journal of Law and Society* 38; R Mulgan, *Holding Power to Account: Accountability in Modern Democracies* (Basingstoke, Palgrave Macmillan, 2003); C Pollitt, *The Essential Public Manager* (London, Open University Press/McGraw-Hill, 2003); T Schillemans, 'Accountability in the Shadow of Hierarchy: The Horizontal Accountability of Agencies' (2008) 8 *Public Organization Review* 175; M Bovens, P 't Hart, and T Schillemans, 'Does Public Accountability Work? An Assessment Tool' (2008) 86 *Public Administration* 225; A Meijer and T Schillemans, 'Fictional Citizens and Real Effects. Accountability to Citizens in Competitive and Monopolistic Markets' (2009) 14 *Public Administration and Management* 254.

[73] M Bovens, 'Analysing and Assessing Accountability: A Conceptual Framework' (2007) 13 *European Law Journal* 447, 450. See too, M Bovens, D Curtin and P 't Hart (eds), *The Real World of EU Accountability. What Deficit?* (Oxford, Oxford University Press, 2010).

[74] M Bovens, P 't Hart, S Dekker and G Verheuvel, 'The Politics of Blame Avoidance: Defensive Tactics in a Dutch Crime-fighting Fiasco' in HK Anheier (ed), *When Things Go Wrong: Failures and Breakdowns in Organizational Settings* (Thousand Oaks, Sage, 1999); KM Hearit, *Crisis Management by Apology: Corporate Response to Allegations of Wrongdoing* (London, Taylor & Francis, 2005); C Hood et al, *The Tools of Government in the Digital Age* (London, Palgrave Macmillan, 2007).

information available may also depend on the working methods of the institution or actor to be held to account.

The European Council meetings are particularly difficult to control for national parliaments because of the *working methods* adopted by the European Council.[75] If there are fewer documents and 'open' debates among the leaders at the Summits themselves, then even those Member States, such as Germany, which provide for very detailed specification of the documents that must be supplied to the national parliament are potentially out of the accountability loop, to some extent at least. The same goes for countries such as the United Kingdom (UK), with an almost exclusively document-based system of EU scrutiny. Moreover, the precision of formal rules on information sharing by the government does not necessarily correlate with the assessment of the parliamentarians themselves about their level of information. Thus, according to one study, in Germany members of parliament still feel a lack of information despite very detailed legal prescriptions.[76] Other countries, in particular the Nordic ones, 'really are well informed on all governmental activities in regard of the (European) Council',[77] and members of the Finnish Committee are even informed during European Council meetings on new issues and initiatives while the summits are ongoing. In the Czech Republic, civil servants from the two houses of parliament actually participate in the government coordination mechanism preparing the European Council by the national government and thus have excellent access to information.[78]

Although publicity is key to democracy, secrecy is currently the practice. A crucial part of the parliaments' pushback against the reality of executive domination is the manner in which they assert their own autonomy over the information in their possession. Do they continue to accept that non-classified information that does not breach data protection or privacy rules, and purely concerns ongoing debates within a variety of EU institutions and committees, needs to be kept secret by them even when that means that they cannot perform a vital part of their role as parliaments and public forums for deliberation and debate as a result? The issue of governments (and EU institutions) insisting that they control 'limited' documents (and under EU internal rules these cannot be put into the public domain other than when the document stamp is lifted) and that parliament must abide by these EU procedural rules is a key one. In the UK House of Commons, for example, an MP (William Cash) who had obtained a limited document considered very important in the context of the economic bailouts at the time was: 'the Speaker, who gave authority for the matter to be exposed in the House of Commons'.[79]

[75] See further, Curtin (n 11) on which this section draws.

[76] Wessels et al, 'Democratic Control in the Member States' (n 42) 33.

[77] ibid.

[78] Wessels et al (n 42) 33.

[79] See, Oral Evidence taken before the European Scrutiny Committee, 'European Scrutiny in the House of Commons', 4 September 2013, available at: www.publications.parliament.uk/pa/cm201314/cmselect/cmeuleg/uc109-iv/uc10901.htm.

Protocol No 1 on the Role of National Parliaments in the European Union provides that the Commission must forward to national parliaments its green and white papers; its communications; its annual legislative programme and any other measures of legislative planning or policy; as well as draft legislative acts. Under the terms of the Framework Agreement between the Commission and the EP,[80] the EP agreed to adapt its internal provisions so as to provide for equivalent internal security standards and for the establishment of a specially established oversight committee. In the event, the EP did so in June 2011 (after the Council had adopted its new security rules) and sought to ensure that its own new security rules would be considered *equivalent* to those of the Commission and of the Council. The EP is clearly keen to reassure both the Council and the Commission that it is very serious about the measures it has taken to ensure the security of classified, and unclassified but sensitive, information that it receives from either institution and that it can be 'trusted'. This established inter-institutional trajectory culminates with the very recent new inter-institutional agreement with the Council.[81] It is early days to know how exactly the EP is applying these rules in practice and clearly the Council is adopting an attitude of wait and see (also by building in provisional and far-reaching rules even for the category of 'Restricted' documents).[82]

It was explicitly stated by the ECB in its response to a recent EP questionnaire that '[t]he ECB is not accountable to national parliaments'.[83] This statement applies to its activities in the areas of both monetary policy and banking supervision. However, when it comes to reporting obligations and an exchange of views, there are differences between these two distinct spheres of activity of the ECB. While in the context of monetary policy there is no legal framework for scrutiny by national parliaments, the supervisory functions of the ECB do entail certain formal reporting obligations along with the opportunity to invite the chair or a member of the Supervisory Board to appear before a national parliament. This is laid down in Article 21 of the SSM Regulation.[84] To what extent these rules will be followed in practice will be seen, as the ECB has assumed its supervisory tasks only since November 2014.

ECB's accountability to the EP in the context of monetary policy is governed by Article 284(3) TFEU which provides that the ECB will send the EP an annual report on its activities and on the monetary policy of both the previous and current year. Moreover, the President of the ECB is to present this report to the EP which then

[80] Framework Agreement on relations between the European Parliament and the European Commission [2010] OJ L304/47.

[81] Interinstitutional Agreement of 12 March 2014 between the European Parliament and the Council concerning the forwarding to and handling by the European Parliament of classified information held by the Council on matters other than those in the area of the common foreign and security policy [2014] OJ C95/1.

[82] ibid Art 6(2).

[83] 'ECB response to the questionnaire of the European Parliament on the troika' published on the ECB website on 10 January 2014, available at: www.ecb.europa.eu/pub/pdf/other/140110_ecb_response_troika_questionnaireen.pdf.

[84] Council Regulation (EU) No 1024/2013 (n 17).

may hold a general debate on the basis of this report. In addition, it is provided that the President of the ECB and the other members of the Executive Board may, at the request of the EP or on their own initiative, be heard by the competent committees of the EP. Rule 113 of the EP Rules of Procedure[85] created the additional requirement of the ECB President appearing before the ECON committee at least four times a year.[86] These appearances of the ECB President before the EP—in plenary and in the ECON committee—is what became known as the Monetary Dialogue.[87] Finally, according to Rule 118 of the EP Rules of Procedure, any Member of the EP may also put a question for written answer to the ECB. Accountability to the EP within the framework of Banking Supervision is governed by Article 20 of the SSM Regulation[88] and the Interinstitutional Agreement signed by the ECB and the EP.[89] Under Article 20 of the SSM Regulation, the Chair of the Supervisory Board is required to present an annual report to the EP in plenary, reply to questions from MEPs and appear before the ECON committee upon request. In addition, she must also divulge sensitive information—although in 'confidential oral discussions behind closed doors'—and cooperate with EP investigations. The Interinstitutional Agreement provides for more detailed arrangements regarding the requirements spelled out in Article 20 SSM Regulation.

C. Debate and Dialogue: National Parliaments and the European Parliament

The second stage is *debate*. For a relation to qualify as an accountability relation, there needs to be a possibility for the forum to interrogate the actor and to question the adequacy of the information or the legitimacy of the conduct. One of the main problems for national parliaments is the amount of information they receive on European Council meetings and the timing of that information, in particular, for *ex ante* accountability practices.

The timing and public or confidential nature of the information received by parliaments also influence the nature and depth of the accountability practices in question. Even the national parliaments in the best-case scenarios (Denmark, Finland, maybe Germany) are engaged only with their own government and

[85] Rules of Procedure of the European Parliament, 7th Parliamentary Term, March 2014 version, available at: www.europarl.europa.eu/sides/getDoc.do?pubRef=-//EP//NONSGML+RULES-EP+20140310+0+DOC+PDF+V0//EN&language=EN.

[86] C Fasone, 'European Economic Governance and Parliamentary Representation. What Place for the European Parliament?' (2014) 20 *European Law Journal* 164, 175.

[87] ibid.

[88] Council Regulation (EU) No 1024/2013 (n 17).

[89] Interinstitutional Agreement between the European Parliament and the European Central Bank on the practical modalities of the exercise of democratic accountability and oversight over the exercise of the tasks conferred on the ECB within the framework of the Single Supervisory Mechanism [2013] OJ L320/1.

are constrained by EU rules (enforced by their governments) to keep salient information secret.[90] If EU 'limited' documents are received by the national parliament from its own government, the national parliament is required to keep them out of the public domain. No genuinely *public* debate is often possible even if there is a trend at the leading edge to more plenary debates in parliaments in advance of important decision-making. The situation is aggravated when it concerns non-EU executive constructions because then the normal scrutiny and information requirements of the respective governments do not generally apply.[91]

Those parliaments that had already been given significant rights on EU affairs, in general, tend to be the ones leading the way regarding parliamentary influence over European Council meetings.[92] For example, if we look at Denmark, it is famous for the fact that its European Affairs Committee has the formal power to provide the different ministers with a negotiation mandate before Council meetings in Brussels, although this power is apparently not used a lot in practice. The same mandating system is, in any event, not mandatory for the control of European Council meetings and the Prime Minister. Yet, due to the political dynamics in Denmark, the minority government needs to take into account the views of the opposition in order to secure majorities in the House. This makes the European Affairs Committee powerful in view of this constant bargaining between government and opposition parties. National parliaments in fact need information on the different negotiation positions of other Member State governments in order to be able to make strategic interventions. The fact that the Danish Parliament has both *ex ante* and *ex post* control of European Council meetings makes it possible for the Danish MPs to hold the government accountable for its negotiation position by referring to the previous statements of the prime ministers. We find something similar in Finland where the Finnish prime minister and government have a constitutional obligation to inform the Grand Committee of parliament, both before and after the European Council meetings, of all the relevant issues and draft decisions. If needed, the prime minister and the government are also in contact with the Grand Committee during the actual European Council meetings when individual government positions can and do change on the hoof during negotiations. In Finland, there have been repeated recent debates in plenary sessions in parliament with the result that the government has been forced to justify and defend its EU policies in public—and this has also occurred when the opposition has attacked the cabinet publicly over the handling of EU matters related to the Euro-crisis in particular.[93]

There is a certain leapfrog effect of 'best practices' discernible among national parliaments and they are, on the whole, all trying hard to 'catch up' with the new and shifting institutional and policy realities. In the Netherlands, for example,

[90] See further, Curtin (n 11) 29.
[91] ibid.
[92] This part draws on the country reports in Wessels et al (n 42).
[93] Wessels et al (n 42) 59.

since the end of 2010, plenary debates have been scheduled in parliament before European Council summits, and this practice has underlined the importance of such summits. It is a big change from the previous situation where plenary sessions were held only *after* European Council summits.[94] Other issues of high political importance were also debated in the plenary, for example, the plans on the emergency fund for the Euro-crisis were on the agenda of the plenary throughout the summer of 2011. Yet a recent debate in the Dutch parliament shows that it too is quite unhappy with the level of information it receives in advance of summits.[95] In the UK, the fact that the country has a largely document-based system means that the House of Commons simply does not get even the information that is available on time in order to engage in an informed manner with government prior to summit meetings.[96]

Moving from the national parliamentary arena to the supranational, the *EP* has, in fact, for some years now, been granted some privileged access to EU information. This access was limited to classified information produced and circulated under the auspices of the EU (unless subject to the principle of originator control), and documents had to be physically consulted on the Council's premises.[97] Early institutional cooperation involved the EP making arrangements to receive and 'handle' sensitive documents in secure reading rooms on the Council's premises as the quid pro quo for being informed on the content of, in particular, the Council's security and defence policy.[98] A security-cleared 'gang of Five' MEPs was also given classified briefings, although little public information is available as to how often these measures were availed of in practice nor—surprisingly—has an internal evaluation ever taken place as to how it operated. It was described by one of the MEPs concerned as being like a 'bad Le Carre novel'.[99]

The EP is in a slightly better position than its counterparts on the national level as it can call in representatives of the European Council (and Council) albeit under the conditions these institutions lay down in their own Rules of Procedure.[100] In addition, the President of the European Council has to present a report to the EP *after* the meetings of the European Council.[101] However, the fact that (as we

[94] See M van der Steeg, 'The European Council's Evolving Political Accountability' in M Bovens, D Curtin and P 't Hart (eds), *The Real World of EU Accountability* (n 73)

[95] Debate with Foreign Minister Timmermans, Dutch Second Chamber documents 22 112, No 1581, 12 March 2013.

[96] In the UK there has been, it seems, only one emergency plenary debate on the Stability Treaty ahead of a European Council meeting in March 2012.

[97] G Rosén, 'Can you Keep a Secret? How the European Parliament got Access to Sensitive Documents in the Area of Security and Defence' (2011) RECON Working Paper 22.

[98] Interinstitutional Agreement of 20 November 2002 between the European Parliament and the Council concerning access by the European Parliament to sensitive information of the Council in the field of security and defence policy [2002] OJ C298/1.

[99] A Rettman, 'Secret Documents Group was Like "Bad Le Carre Novel," MEP Says' (2012) *EUobserver*. Available at euobserver.com/institutional/31296.

[100] Art 230(3) TFEU. See further, A Maurer, 'From EMU to DEMU: The Democratic Legitimacy of the EU and the European Parliament' (2013) IAI Working Papers, available at: www.iai.it/sites/default/files/iaiwp1311.pdf.

[101] Art 15(6)(d) TEU.

have seen) the European Council increasingly meets without formal documents, hinders the role the EP can play in advance of decision-making. These—very thin—powers do not lead to meaningful accountability of the European Council to the EP.[102]

As to Commission dialogue and debate with the EP, Rule 111 of the EP Rules of Procedure[103] gives the President of the Parliament the right to invite the President of the Commission or another Commissioner to make a statement after each meeting of the Commission to explain decisions taken during a meeting and to take part in a debate. Rule 114 prescribes that the Commission must present its recommendation on the broad guidelines of economic policy to the relevant committee, while Rule 115 grants the parliamentary committees the right to ask the Commission questions for oral answers with a debate. In addition, in the area of economic governance, Article 121(5) TFEU lays down the obligation for the President of the Commission (as well as that of the Council) to submit a report on the results of multilateral surveillance to the EP. The most important tool for the Parliament in this respect is the economic dialogue provided for in the five regulations of the 'six-pack'. These dialogues give the competent committee of the EP the opportunity to discuss certain issues with the Commission. Article 15 of Regulation (EU) 473/2013,[104] for example, gives the Parliament the power to invite the Commission to discuss budgetary matters. However, these dialogues are questionable from a legal point of view, 'since it is not clear what happens if the "economic dialogue" fails or if one of the institutions [in this case the Commission] does not fulfil its obligations'.[105]

With respect to ECB dialogue with national parliaments, it is noteworthy that in recent years, the ECB President has appeared before a number of parliamentary forums: the German Bundestag on 24 October 2012; the Spanish Congreso de los Diputados on 12 February 2013; and the French Assemblée Nationale on 26 June 2013. Draghi's visit to the German Bundestag was primarily aimed at explaining and justifying ECB's unconventional measures, while his Spanish and French visits focused largelyon underlining the positive effects of the unconventional measures and emphasising the importance of structural reforms. In his speech at the German Bundestag[106] Draghi stated that '[i]t was rare for the ECB President to speak in a national parliament' and that the ECB was accountable to the EP. However, he stated that the purpose of his visit was to 'explain ECB's policies' and to listen to the views of the parliamentarians. Thus, there are some recent attempts by the ECB to engage in debates on the national level.

[102] Wessels et al (n 42) 22–23. See further, C Fasone, 'The Struggle of the European Parliament to Participate in the New Economic Governance' EUI Working Paper RSC 2012/45, 10, 17; de Schoutheete and Micossi (n 28) 9–10.

[103] Rules of Procedure of the European Parliament, 7th Parliamentary Term (n 85).

[104] Regulation (EU) 473/2013 of the European Parliament and of the Council of 21 May 2013 on common provisions for monitoring and assessing draft budgetary plans and ensuring the correction of excessive deficit of the Member States in the euro area [2013] OJ L140/11.

[105] Fasone, 'European Economic Governance' (n 86) 175.

[106] Opening Statement at Deutscher Bundestag by Mario Draghi, Berlin, 24 October 2012.

As to the EP, in the post-financial crisis years (2009 to 2014), the ECB presidents Trichet and Draghi attended five meetings in plenary. These were all meetings to discuss the *ECB Annual Report*. The structure of the meetings did not really allow for a debate to take place. There was an opening speech, the Parliamentarians expressed their views and concerns and asked the Presidents to elaborate and in some instances justify certain decisions. The Presidents ended the meeting with concluding remarks which covered most of the topic but almost never included specific responses to the critiques. Trichet and Draghi also engaged in a *monetary dialogue* with the Economic and Monetary Affairs (ECON) Committee four times a year. The nature of the monetary dialogues, in general, is informative, but with some room for critique and debate. Draghi usually starts with a speech followed by Parliamentarians asking questions which are immediately answered by Draghi. This setting is rather informal and allows Parliamentarians to react immediately on a response given by Draghi. This provides opportunities for more genuine political debate.[107]

D. Consequences (Sanctions): National Parliament and the European Parliament

The third stage in a full accountability relationship is that the forum, in this instance, the parliament may *pass judgement* on the conduct of the actor (motion of no confidence or otherwise). It may approve of an annual account, denounce a policy, or publicly condemn the behaviour of an official or an agency. In passing a negative judgement, or following it, the forum may impose *consequences* on the actor. These consequences can be highly formalised, such as fines, disciplinary measures, civil remedies or even penal sanctions, but they can also be based on historical conventions, or on informal practices, such as naming and shaming.

National parliaments do not have any formal powers to sanction the European Council. The parliament of each Member State may pass judgement and impose consequences on its respective head of state or government.[108] Yet there are no arrangements for sanctioning the European Council as a collective entity. The fact that since the Lisbon Treaty entered into force the European Council has been a formal institution with a formal President has brought about some changes to political accountability to the national parliaments. We can observe the new phenomenon of the President of the European Council coming to individual national

[107] eg during the Monetary Dialogue of 3 March 2014, Brussels, where Sampo Terho, Pablo Zalba Bidegain and Markus Ferber used this opportunity, or the Monetary Dialogue of 23 September 2013, Brussels, where Sylvie Goulard wouldn't stop after one answer. The best example is the dialogue between Draghi and Philippe Lamberts during the Monetary Dialogue of 9 July 2012, Brussels (which was in fact partly on the accountability of the ECB/Draghi).

[108] This is made explicit by Art 10 TEU which states: 'Member States are represented in the European Council by their Heads of State or Government and in the Council by their governments, themselves democratically accountable either to their national Parliaments, or to their citizens.'

parliaments in order to inform, explain and justify decisions that are being taken by the European Council or in implementation of European Council decision-making. Thus, Van Rompuy has visited a number of national parliaments over the course of the past few years (for example, Cyprus, Malta, Romania, Estonia, Slovenia and France).[109] However, on the whole, these are 'set' speeches and there seems to be little opportunity for real dialogue or debate and there is certainly no possibility of any sanctioning or other consequences attached. Similarly, national parliaments do not have any tangible sanctioning powers over the Commission[110] or the ECB.

Moving from national to the EU level, it must be observed that overall the accountability arrangement between the EP and the European Council is weak and mainly covers, and to a limited extent, the first aspect of accountability (information) and not debate or sanction/consequence. During the parliamentary terms of 2009 to 2014, Van Rompuy has attended 15 debates in plenary. These were almost exclusively meetings on *Conclusions of the European Council* and some on *Economic Governance.* Van Rompuy also visited and debated with the ECON Committee three times during the Parliamentary term of 2009 to 2014. These meetings were more than just informative; however, they can hardly be viewed as effective means of sanctioning by the EP.

With regard to the Commission, it must be stated that the Treaties as well as the EP Rules of Procedure,[111] grant the EP rights to be informed and to participate in a debate with Commission representatives. However, these rights lack pressurising power because there are few real consequences attached to these meetings. The Parliament does hold the power to table a motion for a resolution according to Rule 120 of its Rules of Procedure and a motion for censure under Article 234 TFEU. The latter article probably contains the strongest tool for Parliament, containing a voting procedure which might result in the resignation of members of the Commission.

As to ECB's accountability to the EP, as stated above, in the context of monetary policy it is governed by Article 284(3) TFEU and Rule 113 of EP Rules of procedure. While these two provisions together have given rise to the practice of monetary dialogues, the latter entails information provision and debates rather than true sanctioning powers of the EP over the ECB. This is also true for ECB accountability to the EP within the framework of banking supervision.

[109] Van Rompuy's speech at the Parliament of Cyprus, Nicosia, 28 May 2012; speech at the House of Representatives of Malta, Valletta, 11 July 2013; speech at the Joint Meeting of the Chamber of Deputies and of the Senate of Romania, Bucharest, 25 April 2012; speech at the Estonian Riigikogu, Tallinn, 26 February 2013; speech at the National Assembly of Slovenia, Ljubljana, 25 May 2012; speech at the French Assemblée Nationale, Paris, 9 October 2013.

[110] Although it must be noted that based on Protocol No 2 on the Application of the Principles of Subsidiarity and Proportionality, national parliaments can issue reasoned opinions if they consider that a draft legislative act does not comply with the principle of subsidiarity, after which the Commission may decide to maintain, amend or withdraw the draft.

[111] Rules of Procedure of the European Parliament, 7th Parliamentary Term (n 85).

IV. A REFORM AGENDA: INFORMATION, DEBATE AND CONSEQUENCES

A. Introduction

In terms of an agenda for reform the focus is on the key elements of information, debate and consequences. This boils down to less secrecy with the parameters debated in public (legislation) and more dialogue and learning horizontally by parliaments across the levels of representation.

B. Less Secret Information, More Rule-making?

It goes without saying that some provision must be made for parliaments to keep (highly) classified secrets, but at the European level a public debate on when secrets must be kept and how (a type of EU secrecy law) is missing. As things stand at present, it is a matter of total executive prerogative and internal rule-making that is subsequently also applied to restrict national parliaments.[112] This is a crucial part of a (legislative) reform agenda.

The EP is not really showing the way in terms of forcing the executive institutions to be more public in their ongoing deliberations. The manner in which the EP has allowed itself to be sucked into the secretive vortex of closed-door 'negotiations' on legislation before the first reading in plenary (trilogue meetings), and also accepted Council rules on secrecy in a host of inter-institutional agreements giving it some non-public access, means that the EP is not engaging with the EU-level executive actors in a manner that challenges their domination or that is truly leading. This does not, of course, mean that the EP is not part of the larger answer as Article 10(2) TEU indicates. It is crucial that the EP continues to engage with the collectivity of executive actors at the supranational level (the European Council, the Euro Summit, the Council, the ECB and Europol) and that it does so alongside its evolving relationship with the Commission.

Something may be changing already when it comes to (some) national parliaments. There is, more and more, a realisation of the need to change both their own working practices and to network more intensively with their European counterparts (other national parliaments, the EP) in order to address the reality of executive domination at all levels. It is not just a matter anymore of learning from those national parliaments that have a stronger scrutiny position vis-à-vis their own government (and here the new German law on the Bundestag's participation in matters concerning the EU is innovative and seemingly comprehensive in

[112] D Curtin, 'Judging EU Secrecy' (2012) *Cahiers de Droit Européen* 459.

its reach at least on the books)[113] but also of networking more intensively with their own parliamentary counterparts in order to be better informed and exert countervailing power, both individually and collectively. This is crucial and is beginning to happen in a variety of ways. It is particularly important to obtain information about the positions of other Member State governments that can then be used to enable national parliaments to put together different bits of the puzzle and to begin redressing the informational advantage that all the governments enjoy.

C. More Horizontal Dialogues Between Parliaments

The many recent practices to increase what is termed inter-parliamentary cooperation, among the national parliaments themselves, do attempt to address some aspects of these information asymmetries.[114] The fact that the national parliaments now have representatives in Brussels and that their offices are next to one another provides the possibility of informal but potentially extensive exchanges of information so that when parallel discussions in parliamentary committees and plenaries of the parliaments take place, individual national parliaments are no longer just dependent on the information given by their own government but can rely as well on a more independent sourcing of available information. Of course, as comparative research shows, the degree of re-parliamentarisation strongly depends on the broader pattern of executive–legislative relations in different countries.[115] Courts can help by prodding parliaments and executive actors to change their working practices and interactions, but ultimately it is up to parliaments to assert themselves in a manner that is true to their role in the political system and that is not dictated by government at whatever level.

The fact that one national parliament (the House of Commons in the UK) stands up to its government (and the EU rules) makes it easier for another national parliament to do the same. Will the German Bundestag or the Dutch *Tweede Kamer* be next? A drop must become a trickle before becoming a flow. We have seen that parliaments are increasingly looking to one another and learning from one another. If, in addition, the national parliaments organise themselves bottom-up to discuss how to more collectively, or at least in parallel, exercise more countervailing pressure on the executives individually and jointly, we can see the beginnings of a less executive-dominated future. New institutions are not essential to do this,

[113] Act on Cooperation Between the Federal Government and the German Bundestag in Matters Concerning the European Union 4 July 2013 available at: www.bundestag.de/htdocs_e/bundestag/committees/a21/legalbasis/euzbbg.html. See further, Curtin (n 11) 26–28.

[114] B Crum and J Fossum (eds), *Practices of Inter-Parliamentary Coordination in International Politics. The European Union and Beyond* (Colchester, ECPR Press, 2013).

[115] K Auel and A Benz, 'The Politics of Adaptation: The Europeanisation of National Parliamentary Systems' (2005) 11 *Journal of Legislative Studies* 372.

but existing structures such as the Conference of Parliamentary Committees for Union Affairs (COSAC) could be reinvigorated in a more innovative manner that goes beyond what the governments themselves are suggesting. In other words, it is up to both the national parliaments and the EP to roll up their individual and collective shirtsleeves and ensure that they are the visible vectors for a genuinely *public* and ongoing debate on the front-stage and back-stage activities of executive actors, both European and national. Information and public debate are prerequisites to democratic accountability mechanisms worthy of their name.

Part IV

The Parliamentarisation of the EU and its Critics

11

Towards a New Constitutional Architecture in the EU?

R DANIEL KELEMEN

I. INTRODUCTION

MANY PUNDITS PREDICTED that the Eurozone crisis would destroy the common currency and even tear apart the European Union (EU). They were wrong. Quite to the contrary, the Eurozone crisis has led to perhaps the most rapid period of deepening of integration since the European Communities were founded. Since late 2009, reforms introduced in reaction to the Eurozone crisis have led to dramatic increases in the powers of EU institutions that would have been unimaginable five years ago. These reforms occurred at the same time that the consequences of the Lisbon Treaty (which entered into force in December 2009) were unfolding. The combination of crisis-related reforms and the consequences of the Lisbon Treaty have led to tectonic shifts in the constitutional architecture of the EU, and pressure for further reform continues to build.

The intensifying political strife we observe today in the EU is closely intertwined with the rapid deepening of integration in recent years. Because the EU now wields more power, there is more at stake in EU-level politics. In the wake of steps that advanced the EU's fiscal union, banking union and debt union, we are now witnessing a battle over the future shape of the EU's political union. This chapter explores how the political responses to the crisis, coupled with the entry into force of the Lisbon Treaty, have altered the constitutional architecture of the EU. The chapter assesses where the EU stands today and the choices it now faces. Battles are brewing in Brussels, Strasbourg and Luxembourg that will shape the nature of the EU's political system for years to come. To better understand the nature of the coming shifts in the EU's institutional architecture, Section II begins by reviewing recent steps taken to deepen integration. Section III briefly describes shifts in the institutional balance between the European Council, Commission, Council and Parliament that have occurred over the past three decades. Sections IV and V then evaluate the current effort by the European Parliament (EP) to exert greater control over the European Commission, and the suggestions that national parliaments should be granted a greater role in EU policy-making.

Section VI conversely explores new calls on the EU to play a greater role in protecting democracy and the rule of law within troubled Member States. Finally, Section VII engages in a discussion of the relationship between the deepening of integration and increasing reliance on forms of multi-speed, 'differentiated integration', and Section VIII concludes.

II. THE GREAT DEEPENING

Just how far has the EU come in the past five years? To understand how deeply the EU has integrated in reaction to the crisis, we must consider developments in the intertwined fields of fiscal union, banking union and debt union.[1]

A. Fiscal Union

At the height of the crisis, when a messy Greek default and exit from the Eurozone seemed possible, EU Member States decided to dispense with the Eurozone governance rules put in place in the Maastricht Treaty—including the Stability and Growth Pact,[2] the Excessive Deficit Procedure[3] and the 'no-bailout-clause'.[4] For better or worse, governments decided that the risks posed by adhering to these rules and allowing a Greek default (such as risks of contagion to other peripheral states and risks to core state banking systems) were too great. Among other concerns, EU leaders feared that the default of one Member State could have a domino effect, raising borrowing costs and leading to defaults and bank failures across peripheral Eurozone economies, and leading to major losses for banks in the Eurozone core that were exposed to peripheral sovereign debt.

Instead of allowing insolvent Member States to default, the EU took significant steps toward fiscal union, putting in place a permanent bailout fund, the European Stability Mechanism (ESM), which—subject to conditionality—offers low interest loans to states who cannot borrow on private markets.[5] Also, to prevent excessive deficits and debts from emerging in the first place, new mechanisms have been put in place for tighter EU monitoring of national budgets and strict, judicial

[1] Debt union refers to the pooling of government borrowing activities—such as the joint issuance of bonds.

[2] Art 121 TFEU (ex Art 199 TEC).

[3] Art 126 TFEU and Protocol 12 TFEU (ex Art 104 TEC).

[4] Art 125 TFEU (ex Art 103 TEC).

[5] L Gocaj and S Meunier, 'Time Will Tell: The EFSF, the ESM, and the Euro Crisis' (2013) 35 *Journal of European Integration* 239; B de Witte and T Beukers, 'The Court of Justice Approves the Creation of the European Stability Mechanism Outside the EU Legal Order: *Pringle*' (2013) 50 *Common Market Law Review* 805; E Jones, 'Forgotten Financial Union' in M Matthijs and M Blyth, *The Future of the Euro* (Oxford, Oxford University Press, 2014).

enforcement of national deficit and debt limits.[6] Ultimately, any state—in the Eurozone or beyond—that wanted to have access to the ESM in times of crisis was required to ratify a new Fiscal Compact Treaty, which required signatories to enshrine structural balanced budget rules in domestic law where they can be enforced by domestic courts.[7] Most importantly perhaps, whatever the actual impact of these initiatives, they have created the perception among voters that the EU now plays a significantly more important role in national fiscal policy.

The EU has not been turned into a transfer union[8]—at least not on a scale larger than it already was with existing transfer programmes. Proposals to dramatically increase the size of the EU's budget and the scale of redistribution, or to create a separate Eurozone budget or 'shock absorption fund' have found no traction in the European Council. In the last round of budget negotiations, the Commission's proposal for a modest (5 per cent) increase in the EU budget was firmly rejected.[9] One might be tempted to dismiss the EU's fiscal power, given that the EU's budget of just over €140 billion per year constitutes only approximately 1 per cent of the EU's collective GDP and that the EU's 'own resources' revenues make up only roughly 2 per cent of the total tax revenue collected by EU Member States—percentages which are tiny compared to the fiscal power of even the most

[6] First, the so-called 'six-pack' legislation strengthened the Commission's ability to monitor and enforce the EU's deficit and debt limits—giving the EU much more control over national fiscal policy. (See Regulation 1173/2011/EU on the effective enforcement of budgetary surveillance in the euro area [2011] OJ L306/1; Regulation 1174/2011/EU on enforcement measures to correct excessive macroeconomic imbalances in the euro area [2011] OJ L306/8; Regulation 1175/2011/EU on the strengthening of the surveillance of budgetary positions and the surveillance and coordination of economic policies [2011] OJ L306/12; Regulation 1176/2011 on the prevention and correction of macroeconomic imbalances [2011] OJ L306/25; Council Regulation 1177/2011/EU on speeding up and clarifying the implementation of the excessive deficit procedure [2011] OJ L306/33; Council Directive 2011/85/EU of 8 November 2011 on requirements for budgetary frameworks of the Member States [2011] OJ L306/41). Secondly, the so-called 'two-pack' legislation EU further enhanced EU supervision of Member State budgets. (See Regulation 473/2013/EU on the strengthening of economic and budgetary surveillance of Member States in the euro area experiencing or threatened with serious difficulties with respect to their financial stability [2013] OJ L140/11; Regulation 472/2013/EU on common provisions for monitoring and assessing draft budgetary plans and ensuring the correction of excessive deficit of the Member States in the euro area [2013] OJ L140/1). Among other requirements, all Member States have to submit their draft budgets to the Commission annually by 15 October and the Commission reports on whether it finds each national budget acceptable under EU rules, and the Eurogroup then meets to discuss the Commission's opinion before national budgets are formally adopted.

[7] M Adams, F Fabbrini and P Larouche (eds), *The Constitutionalization of European Budgetary Constraints* (Oxford, Hart Publishing, 2014).

[8] Transfer Union—as the term has come to be used in discussions of the EU—refers to a situation in which the EU would engage in substantial ongoing transfers of wealth from wealthier Member States to economic laggards. See, eg 'We don't want no transfer Union' *The Economist* (2 December 2010); C Reiermann, 'For Richer, For Poorer: Europe on the Verge of Becoming a Transfer Union' *SpiegelOnline*, 1 August 2011, www.spiegel.de/international/spiegel/for-richer-for-poorer-europe-on-the-verge-of-becoming-a-transfer-union-a-777671.html.

[9] J Chaffin and A Barker, 'Leaders Agree Cut to EU Spending', *Financial Times* (London, 8 February 2013).

decentralised federal governments.[10] Nevertheless, we should recall that the EU already engages in redistribution between states, as it has for decades, through structural and cohesion funds, which for many of the recipient countries make up a significant proportion of their infrastructure spending. Moreover, though the EU budget may remain tiny relative to the overall EU economy, the EU's budget (at over €140 billion per year) is bigger in absolute terms than the budgets of 19 of the EU's 28 Member States. Finally, the EU's ability to respond to asymmetric shocks affecting Member States in times of crisis has been enhanced with the establishment of the ESM bailout fund, with a lending capacity of up to €500 billion.

B. Banking Union

Just as the crisis in Greece highlighted risks posed by inadequate controls on national fiscal policy, the crisis in Ireland illustrated the risks to the Eurozone posed by inadequate systems of national banking regulation. The Irish case showed that even the most fiscally prudent state could become insolvent if their banks face a crisis and the state feels compelled to socialise the losses in order to save the financial system.[11] The banking crises that unfolded in Ireland and other Member States also demonstrated that in an integrated financial system like the EU's, lax supervision of banks in one Member State could spark crises with significant negative spillover effects on other Member States. Relying on purely national systems for the regulation of banks, for the resolution of failed banks and for deposit insurance, proved untenable in the context of a single financial market. In response, the EU has taken major steps toward banking union establishing a common banking supervisor for Europe's largest banks (housed in the European Central Bank) and, more recently, agreeing on a common resolution mechanism for failed banks and common minimum rules on deposit insurance.[12]

C. Debt Union

The crisis has led many observers to conclude that the survival of the euro will require not only a fiscal union and a banking union, but also a 'debt union' in which Eurozone countries would pool existing debt (and/or future borrowing)

[10] P Genschel and M Jachtenfuchs, 'How the European Union Constrains the State' (2011) 50 *European Journal of Political Research* 293; RD Kelemen, 'Building the New European State? Federalism, Core State Powers and European Integration' in P Genschel and M Jachtenfuchs (eds), *Beyond the Regulatory Polity* (Oxford, Oxford University Press, 2014).

[11] S Sharma, 'Why Ireland's Luck Ran Out and What this Means for the Eurozone' (2011) 46 *The International Spectator* 115; B Thorhallsson and P Kirby, 'Financial Crisis is Iceland and Ireland: Does European Union and Euro Membership Matter?' (2012) 50 *Journal of Common Market Studies* 801.

[12] See also the contributions by T Beukers and G Lo Schiavo, chs 6 and 7 in this volume.

through the issuance of Eurobonds. There have been a series of proposals whereby a common authority would authorise individual states to issue Eurobonds backed by the Eurozone Member States collectively up to a fixed limit.[13]

Though proposals that the EU issue common Eurobonds have been rejected thus far—above all by Germany—the EU has nevertheless taken indirect steps toward establishing a debt union through the back door. The European Central Bank's (ECB's) purchase of the debt of distressed Member States (its Securities Markets Programme[14] and its Outright Monetary Transactions (OMT)[15] programme) amounts to a back-door version of debt mutualisation, by transforming national bonds into (potentially) quasi-Eurobonds. When the ECB President Mario Draghi promised to do 'whatever it takes'[16] to save the euro and announced that the OMT programme that would purchase potentially unlimited quantities of the bonds of distressed Eurozone countries, the ECB transformed national bonds into quasi-Eurobonds by in effect asserting that they were backed by the EU's central bank. OMT and Draghi's 'whatever it takes' pledge proved effective without ever being put into practice. The assurance that the ECB would stand behind the euro and beleaguered governments proved sufficient to calm financial markets and bring down bond yields.[17] Though these activities required no Treaty amendment and have—at least thus far—proved effective, they have proven controversial and have prompted strong legal challenges in Germany.[18]

D. Other Areas of Deepening

Though the most dramatic and controversial increases in the EU's powers in recent years have come in the areas of economic and monetary union discussed above, the EU has also seen its power increase in a number of other fields—including areas that were traditionally viewed as 'core state powers' associated with the sovereign state.[19] The EU has established more robust institutions in the field of foreign affairs,

[13] See, eg J Delpla and J von Weizsäcker, 'The Blue Bond Proposal', Bruegel Policy Brief, Issue 2010/03, May 2010; E Jones, 'A Eurobond Proposal to Promote Stability and Liquidity while Preventing Moral Hazard', Instituto Per Gli Studi Di Politica Internanzionale (ISPI), Policy Brief No 180, March 2010.

[14] European Central Bank, Press Release, 'ECB Decides on Measures to Address Severe Tensions in Financial Markets', 10 May 2010.

[15] European Central Bank, Press Release, 'Technical Features of Outright Monetary Transactions', 6 September 2012.

[16] M Draghi, President of the European Central Bank, 'Speech at the Global Investment Conference', London, 26 July 2012.

[17] S Bodoni, 'Draghi's Whatever It Takes Bid Saved Euro Area, ECB Says' Bloomberg.com, 14 October 2014; M Wolf, *The Shifts and the Shocks* (London, Penguin, 2014).

[18] E Jones and RD Kelemen, 'The Euro Goes to Court' (2014) 56 *Survival* 15; Bundesverfassungsgericht [BVerfG—Federal Constitutional Court], 2 BvR 2728/13, 14 January 2014, referred by the BVerfG to the European Court of Justice as Gauweiler and Others, ECJ Case C-62/14 (pending).

[19] P Genschel and M Jachtenfuchs (eds), *Beyond the Regulatory Polity?* (Oxford, Oxford University Press, 2013).

above all with the establishment of a new position of 'High Representative' and the creation of an EU diplomatic corps (the European External Action Service).[20] The granting of formal legal status to the Charter of Fundamental Rights in the Lisbon Treaty has enhanced the EU's status as a guarantor of the fundamental rights of European citizens.[21] More generally, the Lisbon Treaty granted the EP enhanced legislative powers in roughly 40 new policy areas, including areas such as asylum, immigration, police and judicial cooperation, agriculture, structural funds and transportation.[22] The dramatic transfer of policy-making and regulatory authority to the EU level in recent years has raised the stakes of EU politics, setting the stage for the battles over the structure of the EU's political union that we are now witnessing.

III. THE SHIFTING INSTITUTIONAL BALANCE

From its founding to the mid-1980s, institutional power at the EU level was divided primarily between the Council and the Commission.[23] The Council was, of course, the most powerful actor, exercising a veto over proposed legislation, but the Commission was able to use its right of initiative and other agenda-setting powers to push forward the process of integration. The EP was a loyal partner to the Commission and could be relied on to support Commission initiatives designed to promote European integration, but it exercised little real influence in its own right. This began to change with the Single European Act, which gave the EP the power to amend legislation (through the cooperation procedure). The Maastricht Treaty took this a step further with the co-decision procedure, which gave the EP veto power, and subsequent treaty revisions have only enhanced the EP's power over the legislative process and—as we shall see below—over the appointment of the EU's executive.

With the gradual empowerment of the EP, the division of authority and institutional balance in the EU shifted from two-headed (bicephalous) to three-headed (tricephalous).[24] Legislative power was divided between the Commission (which

[20] S Vanhoonacker and K Pomorska, 'The European External Action Service and Agenda-setting in European Foreign Policy' (2013) 20 *Journal of European Public Policy* 1316.

[21] F Fabbrini, *Fundamental Rights in Europe* (Oxford, Oxford University Press, 2014).

[22] J Emmanouilidis and C Stratulat, 'Implementing Lisbon: Narrowing the EU's 'Democratic Deficit'?' Policy Brief, European Policy Centre, March 2010.

[23] Some scholars argue that the European Council—the Council formation that since the 1970s has brought together heads of government—should be treated as a separate institution from the 'regular' Councils that bring together ministers in the policy areas under discussion. (See, eg L van Middelaar, *The Passage to Europe* (New Haven, Yale University Press, 2013) arguing that the European Council has played a powerful role in driving the EU agenda.) In my view, while, of course, distinctions between the European Council and regular formations of the Council of Ministers exist, there is little to be gained analytically from treating these as separate institutions, since the ministers meeting in the Council of Ministers in any case represent the governments whose heads meet in the 'European Council' formation.

[24] M Smith and RD Kelemen, 'The Institutional Balance: Formal and Informal Change' (1997) Centre for European Policy Studies, Working Document No 111.

retained its right of initiative), the Council (which remained ultimately the most powerful actor), and the Parliament (which gradually gained co-equal legislative powers in most areas of EU policy-making). As the Parliament gained real legislative power, it gradually distanced itself from the Commission, taking on the oversight role that any parliament in principle is expected to play vis-à-vis the executive. This could be seen in dramatic moments such as when the Parliament forced the resignation of the Santer Commission after scandals involving French Commissioner Édith Cresson and others. It could also be seen in more mundane processes of regulatory policy-making where the Parliament increasingly sought to oversee and control the administrative discretion of the Commission and other EU bodies (such as newly created EU agencies) when they acted to implement EU legislation.[25]

In short, the EU had evolved by the 1990s into a political system that combined a form of separation of powers with federalism. It did not have the directly elected President characteristic of many separations of powers systems, but it did have a clear horizontal separation between legislative power (concentrated in a bicameral legislature made up of the Council and Parliament), executive power (concentrated in the Commission) and independent judicial power (concentrated in the European Court of Justice). Power was, of course, also divided vertically between the quasi-federal centre where EU legislation was adopted and the Member State administrations which were tasked with the implementation of most EU policies. On the whole, the EU emerged as a polity characterised by a high degree of fragmentation of power and the need to secure the approval of multiple veto players in order to adopt common policies.[26] Indeed, it is striking that in his classic book on forms of democracy, Arend Lijphart uses the EU as one of his prime examples of a consensus model of democracy, in contrast to a majoritarian Westminster model of democracy.[27]

Finally, in recent years, many scholars have remarked on the growing executive power of the Council of Ministers and even more so of the European Council.[28] Given the European Council's growing agenda-setting role, many observers would challenge the characterisation presented above of the Commission as the EU's executive organ. However, while the European Council has certainly come to play an increasing role in setting forth the broad parameters of the EU's agenda, it is somewhat misleading to characterise the European Council as the EU's executive. First, with regard to agenda-setting, while the European Council plays a

[25] See RD Kelemen and G Majone, 'Managing Europeanization: The European Agencies' in J Peterson and M Shackleton (eds), *The Institutions of the European Union* (Oxford, Oxford University Press, 2012); RD Kelemen, 'The Politics of Eurocracy: Building a New European State?' in N Jabko and C Parsons (eds), *State of the European Union, Vol 7* (Oxford, Oxford University Press, 2005).

[26] G Tsebelis, *Veto Players* (Princeton, Princeton University Press, 2002).

[27] A Lijphart, *Patterns of Democracy* (New Haven, Yale University Press, 1999).

[28] See, eg the contribution by Puetter, ch 14 in this volume; see also P Ponzano, C Hermanin and D Corona, 'The Power of Initiative of the European Commission: A Progressive Erosion?' (Notre Europe—Jacques Delors Institute, 2012).

powerful role, the Commission retains a (near) monopoly of legislative initiative in EU policy-making. In the unlikely event that the Council called for policy measures that the Commission strenuously opposed, the Commission could refuse to act on these. Secondly, outside the realm of agenda-setting, other key EU executive functions—such as monitoring the implementation and enforcement of EU law—remain concentrated in the Commission. In short, while the Commission may be a weaker agenda-setter than it was in the past, it remains the EU's principal executive body.

IV. TOWARDS PARLIAMENTARY GOVERNMENT?

Under the Maastricht Treaty, governments accorded the EP the right to be consulted on the appointment of the Commission President and to veto the college of Commissioners as a whole.[29] That change proved to be the thin end of a wedge that the EP has been pushing on ever since in an effort to wrest control of the appointment of the Commission away from the Member States in the Council. The EP asserted that based on its power to be consulted on the appointment of the Commission President, it could veto potential nominees. EU Member States eventually accepted this position and affirmed it in the Treaty of Amsterdam.[30] In 2004, the EP demanded that the Council's nominee for Commission President reflect the majority (then centre-right) in the EP, and the Member States eventually acceded to this demand as well.[31] In the run-up to the 2009 EP election, the European People's Party group in the EP went even further, not simply demanding that the Commission president should come from whichever party prevailed in the election, but officially naming their candidate in advance of the vote: they named incumbent Commission President José Manuel Barroso as their candidate

[29] Treaty on European Union Art 158(2) stated:

'The governments of the Member States shall nominate by common accord, after consulting the European Parliament, the person they intend to appoint as President of the Commission.

The governments of the Member States shall, in consultation with the nominee for President, nominate the other persons whom they intend to appoint as members of the Commission.

The President and the other members of the Commission thus nominated shall be subject as a body to a vote of approval by the European Parliament. After approval by the European Parliament, the President and the other members of the Commission shall be appointed by common accord of the governments of the Member States.

[30] Treaty of Amsterdam amended the first two paragraphs of Art 158(2) from the Maastricht Treaty to read as follows:

'The governments of the Member States shall nominate by common accord the person they intend to appoint as President of the Commission; the nomination shall be approved by the European Parliament. The governments of the Member States shall, by common accord with the nominee for President, nominate the other persons whom they intend to appoint as Members of the Commission.'

[31] S Hix, A Noury and G Roland, *Democratic Politics in the European Parliament* (New York, Cambridge University Press, 2007) 16.

for a second term.[32] Immediately after the 2009 election, the Party of European Socialists group in the EP (now called the Socialists & Democrats) made it clear that it planned to follow the European Peoples Party's example and name a candidate for the Presidency in advance of the 2014 election.

Though the Lisbon Treaty did not explicitly endorse the Parliament's demand that the Commission President should come from the party that won a plurality in the EP election, the Treaty did move clearly in that direction. Article 17 of the EU Treaty, as amended by the Lisbon Treaty, states that in proposing a candidate for the Presidency, the European Council would 'take into account the elections to the European Parliament' and hold 'appropriate consultations' with the Parliament, and that the candidate would then have to be approved by a majority in the Parliament.[33] While it was never spelled out precisely what it would mean for the European Council to 'take into account' the EP elections, it was—or at least should have been—clear to everyone involved what the EP had in mind. At minimum, the European Council should name a candidate from the party group that won in the EP election, and—if the Parliament had its way—the European Council would select the specific candidate named in advance by the winning party.

Finally, in the run-up to the 2014 EP elections, the Party groups in the EP sought to realise their new vision of how the Commission President should be selected under the Lisbon Treaty regime. Each major party group named a candidate—a so-called *Spitzenkandidat* (top candidate)—for the presidency in advance of the election, and the parties agreed that the candidate whose party won the most seats would become president. The parties made it clear to the heads of state and government in the European Council that the only candidate they would endorse was the winning *Spitzenkandidat*. In effect, the Parliament sought to leverage its power to approve the candidate for president in order to transform the Commission President into a kind of prime minister selected by the Parliament and serving with the backing of a parliamentary majority.

As the Parliament tried to assert this new power, a battle ensued between it and reluctant Member States in the European Council—above all the UK.[34] Critics characterised the Parliament's move as an illegitimate power-grab, whereby the Parliament was attempting usurp national governments' authority to select the

[32] S Hix, 'What to Expect in the 2009–14 European Parliament' European Policy Analysis 8-2009, Swedish Institute for European Policy Analysis.

[33] Art 17(7) TEU reads, 'Taking into account the elections to the European Parliament and after having held the appropriate consultations, the European Council, acting by a qualified majority, shall propose to the European Parliament a candidate for President of the Commission. This candidate shall be elected by the European Parliament by a majority of its component members. If he does not obtain the required majority, the European Council, acting by a qualified majority, shall within one month propose a new candidate who shall be elected by the European Parliament following the same procedure.

[34] For more detailed discussion of this battle, see RD Kelemen and A Menon, 'Fight Club' Foreign Affairs online, 18 May 2014, www.foreignaffairs.com/articles/141426/r-daniel-kelemen-and-anand-menon/fight-club; D Kelemen, 'A President for the People' Foreign Affairs online, 30 June 2014, www.foreignaffairs.com/articles/141609/r-daniel-kelemen/president-for-the-people.

Commission President. Meanwhile, the Parliament justified its assertion of power as an answer to the EU's supposed 'democratic deficit'. Defenders of the Parliament's approach argued that organising presidential campaigns between rival candidates offering competing platforms and visions for the EU would stimulate voter interest and finally engage them in EU politics.[35] Eventually, this would help create a European public space and the sort of pan-European partisan politics needed to underpin a true political union.

The battle came to a head in the aftermath of the election. After the European People's Party (EPP) won the most seats in the election, Members of the European Parliament (MEPs) agreed that the EPP candidate—Jean Claude Juncker—should become Commission President.[36] A number of national leaders expressed opposition to the *Spitzenkandidat* process, preferring to select the President the old-fashioned way, through behind-closed-door negotiations. Even German Chancellor Angela Merkel briefly appeared ambivalent about Juncker's candidacy. For British Prime Minister David Cameron and eurosceptics in his Conservative Party, the Parliament's gambit was totally unacceptable: basing the selection of the president on the outcome of the parliamentary election was for Cameron a step too far toward a European federal government. At the June 2014 European Council Summit, Cameron sought to block Juncker's appointment—warning that installing him as President might hasten British exit from the EU.[37] Ultimately, however, Cameron lost his battle to block Juncker. After the German press attacked Merkel for failing to respect the outcome of the European election by not supporting Juncker, she changed tack and came out in support of him.[38] Other national leaders then lined up behind Juncker as well, leaving Cameron isolated—backed only by Hungary's Viktor Orbán. In the conclusions of the June 2014 European Council a majority of heads of state and government voted to appoint Juncker as Commission President.[39]

If member governments were unhappy with the EP's most recent power grab, they should hardly have been surprised. The EP's assertions of authority in the 2014 election were not revolutionary—rather they were a simple continuation of the tactics, described above, that the EP has pursued for years in increasing its influence over the selection of the Commission President. Had member governments cared to pay attention they could have seen this coming. Governments who were unhappy with the Parliament's selection of Jean-Claude Juncker as Commission President or more generally with the Parliament's efforts to construct EU level 'presidential' campaigns complete with buses and televised debates, have only themselves to blame.

[35] See also the contributions by C Anthpohler, ch 12 in this volume.

[36] See Kelemen, 'A President for the People' (n 34).

[37] I Traynor and N Watt, 'Britain Closer to EU Exit after Jean Claude Juncker Vote' *The Guardian* (London, 27 June 2014).

[38] A Schmidt, 'Merkel says Juncker can be Approved with "Qualified Majority"' *Reuters* (2 June 2014).

[39] General Secretariat of the Council, European Council Conclusions, EUCO 79/14, 27 June 2014.

While heads of states and governments in the European Council have a clear self-interest in resisting the EP and maintaining control over the selection of the Commission President, one might ask whether there are also principled reasons for them to oppose the Parliament's move. There are indeed. First, Member States never explicitly agreed to give Parliament the power to nominate candidates and determine the Commission President on the basis of the EP election outcome.[40] The idea embedded in the Treaty was that the Commission President would likely come from the party that secured the plurality of seats in the EP, but that the particular person chosen would be a compromise between the EP and the member governments in the European Council.[41] While the EP may have democratic legitimacy, heads of state and government have a democratic mandate too, and there is no principled reason that they should have to surrender their say in the selection of the President.

Secondly, the Parliament's tactics are highly misleading to voters in a crucial respect. By suggesting that the outcome of the election will determine the party affiliation of the Commission President, the Parliament seems to be trying to raise voters' interest by giving them the impression that they are electing a leader who will shift the partisan orientation of the EU's executive branch and thus change the direction of policy.[42] This seems to be based on a majoritarian, Westminster view of democracy, where a party that wins the most seats in the lower chamber of the legislature takes power and governs.

But the EU is not and will never be a Westminster system. It is a consensus democracy that is based on dividing power between multiple institutions, encouraging a wide representation of diverse interests and building broad, multi-party coalitions to govern. Regardless of the partisan affiliation of the Commission President, as long as individual Member States appoint the 27 other members of the Commission, the EU's executive will remain a multi-party body that seeks broad cross-party consensus and does not simply cater to the parliamentary majority on the left or right. Thus, even though the Parliament succeeded in pressuring governments to accept the winning *Spitzenkandidat*, voters in the EP election did not in fact have the opportunity to select a coherently partisan European government of the left or right.[43] This is true not only because the Commission will remain a politically diverse, multi-party body, but also because the Council of Ministers will remain the most powerful legislative actor in the EU and will represent a wide

[40] See also the contribution of A Kocharov, ch 13 in this volume.

[41] That the nomination should be based on a compromise between the European Parliament and European Council was implicit in Art 17(7) of the EU Treaty as amended by the Lisbon Treaty, see n 33.

[42] Critics of past EP elections have complained that the electoral outcomes have not changed the direction of EU politics in a way that voters could observe, and that therefore it appeared that little if anything was really at stake in the elections—which depressed voter interest and turnout. See 'Fight Club' (n 34).

[43] If any national analogue for the Commission is appropriate, it would most likely be something akin to the multi-party Swiss collective executive (the Federal Council). See U Klöti, 'Consensual Government in a Heterogenous Polity' (2001) 24 *West European Politics* 19.

swathe of partisan views. Rather than misleading voters into thinking that a single pan-European election will dramatically alter the direction of EU policies, EU leaders should recognise and admit to voters that the EU is and will remain a consensus democracy—based on compromise between a broad range of democratically elected representatives from national governments and the EP.

V. MORE POWER TO NATIONAL PARLIAMENTS

The Lisbon Treaty included several measures designed to strengthen the role of national Parliaments in the legislative process, and in the wake of the Eurozone crisis there have been renewed calls to further strengthen the role of national parliaments at the EU level based on the notion that increased participation by national parliaments at the EU level will redress the EU's supposed 'democratic deficit'.[44] These views and proposals based on them are misguided. Certainly national parliaments should play a more active role in shaping EU policies, but they should do so in their national capitals, not in Brussels. They should do so by overcoming their domestic impotence and actually controlling—rather than being dominated by—the national governments that are supposedly responsible to them. In short, they should do *less blaming* and *more taming*. Instead of *blaming* Brussels, they should be *taming* their governments.

The most important reform in the Lisbon Treaty designed to strengthen the role of national parliaments was the so-called yellow card procedure. Under this procedure, legislative proposals from the European Commission are forwarded to national Parliaments, which may then issue a 'reasoned opinion' on whether the proposal over-extends EU power in violation of the principle of 'subsidiarity'.[45] If, within eight weeks, one-third of national parliaments decide that a Commission proposal violates the principle of subsidiarity, they can issue a 'yellow card'—calling for a halt to the legislative initiative. The Commission may choose to continue with its legislative initiative in the face of this opposition, but it must offer a reasoned opinion as to why its proposal does not violate subsidiarity and its proposal may still be blocked by a vote of either 55 per cent of the Member States or 50 per cent of votes cast in the EP. National parliaments have made use of the yellow card only twice since the Lisbon Treaty entered into force. In 2012 they yellow carded proposed EU rules on the right to strike (Monti II).

[44] I Cooper, 'A "Virtual Third Chamber" for the European Union? National Parliaments after the Treaty of Lisbon' (2012) 35 *West European Politics* 441; I Cooper, 'Bicameral or Tricameral? National Parliaments and Representative Democracy in the European Union' (2013) 35 *Journal of European Integration* 531; R Bellamy and S Kröger, 'Domesticating the Democratic Deficit? The Role of National Parliaments and Parties in the EU's System of Governance' (2014) 67 *Parliamentary Affairs* 437.

[45] Protocol (No 2) on the application of the principles of subsidiarity and proportionality, annexed to the Treaty on European Union and the Treaty on the Functioning of the European Union by the Treaty of Lisbon of 13 December 2007.

In 2013, national parliaments yellow carded a Commission proposal to create an EU public prosecutor office.[46]

Given the difficulties of coordinating across national parliaments and given that historically few parliaments have demonstrated much interest in closely scrutinising the EU legislative process, it should not surprise us that the yellow card has been used sparingly. Nevertheless, in the wake of the Eurozone crisis, with the EU playing a larger role in shaping national fiscal policies, there have been renewed calls to increase the role of national parliaments.[47] Most recently, Thomas Piketty and a group of collaborators issued a manifesto arguing that the EU should establish a new legislative institution composed of national parliamentarians.[48] Piketty is a brilliant economist and his contribution to the debate on EU institutions suggests he might do well to stick to economics. His group's manifesto explains: 'In this scheme the European Union would have two chambers: the existing European parliament, directly elected by the citizens of the EU 28, and the European chamber, representing the states through their national parliaments.'[49] This proposal for a two chamber legislature seems to ignore the fact that the EU already has a two chamber legislature—composed of the Council of Ministers (the upper chamber) and the EP (the lower chamber).

The proposal also ignores the fact that, at least in principle, the party or coalition that holds a majority in a national parliament is supposed to exercise control over their country's government. So, the governments in the Council of Ministers are supposed to be doing the bidding of their national parliaments (or at least their parliamentary majorities). In some cases (such as with the Danish Folketing) national parliaments are active and exercise real control over their governments. But in most cases, governments in fact dominate their parliaments—both in national capitals and in Brussels.[50] When national MPs call for a greater direct role in the EU legislative process, they are essentially asking the EU to help them make up for their own impotence vis-à-vis their governments. Many national MPs may be keen to blame their weakness and their inability to control their own national government on the EU policy process.[51] But, in reality, the causes of the impotence of most national

[46] The two Commission proposals to be yellow carded were: Proposal for a Council Regulation, 'On the exercise of the right to take collective action' 21 March 2012, COM (2012) 130 final, and Proposal for a Council Regulation, 'On the establishment of the European Public Prosecutor's Office', 17 July 2013, COM (2013) 534 final. The impact of the yellow card seems to extend beyond these two instances in that the Commission now considers, and tries to avoid, the possibility of a yellow card when crafting new legislation. F Fabbrini and K Granat, 'Yellow Card, but No Foul: The Role of the National Parliaments under the Subsidiarity Protocol and the Commission Proposal for an EU Regulation on the Right to Strike' (2013) 50 *Common Market Law Review* 115.

[47] See also the contribution of V Kreilinger, ch 15 in this volume.

[48] Thomas Piketty et al, 'Our manifesto for Europe' *The Guardian* (London, 2 May 2014).

[49] ibid.

[50] On executive dominance in parliamentary systems in general see Tsebelis, *Veto Players* (n 26) 109–15; on executive dominance of national parliaments in the EU context, see P De Wilde, 'Why the Early Warning Mechanism does not Alleviate the Democratic Deficit', Observatory of European Parliaments After the Lisbon Treaty, OPAL Online Paper 6/2012, www.europe-opal.org.

[51] In fact, many national MPs may be jealous of the EP because, despite all of its flaws, it is clearly a powerful legislative actor that decisively shapes—and does not simply rubber stamp—legislation proposed by the executive.

parliaments in Europe are domestic, rooted in the dynamics of party discipline that so often enable the party leaders in government to dominate back bench MPs. Giving national MPs a direct role at the EU level will not change this.

By all means, national parliaments should work to become more engaged in debating EU issues, scrutinising draft legislation and holding their government ministers to account for what they do in Brussels—but this does not mean parliaments should be represented in Brussels separately from their governments. In fact, proposals designed to heighten participation of national parliaments in EU governance might have perverse consequences. Consider, for instance, the yellow card issued against the European Public Prosecutor's Office (EPPO) proposal. The French Senate's opposition to the Commission Proposal[52] was pivotal to the success of the yellow card procedure in this case. However, in opposing the EPPO proposal the French Senate was acting against the position of the French National Assembly and the French government.[53] This illustrates how the yellow card may serve to empower upper chambers vis-à-vis lower chambers and the governments linked to them. Given that upper chambers are often less democratically representative than lower chambers, it is by no means clear that this sort of empowerment would be a 'win' for democracy.

VI. ADDRESSING THE OTHER DEMOCRATIC DEFICIT

In recent years, democracy and the rule of law have come under serious threat in Romania, Bulgaria and above all, Hungary. These developments have turned the democratic deficit debate on its head. For years, critics have argued that the EU suffers from a democratic deficit, namely a lack of public engagement and political accountability at the EU level.[54] According to this view, the growing power of the rather undemocratic EU undermines existing national democracies. While the EU may have its democratic shortcomings, today the greatest challenges to democracy in the EU can be found at the national level, not the EU level.[55] Developments in Hungary, Romania and Bulgaria remind us that rather than posing a threat to democracy in Europe, the EU may be crucial in defending democracy and the rule of law.

And yet, while the EU has faced calls to step in to defend democracy, it has found its toolkit for dealing with democratic backsliding in EU Member States

[52] Reasoned Opinion of the French Senate on the proposal for a Council regulation on the establishment of the European Public Prosecutor's Office (COM (2013) 534—2013/0255 (APP)).

[53] H Brady, 'The EU's "Yellow Card" Comes of Age: Subsidiarity Unbound?' Centre for European Reform, 12 November 2013.

[54] The literature on the democratic deficit is, of course, voluminous. For one well-known work asserting the existence of a democratic deficit at the EU level, see A Follesdal and S Hix, 'Why There is a Democratic Deficit in the EU: A Response to Majone and Moravcsik' (2006) 44 *Journal of Common Market Studies* 533.

[55] See also the contribution by C Calliess, ch 3 in this volume.

to be very limited. The EU possesses a 'nuclear option' under Article 7 of the EU Treaties of suspending the voting rights of a Member State that breaches the EU's fundamental values.[56] But the political hurdles to deploying Article 7 are very high and short of taking that dramatic step, the EU has limited tools at its disposal to address threats to democracy and the rule of law at the national level.

For instance, in Hungary the EU has had limited success in restraining the Orbán regime's drive remove all checks and balances and to consolidate one-party rule.[57] Lacking tools to address these threats head on, the primary EU response has been for the European Commission to launch a series of infringement proceedings against Hungary before the European Court of Justice, cases which focus on ostensibly technical issues of compliance with EU law—rather than targeting the underlying attacks on the rule of law and democratic pluralism that are at stake. For instance, when Orbán's government lowered the retirement age of judges in a thinly veiled effort to purge the judiciary and open up space for the appointment of Fidesz party loyalists, the Commission could only respond by bringing a case claiming that this policy violated EU rules on age discrimination.[58] While EU pressure has prompted Orbán to make some tactical concessions, it has by no means halted his drive to consolidate power.

The EU's shortcomings in confronting the Orbán regime raise doubts about the EU's ability and willingness to take the steps needed to uphold EU values when they are threatened by governments. This has people asking troubling questions, such as whether we might witness the rise of an autocratic regime inside the EU. More powerful tools and graded sanctions may be needed if the EU is to act effectively to prevent this outcome. Commission President Barroso and Members of the EP have highlighted the importance of empowering the EU with more instruments to intervene and safeguard democracy and the rule of law at the Member State level where these are under threat.[59] The EP has taken a leading role in condemning actions of the Orbán government, and in calling for concerted action by European institutions to prevent further erosion of democracy and the rule of law in Hungary.[60] The Commission recently proposed a Rule of Law

[56] Art 7 provides that the EU may suspend the voting rights of a state deemed by the European Council to be in serious and persistent breech of values enshrined in Art 2 of the Treaty—namely respect for human dignity, freedom, democracy, equality, the rule of law and respect for human rights. See W Sadurski, 'Adding Bite to a Bark: the Story of Article 7, EU Enlargement and Jörg Haider' (2010) 16 *Columbia Journal of European Law* 385.

[57] KL Scheppele, 'Guest Post: Constitutional Revenge' The Conscience of a Liberal Blog, *New York Times*, (New York, 1 March 2013).

[58] Case C-286/12, *European Commission v Hungary* [2013] 1 CMLR 44.

[59] JW Müller, 'What, if Anything, is Wrong with a Copenhagen Commission?' Transatlantic Academy Working Paper, 24 July 2013.

[60] See the *Tavares Report* (Report of 25 June 2013 on the situation of fundamental rights: standards and practices in Hungary—pursuant to the European Parliament resolution of 16 February 2012 (2012/2130(INI)), prepared by the European Parliament's Committee on Civil Liberties, Justice and Home Affairs and endorsed by the Parliament's plenary in July 2014; see also E Balazs, 'European Lawmakers Criticize Hungarian Government' *Bloomberg News* (3 July 2013), www.bloomberg.com/news/articles/2013-07-03/european-lawmakers-criticize-hungarian-government.

initiative[61] that establishes a series of intermediary steps, warning a state that it is on track for an Article 7 procedure and ratcheting up the pressure.

But EU legal actions alone will not stop democratic backsliding in Hungary, or elsewhere, if politicians at the European level are willing to coddle the national leaders responsible. The behaviour of leaders of the European People's Party in the run-up to the 2014 EP election illustrates this problem. Orbán's Fidesz party remains a member in good standing of the EPP. In the run-up to the recent election, leading figures in the EPP, above all Joseph Daul, the French Union for a Popular Movement (UMP) politician who leads the EPP group party, sheltered the Orbán regime from criticism in the name of partisan politics. In the interest of party loyalty and of winning a majority in the upcoming EP elections (for which they needed Fidesz' seats), many EPP politicians were willing to tolerate Orbán's violations of democratic values—even in the face of sustained international criticism of his actions. Thus, ironically, the drive to enhance EU democracy by politicising the selection of the Commission Presidency may actually create incentives for EU leaders to tolerate threats to democracy at the national level. This is equally true whether it is the EPP protecting Orbán today or the Socialists protecting one of their own—as they did during the 2012 Romanian constitutional crisis. Indeed, the experience of other democracies—from Mexico, to Argentina, to the United States in the era of the 'Solid South'[62]—suggests that so long as party leaders are willing to put partisan interests above democratic values, they may allow local pockets of autocracy to persist for decades within otherwise democratic political systems.

VII. DEEPENING AND FRAGMENTATION

While the EU is sure to move forward with the deepening of its economic and political union in the years to come, it is uncertain whether all EU Member States will be willing to go along with these steps. In particular, the UK government has made it clear that it will not participate in several of the moves toward deeper integration currently under consideration, and the Conservative Party has even pledged that if it wins the 2015 general election, it will then hold an 'in-or-out' referendum on the question of the UK's continued membership in the EU. More generally, there is a risk that a divide may be opening up between EU members in the Eurozone and those outside it. Many suggest that multi-speed arrangements, sometimes called 'differentiated integration'[63] or 'variable geometry', offer a way out of this conundrum. Recent reports on the future of Europe by European

[61] Communication from the Commission to the European Parliament and the Council, 'A New EU Framework to strengthen the Rule of Law', 3 November 2014, COM (2014) 158 final.

[62] E Gibson, *Boundary Control* (New York, Cambridge University Press, 2012).

[63] D Leuffen, B Rittberger and F Schimmelfennig, *Differentiated Integration* (London, Palgrave Macmillan, 2012).

Council President van Rompuy,[64] Commission President Barroso[65] and the Member State foreign ministers participating in the 'Future of Europe' group[66] all suggested that those states (in particular euro area states) who were willing to move ahead on closer economic and political union could do so through some form of 'enhanced cooperation', and they maintained that this would not endanger the unity of EU or its Single Market. The notion that fundamental disagreements over the pace and scope of integration can be massaged away with differentiated, multi-speed arrangements is untenable. Multi-speed arrangements are no panacea. Enhanced cooperation among the Eurozone states or other subsets of states threatens to undermine the integrity of the EU and the unity of the Single Market. The EU was already turning to multi-speed arrangements, either in the form of enhanced cooperation of vanguard groups of states or opt-outs for the recalcitrant, in order to overcome legislative impasses before the crisis—as illustrated by the operation of the euro area and Schengen. But if voluntary opt-outs and opt-ins become the norm, then EU membership may eventually come to constitute an inchoate assemblage of voluntary clubs, rather than a Union with a distinct legal order. This trend might also intersect in troubling ways with other challenges to the coherence of the EU legal order being posed by mounting tensions between some national judiciaries and the European Court of Justice.[67]

VIII. CONCLUSION

Over the past two years, constitutional architecture of the EU has changed in important ways. The EU remains—as it has been since the 1990s—a constitutional order characterised by the consensus model of democracy replete with veto players and combining a form of separation of powers with federalism. But within those broad parameters, a great deal has changed. The EU has strengthened its authority in a range of sensitive policy areas that were traditionally viewed as the preserve of Member State governments. The EP successfully asserted control over the selection of the Commission President in 2014, further politicising the

[64] H van Rompuy, in close collaboration with J M Barroso, J-C Juncker and M Draghi, 'Towards a Genuine Economic and Monetary Union' 5 December 2012, www.consilium.europa.eu/uedocs/cms_data/docs/pressdata/en/ec/134069.pdf.

[65] JM Barroso, President of the European Commission, State of the Union 2012 Address, 12 September 2012, Speech/12/596.

[66] Final Report of the Future of Europe Group of the Foreign Ministers of Austria, Belgium, Denmark, France, Germany, Italy, Luxembourg, Netherlands, Poland, Portugal and Spain, 17 September 2012.

[67] See, eg A Dyevre, The German Federal Constitutional Court and European Judicial Politics' (2011) 34 *West European Politics* 346; A Dyevre, 'Judicial Non-Compliance in a Non-Hierarchical Legal Order', Max Planck Institute for International and Comparative Law Working Paper, 2012; M Bobek, 'Learning to Talk: Preliminary Rulings, the Courts of the New Member States and the Court of Justice' (2008) 45 *Common Market Law Review* 1611. On the looming showdown between the ECJ and the German Federal Constitutional Court over the question of *Kompetenz Kompetenz*, see E Jones and RD Kelemen, 'The Euro Goes to Court' (n 18).

Commission and pushing the EU at least a small step in the direction of supranational parliamentary government.[68] Though EU leaders declared after Juncker's selection that they would reconsider the process of appointment of the president in the future,[69] they are unlikely to sever the link between the pan-European election and the Commission presidency that the EP has established. The EU has also begun to contemplate actions aimed at addressing democratic deficits and threats to the rule of law at the national level,[70] though it remains to be seen whether the EU will take robust actions in this regard. While the EU has deepened and taken steps to address democratic deficits at both the EU and national levels, greater power and greater politicisation have not made the EU more popular, and they have brought with them new sets of challenges.[71]

While many Europhiles may view recent steps to deepen and democratise the Union as forms of progress, these steps will not come without costs and unintended consequences. The rapid deepening the EU has just experienced will encourage some fragmentation within the Union and heighten tensions between Eurozone members and Member States outside the common currency zone.[72] Ultimately, such tensions may test just how far the EU can proceed based on a model of differentiated, multi-speed integration.[73] Such arrangements cannot resolve all the tensions between a Union committed to further deepening and particular Member States—above all the United Kingdom—who seem unwilling to go along with such initiatives. If such tensions cannot be resolved, the exit from the EU of one or more Member States in the years to come is possible (if still unlikely). Finally, the effort to address the EU's supposed democratic deficit by politicising the selection of the Commission President may have negative consequences. First, as noted above, heightened pressure on party groups in the EP to maintain a parliamentary majority may lead them to tolerate abuses of democracy by national parties that are part of their coalition. Politicisation of the Commission may also undermine its legitimacy as an independent and neutral enforcer of EU law.

The EU's process of constitutional change is ongoing, and the EU has by no means arrived at a stable constitutional settlement.[74] Recent developments in

[68] The shift of the Commission from being seen as an independent technocratic regulatory body to a politicised executive was a process already well underway before the EP's latest moves to increase control over the selection of the Commission President. As I have discussed elsewhere, the increasing delegation of routine regulatory tasks to new EU agencies has facilitated this process, allowing the Commission to focus on more political functions. See RD Kelemen, 'European Union Agencies' in E Jones, A Menon and S Weatherill (eds), *The Oxford Handbook of the European Union* (Oxford, Oxford University Press, 2012).

[69] See Kelemen, (n 34).

[70] See n 60 and n 61 and accompanying text.

[71] M Matthijs and RD Kelemen, 'Europe Reborn' (2015) 94 *Foreign Affairs* 96.

[72] RD Kelemen, 'Saving the Euro, Dividing the Union' *Foreign Affairs* online, 21 January 2013, www.foreignaffairs.com/articles/138768/r-daniel-kelemen/saving-the-euro-dividing-the-union.

[73] Leuffen, Rittberger and Schimmelfennig *Differentiated Integration* (n 63).

[74] See A Moravcsik, 'The European Constitutional Compromise and the Neofunctionalist Legacy' (2005) *12 Journal of European Public Policy* 349, arguing that the EU had by the mid-2000s arrived at a stable constitutional equilibrium.

the EU's constitutional architecture have provided advocates of deepening and democratisation of the Union an object lesson in the old adage, 'Be careful what you wish for'. As many Europhiles had long hoped, the EU has become more deeply integrated in terms of substantive policies and its political institutions have become more democratic in some respects—particularly with the enhanced role of the Parliament in the selection of the Commission President. But these very achievements bring with them new risks such as the risk of greater fragmentation between Eurozone insiders and other Member States and the risk that politicisation of the Commission may undermine its existing base of legitimacy and may lead to destructive forms of partisanship.

12

Enhancing European Democracy in Times of Crisis?—The Proposal to Politicise the Election of the European Commission's President

CARLINO ANTPÖHLER*

I. INTRODUCTION

THE RECENT EUROPEAN Parliament (EP) elections of 2014 have been subject to a major institutional reform, the so-called *Spitzenkandidaten* process. The EP in particular innovatively made use of Article 17(7) of the Treaty on European Union (TEU), which makes the European Council 'tak[e] into account the elections to the European Parliament'. It succeeded in imposing a duty on the European Council to propose the leading candidate of the largest parliamentary group. This changes European democracy, arguably, more 'than anything proposed in the defunct Constitution'.[1] It is open to debate whether this is for the better or for worse. Over the past years, there has been intense institutional and scholarly debate on the merits of the reform proposal.[2] It is not the aim of this paper to simply reiterate the thoughtful discussions on the proposal. Instead, I will highlight two important aspects which have so far only marginally been touched upon in the debate: a European legal principle of democracy as a yardstick, and the developments during the crisis as a backdrop for the evaluation.

The debate has been conspicuously absent for a long time from legal scholarship.[3] This was all the more striking as it stood in stark contrast to lively

* For valuable comments and critique I am indebted to the participants of the Heidelberg Working Group on Public Law, Professor Dr Armin von Bogdandy in particular, and the participants of the workshop 'What Form of Government for the EU and the Eurozone?' in Tilburg, the Netherlands, June 2014.

[1] JHH Weiler, 'Editorial—European Parliament Elections 2014: Europe's Fateful Choices' (2013) 24 *European Journal of International Law* 747, 750.

[2] Most notably invigorated by S Hix, *What's Wrong With the European Union & How to Fix it* (Cambridge, Polity Press, 2008).

[3] Notable exceptions are P Craig, 'The Lisbon Treaty, Process Architecture and Substance' (2008) 33 *European Law Review* 137, 154; M Dougan, 'The Treaty of Lisbon 2007: Winning Minds, not Hearts' (2008) 45 *Common Market Law Review* 617, 693.

debates in other disciplines and within the European institutions. The discussion only caught the attention of legal academia shortly before it was implemented.[4] Analysing the reasons for the delay of the legal debate might offer a better understanding of the way the reform proposal might be addressed in legal terms. There has been a certain reluctance among legal scholars to address a reform which touches the very core of the political system, the election process. Judicial reasoning derives authority from perceived neutrality and thus a detachment from politics. The more political an issue becomes, the more restraint legal scholars are in their assessment. While there are obviously many contested issues of legal politics which are debated amongst legal scholars, the election process is a core political issue which prevents legal scholars from participating in the debate. This restraint should not simply be couched in terms of a virtue or a vice. Positively, it can be argued that legal scholarship does not offer the methods to assess the reform proposal thoroughly and that the legal minimalism, correctly, allows for ample room for the political process. This, however, ought not to come at the price of a complete isolation of legal scholarship from such an important societal debate. A vantage point is thus needed that simultaneously respects legal restraint yet offers normative guidance in assessing the reform. The principle of democracy enshrined in Articles 9 to 12 TEU provides such an approach. This yardstick derived from positive law rather than from democratic theory sufficiently distinguishes my legal approach from that of a political scientist or democratic theorist.[5] *Jürgen Habermas* has in recent years fervently criticised the move towards intergovernmentalism and post-democratic executive federalism.[6] This paper argues that a legal analysis can contribute to this debate by applying a judicial yardstick to the reforms. The insights of political theory can be incorporated into the interpretation of a principle of democratic legitimacy.

Secondly, I propose to take the developments in response to the financial crisis in the European legal sphere as the factual backdrop for the debate. This alleviates a weakness in recent debates on the proposal. Papers on democracy in the European crisis reiterate the demand for politicising the European Commission President without taking into account the changes the European Commission has already undergone, and their effects on the debate.[7] To proceed in this manner takes insufficient stock of the profound institutional changes that have occurred in response to the crisis. This is not to say that earlier debates are meaningless,

[4] See for a recent very elaborate judicial call for the reform, MP Maduro, B de Witte and M Kumm, 'The Euro Crisis and the Democratic Governance of the Euro' (2012) 8 *RSCAS Policy Paper* 4.

[5] A von Bogdandy, 'National Legal Scholarship in the European Legal Area—A Manifesto' (2012) 10 *International Journal of Constitutional Law* 626. A social science concept to address the reform might be the concept of politicisation, developed particularly by M Zürn (ed), *Die Politisierung der Weltpolitik* (Berlin, Suhrkamp, 2013).

[6] J Habermas, *Zur Verfassung Europas* (Berlin, Suhrkamp, 2011) 48; J Habermas, 'The Crisis of the European Union in the Light of a Constitutionalisation of International Law' (2012) 23 *European Journal of International Law* 335.

[7] See, eg I Pernice et al, 'A Democratic Solution to the Crisis—Reform Steps towards a Democratically Based Economic and Financial Constitution for Europe (Baden-Baden, Nomos, 2012)' 136.

but their arguments ought to be critically reflected once more. The role of the European Commission has transformed during the crisis: from an agenda-setter of new acts to depolitically overseeing the implementation of decisions by the European Council. This change has repercussions for the debate on the *Spitzenkandidaten* reform. Vice versa, the repercussions of the reform on crisis policy seem even more important. Will politicising the Commission President support changes to the Troika or diminish inter-governmentalism? This paper aims to go beyond previous debates insofar as it assesses the interplay between the crisis response and the *Spitzenkandidaten* process.

With this in mind, I argue that the politicisation of the European Commission President convincingly challenges depoliticised crisis management thereby contributing to strengthening the democratic credentials of decision-making in the EU.

I will start by developing the principle of European democracy and the way it might be applied in legal discourse more thoroughly (Section II). Next, I will assess how the *Spitzenkandidaten* process has evolved and what has led to a leading candidate eventually becoming President of the European Commission (Section III.A). Furthermore, I will highlight the shortcomings of assessing the reform on the basis of a legal/illegal dichotomy (Section III.B). The paper proceeds by introducing the backdrop of the response to the financial crisis. It is argued that the new European economic governance can be assessed through the paradigms of inter-governmentalism and de-politicisation (Section IV). Next, I will apply the standard of democratic legitimacy developed previously. I will arrive at the conclusion that the crisis response rests on weak democratic credentials (Section V). The *Spitzenkandidaten* reform, it is argued, alleviates these democratic shortcomings and strengthens the Community method (Section VI).

II. A LEGAL YARDSTICK TO ASSESS THE REFORM: THE PRINCIPLE OF DEMOCRACY

The Lisbon Treaty spells out a detailed principle of democracy in its Articles 9 to 12 TEU. Unfortunately, with the exception of Union citizenship and precise prerogatives of the EP these norms have not been applied by the Court of Justice of the European Union (CJEU).[8] In my view, Articles 9 to 12 TEU offer immense potential. This chapter examines the recent reform of transnational democracy through the *Spitzenkandidaten* process in light of the European judicial principle of democracy, preventing unwarranted analogies to nation states. As the state is still the most common form of political organisation, many scholars implicitly

[8] See, however, K Lenaerts, 'The Principle of Democracy in the Case Law of the European Court of Justice' (2013) 62 *International & Comparative Law Quarterly* 281 with further reference to jurisprudence. On the application in the field of Union citizenship and an innovative reform proposal, see A von Bogdandy et al, 'Reverse Solange—Protecting the Essence of Fundamental Rights against EU Member States' (2012) 49 *Common Market Law Review* 489.

or explicitly compare the EU with nation states,[9] which has been repeated in the debate on the *Spitzenkandidaten*.[10] The EU has arguably gone beyond the state/non-state dichotomy. This becomes particularly clear when examining the principle of democracy. One of the core concepts of European democracy is the concept of dual legitimacy enshrined in Article 10(2) TEU: the individual is represented in the European democratic process simultaneously as Union citizen and as a citizen of a Member State.[11] Representation is mediated via the EP or national governments. Debates as to whether the EU should become a state, and the threshold needed, fail to address the particular characteristics of European democracy that are likely to prevail for some time to come. Instead, it might be more useful to explore in detail the intermediate status between a nation state and a classical international organisation coordinating Member States' interests. By using the concept of democracy contained in the Treaties we avoid implicit nation state analogies. European democracy has evolved considerably differently from democracies known in Member States. This is not to say that Member States' democratic practices cannot offer important inspiration for the development of European democracy. By highlighting the distinction, however, we ensure that the differences of democracy on the different levels come to the fore more explicitly.

In legal discourses, the European principle of democracy can be applied in three different ways. The stronger the conflict with the principle of democracy, the harsher the legal consequences for the act in question. First, a European legal act is void if it violates the core of the principle. The *Spitzenkandidaten* reform does not reach this high threshold. More interesting is the second category: I argue that there is an interpretation rule that *in dubio* a reading should be applied that strengthens European democracy. The third category has the smallest consequences but has the benefit of offering a yardstick for most developments within the EU. Here, I argue that the European principle of democracy contains a standard of democratic legitimacy. An encroachment on this part of the principle might not lead to an assessment on the legality of an act, but still offers an important way to assess the legitimacy of it. For example, in a reform debate the approach might be identified that is most beneficial for European democracy. This paper will conduct such an analysis for the *Spitzenkandidaten* process in light of legal developments during the financial crisis.

[9] For the limits of such comparison, see C Schönberger, 'Die Europäische Union als Bund—Zugleich ein Beitrag zur Verabschiedung des Staatenbund-Bundesstaat-Schemas' (2004) 129 *Archiv des öffentlichen Rechts* 83.

[10] See, eg the contribution by Kocharov, ch 13 in this volume.

[11] J von Achenbach, 'Vorschläge zu einer Demokratietheorie der dualen Demokratischen Legitimation Europäischer Hoheitsgewalt' (2012) 127 *Archiv für Rechts und Sozialphilosophie* 212; A von Bogdandy, 'Founding Principles' in A von Bogdandy and J Bast (eds), *Principles of European Constitutional Law*, 2nd edn (Oxford, Hart Publishing, 2009) 49; J Habermas, 'Zur Prinzipienkonkurrenz von Bürgergleichheit und Staatengleichheit im supranationalen Gemeinwesen—Eine Notiz aus Anlass der Frage nach der Legitimität der ungleichen Repräsentation der Bürger im Europäischen Parlament' (2014) 53 *Der Staat* 167, 181.

III. WHAT HAS HAPPENED SO FAR—THE SUCCESS IN PRACTICE AND THE INSUFFICIENCY OF LEGAL ASSESSMENT

A. The Success of the *Spitzenkandidaten* Model in Practice

On 15 July 2014, the EP elected Jean-Claude Juncker, who had earlier been proposed by the European Council, as European Commission President.[12] Prior to the election there had been intense inter-institutional disagreement on how the European Commission President ought to be chosen. Article 17(7) TEU states that the European Council proposes its candidate for the post 'taking into account the elections to the European Parliament'. The provision is the result of a compromise in the negotiations on the Constitutional Treaty: While the EP claimed the right to elect the President itself, the Member States were unwilling to render their roles meaningless.[13] As the 2014 EP election was the first conducted under the Treaty of Lisbon, the precise potential of the provision had remained unclear. Its 'realisation [depended] ultimately upon political action'.[14] The European Commission as well as the EP made use of the provision's potential.[15] After the Lisbon Treaty entered into force, the EP in particular, set into motion a process which eventually led to the successful *Spitzenkandidat* being proposed by the European Council for President of the European Commission. The EP as well as the European Commission issued recommendations, calling for the full exploitation of the provision by 'linking the votes of EU citizens and the election of the President of the European Commission'.[16] Six European parties followed suit and nominated candidates for the President of the European Commission.[17] Before the election, the three largest groups within the EP had already agreed that the candidate for the post ought to be chosen among the parties' candidates for the post.[18] The candidate from the largest group was supposed to have the chance to form the required majority. Eventually the procedure took a slightly different turn. As the European Council failed to agree on a candidate a few days after the elections, the EP was concerned to lose momentum in the appointment procedure. Accordingly, the agreement upon a common candidate within the EP took place prior to the

[12] European Parliament, Press Release, 15 July 2014, 'Parliament elects Jean-Claude Juncker as Commission President'; European Council, Conclusions of meetings 26/27 June 2014, EUCO 79/14.

[13] Craig, 'The Lisbon Treaty' (n 3) 154.

[14] Dougan, 'The Treaty of Lisbon 2007' (n 3) 693.

[15] European Commission Recommendation of 12 March 2013 on enhancing the democratic and efficient conduct of the election to the European Parliament, (2013) 1303; European Parliament Resolution of 13 March 2014 on the implementation of the Treaty of Lisbon with respect to the European Parliament, 2013/2130(INI).

[16] European Commission Communication of 12 March 2014 on preparing for the 2014 elections: further enhancing their democratic and efficient conduct, COM (2013) 126, 5.

[17] European Commission Report of 27 March 2014 towards more democratic EP elections, COM (2014) 196, 5. Two parties declined to nominate a candidate.

[18] Joint Declaration by the EPP, S&D and ALDE Groups on the election of the President of the European Commission, available at: www.eppgroup.eu/press-release/EPP,-S%26D,-ALDE-Groups-on-election-of-EU-Commission-President.

candidate actually forming the required majority. The negotiations were left to the phase after the European Council had made its proposal. Eventually, Jean-Claude Juncker was proposed and elected by a broad majority.

In general, the EP and the European Commission thus succeeded in making the EP election an election for the President of the European Commission. The European Council, however, has been adamant on its right for future elections to refrain from proposing one of the *Spitzenkandidaten*.[19] It seems more likely though that the 2014 elections have enduringly changed the way the President of the European Commission is elected.

B. The Insufficiency of the Legal/Illegal Dichotomy

In the ongoing judicial debate on the merits of the *Spitzenkandidaten* process, some commentators have made arguments based on the phrase 'taking into account the election to the EP' in Article 17(7) TEU. It has been argued that the pressure of the EP on the European Council to accept the *Spitzenkandidat* violates the 'letter and spirit of the Treaty'.[20] Conversely, it has been argued that there is a legal duty of the European Council to propose a *Spitzenkandidat* if certain conditions are met.[21] While these views mark opposite ends of the understanding of European democracy, they share an extensive reading of law. This runs contrary to the wording of Article 17(7) TEU and the role law ought to play in structuring the debate. Article 17(7) provides for the European Council and the EP to elect the European Commission's President on an equal footing. It gives neither institution the power to elect a person without the support of the other.[22] The provision spells out the principle of dual legitimacy in more detail for the election of the European Commission's President. For any act to be legitimate, including the election of officials, both democratic strands ought to be represented. The provision, however, does not go beyond formally assigning the roles in the election process: There is no duty for the institutions to behave in a certain manner.[23] Rather, the provision offers a framework for the political process to function. It is for the European democratic process and the inter-institutional discourse to determine how the elections are actually to be taken into account. The EP and the European

[19] European Council, Conclusions of meetings 26 and 27 June 2014, EUCO 79/14, 27.

[20] See the contribution by Kocharov, ch 13 in this volume; M Rossi, 'Politisierung durch Personalisierung—Demokratisierung der Union oder Ignorieren des Rechts?' (2014) 25 *Europäische Zeitschrift für Wirtschaftsrecht* 282.

[21] M Kumm, 'Why the Council is Under a Legal Duty to Propose Juncker as a Commission President' *Verfassungsblog*, (6 June 2014) available at: www.verfassungsblog.de/en/der-europaeische-rat-ist-verpflichtet-juncker-vorzuschlagen/.

[22] Similarly, Weiler, 'European Parliament Elections 2014' (n 1) 750; K Armstrong, 'Why Kumm is Wrong and There is Not in Law a Duty to Appoint Juncker' *Verfassungsblog* (13 June 2014) available at: www.verfassungsblog.de/en/kumm-wrong-law-duty-appoint-juncker/.

[23] There is a duty on both institutions to consult laid down in Declaration 11 of the Treaty on European Union. This obligation, however, does not impose an obligation to accept a certain result.

Commission have made very effective use of the provision's potential through the *Spitzenkandidaten* process, but did so within the scope of that provision. It would also have been legal for the European Council to propose someone different than a *Spitzenkandidat*. This view is also the only one compatible with the historic compromise: the EP wanted to gain the sole right to elect the President, while the European Council was very reluctant to grant that right. In my view it is hence more convincing to refrain from an extensive reading of the law and leave the process leading up to the election of the President for the political process to decide. Usually, legal analyses of the reform either end at this point, or switch to assessing the merits of the reform politically. Articles 9 to 12 TEU and the principle of democracy also offer a different route, however.

IV. THE TURN TO INTER-GOVERNMENTALISM AND THE DE-POLITICISATION DURING THE CRISIS

In the next sections, it is argued that a European principle of democracy favours politicising the European Commission. The European response to the crisis can largely be understood through two paradigms: the turn to inter-governmentalism and the involvement of EU institutions in depoliticised decision-making procedures. Both developments, I will argue, fall short of justification in light of a legal European principle of democratic legitimacy contained in the Treaties. Mitigating the effects of the turn to inter-governmentalism and de-politicisation will thus enhance democratic legitimacy. As politicising the European Commission contributes to an increased political supranationalism, the proposal will be assessed positively.

A turn to inter-governmentalism has been one of the striking features of the European response to the crisis.[24] As early as in 2010 Angela Merkel announced the advent of a new Union method.[25] Pivotal new regimes were, subsequently, decided outside the scope of EU law, the Treaty establishing the European Stability Mechanism (TESM)[26] and the so-called Fiscal Compact (TSCG) in particular. The ESM offers financial assistance to its members subject to strict conditionality if that is indispensable for the stability of the euro area as a whole.[27] Due to a perceived lack of competence,[28] the TESM was established inter-governmentally.

[24] For an account of inter-governmentalism, see AJ Menéndez, 'Editorial: A European Union in Constitutional Mutation?' (2014) 20 *European Law Journal* 127; E Chiti and PG Teixeira, 'The Constitutional Implications of the European Responses to the Financial and Public Debt Crisis' (2013) 50 *Common Market Law Review* 683.

[25] A Merkel, Speech at the opening ceremony of the 61st academic year of the College of Europe in Bruges, 2 November 2014 available at: www.bruessel.diplo.de/contentblob/2959854/Daten/.

[26] The development here focuses on the TESM for reasons of simplification. The argument could similarly be made for the earlier temporary intergovernmental regimes which made use of the Troika, the Greek Loan Facility and the European Financial Stability Facility in particular.

[27] Art 3 TESM.

[28] ECJ Case C-370/12 *Pringle v Government of Ireland, Ireland and The Attorney General*, judgment of 27 November 2012, not yet reported, 66.

The Fiscal Compact is aimed at strengthening, in particular, the budgetary discipline of Member States whose currency is the euro.[29] The TSCG was also decided inter-governmentally due to the resistance to an amendment of the Treaties by a few Member States. The EP, as well as the European Commission, only played a marginal role in establishing both new treaties.[30] Less publicly visible but similarly striking, is the involvement of the European Council in those acts which came into being through the Community method, especially the six- and two-pack.[31] The six-pack focuses on the prevention of future crises by strengthening the deficit criteria and supranational surveillance, inter alia by the codification of the European Semester, as well as introducing a new procedure against macro-economic imbalances. The drafting of the six-pack within the European Commission was overseen in detail by a working-group of the European Council.[32] The two-pack partially aligns the financial assistance regime with Union law. It came into being long after the assistance regime was set up inter-governmentally and changed it merely marginally. The European response to the crisis was thus to a great extent a product of the inter-governmental paradigm.

A second paradigm is relevant when assessing, in particular, the role of the European Commission in responding to the crisis. The de-politicisation paradigm marks the transformation of the European Commission's main focus from an agenda-setter of new acts to overseeing implementation by Member States of policies that were decided by the European Council. The European Commission is involved in de-politicised as well as politicised decision-making processes. A politicised decision-making process is characterised by contestation, which is publicly visible.[33] Public contestation is absent in regimes that respond to the crisis by granting the European Commission new implementing powers. The most important illustration of the trend towards de-politicisation is the unparalleled authority of the Troika over large parts of domestic policy, which so far were deemed cornerstones of national sovereignty. The Memoranda of Understanding

[29] Art 1(1) TSCG.

[30] For the parliamentary involvement, see C Fasone, 'European Economic Governance and Parliamentary Representation. What Place for the European Parliament?' (2014) 20 *European Law Journal* 164.

[31] On the six-pack and two-pack, see C Antpöhler, 'Emergenz europäischer Wirtschaftsregierung—Das Six Pack als Zeichen supranationaler Leistungsfähigkeit' (2012) 72 *Zeitschrift für ausländisches öffentliches Recht und Völkerrecht* 353; M Ioannidis, 'EU Financial Assistance after Two Pack' (2014) 74 *Zeitschrift für ausländisches öffentliches Recht und Völkerrecht* 1.

[32] On the predominance of the European Council, see U Puetter, *The European Council and the Council: New Intergovernmentalism and Institutional Change* (Oxford, Oxford University Press, 2014); M Chang, 'Constructing the Commission's Six Pack Proposals—Political Leadership Thwarted?' in M Chang and J Monar (eds), *The European Commission in the Post-Lisbon Era of Crises* (Brussels, Peter Lang, 2013) 168.

[33] This definition draws partially on P de Wilde, 'No Polity for Old Politics? A Framework for Analysing Politicisation of European Integration' (2011) 33 *Journal of European Integration* 566; P de Wilde and M Zürn, 'Can the Politicisation of European Integration be Reversed' (2012) 50 *Journal of Common Market Studies* 137.

(MoU) have severe redistributive impacts,[34] for example, in the field of social, labour and health policy.[35] The decision-making process within the Troika is depoliticised. The two other institutions in the Troika, the European Central Bank (ECB) and the International Monetary Fund (IMF) act with a technocratic mindset. The collaboration with these institutions within the Troika shapes the characteristics of the European Commission's decision-making. Furthermore, the positions taken by the Troika are inseparable as the decision-making processes are entirely removed from the public. The involvement of the Board of Governors and the Council fails to alter the depoliticised nature of the process, as no meaningful early public involvement of these bodies takes place.[36] Neither is it convincing to construe the conditions attached to financial assistance as autonomous political sovereign acts of the Member State in need of financial assistance. It would, however, also be flawed to describe conditionality as a process where lenders unilaterally impose policies upon recipient states.[37] The precise distinction between coercion and autonomy is not relevant for our purposes, however. It is sufficient to conclude that the transnational institutions have perceivable authority in pivotal fields of national policies.[38] Thus, there decision-making takes place on the transnational level, which is executed depolitically.

The six-pack as well as the Fiscal Compact adds another layer to the phenomenon of de-politicised decision-making.[39] Impacts on national economic policy are a lot less profound than in the case of the Troika. So far, only a minor part of the recommendations issued within the Macroeconomic Imbalance Procedure (MIP) were enforced within Member States.[40] Furthermore, the sanctions regime of neither the six-pack nor the Fiscal Compact has so far been applied. The redistributive potential of the regimes, however, is immense. The material scope and the countries which the procedure applies to are only marginally contained.[41]

[34] For the criterion 'redistributive', see D Chalmers, 'The European Redistributive State and a European Law of Struggle' (2012) 18 *European Law Journal* 667; G Majone, 'Europe's "Democratic Deficit": The Question of Standards' (1998) 4 *European Law Journal* 28.

[35] For a number of consequences of the MoU, see A Fischer-Lescano, 'Human Rights in Times of Austerity Policy' Legal Opinion commissioned by the Chamber of Labour, Vienna, 21 ff.

[36] Art 13(3) TESM; Art 7 Regulation 472/2013.

[37] The EU has in its crisis response been adamant to highlight ownership of the country receiving financial assistance. The concept, however, falls short of assessing realistically the negotiations leading to the MoU. See MoU—Greece, available in the European Commission Occasional Papers on European Economy 94 (2012): 'the ownership of the programme and all executive responsibilities in the programme implementation remain with the Greek Government'. Furthermore, Michael Ioannidis points out that the language of all legal acts is phrased with utmost carefulness to avoid the impression of coercion (Ioannidis 'EU Financial Assistance after Two Pack' (n 31) 32).

[38] Similarly K Tuori and K Tuori, *The Eurozone Crisis* (Cambridge, Cambridge University Press, 2014) 210 f; Ioannidis (n 31) 35.

[39] On a detailed analysis of both regimes, see Antpöhler, 'Emergenz europäischer Wirtschaftsregierung' (n 31).

[40] European Parliament, Directorate General for Internal Policies, Background Note, Country Specific Recommendations 2012 and 2013: comparison and overview of implementation.

[41] The procedures apply to all euro area Member States, not only countries in financial difficulties, and partially beyond the euro area. Additionally, recommendations in the deficit procedure as well as the MIP can impact all fields of domestic social and economic policy.

Furthermore, policy requests can be enforced through sanctions, although a lengthy prior procedure is needed. To enhance the effectiveness of these procedures, a reverse qualified majority was introduced.[42] Member States of the Eurozone commit to follow the proposals of the European Commission unless a qualified majority opposes the step. The aim of the reform is the automatic sanctioning of deficits and excessive imbalances. The impact of political considerations in the Council is reduced. The decision-making process is thus less politicised. This is even more the case with the new MIP. The European Commission bases its analysis of Member States' economic policy on a set of technical indicators contained in a so-called scoreboard, drawn up by the European Commission itself.[43] Highly contested questions on the core of Member States' economic policy, such as the minimum wage or the retirement age, are thus addressed through depoliticised indicators. In conclusion, the six-pack and the Fiscal Compact add significantly to the process of de-politicisation through changes in decision-making and substantive criteria. Although not as harsh as the conditions attached to financial assistance, these processes complete the picture by extending the de-politicisation developments to decisive parts of all Member States' policy. The new oversight of national economic policy is thus comprehensively determined by the de-politicisation paradigm.

V. WHY RECENT DEVELOPMENTS ARE A PROBLEM FOR THE PRINCIPLE OF DEMOCRATIC LEGITIMACY

How can we assess the trends towards inter-governmentalism and de-politicisation in light of the principle of democratic legitimacy? A prerequisite for responding to the question is the applicability of Union law and the principle of democracy accordingly, which will be addressed first. Next, I will argue that supranational political decision-making would rest on stronger democratic legitimacy than the current regime.

It might be questioned whether the principle of democratic legitimacy contained in the Treaties is relevant to the assessment of the developments described, as most responses to the crisis were taken outside the scope of EU law. The ESM and the Fiscal Compact were established on the basis of international law. Beyond doubt is the applicability of the democratic principle of Articles 9 to 12 TEU for those acts which are part of the EU legal order: the six-and the two-pack. The principle is also applicable, albeit weaker' outside the scope of Union law. Article 2 TEU provides for the respect of, inter alia, democracy. Respect for the values enshrined in Article 2 is the precondition for a Member State to accede to the Union according to Article 49 TEU. Furthermore, Article 7 TEU shows that Member States actions

[42] Art 7 TSCG; Art 4(2), Art 5(2), Art 6(2) Regulation 1173/2011; Art 3(3) Regulation 1174/2011. On this point, see Antpöhler (n 31) 365; R Palmstorfer, 'The Reverse Majority Voting under the "Six Pack": A Bad Turn for the Union?' (2014) 20 *European Law Journal* 186.

[43] Arts 3 and 4 Regulation 1176/2011/EU.

can also be assessed in light of Article 2 TEU. It is undisputed that the provision applies to all public authority exercised within Europe.[44] There is no limitation in Article 2 TEU as is contained in Article 51(1) Charter of Fundamental Rights of the European Union (CFREU). A Member State needs to respect the democratic principle irrespective of whether Union law applies. Domestic law can, hence, be assessed by the yardstick of Article 2 TEU. This applies equally to international treaties of the Member States. If international law was not covered, Member States could escape their responsibility for Article 2 TEU by including a provision in an international treaty. In principle, the TESM and the Fiscal Compact can thus be assessed by the yardstick of Article 2 TEU. The standard of Article 2 TEU, however, is less strict than the fully-fledged principle contained in Articles 9 to 12 TEU. Within the scope of EU law, every act needs to comply fully with the democratic standard enshrined in Articles 9 to 12 TEU. As Article 2 TEU is the condition for membership in the Union, it can only encompass a core of the democratic principle. Furthermore, not every provision of international law can be assessed by the yardstick. Different criteria ought to be used to assess whether a particular regime must comply with the reduced principle of democratic legitimacy contained in Article 2 TEU. First, an application of the principle is only convincing if the regime is essential for the lives of concerned individuals. This is a standard commonly found in European law.[45] For the application of Article 2 TEU the actions within a regime need to significantly affect fundamental rights of individuals. Secondly, a European principle of democracy can only apply if there is sufficient connection with the EU legal sphere. Most significant in this regard is the overlap of membership between the EU on the one hand, and the regime under scrutiny on the other hand. If a significant number of state parties to an international treaty are Member States of the EU, Article 2 TEU ought to apply. This is, for example, the case for the Council of Europe.[46] If these conditions are met, the standard of democratic legitimacy contained in Article 2 TEU is applicable and the establishment and functioning of the international regime can be assessed on the basis of the European principle of democracy. Beyond including only essential provision with a sufficient link to the EU the yardstick applied in Article 2 TEU cases remains less

[44] F Schorkopf, *Homogenität in der Europäischen Union—Ausgestaltung und Gewährleistung durch Art. 6 Abs. 1 und Art 7 EUV* (Berlin, Duncker & Humblot, 2000) 69 f, 99 ff; A Verhoeven, 'How Democratic Need European Union Members Be?' (1998) 23 *European Law Review* 217, 222 ff, 234; Declaration of the Presidency of the Convention, 6 February 2003, CONV 528/03, 11; European Commission, Communication to the Council and the European Parliament of 15 October 2003 on Article 7 of the Treaty on European Union: Respect for and Promotion of Values on which the Union is based, COM (2003) 606, 5.

[45] Art 290(1) TFEU. In the context of Art 2 TEU in contrast to Art 290 TFEU, however, it is more convincing to give the essential-condition an individualistic reading as the democracy principle aims at protecting the individual (for the interpretation prior to Art 290 TEU, see ECJ, Case C-240/90 *Germany v Commission* [1992] I-05383, 37). This is similar to the standard contained in Art 52(1) CFREU.

[46] For an application of the principle in the realm of the Council of Europe, see A von Bogdandy and C Krenn, 'How to Select Europe's Judges: A Principled and Comparative Reconstruction' in M Bobek (ed), *Selecting Europe's Judges. A Critical Review of the Appointment Procedures to the European Courts* (Oxford, Oxford University Press, forthcoming).

strict than the fully-fledged principle of democracy of Articles 9 to 12 TEU. First, not all elements of the democratic principle apply outside the scope of Union law. The provisions on citizenship, for example, are limited to the scope of Union law. Furthermore, the elements of the democratic principle applying outside the scope of Union law comprise a less detailed standard. The transparency rule contained in Article 10(3) TEU, for example, was spelt out in great detail for the public access to documents of EU institutions.[47] As the transparency rule is an important part of the democratic principle, it is also contained in the standard of Article 2 TEU. One could argue that the access to documents is already enshrined in Article 10 TEU and is only laid down in the respective regulation. Accordingly, access to documents via Article 2 TEU would apply outside the scope of Union law. This would, however, neglect the limited standard of Article 2 TEU. Only the core of the transparency rule applies outside the scope of Union law. If we apply these criteria to the acts in question, the TESM and the Fiscal Compact come within the ambit of Article 2 TEU. The conditions attached to financial assistance within the TESM have intense redistributive effects. They affect all aspects of Member States' policy thoroughly and thus impact the lives of the concerned individuals and their affected fundamental rights significantly.[48] This has been less the case for the Fiscal Compact so far. However, it too has significant redistributive potential, as the recommendation issued within the enforced deficit procedure affects all areas of Member States' policy. Furthermore, both regimes are established exclusively by Member States of the EU, and a significant majority of Member States have joined both regimes.[49] Article 2 TEU can thus be used to pass judgement on the democratic legitimacy of the European Stability Mechanism and the Fiscal Compact.

Dual legitimacy via the EP and the representative bodies of Member States is a core principle of European democracy. It might, however, be objected that the dual legitimacy standard contained in Article 10 TEU is meaningless as it has not been fulfilled within EU law. There are numerous exceptions to parliamentary co-decision in special legislative proceedings within the Treaties. The standard is not rendered meaningless, however. Instead, I propose to give it a reading as a constitutional manifesto.[50] It defines an ideal state of democracy, which European practice seeks to conform to gradually through future reforms of the Treaties. Articles 9 to 12 TEU hence contain an enforceable standard of dual legitimacy. Can that standard be applied outside the scope of Union law? Dual legitimacy is

[47] Regulation 1049/2001 regarding public access to European Parliament, Council and Commission documents.

[48] D Schraad-Tischler and C Kroll, 'Social Justice in the EU—A Cross-National Comparison' (2014) *Social Inclusion Monitor Europe (SIM)—Index Report.*

[49] The ESM is comprised of the 19 euro area Member States; the Fiscal Compact was ratified by 25 countries initially. The Czech Republic is in the process of ratification.

[50] On the concept of constitutional manifesto, see A von Bogdandy, 'The European Lessons for International Democracy' (2012) 23 *European Journal of International Law* 333; J Bast, 'The Constitutional Treaty as a Reflexive Constitution' (2005) 6 *German Law Journal* 1451; G Frankenberg, 'The Return of the Contract: Problems and Pitfalls of European Constitutionalism' (2000) 6 *European Law Journal* 261.

at the very core of European parliamentary democracy. It would be odd to apply the democratic standard of Article 2 TEU outside the scope of EU law but leave dual legitimacy aside. Furthermore, arguments from political theory support the argument for application outside the scope of Union law. The EP is the only institution directly accountable to EU citizens. It can therefore provide for a stronger link between its decision-making and public discourse in Member States.[51] Furthermore, only the EP can provide for a pluralist representation at the supranational level.[52] Within the Council, Member States are represented only by their governments. While the Council and European Council can provide democratic legitimacy, their democratic capacity needs to be supplemented by parliamentary involvement.[53] It is thus desirable to understand the principle of European representative democracy in ways that support dual legitimacy. This militates for an application outside the scope of Union law. Remaining doubts can be cast aside by limiting the consequences of a breach of the principle of dual legitimacy. At present, it would go beyond Article 2 TEU to rule the international law responses to the crisis unlawful because of the absence of meaningful involvement of the European Commission and the EP. Instead, Article 2 TEU can be used outside the scope of Union law only to assess the democratic legitimacy of a particular measure.

An act with the involvement of both, the EP and the Council, is thus democratically more legitimate than acts without such involvement and the Community method therefore enjoys more democratic legitimacy than the Union method. The turn to inter-governmentalism hence undermines democratic legitimacy, but does not lead as such to the acts being unlawful.

It might be objected that lack of Union competence meant that there was no possibility to proceed based on dual legitimacy. It is beyond this paper to assess comprehensively whether the TESM and the Fiscal Compact exceed the Union's competences.[54] However, even if that was the case, the EP could have been involved in the negotiations on the acts outside the Union context. Both regimes entail the involvement of Union institutions outside the EU context: The Troika consists of the European Commission and the ECB. The European Commission is involved in the Fiscal Compact by proposing common principles for the correction mechanism in case of deviations from the balanced budget rule.[55]

[51] On the importance of the link of the public with legislative proceedings, see J Habermas, *Faktizität und Geltung* (Frankfurt, Suhrkamp, 1992) 188.

[52] On the importance of a pluralistic representation on the international level, see I Ley, 'Opposition institutionalisieren—Alternativität und Reversibilität als Elemente eines völkerrechtlichen Legitimationskonzepts' (2014) 53 *Der Staat* 241.

[53] For a strong theoretical reconstruction of the importance of parliamentary involvement, see J von Achenbach, *Demokratische Gesetzgebung in der Europäischen Union* (Heidelberg, Springer, 2014) 424. The German Federal Constitutional Court unconvincingly approaches democratic representation by the EP more cautiously, FCC, Case Lisbon-Treaty, (2010) 123 *Entscheidungen des Bundesverfassungsgerichts* 267, para 262, 271.

[54] See on this point Antpöhler (n 31) 391.

[55] Art 3(2) TSCG. The European Court of Justice is equally involved (Art 8 TSCG). The case differs, however, as Art 273 TFEU explicitly allows for the Court to have jurisdiction outside the scope of Union law.

If the political will had been existent, it would thus have been possible to involve the EP in a similar manner.

So far, we have come to the conclusion that the intergovernmental establishment of the acts provides them with weak democratic credentials. The principle of democratic legitimacy, furthermore, enables us to assess not only the initial establishment of the TESM and the Fiscal Compact but also the functioning within the new regimes. As was argued above, the functioning within the regimes is determined by the de-politicisation paradigm. This is also at odds with the principle of democratic legitimacy. It is appropriate to read the principle of representative democracy contained in Article 10(1) TEU in light of the separation of powers. Accordingly, the legislature ought at least to have the power to decide on matters that impact significantly upon the fundamental rights of individuals.[56] Pivotal decisions can, therefore, not be delegated to the executive.[57] In the six-pack, the European Commission was given a wide array of powers with potential redistributive effects. It can issue recommendations on all fields of domestic policy, which, after a lengthy procedure, can be enforced with sanctions. The Council can block these only with a qualified majority. Furthermore, the European Commission draws up the criteria for its interference in national policy independently. It would be more democratically legitimate if the legislative adopted at least a framework for the conditions of the interference and the sanctioning powers. This standard prima facie seems to be met in the European Stability Mechanism. The Board of Governors ultimately decides on the MoU according to Article 13(4) TESM. However, decisions of the Board of Governors ultimately appear to be a formality. The entire procedure evokes the pretence that indeed the Troika was responsible for the conditions attached to financial assistance. The Troika negotiates the MoU and the European Commission ultimately signs it.[58] A more transparent separation is needed and pivotal decisions ought to be taken by a legislative body within the European Stability Mechanism for it to be democratically legitimate.

VI. HOW POLITICISING THE EUROPEAN COMMISSION WILL MITIGATE THE EFFECTS OF THE INTER-GOVERNMANTALISM AND DE-POLITICISATION

How are the democratic shortcomings of the crisis response related to the election process of the European Commission? In the past, the European Commission has not been able to counter the turn to inter-governmentalism effectively. Instead, it has tacitly accepted the predominance of the European Council. The European Council even intervened substantially in the European Commission's pivotal prerogative, the agenda-setting for supranational acts. Simultaneously, the European

[56] C Möllers, *The Three Branches* (Oxford, Oxford University Press, 2013) 118.

[57] This is different from the question which is dealt with in Art 291 TFEU. The acts in question concern the enforcement of acts vis-à-vis the Member States. Accordingly, the powers of the European Commission in the six-pack are not designated as implementing powers.

[58] Art 13(3) and (4) TESM.

Commission has been actively engaged in the process of de-politicisation. De-political decision-making in central fields rests on the perceived neutrality of the European Commission. Both trends have been characterised as a threat to democratic legitimacy. The turn towards inter-governmental and de-political decision-making is the central challenge for the development of supranational democracy in the coming years.[59] A European Commission with increased democratic credentials could challenge the European Council's predominance more effectively. One of the central insights of democratic discourse theory is the strong link between the public at large and democratic procedures.[60] Administrative power results from public discourse and ought to be so limited. The European Council could only be so dominant, due to the weak presence of the European Commission in the public sphere. The *Spitzenkandidaten* process has increased the public visibility of the European Commission's President. By relying on public support, the European Commission will be able to resist the turn to inter-governmentalism more effectively.[61] It is for the social sciences to point out retrospectively how the shift back to the European Commission evolved precisely. For this paper it is sufficient to observe that the *Spitzenkandidaten* process contributes to strengthening the Community method.[62] This is not to say that the *Spitzenkandidaten* process is the cure for all the problems of remodelled European economic governance. However, it might contribute to re-establishing the equilibrium of the Union and the Community methods. The exact effects of this shift are difficult to predict. The European crisis' response and its recent developments offer some indications. A possible route towards strengthening supranational decision-making is offered by Article 16 TSCG, which allows for the incorporation of the Fiscal Compact into Union law. For the European Stability Mechanism, the discussion on a European Monetary Fund might offer an opportunity to invigorate parliamentary involvement.[63] These reform options might also alleviate de-politicisation, the second weakness in light of the principle of democracy. It has often been pointed out as a weakness of the *Spitzenkandidaten* reform that the European Commission might not be able to fulfil its role as neutral watchdog anymore.[64] While this is certainly a danger in certain areas, for example, in infringement proceedings, it might be beneficial to the democratic legitimacy of the responses to the crisis. The

[59] MP Maduro, 'A New Governance for the European Union and the Euro: Democracy and Justice' (2012) 11 *RSCAS Policy Paper* 5.

[60] Habermas (n 51) 188.

[61] The *Spitzenkandidat* has been most visible in only a number of states, among them Germany. It might be questioned that he will raise visibility beyond these few states. As Germany in particular, has been at least one of the dominant forces of the current crisis response, even a shift in the German public debate might challenge the turn to inter-governmentalism.

[62] Coming to a similar conclusion, MP Maduro, 'Democracy and Justice' (2012) 11 *RSCAS Policy Paper* 18.

[63] Reuters, 'Brussels considers scrapping troika supervising Greece' *The Guardian* (London, 5 August 2014); M Schwarz, 'A Memorandum of Misunderstanding—The Doomed Road of the European Stability Mechanism and a Possible Way Out: Enhanced Cooperation' (2014) 51 *Common Market Law Review* 389.

[64] Maduro, 'Democracy and Justice' (n 62) 19.

European Commission already decides on highly contingent political questions of a redistributive nature. It is conducive for the European political debate if these decisions are seen to be political again. Within the reform debate, it might even lead to the political decision being taken by the legislature, which is superior from the perspective of representative democracy.

The *Spitzenkandidaten* reform contributes to alleviating the effects of inter-governmentalism and de-politicisation, currently the two most imminent challenges to European democracy. The European principle of democracy, therefore, suggests that the European Commission President should be directly linked to outcomes of EP elections.

VII. CONCLUSION

This chapter has assessed the efforts to politicise the election of the European Commission's President in light of a principle of European democratic legitimacy. The principle allows for a judicial analysis of the reform. Although resting firmly in the legal sphere, it is open to interdisciplinary insights. In this paper I argued that the proposal is well suited to oppose the inter-governmental and de-politicised crisis response and thereby contribute to the re-establishment of the equilibrium of Community and Union modes of decision-making in the EU. The response of the EU to the financial crisis has been characterised by the paradigms of inter-governmentalism and de-politicisation. All major decisions were taken within the European Council without meaningful involvement of the EP and the European Commission. Within the new regimes, the European Commission was given extensive powers, which are executed in a de-politicised manner. In light of democratic theory, the European principle of democracy ought to be interpreted in a manner that supports dual legitimacy as a core principle of European representative democracy. This applies via Article 2 TEU outside the scope of Union law. Accordingly, the European Stability Mechanism and the Fiscal Compact come within the ambit of the European principle of democracy. Establishing pivotal acts inter-governmentally falls short of the need for dual legitimacy. Deciding on redistributive matters depolitically, particularly within the Troika, conflicts with representative democracy. The crisis response rests, therefore, on weak democratic credentials. Politicising the election of the President of the European Commission will alleviate these shortcomings. A European Commission with increased democratic credentials and stronger standing in public could challenge the European Council's predominance more effectively. Furthermore, the rise of de-politicised decision-making processes with the involvement of the Commission might be stopped. Responding to the threats of inter-governmentalism and de-politicisation are currently major challenges for European democracy. Politicising the election of the President of the European Commission contributes to mitigating these detrimental effects for European democracy, which is an important step in ongoing efforts to develop transnational democracy.

13

In the Image of State: Constitutional Complexities of Engineering a European Democracy

ANNA KOCHAROV

Se non ci siamo anche noi, quelli ti combinano la repubblica.
Se vogliamo che tutto rimanga come è, bisogna che tutto cambi.
Mi sono spiegato?

Giuseppe Tomasi di Lampedusa, Il Gattopardo

I. INTRODUCTION

IN THE COURSE of the 2014 elections to the European Parliament (EP), the main European political parties nominated their candidates for president of the European Commission (the so-called *Spitzenkandidaten*) and the candidate of the party that won most seats in the EP was appointed as President of the Commission despite a contrary vote by two Member States. Two claims are made in this regard. First, that giving direct voice to citizens on Union level would increase democratic legitimacy of the Union; secondly, that the *Spitzenkandidaten* arrangement respects the Treaties.

This contribution will analyse both claims. It is argued that under the current Treaties, legitimacy of the Union and its policies cannot be separated from the national political processes. By twisting the letter and spirit of the Treaties, linking the presidency of the Commission to EP elections constitutes a further step towards engineering a democratic process in Europe. This strikes against the constitutional construct for Europe established in the Treaties, which leaves decisive policy-making power with national governments acting in the European Union. Accountability needs to follow the *locus* of power. To the extent that European democracy sidelines and bypasses accountability on the national level, legitimacy of both the Union and national governments is undermined.

The argument is presented in four parts. First, the background of the *Spitzenkandidaten* arrangement is examined. Even before its invention, the Commission was accountable to the EP, and the Parliament exercised this power. Secondly, the text of Union Treaties is scrutinised to establish the exact procedure for nomination of the Commission it contains. The obligation to take into account the outcome of EP elections when nominating the President of the Commission is taken out of context of this procedure and disregards the institutional balance established in the Treaties. Thirdly, the broader constitutional context is examined. The project of European integration is based on a messianic promise to ensure peace between 'the peoples of Europe' implying preservation of European peoples as opposed to merging them into one; establishing the democratic process directly at Union level would amount to the opposite result. Fourth, an alternative solution is considered. Legitimacy of the Union and national systems of democracy are inseparably intertwined. Linking EP elections to the performance of national governments in the Council and national members of the EP would enhance democratic legitimacy of both national and European policies.

II. THE *SPITZENKANDIDATEN* INVENTION

On 27 June 2014 the President of the European Commission was appointed against an express vote of two Member State governments for the first time. This nomination followed the practice proposed by the EP a year earlier, whereby the European political parties nominate their candidates for presidency of the European Commission ahead of the 2014 elections to the EP, with the candidate put forward by the party that wins the most seats to 'be the first to be considered' for the post of President of the European Commission.[1]

This practice completes attempts to construct venues for voice of citizens directly on Union level through increasing the powers of the EP. Originally under the EC Treaty, the members of the Commission were appointed by common accord by the governments of Member States,[2] while the President of the Commission was to be appointed from Commission members after consultation of the entire college.[3] The Assembly (which preceded the EP) could pass a motion of censure of the Commission obliging it to resign as college;[4] the Court of Justice could compulsorily retire individual members of the Commission.[5]

The Maastricht Treaty reversed the order of appointment procedure. Under Article 158(2) EC as amended:

> The governments of the Member States shall nominate by common accord, after consulting the European Parliament, the person they intend to appoint as President of the Commission … The President and the other members of the Commission … nominated [by governments in consultation with the nominee for President of the Commission] shall be subject as a body to a vote of approval by the European Parliament.

[1] European Parliament Rresolution of 4 July 2013 on improving the practical arrangements for the holding of the European elections in 2014 (2013/2102 INL).

[2] Art 158 EC Treaty 1957.

[3] ibid Art 161.

[4] ibid Art 144.

[5] ibid Art 160.

This procedure was followed for the appointment of the Santer Commission in January 1995. The Court of Justice remained in charge of compulsory retirement of individual members of the Commission, while the possibility of the Council to suspend Commissioners was removed.[6] The power of the EP to censure the Commission as a college remained intact; while a motion of censure was never carried, the mere threat thereof caused the Santer Commission to resign in March 1999.

The Amsterdam Treaty increased parliamentary control over the Commission further. The new Article 214(2) EC required not only consultation of the EP when nominating the President of the Commission but also EP approval; the provision on approval by the EP of the Commission as a whole remained unchanged. The Prodi Commission was appointed using this procedure in September 1999. The EP retained its power to dismiss the Commission as college. Article 219 EC as amended by the Amsterdam Treaty, specified that the Commission President shall provide 'the political guidance' for work of the Commission.

A further amendment to Article 214(2) EC followed with the Treaty of Nice. While leaving the powers of the EP unaltered, the procedure for appointment of all Commissioners was changed from common accord to qualified majority vote (QMV) in the Council. At the same time, the EP exercised its power of approval of the Commission as college postponing the appointment of the first Barroso Commission from October to November 2004.[7] The Parliament exercised this power again during the appointment of the second Barroso Commission in early 2009. Both in 2004 and 2009, the political stripe of the President of the Commission followed the European party with most seats in the EP as well as the governments of most Member States in the Council, although both times the support of other parties in the EP was necessary since no one party ever held an absolute majority in the Parliament. The Treaty of Nice also introduced the power of the Commission President to request the resignation of individual Commissioners 'after obtaining the approval of the College'.[8]

Therefore, already prior to the Lisbon Treaty, the Commission was accountable to the EP both as college and its individual members,[9] while nomination of the President of the Commission and the college required approval of majority in the Parliament. On several occasions the EP exercised these powers.

Despite these developments, the Laeken Declaration of the European Council restated the link between the democratic deficit of European institutions and the procedure of appointment of President of the Commission.[10] The draft Treaty

[6] ibid Art 160, as amended in Maastricht.

[7] For a detailed account, see MEP A Duff, 'How the European Parliament approves the European Commission' AFCO Working Document by (30 November 2004) DT/548974EN.

[8] Art 217(4) EC.

[9] Framework Agreement on relations between the European Parliament and the European Commission [2010] OJ L304/47, Point II(5).

[10] Annexes to the Presidency conclusions, European Council meeting in Laeken 14 and 15 December 2001, SN 300/1/01 REV 1 22–23.

establishing a Constitution for Europe introduced new phrasing[11] that was carried over into the Constitutional Treaty Article I-27:

> The President of the European Commission
>
> 1. Taking into account the elections to the European Parliament and after having held the appropriate consultations, the European Council, acting by a qualified majority, shall propose to the European Parliament a candidate for President of the Commission. This candidate shall be elected by the European Parliament by a majority of its component members. If he or she does not obtain the required majority, the European Council, acting by a qualified majority, shall within one month propose a new candidate who shall be elected by the European Parliament following the same procedure.
> 2. The Council, by common accord with the President-elect, shall adopt the list of the other persons whom it proposes for appointment as members of the Commission. They shall be selected, on the basis of the suggestions made by Member States, in accordance with the criteria set out in Article I-26(4) and (6), second subparagraph.
>
> The President, the Union Minister for Foreign Affairs and the other members of the Commission shall be subject as a body to a vote of consent by the European Parliament. On the basis of this consent the Commission shall be appointed by the European Council, acting by a qualified majority.
>
> 3. The President of the Commission shall:
>   (a) lay down guidelines within which the Commission is to work;
>   (b) decide on the internal organisation of the Commission, ensuring that it acts consistently, efficiently and as a collegiate body;
>   (c) appoint Vice-Presidents, other than the Union Minister for Foreign Affairs, from among the members of the Commission.
>
> A member of the Commission shall resign if the President so requests. The Union Minister for Foreign Affairs shall resign, in accordance with the procedure set out in article I-28(1), if the President so requests.[12]

With the Lisbon Treaty, the first paragraph of this article became Article 17(7) TEU:

> Taking into account the elections to the European Parliament and after having held the appropriate consultations, the European Council, acting by a qualified majority, shall propose to the European Parliament a candidate for President of the Commission. This candidate shall be elected by the European Parliament by a majority of its component members. If he does not obtain the required majority, the European Council, acting by a qualified majority, shall within one month propose a new candidate who shall be elected by the European Parliament following the same procedure.
>
> …

[11] Art 26 (18 July 2003) CONV 850/03.
[12] [2004] OJ C 310/3.

> The President ... and the other members of the Commission shall be subject as a body to a vote of consent by the European Parliament. On the basis of this consent the Commission shall be appointed by the European Council, acting by a qualified majority.

The European Commission reinterpreted this provision. In order 'to foster the emergence of a genuine European political sphere', the Commission called on the political parties to nominate their candidates for the President of the Commission in the context of 2014 elections.[13] The following year the Commission was even more explicit:

> Each political party *should* make known its candidate for President of the Commission during the election process. In accordance with the Treaty, the outcome of the European elections *should* play a key role in determining which candidate becomes President of the Commission.[14]

The EP took up the idea and urged 'the European political parties to nominate candidates for the Presidency of the Commission' with the expectation that 'those candidates ... play a leading role in the parliamentary electoral campaign, in particular by personally presenting their programme in all Member States of the Union'.[15] In the same Resolution, the Parliament called 'for as many members of the next Commission as possible to be drawn from Members of the European Parliament, to reflect the balance between the two chambers of the legislature'.

Neither Commission Communications nor Resolutions of the EP produce legal effects and as such cannot be challenged before the Court of Justice of the EU (CJEU).[16] Further, the Council did not issue any document in response to this initiative to express its formal opinion or consent. Thus, while a political agreement between the Commission and the Parliament is in place, there is no formal inter-institutional agreement between them and nothing documents any legal, formal or political agreement on the proposed arrangement between these two institutions and the Council. Therefore, unlike previous cases where the Council indicated its readiness to challenge inter-institutional arrangements between the Commission and the EP,[17] no such formal challenge is possible for the *Spitzenkandidaten*

[13] Commission 'A blueprint for a deep and genuine economic and monetary union: Launching a European Debate', 28 November 2012 COM (2012) 777 final/2, 37.

[14] Commission to the European Parliament, the Council and the European Economic and Social Committee and the Committee of the Regions 'Preparing for the 2014 European elections: further enhancing their democratic and efficient conduct', 12 March 2013 COM (2013) 126 final 6 (emphasis added).

[15] European Parliament Resolution of 22 November 2012 on the elections to the European Parliament in 2014 2012/2829(RSP).

[16] Art 263 TFEU.

[17] For instance, as regards the Framework Agreement on relations between the European Parliament and the European Commission [2010] OJ L304/47, the Council indicated readiness to commence infringement proceedings against the Commission and the EP for 'modify[ing] the balance established in the Treaties between the institutions' to the prejudice of the Council, for 'accord[ing] powers to the Parliament not conferred in the Treaties' and for 'limit[ing] the autonomy of the Commission and its President', see Council of the European Union, Opinion of the Legal Service on the Draft Framework Agreement between the European Parliament and the Commission, 18 October 2012, doc 15018/10.

arrangement. Nevertheless, the CJEU could 'ensure that in the interpretation and application of the Treaties the law is observed'[18] by reviewing the act of appointment of the President of the Commission by the European Council under the last paragraph of Article 17(7) TEU: this is an act that produces legal effects and could change the inter-institutional balance established in the Treaties.[19]

III. THE LETTER OF THE TREATIES: CONSTITUTIONALITY OF THE ARRANGEMENT

It is against this background that the *Spitzenkandidaten* scheme was introduced. The phrase '[t]aking into account the elections to the European Parliament' contained in Article 17(7) TEU was taken out of context of the Treaties and the inter-institutional balance established therein. The procedure for appointing the President of the European Commission contained in Article 17(7) TEU is as follows:

1. The European Council proposes the candidate by QMV.
2. The EP elects the candidate by absolute majority.
3. The Council, on the basis of suggestions made by Member States and by common accord with the President pre-elect, proposes the college.
4. The EP consents to the entire college (the President of the Commission included) by absolute majority.
5. The European Council appoints the college by QMV.

This procedure amounts to co-decision between the Member States in the European Council and Council on the one hand and the EP on the other. This interpretation is corroborated by Declaration 11 on Article 17(6) and (7) TEU attached to the Treaty of Lisbon. While not legally binding, Declaration 11 obliges the two institutions to collaborate on the nomination, placing the responsibility for 'the smooth running of the process leading to the election of the President of the European Commission' jointly on the EP and Council.

Article 17(7) TEU unequivocally reserves the power to propose candidates for President of the European Commission to the European Council: 'the European Council ... shall propose to the European Parliament a candidate for President of the Commission'. There is no priority given to any candidates advanced by the EP or any other institution or political party. Giving the Parliament an upper hand in nominating the candidate for President of the European Commission would reverse the procedure set out in the Treaties, a change requiring a formal Treaty amendment.

The obligation to take account of EP elections should be read together with the remainder of Article 17(7) TEU, which provides that the candidate gather majority

[18] Art 19(1) TEU.

[19] I am indebted to Enzo Moavero Milanesi for pointing this out.

support in the EP. The purpose of the requirement to take account of EP elections is to ensure that the Council nominates a candidate who can realistically gather majority support in the Parliament, as opposed to nominating minority candidates who a priori cannot be expected to meet this requirement. The importance of this joint reading of the two provisions becomes especially apparent once the first candidate for President of the Commission does not gather a simple majority in the EP, since the European Council has a one-month time limit to propose each subsequent candidate.[20] The obligation to take account of the political composition of the EP therefore aims to expedite the appointment procedure.

The requirement to take account of EP elections is not a special rule for the appointment procedure but a specific application of the general principle of sincere mutual cooperation between the EU institutions contained in Article 13(2) TEU:

> Each institution shall act within the limits of the powers conferred on it in the Treaties, and in conformity with the procedures, conditions and objectives set out in them. The institutions shall practice mutual sincere cooperation.

This reading is corroborated by the fact that the two obligations—to take account of EP elections in nominating the candidate for Presidency of the Commission on the one hand, and the duty of sincere mutual cooperation between EU institutions on the other—converge in their historic origins. Both were introduced into the Treaties with the draft Constitution and, in their legally binding form, in the Lisbon Treaty—yet both obligations have pre-Constitution origins in inter-institutional practice. As regards the political affiliation of the President of the Commission, prior to 2014, in all the cases where election by the EP was required, the appointee belonged to the party with most seats in the EP (although this also coincided with the governing parties in most Member States). Giving priority to the candidate of the party that wins the most seats in the EP would open the door—at least hypothetically—to majorities for Eurosceptics. While Eurosceptics are not outlawed from the political process in the EU or any Member State (unlike the more extreme right-wing parties in some Member States), their candidates would be precluded from consideration not only for presidency of the Commission,[21] but also for any member of the college by virtue of Article 17(3) TEU,

> The members of the Commission shall be chosen on the ground of their … European commitment.

The *Spitzenkandidaten* arrangement could lead to a major inter-institutional crisis because the President of the Commission cannot nominate the Commissioners

[20] Para 1 Art 17(7) TEU.

[21] This is also because, according to European Parliament Resolution of 4 July 2013 on improving the practical arrangements for the holding of the European elections in 2014 (2013/2102 INL), the candidates for President of the Commission would be nominated by European parties, while not all the political forces competing in EP elections qualify as European parties under Art 3 Regulation 2004/2003/EC on the regulations governing political parties at European level and the rules regarding their funding as amended by Regulation 1524/2007/EC [2007] OJ L343:5.

but only accord on nominations made by Member States,[22] what José Manuel Durão Barroso famously called 'a blind date'.[23] Even if the party that gains the most seats in the EP nominates a candidate who gathers support of the majority in the Parliament and qualified majority in the Council, this President might not be able to wrestle 28 governments appointing Commissioners from other parties. Where a partisan President of the Commission belongs to a political denomination different from most governments in the Council, a disagreement on the college could delay appointment of the Commission; once a college comprising Commissioners from different political parties is appointed, they might not necessarily follow the policies put forward by a partisan President. Partisan discord could undermine collegiality of the Commission, which its President has a duty to ensure.[24] It could also be more difficult for a partisan President of the Commission to request resignation of individual Commissioners who belong to different parties, as this could be seen as a bet on new appointees closer to her political preference.[25] In addition, censuring the Commission by the EP could become more difficult.[26] A Commission President belonging to the party that wins most seats in the EP is bound to pose questions of democratic legitimacy: can minority parties in Parliament collude to dismiss the President nominated by the party with most seats, that is, elected by Union citizens? The proposal that the Parliament be able to dismiss the Commission only when the EP can propose a new candidate for President would not solve this problem.[27]

The importance of sincere mutual cooperation between European institutions was recognised by the CJEU on the basis of a joint declaration by the EP, the Council and the Commission.[28] Both pertain to the functioning of the Union and its institutions as well as to the conferral and division of powers between them according to the provisions of the Treaties.[29] The CJEU might therefore be able

[22] Art 17(7) TEU.

[23] *European Voice* (3 December 2009) 6 cited in J Peterson 'The College of Commissioners' in J Peterson and M Shackleton (eds), *The Institutions of the European Union* (Oxford, Oxford University Press, 2012) 108.

[24] Art 17(6)b TEU. In this regard, the Code of Conduct of Commissioners C (2011)2904:3 specifies that 'Commissioners are expected to defend and support the decisions taken by the College. Their Commission duties must prevail over party commitment.'

[25] Art 17(6) TEU.

[26] Art 17(8) TEU.

[27] Speech of Commission President Barroso at Humboldt University Berlin (8 May 2014) SPEECH/14/355, 16.

[28] Joint Declaration by the European Parliament, the Council and the Commission of 30 June 1982 on various measures to improve the budgetary procedure [1982] OJ C194/1 (which opens with the phrase 'Whereas harmonious cooperation between the institutions is essential to the smooth operation of the Communities') and Case 204/86, *Greece v Council* [1988] ECR 5323, para 16; see also Case C-65/93, *EP v Council* [1995] ECR I-00643, para 23 on the 'mutual duty of sincere cooperation' in the course of inter-institutional dialogue.

[29] It is significant in this regard that proposals to amend the wording 'Taking into account the elections to the European Parliament' and the role of the EP in nominating the Commission President contained in Art 26 of the draft Constitution in a way that would reverse the institutional balance giving the power to nominate candidates for President of the Commission to the European Parliament and leaving the European Council the role of confirming the President-elect, were not carried into the final

to review the act of appointment of President of the Commission for compliance with Article 13(2) of the Treaty on European Union (TEU) in view of the institutional balance observed in the course of this appointment.[30]

Nor would the linking of Commission's policies to EP elections be desirable in democratic terms—if the democratic process were established on Union level. Winning the most seats in the Parliament—the requirement for giving priority to one party candidate over others—is not the same as absolute majority. Even if the other parties back the candidate for President of the Commission so that the absolute majority required for appointment is gathered, this would be an arrangement very different from coalition governments formed in Member States. Since the President of the Commission can only accord with nomination of the college by Member States but has no power to propose own candidates, the composition of the college is not likely to reflect majority coalition in the EP. Were a partisan President of the Commission to shape the policy agenda of the Union along her party lines—as opposed to merely 'lay down guidelines within which the Commission is to work'[31]—such agenda-setting could disempower the other parties in the Parliament, especially the smaller parties who cannot hope to be the largest in the EP. This risks reducing the EU (and, by implication also the national political processes) to a two-party system, muting the votes of citizens who vote for medium and smaller parties, and concentrating excessive power in a single office. Failing to further the lines of her coalition party (for instance because none of the Commissioners share the latter) might risk a loss of support for the President of the Commission in the Parliament and a motion of censure for the entire college. This would not be undemocratic because, however democracy is defined, a party that gathers less than 50 per cent support from citizens should not be imposing its views on the majority.

version of the Constitution. Proposals to reduce or even eliminate the role of the EP were also rejected, see: european-convention.europa.eu/EN/amendments/amendmentsf9f8.html?content=41899&lang=EN (6 June 2014) The relevance of *travaux preparatoires* for identifying the purpose of Treaty provisions has been confirmed in Case C-370/12, *Pringle v Government of Ireland, Ireland and The Attorney General*, judgment of 27 November 2012, not yet reported, para 58.

[30] In Case C-28/12, *Commission v Council* (unreported), the Commission inter alia alleges that 'the Council infringed … the principle of sincere cooperation laid down in Article 13(2) TEU. The Council should have exercised its powers so as not to circumvent the institutional framework of the Union and the Union procedures set out in Article 218 TFEU' insofar as 'it transpires from Article 218(2) and (5) TFEU that the Council is the institution designated to authorize the signing and provisional application of agreements. Therefore, the decision should have been solely taken by the Council and not also by the Member States, meeting within the Council.' (case pending) For an opinion that 'institutional balance does not entail a kind of one-way traffic in favour of the European Parliament' see S Prechal, 'Institutional Balance: A Fragile Principle with Uncertain Contents' in T Heukels, N Blokker and M Brus (eds), *The European Union after Amsterdam: A Legal Analysis* (Deventer, Kluwer, 1998) 278; and M Klamert, *The Principle of Loyalty in EU Law* (Oxford, Oxford University Press, 2014) 216: 'always favouring the legal basis granting more rights of participation to the Parliament is not supported by arguments of institutional balance'.

[31] Art 17(6)(a) TEU.

IV. THE SPIRIT OF THE TREATIES: DEMOCRACY IN THE UNION

A systemic issue lurks behind these provisions. The *Spitzenkandidaten* scheme was introduced in order to enhance democratic legitimacy of the Union and its policies. 'Giving a face to EP elections'[32] aimed to create a 'difference to Europe and in Europe whether and how the people vote for the European Parliament'.[33] Establishing a more direct link between the outcome of EP elections and the nomination of President of the Commission was supposed to connect EP elections to Union policies, raise the plummeting turnout in EP elections, and ensure democratic accountability of EU institutions.[34] While an increase in voter turnout has failed to materialise,[35] with legitimacy of the Union increasingly questioned by the rise of the Eurosceptics, modelling accountability for Union policies on the state—even if a federal state—is inadequate for the EU. The European Communities were founded with the finality of European integration and a mission to ensure prosperity and peace between Member States. Throughout the process of European integration, one of the main concerns has been to prevent the domination of some Member States over others. Supranational democracy was not only absent from the European project but it was so on purpose: the Union would enable Member States to counteract the eventuality of another Hitler coming to power through a democratic political process. For this, an intergovernmental Community would counterbalance the democratic nation state.

With the expansion of Europe's powers and the passage from unanimous and majoritarian decision-making in the Single European Act and the Maastricht Treaty, concerns over legitimacy of the Union flourished.[36] These concerns and sources of legitimacy can be broken down into the following categories:[37]

[32] J Borrell Fontelles, 'The Future Role of the European Parliament' in L Tsoukalis and JA Emmanouilidis (eds), *The Delphic Oracle on Europe: Is There a Future for the European Union?* (Oxford, Oxford University Press, 2011) 54.

[33] For analysis of the 'opportunities and possible risks related to prospect of turning the European elections into personalized contest for the presidency of the European Commission' see JHH Weiler, 'Challenges to electoral participation in the European elections of 2014. Restoring Electoral Faith: Prospects and Risks' in AFCO Report 'Strengthening European Democracy: Citizens' Participation. Which challenges do we face at the European Elections of 2014?' (2013) European Parliament doc. PE 493.036.

[34] JHH Weiler, 'The Political and Legal Culture of European Integration: An Exploratory Essay' (2011) 9 *International Journal of Constitutional Law*, 678–94 and 'Editorial: European Parliament Elections 2014: Europe's Fateful Choices' (2013) 24 *European Journal of International Law* 747–53.

[35] H Mahony, 'EU Election Turnout at Record Low After All' *EU Observer* (6 August 2014) available at: euobserver.com/political/125198.

[36] *Ex multis*, A Moravcsik, 'Reassessing Legitimacy in the European Union' (2002) 40 *Journal of Common Market Studies* 603–24; G Majone, 'The Common Sense of European Integration' (2006) 13(5) *Journal of European Public Policy* 607–26; A Foellesdal and S Hix, 'Why There is a Democratic Deficit in the EU: A Response to Majone and Moravcsik' (2006) 44 *Journal of Common Market Studies* 533–62; for European institutions and the EP specifically, see P Dann, 'The Political Institutions' in A von Bogdandy and J Bast (eds), *Principles of European Constitutional Law* (Oxford, Hart Publishing, 2010); for the view that EU need not be democratic along the model of nation states, see G Majone, *Dilemmas of European Integration: The Ambiguities and Pitfalls of Integration by Stealth* (Oxford, Oxford University Press, 2005) ch 2.

[37] M Adams, F Fabbrini and P Larouche (eds), 'Introduction' in *The Constitutionalization of European Budgetary Constraints* (Oxford, Hart Publishing, 2014) 4–6; A Kocharov, 'This Time It's

1. *Formal legitimacy or consent* concerns whether the powers were constituted and laws enacted following formal rules, procedures, and constitutional guarantees. It is the legalistic side of process legitimacy that does not necessarily translate into the acceptance of resulting rules.[38] However, lack of compliance with the constitutional letter and spirit of the Treaties would undermine this legitimacy source.
2. *Substantive or output legitimacy* links the acceptance of public power to the results that this power achieves. It is also the extent to which the polity is capable of autonomous self-governance.[39] Output legitimacy will be high for popular measures that achieve their promised results and low for unpopular policies or failure to deliver (the latter will also undermine messianic legitimacy). The onset of financial crisis and the need for unpopular austerity measures have undermined this source of legitimacy for the EU.
3. *Process or input legitimacy* seeks to achieve acceptance of public power through ensuring interest representation and participation in the political process. Direct elections of the EP and the increase in its powers, citizens' initiative and subsidiarity review by national parliaments seek to further process legitimacy by giving citizens voice directly at Union level. Process legitimacy, to be effective, needs to be backed up by accountability and the power to enforce limited government in court. Accountability is the capacity of citizens to remove the government from power when the latter no longer represents their voice, usually through elections.[40] Adjudication protects the legitimacy of the political process by protecting minorities from majorities by enforcing citizens' and fundamental rights.[41]
4. *Messianic or promise legitimacy* corresponds to the original promise of Europe to deliver peace and prosperity. Economic revival after World War II and lasting peace between 'the peoples of Europe' are part of this promise[42]—but so is preservation of multiple European peoples.[43]

Different? Constitutional Complexities of the Spitzenkandidaten Arrangement' (12 June 2014) *Berlin e-Working Papers on European Law* 95 Feie Universität Berlin available at: portal-europarecht.de/index.php?option=com_jdownloads&Itemid=17&view=finish&cid=21822&catid=5.

[38] JHH Weiler, 'The Transformation of Europe' (1991) 100 *Yale Law Journal* 2469.

[39] N Walker, 'Constitutionalizing Enlargement, Enlarging Constitutionalism' (2003) 9 *European Law Journal* 368, citing F Scharpf, *Governing in Europe: Effective and Democratic?* (Oxford, Oxford University Press, 1999) ch 1.

[40] JHH Weiler, U Haltern and F Mayer, 'European Democracy and its Critique Five Uneasy Pieces' EUI Working Paper RSC 95/11, 9: 'In its present state, no one who votes in the European elections has a strong sense at all of affecting critical policy choices at the European level and certainly not of confirming or rejecting European governance.'

[41] M Poiares Maduro, 'Sovereignty in Europe: the European Court of Justice and the Creation of European Political Community' in ML Volcansek and JF Stack Jr (eds), *Courts Crossing Borders. Blurring the Lines of Sovereignty* (Durham, Carolina Academic Press, 2005); G de Búrca and O Gerstenberg, 'The Denationalization of Constitutional Law' (2006) 47 *Harvard International Law Journal* 1.

[42] Recital 8, Preamble to the 1957 EEC Treaty; *The Schuman Declaration* (Paris, 9 May 1950) Selection of texts concerning institutional matters of the Community from 1950 to 1982. Luxembourg: EP Committee on Institutional Affairs (1982) 561, 47–48.

[43] JHH Weiler, 'The Political and Legal Culture of European Integration' (n 34) 683.

5. *Social legitimacy* is the result of all the previous methods of increasing the authority of public power as reflected in public opinion surveys[44] and in the actual acceptance of the resulting norms.[45] Here, the 2013 surveys were worrying: only 30 per cent of Europeans expressed trust in the European Parliament while 48 per cent distrusted it, and 12 per cent said that they expect nothing from the EU.[46]

Two structural features of Europe's Union determine the constitutional construct of legitimacy of the EU. The first concerns the reach of Union's policies and powers and can be termed as policy interdependence.[47] Policy interdependence takes place independently from the decision-making procedure at Union level (unanimity, consensus or majority rule) and refers to the factual capacity of each national polity to regulate within its jurisdiction (to implement a policy choice). This capacity can be undermined as a result of externalities and interdependence between national polities created by European integration, whereby regulatory decisions by one polity may affect the regulatory capacity of the other. Good examples of policy interdependence are the Schengen area and the euro, where immigration and budgetary decisions respectively of one Member State may produce effects on the policies pursued by another Member State. The problem caused by policy interdependence can be resolved by shifting policy-making from the national level to the Union. National polities and national political processes would then lend their legitimacy to the Union and its policies[48] as long as these are adopted by unanimity or consensus.

The second structural feature of Europe's Union is the method of decision-making. The passage from unanimity or consensus to QMV in the Council implies that Union policies no longer derive legitimacy from the national political process because individual Member States may find themselves bound against their will as represented by their governments in the Council. This creates interdependence between the national political processes whereby policy preferences elaborated in the course of one national political process and represented by its government in the (European) Council can overpower policy preferences developed in another national political process that remains outvoted on Union level. As long as the peoples of Europe identify themselves as Member State nationals before European citizens[49]—as long as the national political process retains importance in

[44] Weiler, 'The Transformation of Europe' (n 38) 2469.

[45] What Tuori calls 'empirical legitimacy', see K Tuori, *Critical Legal Positivism* (London, Ashgate, 2002) 244.

[46] European Commission 'Standard Eurobarometer 80' Autumn 2013 *European Citizenship* 7.

[47] Chronologically, this is the second element that gained prominence with the abolition of internal borders and the introduction of the single currency.

[48] Art 10(2) TEU secures representative democracy in the Union on two levels: 'Citizens are directly represented at Union level in the European Parliament. Member States are represented in the European Council by their Heads of State or Government and in the Council by their governments, themselves democratically accountable either to their national Parliaments, or to their citizens.'

[49] Standard Eurobarometer 81 June 2014 *European Citizenship* 10: 'More than half the respondents defined themselves first by their nationality and then by their European citizenship (51 per cent, +4

the eyes of Union citizens—interdependence between the national political processes requires preservation and enhancement of national political processes, not the substituting or dismantling thereof. This form of interdependence raises the importance of the capacity of each national political process to factor in interests from other Member States.

The Lisbon Treaty preserves and strengthens the national political processes in three ways. First, it codifies the pre-existing practice of having policy choice made by national governments in the European Council.[50] Although not endorsed with legislative powers, the European Council is now an official institution of the Union responsible for providing 'the Union with the necessary impetus for its development' and defining 'the general political directions and priorities thereof'.[51] These policy-making choices are taken in the European Council by consensus.[52] For Union policies without functional Treaty objectives to direct European policy choice,[53] national policy preferences elaborated in the course of the national political process feed into the development of shared European policies through national governments acting in the EU. This underlines the importance of accountability of governments at the national level.

Secondly, the Lisbon Treaty introduced *pluralism* as one of the foundations of Europe's constitutional construct alongside democracy, equality and the rule of law.[54] Followed by EU's commitment to 'equality of Member States before the Treaties' and respect for their national identities, constitutional and political,[55] pluralism thus refers to plurality of national constitutions and the national political processes that these constitutions regulate. Equality of Member States before the Treaties implies equality of policy choices elaborated in their national political processes, so that no national policy preference can legitimately dominate others.[56] It is this plurality of national policy preferences and 'competing interpretations of the common good' that feed into the process of developing European policies.[57]

percentage points); the proportion of respondents who say that they define themselves first by their European citizenship and then by their nationality is still small (6 per cent, +1); only 2 per cent say that they see themselves solely as European citizens (no change).'

50 Arts 15, 16(6), 22, 26 TEU, Arts 68, 121, 148 TFEU, as well as the capacity of national governments to enter between themselves into international treaties outside EU law, such as the Fiscal Compact.

51 Art 15(1) TEU.

52 Art 15(4) TEU.

53 For an example of such Union policy, see A Kocharov, 'Subsidiarity after Lisbon: Federalism without a Purpose?' in L Azoulai, L Boucon and F-X Millet, 'Deconstructing EU Federalism through Competences' EUI Working Paper LAW 2012/06; S Piedrafita and S Blockmans, *Shifting EU Institutional Reform into High Gear* (Brussels, Centre for European Political Studies, 2014) 14–15.

54 Art 2 TEU.

55 Art 4(2) TEU: 'The Union shall respect the equality of Member States before the Treaties as well as their national identities, inherent in their fundamental structures, political and constitutional, inclusive of regional and local self-government. It shall respect their essential State functions, including ensuring the territorial integrity of the State, maintaining law and order and safeguarding national security.'

56 M Poiares Maduro, 'Il rischio del 'maggioritarismo intergovernativo' (3 September 2003) *Quaderni costituzionali* XXIII, 657.

57 M Poiares Maduro, 'In Search of a Meaning and not in Search of the Meaning: Judicial Review and the Constitution in Times of Pluralism' (2013) *Wisconsin Law Review* 544.

In this way, legitimacy and good functioning of the national political processes is intertwined with the legitimacy of the EU. Accountability at the national level is therefore fundamental for the legitimacy of Union's policies.

Thirdly, Union law recognises and advances the importance of the proper functioning of the national political process in Europe's constitutional construct. Democracy, rule of law, respect for human rights and protection of minorities are integral parts of the Copenhagen criteria that must be fulfilled before joining the EU.[58] The fulfillment of these criteria ensures that the national political process of all Member States leads to elaboration of legitimate national preferences for policy choice, preferences that feed into the policies shaped at Union level. Through operation of Union law, membership in the European legal order eliminates 'externalities' between the national political processes.[59] This is achieved by securing non-discrimination on the grounds of nationality in cross-border situations, where the interests that belong to one national political process fall under the regulatory reach of another national political process. This corrects the shortcomings in interest representation in national political processes, thereby enhancing their functioning and legitimacy.

Accountability of politicians in the national political process emerges as key for the legitimacy of the Union. Legitimacy of the Union and its policies appears inseparable from legitimacy of national democracies. Following the signing of the Maastricht Treaty, it has been noted that in politically sensitive policy fields national governments are tempted to avoid political accountability for contested policy choices by shifting decision-making to Brussels.[60] To ensure that accountability follows power, as opposed to personifying accountability without a corresponding power shift, the agenda-setting power would need to be shifted from the European Council to the Parliament, which cannot take place without amending the Treaties. Appointing an EU 'face' who could be sanctioned for failures of collective policies pursued by national governments on Union level reduces accountability. Member State governments could evade democratic accountability in the national political process by shifting regulation from the national level to the EU, while the person accountable for possible failures of Union policies would be the President of the European Commission—an institution that does not direct European policy choice.[61] Considering the importance of the national political process

[58] European Council in Copenhagen 21–22 June 1993 Conclusions of the Presidency SN 180/1/93 REV 1, 13.

[59] M Poiares Maduro, *We the Court* (Oxford, Hart Publishing, 1998) 156–57.

[60] GA Bermann, 'Taking Subsidiarity Seriously: Federalism in the European Community and in the United States' (1994) 94 *Columbia Law Review* 361; for the latest, see Weiler, 'Challenges to electoral participation in the European elections of 2014' (n 33) 6 and Speech of Commission President Barroso (n 27) 11.

[61] 'The introduction of the co-decision procedure in the EU decision-making and the functioning in practice of the inter-institutional system have transformed the role of the Commission from that of an autonomous initiator to that of a reactive initiator.' P Ponzano, C Hermanin and D Corona, 'The Power of Initiative of the European Commission: A Progressive Erosion?' (2012) (Notre Europe—Jacques Delors Institute, 2014) available at: www.notre-europe.eu/media/commission_power_of_

in the constitutional construct of Europe sealed in the Treaties, shifting political accountability from Member States to the EU undermines democracy and legitimacy at both levels of power.

The original role of the European Commission in Europe's constitutional construct was to act as a neutral guarantor of common European interest and equality between Member States—between national political processes. The nature and institutional setting of the Union established in the Treaties renders the Commission very dissimilar to the governments even in federal states, reflecting the fact that the EU is a 'union among the peoples of Europe'. The role of the Commission is not equivalent or comparable to a national government: the Lisbon Treaty reserves the power to set the policy agenda to the European Council, so the functions exercised by Member State governments are effectively split between the European Council and the Commission. The Council and EP are different from, for example, the Senate and the House of Representatives in the United States (US) because the representation in both EU 'chambers' reflects both Member States and their populations. This leaves small Member States more vulnerable than less populous states of the US,[62] requiring a special role for the Commission. In view of this role in the constitutional construct of Europe:

> The members of the Commission shall be chosen … from persons whose independence is beyond doubt.
>
> In carrying out its responsibilities, the Commission shall be completely independent … the members of the Commission shall neither seek nor take instructions from any Government or other institution, body, office or entity. They shall refrain from any action incompatible with their duties or the performance of their tasks.[63]

Independence of the Commission is crucial for its ability to fulfill the institutional role assigned to it in the Treaties. The Commission has a number of tasks that require a high level of actual and perceived independence, including:

> The Commission shall promote the general interest of the Union and take appropriate initiatives to that end. It shall ensure the application of the Treaties, and of measures adopted by the institutions pursuant to them. It shall oversee the application of Union law under the control of the Court of Justice of the European Union. It shall execute the budget and manage programmes. It shall exercise coordinating, executive and management functions, as laid down in the Treaties. With the exception of the common

initiative_ne_feb2012.pdf?pdf=ok. See also T Christiansen, 'The European Union after the Lisbon Treaty: An Elusive "Institutional Balance"?' in A Biondi, P Eeckhout and S Ripley (eds), *EU Law After Lisbon* (Oxford, Oxford University Press, 2012) 237.

[62] Under the Lisbon Treaty, the relative importance of small Member States fell while the relative importance of medium and large Member States increased. The qualified majority voting rules in force from 2014 provide that three large Member States (representing 35% of Union population) may block the adoption of secondary EU law. This leaves small Member States little leverage while Member States with large populations retain much of their power despite the passage from unanimity to qualified majority voting.

[63] Art 17(3) TEU.

> foreign and security policy, and other cases provided for in the Treaties, it shall ensure the Union's external representation. It shall initiate the Union's annual and multiannual programming with a view to achieving interinstitutional agreements.[64]

Both the President of the Commission and individual Commissioners 'shall refrain from any action incompatible with their duties' and 'may not, during their term of office, engage in any other occupation, whether gainful or not'.[65] A failure to fulfill 'the conditions required for the performance of his duties' by any member of the college enables the CJEU 'on application by the Council acting by a simple majority or the Commission, [to] compulsorily retire him'.[66]

The purpose of the *Spitzenkandidaten* scheme is to create a more direct link between the outcome of EP elections and policies of the Union.[67] Yet, in no part do the Treaties provide for such a direct link. While '[t]he functioning of the Union shall be founded on representative democracy' with direct representation of citizens 'at Union level in the European Parliament',[68] the latter does not have the power to set policy direction for Union acts. On the contrary, were such a direct link established, it would mutate accountability of the Commission to the Parliament into 'taking instructions',[69] failing to respect the balance between accountability and independence of the European Commission set out in the Treaties.[70] Because the EP votes on the candidate for President of the Commission twice—first individually and subsequently on the whole Commission as college—this amounts to an instruction to the President-elect from the EP to form a certain type of Commission (where the coalition parties forming the absolute majority are represented). This instruction is further backed by the possibility to sanction the President-elect together with the entire college on the second vote. This also gives minority parties in the Parliament new bargaining power over the nomination of the college, shifting the power to propose all candidates for membership of the Commission from the Council to the EP—a shift not contained in the Treaties. Instruction from the EP to the Commission appears necessary to ensure accountability under the *Spitzenkandidaten* scheme.

The *Spitzenkandidaten* arrangement also draws the attention away from other criteria the candidate must fulfill. One major requirement is that 'the members of the Commission shall be chosen on the ground of their general competence'.[71]

[64] Art 17(1) TEU. Supervisory powers of the Commission also include competition (Arts 96, 106, 108 TFEU) and budgetary oversight (Art 126 TFEU).

[65] Art 245 TFEU.

[66] Art 247 TFEU.

[67] European Parliament, Resolution of 4 July 2013 'Practical arrangements for the holding of the European elections in 2014 European Parliament' 2013/2102(INI) P7_TA-PROV(2013)0323. For a discussion of this objective in light of the Union structure contained in the Treaties see Weiler, 'European Parliament Elections 2014' (n 34) 24.

[68] Art 10 TEU.

[69] Art 17(3) TEU.

[70] A Dashwood, D Edward, J Lever and J Temple Lang, 'Independence of EU Commission at Risk Over Spitzenkandidat Process' *EU Observer* (26 June 2014) available at: euobserver.com/opinion/124768.

[71] Art 17(3) TEU.

This includes the President of the Commission. Declaration 11 lists the 'backgrounds of the candidates' as a focus factor in choosing the nominee, alongside the EP elections. Additionally, the nomination should 'respect the geographical and demographic diversity of the Union and its Member States', balancing with the nominations for President of the European Council and High Representative of the Union for Foreign Affairs and Security Policy.[72] All these criteria add to legitimacy and should be included in the democratic debate over candidates.

V. DEMOCRATIC LEGITIMACY IN THE EUROPEAN CONSTITUTIONAL CONSTRUCT

On its face, linking Presidency of the Commission to the outcome of EP elections changes little for representation and accountability. Before the Treaty of Lisbon, the Commission was already accountable to the EP, both its President and the entire college had to be approved by the Parliament, while the President of the Commission belonged to the party with the most seats in EP. However, on closer inspection, the arrangement is incompatible with the letter and spirit of the Treaties. It changes the institutional balance of the Union and alters its nature so deeply as to amount to treaty amendment outside the procedure provided in the Treaties. Such twisting of the procedure established in Article 17(7) TEU imperils impartiality of the Commission, could result in major institutional crises and replicate at Union level the malfunctions of national democracies against which the Union is supposed to guard. In seeking to establish a link between EP elections and Union policies, the *Spitzenkandidaten* scheme leans towards creating a democratic process directly on Union level. To the extent that direct European democracy comes to bypass or substitute the national political processes, 'it would be more than ironic if a polity set up as a means to counter the excesses of statism ended up coming round full circle and transforming itself into a (super) state'.[73]

Projects to engineer a democratic process in Europe modelled on the state ignore the absence of a shared perception on the part of Union citizens as a single unified group for the purpose of majority rule and undermine formal and output legitimacy.[74] These projects strike against the letter and spirit of current EU constitutional design and undermine process legitimacy. Creation of accountability for Union policies directly at Union level requires a Treaty change. Under the current Treaties and the constitutional construct that they contain, legitimacy of the Union derives from the national political processes, which are enhanced through Union law. Legitimacy of the Union and national systems of democracy

[72] Declaration 6 on Arts 15(5) and (6), 17(6) and (7) and 18 TEU attached to the Lisbon Treaty.

[73] JHH Weiler, *The Constitution of Europe: 'Do the New Clothes have an Emperor?' and Other Essays on European Integration* (Cambridge, Cambridge University Press, 1999) 341.

[74] See Standard Eurobarometer 80 (n 46).

are inseparably intertwined. Far from being 'second-order elections',[75] national campaigns for the EP could re-position the prevailing domestic issues[76] in a European context, focusing on the performance of national politicians in the EU, both national governments in the Council and European Council and national MEPs. This would require transparency in the work of the Council and the European Council so that a meaningful debate about it can take place at the national level. Such an arrangement would enhance national political processes, bolster accountability, and raise legitimacy of both national and European policies. Linking EP elections to the performance of national governments and MEPs on EU issues is exactly the opposite of decoupling national governments and the EU at the heart of the *Spitzenkandidaten* scheme.

[75] K Reif and H Schmitt, 'Nine Second-Order Elections–A Conceptual Framework for the Analysis of European Elections Results' (1980) 8 *European Journal of Political Research* 3; F Jacobs, 'European Parliament Elections in Times of Crisis' (2014) 1 *Intereconomics* 7: 'A related risk often referred to by political scientists is that voters may perceive these as 'second-order elections' in which national governments are not directly at stake and that this will either lead to indifference and abstention or else provide an ideal opportunity to register a protest vote against incumbent governments and establishment parties.'

[76] S Piedrafita and V Renman, 'The "Personalisation" of the European Elections: A Half-Hearted Attempt to Increase Turnout and Democratic Legitimacy?' (April 2014) *EPIN Paper (CEPS)* 37, 3: 'elections to the EP to second-order elections largely focused on domestic rather than European issues'.

Part V

New Institutional Developments

14

New Intergovernmentalism: The European Council and its President

UWE PUETTER

I. INTRODUCTION

THIS CHAPTER BUILDS on two recent projects of the author and evaluates their implications for contemporary European Union (EU) governance and the Union's future constitutional architecture.[1] The key argument runs as follows: the Maastricht Treaty marked a watershed in EU integration as it contained the boldest political commitment so far to expand integration to all key areas of public policy-making including areas of core state sovereignty. However, the Maastricht Treaty also stipulated that key new areas of EU activity would be governed by policy coordination and intergovernmental agreement rather than through legislative decision-making under the classic Community method. Member State governments were eager to pursue further integration, yet they remained sceptical, if not hostile, to a further delegation of ultimate decision-making competences to the supranational level. The simultaneous insistence on intensified EU integration and on rejecting further delegation constitutes an integration paradox. This integration paradox constitutes the basis of a powerful institutional dynamic within the post-Maastricht period: the new intergovernmentalism. This dynamic revolves around the empowerment and transformation of key intergovernmental actors in EU governance comprising the European Council and influential forums for policy coordination led by senior cabinet ministers such as the Eurogroup, the Economic and Financial Affairs Council (ECOFIN) and the Foreign Affairs Council. The reason for this empowerment is the absence of a central supranational enforcement and implementation mechanism for

[1] *cf* U Puetter, *The European Council and the Council: New Intergovernmentalism and Institutional Change* (Oxford, Oxford University Press, 2014) on how the EU's core intergovernmental decision-making forums have undergone a process of institutional adjustment and became central to the governance of the EU's new areas of EU activity; and C Bickerton, D Hodson and U Puetter, 'The New Intergovernmentalism: European Integration in the Post-Maastricht Era' (2015) 53 *Journal of Common Market Studies*; as well as C Bickerton, D Hodson and U Puetter (eds), *The New Intergovernmentalism: States, Supranational Actors, and European Politics in the Post-Maastricht Era* (Oxford, Oxford University Press, 2015).

collectively agreed policies in prominent new areas of EU activity such as economic governance under Economic and Monetary Union (EMU), the Common Foreign and Security Policy (CFSP), the Common Security and Defence Policy (CSDP) and the domains of employment and social policy coordination. As Member State governments are ultimately responsible for the implementation of collectively agreed policy objectives, defection from these goals is relatively easy. In this context intensive policy coordination and consensus-based decision-making at all stages of the policy process become a prerequisite for EU governance. The post-Maastricht institutional architecture of the European Council and the Council and the practice of inter-institutional relations reflect this. Thus, there is a process of profound institutional change detectable which includes the modification of working methods and decision-making routines. The European Council assumes a central role in this context as many decisions cut deep into domestic politics and/or concern key areas of state sovereignty. It is only through the direct personal agreement among the heads of state and government that decisions stand a chance of implementation and do not come under attack domestically from ruling political elites for constituting an illegitimate interference with core aspects of state sovereignty.

The chapter pursues this general argument further and considers its implications for the current and future constitutional architecture of the Union by discussing five strands of the argument. First, it explores the connection between the integration paradox and institutional change, notably the focus on consensus-based policy coordination and policy deliberation. Secondly, it outlines the central role of the European Council in contemporary EU governance and summarises the evidence for how much this lead role is informed by the growth of prominent new areas of EU activity. Thirdly, it focuses on the changed working methods of the European Council and the Council and attributes them to the institutionalisation of policy deliberation and consensus generation routines. Fourthly, this argument is further illustrated with particular reference to the role of the full-time president of the European Council. Fifthly, and finally, this chapter concludes by cautioning against considerations that the identified new institutional dynamics could be altered by a quick fix of the European Council's constitutional mandate which would redefine key institutional responsibilities either by bringing some of the most dynamic areas of contemporary EU integration under the Community method and/or by formalising and further regulating intergovernmental relations.

II. MORE INTEGRATION WITHOUT DELEGATION

The integration paradox constitutes the entry point for understanding the post-Maastricht period of European integration. Though periodisation is not without problems there are important arguments for engaging with Maastricht as a particular moment in the EU's constitutional development. The Maastricht Treaty constitutes the most important step towards a Union which comprises almost all domains of public policy-making and departs from the idea that European integration predominantly revolves around the idea of market integration and de- and re-regulation. Yet, Maastricht also revealed how difficult agreement on new major transfers of ultimate decision-making responsibilities within the framework of the classic Community method had become. This was reflected in the institutional design of three prominent new areas of EU activity: economic governance under EMU, the CFSP and justice and home affairs. All of them were based on the principle of intergovernmental policy coordination rather than Community method decision-making.

The architects of the Maastricht Treaty may not have realised that they effectively defined the constitutional template for the development of new EU activities for a long time to come. Yet, all Treaties following Maastricht confirmed the institutional architecture of the new areas of EU activity. The Amsterdam Treaty added employment policy coordination and the Nice Treaty further institutionalised the broadening of the EU's coordination approach within many domains of social policy which so far had not been subject to community legislation or within which Member States had failed to agree on further legislative action. Social inclusion policy coordination is an important case in point in this regard.[2] The Lisbon Treaty, including the failed Constitutional Treaty and the European Convention, further consolidated the co-existence of Community method decision-making within previously existing domains and the policy coordination approach of the new areas of EU activity. In a similar vein, Sergio Fabbrini has referred to the Lisbon Treaty as 'the dual constitution'.[3]

The deep institutionalisation of a method of integration alternative to the Community method is remarkable in several respects. First of all, the post-Maastricht period is not characterised by a return to a form of intergovernmentalism which is characterised by stagnation or integration fatigue, as was the case during the 1970s. Ever since Maastricht, the EU has in fact expanded its policy portfolio quite substantially. The post-Maastricht period is also not marked by a continuation of the intergovernmentalism identified by Andrew Moravcsik and which he saw behind the agreement of the Single European Act and the period during the run-up to the Maastricht Treaty.[4] Instead of 'grand bargains' we have been witnessing constant incremental growth of a complex intergovernmental policy coordination agenda and a deepening of most of the policy coordination portfolios.

In short, there is an intensification of intergovernmental policy coordination resulting in collectively agreed EU policies which increasingly have far-reaching repercussions for domestic politics as the Euro-crisis illustrated quite clearly. This is why the author, together with Chris Bickerton and Dermot Hodson, has referred

[2] K Armstrong, *Governing Social Inclusion* (Oxford, Oxford University Press, 2014).

[3] S Fabbrini, 'Intergovernmentalism and its Limits: Assessing the European Union's Answer to the Euro Crisis' (2013) 46 *Comparative Political Studies* 1003, 1005.

[4] A Moravcsik, 'Preferences and Power in the European Community: a Liberal Intergovernmentalist Approach' (1993) 31 *Journal of Common Market Studies* 473.

to post-Maastricht intergovernmentalism as the 'new intergovernmentalism'.[5] It is a distinct integration dynamic which has not been witnessed in EU integration before. Moreover, we argued that the new intergovernmentalism is far from being a short-term phenomenon. We have attributed this to deeply rooted problems with delegation under the classic Community method. What may have appeared at Maastricht mainly as a conflict between euro federalists and less enthusiastic Member State governments in fact became a broad trend in almost all EU Member States in the post-Maastricht period. National governments have been faced with increasingly pronounced push-backs from euro sceptical public opinion. At least they could not count on what once was referred to as the permissive consensus on European integration. At the same time national elites started to realise that with the eventual implementation of the single market agenda European integration cut deeper and deeper into almost all areas of domestic public policy. While differences between leading political elites within and across Member States remain as regards preferences for specific institutional options when it comes to the further development of particular policy domains, the subsequent rounds of Treaty change in Amsterdam, Nice and Lisbon, as well as the European Convention, have confirmed that there is broad agreement among Member State governments to limit the role of traditional supranational 'engines of European integration'[6]—notably the Commission and the Court of Justice—to control policy initiation and implementation processes alike.[7] Instead, Member State executives have preferred to be seen to be in tight and direct control over EU-level decision-making and have insisted on strong agenda-setting powers on the part of the European Council and the Council as the Treaty provisions on EMU economic governance, CFSP, CSDP and employment and social policy coordination demonstrate. Even the field of justice and home affairs which was gradually brought under legislative decision-making procedures, reveals some important modifications of the classic Community method, notably the oversight role of the European Council and the central role of the Council.

Yet, there are also important developments which may explain why the deeply seated scepticism towards new major acts of competence delegation under the Community method has not coincided with integration fatigue. Member State governments face very similar policy challenges and often need to adopt collective policy stances under conditions of uncertainty. The advancement of European integration so far has reinforced interdependencies between domestic policy decisions but has also coincided with a prolonged period of profound policy adjustment related to the departure of post-World War II welfare state policies and

[5] Bickerton, Hodson and Puetter (n 1).

[6] M Pollack, *The Engines of European Integration. Delegation, Agency, and Agenda Setting in the EU* (Oxford, Oxford University Press, 2003).

[7] On the European Convention and its work on EMU economic governance *cf* U Puetter, 'Intervening from Outside: The Role of EU Finance Ministers in the Constitutional Politics' (2007) 14 *Journal of European Public Policy* 1293 and European Convention (2002), Final Report of Working Group VI on Economic Governance, CONV 357/02, Brussels, 21 October 2002.

politics in Western Europe. In this regard Chris Bickerton has diagnosed a powerful underlying dynamic which has gradually transformed European nation states into Member States, as he argues, in the post-war period, that is, states which are inherently focused as regards their internal organisation on defining domestic policies in a larger context of collective European decision-making.[8] Moreover, national governments can no longer be sure of representing core social actors and to enjoy the support of these actors in domestic politics in return for catering for specific interests, which makes the formation of clearly identifiable national preferences problematic. Though there always have been and still are marked differences as regards domestic conditions and causes of policy change, the run-up to EMU showed important patterns of policy convergence—notably as regards the drive for sound public finances. The Euro-crisis has again exacerbated divergences between individual Member State governments and between different parts of the Union. Yet, disputes about appropriate policy responses tend to revolve around the issue of how to interpret and how to adjust an otherwise shared policy doctrine to the particular circumstances of the crisis and how to deal with the redistributive aspects and burden-sharing dimension of crisis management. Again, the point here is not to ignore the tensions between Member State governments but to acknowledge the centripetal forces which push them towards closer integration.

Thus, we are left with the post-Maastricht integration paradox that Member State governments are eager to pursue further integration in order to respond to policy interdependencies and common policy challenges while being reluctant to delegate further legislative decision-making competences to the EU-level. The integration paradox seems to be deeply rooted in the politics surrounding European integration and tied to transformative processes regarding the European nation state. It is thus unlikely that in the foreseeable future Member State governments will fundamentally change their stance on European integration unless they retreat from integration altogether—an option which is currently only openly contemplated by British Prime Minister David Cameron and parts of the British Conservative political elite. The implications of the integration paradox for institutional choice in contemporary EU governance are thus not so much attributed to a lack of further and more decisive institutional reform but are understood to prevail even beyond particular moments of Treaty change. It is rather that Treaty reform since Maastricht is seen to have codified further what the essence of the Maastricht Treaty was: a preference for decentralised decision-making within the new areas of EU activity against the background of fresh political commitment to closer integration.

In fact, post-Maastricht institutional change—whether it is formal or informal—does not revolve around the question of whether and how the new areas of EU activity can be communitarised.[9] Institutional change rather takes place at the

[8] C Bickerton, *European Integration. From Nation-States to Member States* (Oxford, Oxford University Press, 2012).

[9] A notable exception is justice and home affairs though the Lisbon Treaty incorporates important elements of European Council supervision into the new framework.

level of intergovernmental relations within the European Council and the Council. The reason for this is that decision-making within the decentralised governance contexts of the new areas of EU activity cannot rely on the eventual codification of decisions through EU law. Instead self-commitment on the part of national governments towards commonly stipulated policy objectives is crucial. Even more formal requirements, such as the excessive deficit rule of the Maastricht Treaty and the extended requirements for budgetary policy coordination under the original and reformed Stability and Growth Pact, are in danger of not being followed. This leads to a particular quest for permanent consensus-seeking which goes beyond what is known from areas of legislative decision-making.[10] Most importantly, consensus generation is required at all levels, notably among the most senior representatives of Member State governments and the Commission. Indeed, these changes can be traced empirically. Starting with the creation of the informal Eurogroup in 1998 as a forum for close and informal policy debate among euro area finance ministers, the Commission and the ECB, greater emphasis has been placed on institutionalising collective consensus generation practices up to the highest level—the European Council. This means that forums for high-level policy dialogue are reformed and working methods are adapted so to increase the consensus generation potential of particular contexts of decision-making. This institutional dynamic is referred to as deliberative intergovernmentalism.[11] Deliberative intergovernmentalism does not understand policy coordination as a harmonious exercise but rather holds that Member State governments are strongly committed to engaging in policy dialogue even at times of severe disagreement.

III. WHY AND HOW THE EUROPEAN COUNCIL PRESIDES OVER EU GOVERNANCE

There is little doubt that the European Council has been playing a key role in EU integration for a very long time and it certainly has proved to be the crucial venue for finding agreement on major steps in EU integration and on how to advance from crisis situations.[12] In fact, the European Council was originally created with a view to resolving stalemate in European integration. Its construction revealed the depoliticised nature of EU institutions as far as they were conceived by the Treaty of Rome. It is telling that the European Council was not mentioned within the Treaties until the signing of the Maastricht Treaty, and only acquired the formal status of an EU institution with the Lisbon Treaty. Though the Maastricht Treaty

[10] See on the notion of consensus and policy deliberation in relation to EU legislative processes, the seminal work of C Joerges, 'Deliberative Supranationalism—Two Defences' (2002) 8 *European Law Journal* 133.

[11] U Puetter, 'Europe's Deliberative Intergovernmentalism: The Role of the Council and the European Council in EU Economic Governance' (2012) 19 *Journal of European Public Policy* 161.

[12] *cf* the seminal study on pre-Maastricht European Council activity by S Bulmer and W Wessels, *The European Council. Decision-making in European Politics* (Basingstoke, Macmillan, 1987).

stopped short of assigning the European Council the formal status of an EU institution, it made substantial reference to the high-level forum and assigned it key policy-making and oversight roles. All of these provisions can be found in those parts of the Treaties which deal with the newly constituted areas of EU activity: EMU governance, CFSP and justice and home affairs cooperation.

What may have not been fully clear to the architects and early analysts of the Maastricht Treaty is, however, evident from agenda analysis of European Council activity during the last two decades of European integration, as the author has shown in greater detail elsewhere.[13] There are two main observations to highlight here: the European Council meets much more often and meetings are dominated by the above listed new areas of EU activity. Whereas the European Council met three times per year until the mid-1990s, the number of gatherings started to rise from the second half of the 1990s onwards. While the base number of meetings was first increased to four per year there were several occasions on which additional European Council meetings were convened to deal with urgent foreign affairs or major economic governance issues. Since 2008 at least seven European Council meetings are logged per year—more than twice as many meetings as during the time when the Maastricht Treaty was adopted. In the years 2010 and 2011 the number of European Council meetings peaked as the EU sought to address the Euro-crisis. In 2011 there were 11 meetings altogether of the full European Council and its euro area meeting format—which is now referred to as the Euro Summit (see below).

Yet, there is more evidence to present that explains why the increase in European Council meeting activity is directly related to the launch of new areas of EU activity at Maastricht and beyond, which were based on the principle of policy coordination rather than legislative decision-making under the classic Community method. During the period from 1992 until 2013 EMU economic governance emerges as the most frequently recorded agenda item with 90 occurrences, closely followed by the foreign, security and defence policy portfolio. Indeed, there were hardly any European Council meetings during which these agenda items did not feature. Moreover, though not as prominent as economic governance and foreign affairs, social and employment coordination as well as justice and home affairs cooperation are next in line when it comes to prominent European Council agenda items. Each of them ranks at about the same level as agenda items which are related to Treaty reform and other prominent institutional issues which can be considered to have a constitutional dimension. In contrast, none of the classic domains of single market and Community method integration features prominently on the European Council agenda. This should not be surprising as the European Council was not meant to act as a legislative institution. Even the recurrent budget negotiations are just one aspect on the European Council agenda.

[13] Puetter, *The European Council and the Council* (n 1) 91–111. All European Council agenda data referred to in this chapter is based on the European Council agenda data set developed by the author and first presented in the cited publication.

These findings are also confirmed through interviews with senior civil servants who prepare European Council meetings and assist heads of state and government.[14] It is estimated that on average the heads of state and government spend more than half of their time discussing economic governance issues, which is more than twice as much time as allocated to foreign affairs, the next most time-consuming agenda item. The profile of the European Council has thus changed over time. While at the time of negotiation of the Maastricht Treaty the European Council was mainly a forum for agreeing long-term institutional change and resolving decision-making impasses, it has developed into a regular policy-making forum which also does not shy away from interfering with day-to-day issues in EU decision-making which traditionally would have been dealt with by ministers in the Council. The reason for this is that many issues are politically highly controversial. For example, during the Euro-crisis the European Council dealt with all major bailout decisions and only left the adoption of the 2013 financial assistance package for Cyprus to euro area finance ministers within the Eurogroup.

The European Council indeed plays a lead role in contemporary EU politics. Yet, this role is closely linked to the new areas of EU activity. For these areas it can be said that the European Council presides over the relevant coordination processes. Both the Treaties as well as the European Council through its own decisions have institutionalised this lead role. For example, the Lisbon agenda and its successor the European semester have been built around European Council leadership. The practice of holding European Council spring meetings entirely devoted to socio-economic governance issues emerged from the launch of new and more complex coordination regimes in this policy domain. The centrality of the European Council for high-level consensus seeking is also evident from the fact that since the late 1990s the number of European Council meetings per year steadily increased. In other words coordination failure so far has not led to disintegration but rather resulted in increased efforts for consensus-seeking. This is evident from the experience of the Euro-crisis during which governments responded to difficulties in finding agreement and to perceived deficiencies of the existing coordination set-up by an intensification of high-level political dialogue in the European Council, the Council and the Eurogroup rather than through defecting from the integration process. These activities may well be considered as having done just enough to stop the further spiralling of the crisis rather than providing a more fundamental overhaul of the EMU set-up which would make it more resistant to future crises. A similar tendency is detectable in the domain of foreign and security policy. This confirms one of the key claims of deliberative intergovernmentalism, namely that Member State governments are committed to fostering policy dialogue and deliberation as much as they are committed to further integration within the context of the new areas of EU activity in principle. This claim is not one about the effectiveness but one which acknowledges the link between the paradoxical attitude of Member State governments towards integration and contemporary patterns of institutional change.

[14] As quoted in Puetter (n 1) 91–111.

IV. INSTITUTIONALISING HIGH-LEVEL POLICY DELIBERATION

Deliberative intergovernmentalism holds that this broader trend is also detectable at the level of micro-institutional developments, that is, decision-making routines, working methods and procedures which are used in the context of EU intergovernmental decision-making so to enhance the consensus generation capacity of a particular decision-making context. The European Council can be considered an institution which was originally built on the idea that an intimate setting for confidential face-to-face dialogue would allow the heads to reach political agreement on how to drive integration forward. The main initiators of early summit meetings in the 1970s—French President Valéry Giscard d'Estaing and German Chancellor Helmut Schmidt—apparently wanted to model European summits on the model of G7 fireside chats. Yet, as the European Council developed into an important venue for agreeing on major EU institutional reforms and for dealing with broad agenda-setting it also faced a number of challenges to the original idea of an informal discussion environment. Most importantly, European Council meetings—or summits as they were referred to—were populated not only by the heads but also their foreign ministers who often acted as the domestic coordinators of European-level policy and institutional issues. Moreover, the growing prestige of the European Council also meant that the rotating presidency sought to use the meetings, which took place in the relevant country holding the European Council and Council presidencies, to flag important policy initiatives of national or regional relevance.

Again, institutional change with regard to these features of the European Council working method becomes detectable by the end of the 1990s and early 2000s when the new areas of EU activity gathered momentum and policy coordination intensified. Foreign ministers were gradually excluded from the meetings with more and more meeting time being allocated to exclusive debates among the heads. Today, European Council meetings are no longer held together with the foreign ministers. The Lisbon Treaty acknowledges this change in practice and only includes the participation of ministers as a possibility. This adjustment in the European Council working method reflects the focus on face-to-face debate. Moreover, starting in 2002 more and more European Council meetings were held in Brussels rather than in the country holding the rotating presidency. The Lisbon Treaty finally also ended the practice of having at least one European Council outside Brussels per presidency term. Again, this arrangement made European Council meetings more focused and made them logistically much easier to convene.

This leads to another feature of current European Council working practices. Agenda planning is relatively flexible and the European Council is convened much more often on short notice—an important aspect when it comes to dealing with crisis situations or when unresolved problems in decision-making require a continuation of debate. The European Council also operates a strict confidentiality regime which again emphasises the importance attached to frank and open face-to-face debate among the heads. European Council meetings are split into two parts of which only the first part is held in a larger meeting room with interpreters being present in the interpreter booths. This setting is normally used for the exchange with the president of the EP which is followed by a separate short press conference and the so-called family photo. This part of the meeting is normally kept relatively short and the heads gather on the so-called eightieth floor of the Justus Lipsius building in Brussels—the home of the Council and the European Council. The heads are alone in a room to which no civil servant has access except the General Secretary of the Council who personally assists the European Council president. Interpreters are placed in a different room and cannot see the heads while they are talking.

V. THE EUROPEAN COUNCIL PRESIDENT

The introduction of the office of a full-time president was met with different expectations as to what role the new office-holder would play in EU politics. This was not least related to the debate surrounding the creation of the position in the context of the European Convention. The creation of the post was urgently demanded by the British Prime Minister Tony Blair, French President Jacques Chirac, and German Chancellor Gerhard Schröder.[15] Yet, the Commission and several smaller and medium-sized Member States opposed the creation of such a position.[16] The debate continued when the trading of names for the position started ahead of the December 2009 entering into force of the Lisbon Treaty. British Prime Minister Tony Blair himself became a frequently mentioned name, and observers associated with his name the idea that the EU would be represented by an internationally well-known and charismatic leader who could make difference on the international stage. The Belgium Prime Minister Herman Van Rompuy who then became the first elected European Council President was not considered to possess such qualities though commentators praised his skills in pulling off agreements in the difficult context of Belgian domestic politics.

These views are partially also reflected in the academic literature on leadership within the EU institutions. Rational choice institutionalists conceive of the chair function as a formal leadership role which comes with empowerment.[17] This transfer of power to the chair, they argue, is accepted by the members of the relevant decision-making forum as the latter ones in turn hope for a more effective

[15] Y Devuyst, 'The European Union's Institutional Balance after the Treaty of Lisbon: "Community Method" and "Democratic Deficit" Reassessed' (2008) 39 *Georgetown Journal of International Law* 247 290.

[16] J Tallberg, *Leadership and Negotiation in the European Union* (Cambridge, Cambridge University Press, 2006) 225.

[17] *cf* among many others, Tallberg, *Leadership and Negotiation* (n 16) and S Blavoukos, D Bourantonis and G Pagoulatos, 'A President for the European Union: A New Institutional Actor in Town' (2007) 45 *Journal of Common Market Studies* 231.

decision-making process and greater continuity in the external representation of collective positions. The office of the full-time European Council president was thus also seen as a potential source of a principal–agent dilemma.[18] This implies that the office holder may pursue their own political agenda or even act as a policy entrepreneur independent of the Member State governments represented within the European Council. A more recent perspective on the European Council presidency proposed by Federico Fabbrini,[19] suggests responding to power asymmetries in the European Council by the (further) politicisation of the role of the European Council president through the election by EU citizens. Though this argument is reviewed again towards the end of the chapter it is noteworthy here, as it also associates a strong political agenda-setting role with the role of the European Council president.

Yet, evidence from the two terms of Herman Van Rompuy's presidency suggests that none of the above interpretations of formal leadership in relation to the office of European Council president is really adequate. Deliberative intergovernmentalism offers an alternative explanation. Next to the above outlined measures of modifying the European Council's working methods, so to enhance the forum's capacity to generate agreement among the EU's most senior decision-makers, the creation of the office of a full-time European Council president is seen as an important act of institutional engineering which has the very same objective. Here again, deliberative intergovernmentalism attributes the developmental trajectory of the European Council presidency after the entering into force of the Lisbon Treaty to the institutional dilemmas associated with the integration paradox. As Member State governments insist on keeping delegation to the absolute minimum but at the same time are keen to enhance their ability to respond collectively to common policy challenges the intensification of intergovernmental policy coordination becomes a key objective and consensus is considered almost as an end in itself,[20] as consensus stands for the EU's ability to act.

Van Rompuy indeed personified this approach. This became clear with one of his first major programmatic speeches when he declared that his key priority was to ensure that Europe was united in its policy approach within the two most prominent new areas of EU activity: economic governance and foreign and security policy.[21] Most importantly, Van Rompuy refrained from being seen as being associated with a particular policy stance other than the one emerging from European Council discussion. Van Rompuy concluded at the end of his second

[18] W Wessels and T Traguth, 'Der hauptamtlich Präsident des Europäischen Rates: "Herr" oder "Diener" im Haus Europa?' (2010) 33 *Integration* 297.

[19] F Fabbrini, 'Austerity, the European Council and the Institutional Future of the EU: A Proposal to Strengthen the Presidency of the European Council' (2015) 22 *Indiana Journal of Global Legal Studies*.

[20] Bickerton, Hodson and Puetter (n 1).

[21] H Van Rompuy, 'The Challenges for Europe in a Changing World', speech delivered at the College of Europe, European Council Press Release PCE 34/10, Bruges, 25 February 2010.

term that his original idea of how the mandate of the president of the European Council should be exercised was still valid and reiterated a statement given during his inaugural speech following his appointment in November 2009:

> As President of the [European] Council, I will listen to everyone and ensure that our deliberations yield results for all parties ... [M]uch has been said about the profile of the President of the [European] Council, but only one profile is possible, and that is one of dialogue, unity and action. The image of the [European] Council is based on the results achieved.[22]

It would be misleading to consider Van Rompuy a weak president though he certainly did not act as a supranational policy entrepreneur—a quality which is in EU studies rightly or wrongly often attributed to Jacques Delors' role at the helm of the Commission during the 1990s.[23] Next to the apparent ambition not to be seen as a political president with his own policy agenda, Van Rompuy also avoided developing a particularly visible profile as a, or even the, lead EU spokesperson within the domain of international affairs. This also meant that, contrary to many expectations, open conflict and inter-institutional competition with the High Representative Catherine Ashton were absent from Van Rompuy's two terms.

That he enjoyed at least some authority in his role as a facilitator of agreement among the heads of states and government may be also documented by the fact that his role at no point was openly challenged—something which seemed at least a possibility after the public controversies surrounding his appointment. In fact, Van Rompuy was neither accused of imposing a particular position on the members of the European Council nor did he draw criticism for being weak or ineffective in his role as president. He was re-elected to serve for a second term in 2012. It, of course, could be said that the heads were happy to have a president who did not aspire to challenge them in their own roles as national leaders who are eager to portray themselves as leading within the field of EU politics too. Yet, again it would be misleading to assume that the European Council could have operated in the same way it did in the years following Van Rompuy's first appointment without a full-time president. A further hint that the members of the European Council were also very well aware of the important role of the full-time president was provided with the selection of Van Rompuy's successor. After the European Parliament elections in May 2014 two names were circulating for a considerable period of time as potential successors: the Danish Prime Minister Helle Thorning-Schmidt and the Polish Prime Minister Donald Tusk who eventually became European Council president. Both politicians were far from being seen as weak or unknown in EU politics. At the same time, they both played actives roles in the domestic politics of their countries and needed to consider leaving their careers at home in exchange for the European Council presidency. Moreover, both were

[22] H Van Rompuy, 'Calm Stability in Times of Crisis', speech delivered at the University of Leiden, European Council Press Release EUCO 240/14, Leiden, 10 October 2014.

[23] *cf* especially G Ross, *Jacques Delors and European Integration* (Cambridge, Polity Press, 1995).

associated with playing a supportive behind-the-scenes role during the respective Council presidencies of their home countries and were considered to be skilful negotiators and bridge-builders.

Deliberative intergovernmentalism indeed interprets the role of the full-time European Council president, as exemplified by the role exercised by Van Rompuy during his two terms, as the one of a chief institutional engineer. This notion relates to the idea of institutional engineering as a key motive in processes of institutional change, that is, the deliberate attempt to modify political institutions and their internal structures or modes of operation so as to influence the outcome of decision-making processes.[24] The role of the full-time European Council president is exactly this. There are several instruments and types of activity characteristic of this role. The most obvious one, which is well-known from the time of the rotating presidency, is the one of a mediator, honest-broker and someone who prepares or follows up on the actual collective policy debate through bilateral conversations with individual heads in between the European Council meetings. Here, the advantage of the permanent president is that he cannot get distracted by a simultaneous role in domestic politics. Van Rompuy spent more time on bilateral diplomacy than any other previous European Council president. In fact, there are strong indications that this role within the context of the Euro-crisis was so time-consuming that there was indeed very little room for defining the presidency in a radically different way than Van Rompuy did. An interesting example in this regard is the role of the High Representative who has similar responsibilities to the European Council president with regard to coordinating and leading the work of the Foreign Affairs Council. Yet, in contrast to the European Council president, her mandate leaves little doubt that the role of the chair is only one of her various obligations—notably the ones as the EU's external spokesperson on external affairs and as head of the European External Action Service. As a consequence of these multiple tasks, the first High Representative, Catherine Ashton, found herself often being accused of fulfilling none of these roles to the full satisfaction of her peers.

Next to bilateral coordination activities, another key activity of the European Council president, as Van Rompuy's two terms showed, is to organise and reorganise the work of the European Council as a forum for policy deliberation and joint decision-making. Agenda-setting and the organisation of the European Council working methods are the key aspects to be considered here. Again, the agenda-setting powers of the president are often associated with the opportunity to pursue their own political agenda. There is very little evidence that Van Rompuy sought to do this, yet he clearly concentrated the work of the European Council on the domains of economic governance and foreign policy. For example, there was a risk that the latter domain was neglected in the context of the European Council's

[24] The notion of institutional engineering is borrowed from and built on the term 'constitutional engineering' coined by Giovanni Satori. G Satori, *Comparative Constitutional Engineering: An Inquiry into Structures, Incentives, and Outcomes* (New York, New York University Press, 1994).

involvement in Euro-crisis management, a development Van Rompuy sought to address through agenda-setting. Moreover, Van Rompuy introduced a mix of strategic and informal orientation debates which were deliberately not aimed at decision-making, on the one hand, and discussions which were geared towards achieving exactly this. The former mode of interaction can be highly relevant in a context in which policy-makers seek to react to common policy challenges in relation to which there is uncertainty about the appropriateness of particular policy responses. Orientation debates make the heads aware of how others think about a particular policy challenge and whether there is room for common action given diverging views on a particular issue. The fact that no final decisions need to be taken at the meeting makes it easier to explore policy options.

The search for responses to the Euro-crisis during the years 2008 to 2012 probably involved the most intensive decision-making activities of the European Council so far. At the same time, uncertainty about the appropriateness of certain policy was coupled with redistributive conflicts over sharing the burdens of crisis management. The appointment of Van Rompuy as European Council president coincided with a particularly critical phase within the Euro-crisis. Until the end of 2009, severe problems with the refinancing of Greek government debt had become apparent and concerns grew rapidly that the crisis, which so far was mainly perceived as a global financial crisis, could threaten the integrity of the euro area. Among Van Rompuy's various activities as a chair, there are two important episodes which are particularly noteworthy as they involve a combination of all key roles of the president as an institutional engineer: the creation of the routine of special meetings of the euro area heads, and the so-called Van Rompuy Task Force dealing with institutional reform.

In October 2008 when the EU just had started to get on its feet to think more seriously about collective responses to the spreading banking crisis, French President Nicolas Sarkozy, in his capacity as holder of the then still rotating European Council presidency, called an emergency summit in Paris of the EU's G8 members and the presidents of the Eurogroup, the Commission and the ECB. The meeting was considered to have constituted an important political statement—though the outcome was of little substance in terms of concrete policy choices—that the EU would address the consequences of the global financial crisis in the months ahead. Yet, the gathering also proved controversial with many Member State governments as it threatened the unity of the European Council as an institution which equally represents all Member State governments. In the following year, the French government in particular, advocated exclusive meetings of the euro area members of the European Council to deal with crisis management as discussions among all EU Member States were seen as being too cumbersome and slow. Yet, many governments were sceptical including the German government and governments from Central and Eastern Europe as Hungary and Latvia had been the first countries to receive financial aid in response to occurring refinancing problems. Moreover, increasing G-20 coordination implied that the European Council took decisions on the common EU position within this forum which in turn had repercussions for all Member States and not just the euro area.

The situation rapidly changed only a few months after Van Rompuy took office in November 2009. The first quarter of 2010 was the time when the EU could no longer avoid a statement to pledge financial aid to Greece. Yet, decision-making proved difficult as the move was essentially seen as an act of defending the integrity of the euro area rather than of the EU. The UK and other non-euro area Member States showed little intention to become financially involved. Decision-making within the euro area was difficult too, as the pledge of financial aid in this situation was seen to undermine EMU's so-called no-bailout clause, which prevents a euro area Member State from becoming responsible for the repayment of debt of another euro area Member State. Moreover, the required financial resources implied difficulties for a number of euro area countries as governments faced hostile public opinion on the issue. It was in this situation that Van Rompuy called the first informal meeting of the euro area members of the European Council including the president of the Commission. The gathering took place in the context of the regular spring meeting of the European Council at the end of March 2010 and had not been officially announced ahead of the summit.[25] It produced the first clear statement that the euro area Member States were ready to provide financial assistance to Greece.[26] A more general statement by the full European Council on the same issue in February of the same year had failed to calm financial markets.[27]

Van Rompuy used this meeting format several times in 2010 and 2011 as the main forum for negotiating the various financial assistance packages which were assigned to Greece, Ireland, Portugal and Spain. In his capacity as European Council, president Van Rompuy lent legitimacy to the euro area meetings and, yet, was able to bridge the divide as far as possible. It was eventually in October 2011 when the new informal meeting format was given the name 'Euro Summit' and Van Rompuy was officially appointed as president of the Euro Summit.[28] This act of self-empowerment by the Euro Summit was later also codified by Article 12 of the Treaty on Stability, Coordination and Governance in the EMU, which was signed in March 2012 as an intergovernmental treaty outside EU law and which is also known as the Fiscal Compact. Contrary to some expectations, Euro Summit meeting activity decreased rapidly after the main financial assistance packages had been negotiated and the full European Council, rather than the Euro Summit, dealt with most of the EMU economic governance agenda items during the years 2012, 2013 and 2014. The alternative meeting format was important in giving euro area Member States the opportunity to address their internal controversies surrounding the pledge of financial assistance to crisis-hit countries, and equally

[25] As reported by Agence Europe, 24 and 25 March 2010.

[26] *cf* 'Statement by the Heads of State and Government of the Euro Area', 25 March 2010, available at: www.consilium.europa.eu/uedocs/cms_data/docs/pressdata/en/ec/113563.pdf.

[27] *cf* 'Statement by the Heads of State and Government of the European Union', 11 February 2010, available at: www.consilium.europa.eu/uedocs/cms_data/docs/pressdata/en/ec/112856.pdf.

[28] *cf* 'Euro Summit Statement', 26 October 2011, available at: www.consilium.europa.eu/uedocs/cms_data/docs/pressdata/en/ec/125644.pdf.

to display political will and unity by showing their ability to reach consensus on this key aspect of crisis management.

Van Rompuy's role as European Council president in the context of Euro-crisis management is further illustrated by the work of the Van Rompuy Task Force which was also created at the March 2010 meetings of the European Council and the euro area heads in Brussels. The group consisted of all EU finance ministers, the Commission and Van Rompuy as chair of the group and was mandated to develop concrete proposals for EMU institutional reform. The so-called six-pack of reforms to the Stability and Growth Pact and EMU's coordination and surveillance regime is one of the outcomes of this work. During the period May 2010 to October 2010 the group met six times. Van Rompuy subsequently reported to the European Council about the work of the Task Force and in turn worked towards reaching final agreement among the heads on the envisaged reform package. The approach not only represented an unprecedented approach towards relations with finance ministers on part of the European Council but also implied that EU governments monopolised policy initiative and thus reduced the role of the Commission to the one of an implementing actor. These dynamics were fully in line with the new intergovernmentalism prevailing within the domain of EMU.

Here again, Van Rompuy refrained from aggressively pushing his own policy preferences but primarily worked as someone who sought to constitute a particular platform for collective decision-making. In a similar way, Van Rompuy worked with the presidents of the Eurogroup, the Commission and the ECB in the second half of 2012 on proposals for further reforms related to the EMU policy coordination regime and the creation of a European Banking Union. The process led to the decision of the European Council of December 2012 to press ahead with Banking Union and the so-called two-pack, which complemented the original six-pack of legislative acts reforming EMU's policy coordination and surveillance regime. Here again, Van Rompuy ensured that the European Council exercised close oversight over policy initiation processes and that the heads moved towards a final decision despite existing differences in opinion about the scope and direction of reforms. By all EU standards both reform processes were fast.

VI. THE FURTHER DEVELOPMENT OF THE NEW INSTITUTIONAL ARCHITECTURE

There is little doubt that the new institutional architecture of post-Maastricht European integration triggers debate about the further development of decision-making routines and institutional mandates and roles. Most importantly, the new role of the European Council as the political centre of Europe's new intergovernmentalism triggers questions about changes in the relative importance of other institutional actors, the relations between Member States and EU democracy. An important concern is that the emphasis on elite consensus within the European

Council may compromise 'the EU's ability to be politically responsive'[29] and to undermine core legal principles on which the EU's political order has been based so far. Moreover, the empowerment of the European Council takes place within an institutional environment which has seen a sustained growth in executive power throughout the post-Maastricht period, not only at the level of the heads.[30] This raises the question of whether and how non-executive actors, notably national parliaments and the EP, are still in a position to fundamentally challenge executive power.[31] The roles of the European Council in Euro-crisis management outlined above seem to reinforce all these concerns. Another lacuna in the discussion about the rising power of the European Council is opened up with regard to the question of whether the particular style of European Council decision-making further enables certain Member States to play a dominant role in EU politics in relation to others. Notably, Germany is seen to have played such a role in the context of the Euro-crisis. Here, formal mechanisms are seen as missing which would ensure equal representation of all Member States regardless of their size and budgetary position.[32]

Several of these aspects are debated in greater detail in other chapters of this book. However, it is worth focussing attention on one particular issue: the question of whether adjustments to the formal institutional framework for European Council action or, in other words, its constitutional mandate could correct some of the diagnosed difficulties. The answer is that this is unlikely in the current context of European integration. The argument here is that the new intergovernmentalism is based on a post-Maastricht integration paradox. It does not represent a political architecture which is one of clear political choice but is one which has developed to considerable extent through practice. As highlighted above, the architects of the Maastricht Treaty and many of the political and legal analysts of the time were not or at least not fully aware of the consequences for institutional design the 1992 Treaty would have. Most importantly, they were still seeing intergovernmental policy coordination as a transitory phenomenon in EU governance which would be replaced by a gradual communitarisation of the new policy domains at some point. This so far has not happened. Yet, integration has moved on.

The backlash against delegation along traditional lines which the EU has witnessed over the last two decades of integration may not be that unusual for a highly developed system of multi-level governance—what the EU certainly has become. It is the very fact that the EU today is a more powerful source of policy-making than it ever was before, which in turn motivates national governments' preference

[29] M Dawson and F de Witte 'Constitutional Balance in the EU after the Euro-crisis' (2013) 76 *The Modern Law Review* 817.

[30] D Curtin 'Challenging Executive Dominance in European Democracy' (2014) 77 *The Modern Law Review* 1.

[31] See also the contribution by D Curtin, ch 10 in this volume.

[32] Fabbrini, 'Austerity' (n 19).

for tightly controlling all stages of EU decision-making and leaving little room for autonomous supranational policy initiative. Closer intergovernmental relations are in no contradiction to this phenomenon as other multi-level policies such as Canada show. The rejection of delegation is not necessarily identical to the rejection of the idea that common policy challenges and growing policy interdependencies require collective action. The very fact that closer intergovernmental policy coordination develops in response and in parallel to a centralised and established system of regulation, constitutionalism and collective decision-making makes them difficult to control. Yet, intergovernmental structures as alternative venues for collective action allow Member State governments to preserve their status as formally sovereign political actors.

The point here is not to project a teleological argument about the future of the EU. Political institutions may indeed be subject to more radical overhaul should the politics of European integration change more fundamentally—and this may be in one or the other direction as the Euro-crisis showed. However, there is little evidence for this currently to take place. For this reason there is little room for a communitarisation of economic governance nor for modifying decision-making dynamics within the European Council through a politicisation of the office of the European Council president to making it subject to EU-wide electoral competition, as Federico Fabbrini suggests. As argued in this chapter, the role of the European Council president as an institutional engineer rather than one of a supranational policy entrepreneur was no coincidence, but part of the wider institutional dynamic of deliberative intergovernmentalism which developed as a consequence of the integration paradox. Again, the emergence of these new institutional structures is not free of contradictions as much as the underlying context of European integration from which they emerge is of a paradoxical nature. The point here is to acknowledge the persistence or stickiness of this paradoxical nature in contemporary EU politics and not to reject quite appropriate concerns about the long-term sustainability of these institutional arrangements. Indeed, the author, together with Chris Bickerton and Dermot Hodson, has argued that the EU's institutional architecture as it has emerged within the context of post-Maastricht new intergovernmentalism is in a constant state of disequilibrium.[33]

[33] *cf* the sixth hypothesis of the new intergovernmentalism as outlined in C Bickerton, D Hodson and U Puetter (n 1).

15

Inter-Parliamentary Cooperation and its Challenges: The Case of Economic and Financial Governance

VALENTIN KREILINGER*

I. INTRODUCTION

THE TREATY ON Stability, Coordination and Governance (TSCG) has provided for the creation of an inter-parliamentary conference in order to discuss budgetary policies and other issues covered by that treaty.[1] Fiscal and economic policy coordination in the Economic and Monetary Union (EMU) has become much more intense and takes place between the European Commission and national governments in the Council. The pressure put on Member States is based on a stronger legal framework, composed of the 'six-pack', the TSCG and the 'two-pack',[2] and is visible in the functioning of the 'European Semester'.[3] In this framework, parliamentary scrutiny of budgetary policies by individual national parliaments and by the European Parliament (EP) is limited.[4]

To address this state of affairs, increasing pressures have mounted to strengthen cooperation between the EP and national parliaments. According to many, inter-parliamentary cooperation and scrutiny could compensate national parliaments for the transfer of power from the national to the European level and for the transfer of power from national parliaments to their governments with respect to fiscal

* I would like to thank Federico Fabbrini, the participants of the conference at Tilburg University in June 2014, and Christian Deubner for very helpful comments on earlier drafts of this chapter.

[1] See Art 13 TSCG.

[2] For a detailed account, see P Craig, 'Economic Governance and the Euro Crisis: Constitutional Architecture and Constitutional Implications' in M Adams, F Fabbrini and P Larouche (eds), *The Constitutionalization of European Budgetary Constraints* (Oxford, Hart Publishing, 2014).

[3] The European Semester is foreseen by Art 2(a) Regulation 1466/97 amended by Regulation 1175/2011.

[4] See D Chalmers, 'The European Redistributive State and a European Law of Struggle' (2012) 18 *European Law Journal* 667, 693 (stating that a 'zone of influence dominated by the Commission and ECOFIN is established, with political conflicts taking place within these, but the atrophying of local democracy leads to a hollowing out of domestic processes so that these become little more than administrative containers'.)

and economic policy.[5] It could also allow the EP to exert influence in an area with little legislative activity and an only marginal role of the EP. However, inter-parliamentary cooperation in the area of economic and financial governance has met several challenges and has so far moved forward slowly.

The challenges of inter-parliamentary cooperation in economic and financial governance reflect those that have been encountered in foreign and security policy,[6] but might be even more difficult to resolve, because the general relationship between the two parliamentary levels is still characterised by conflict, rather than cooperation.[7] But the executive dominance in fiscal and economic policy coordination could put pressure on national parliaments and the EP to work together against their declining influence and 'exert countervailing power, both individually and collectively'.[8] This chapter puts forward the idea that the purpose of a *joint scrutiny* inter-parliamentary cooperation should be to 'discuss' matters of common interest and to 'control' in areas with weak parliamentary scrutiny. However, inter-parliamentary settings should *not* 'decide', because assigning decision-making power to an inter-parliamentary conference would significantly alter the EU inter-institutional equilibrium.

The chapter is structured as follows: Section II describes inter-parliamentary cooperation as it is defined in the treaties and by inter-parliamentary practices. Although the Members of the European Parliament (MEPs) and members of national parliaments (MPs) meet regularly in organised settings, the meaning of inter-parliamentary cooperation is ill-defined and two contradictory concepts co-exist: Inter-parliamentary cooperation as 'centralised scrutiny' dominated by the EP, with only very limited input by national parliaments; and inter-parliamentary cooperation as 'joint scrutiny' by national parliaments and the EP.[9] Section III examines the concept of centralised scrutiny defended by the EP that aims at keeping inter-parliamentary cooperation weak. Section IV reviews the idea of joint scrutiny endorsed by many national parliaments, although not the national parliaments of all 28 Member States.[10] Here, the cases of the parliaments of Denmark,

[5] See, eg C Deubner, 'Stärkere Parlamente in der neuen WWU-Gouvernanz?' (2014) 37 *integration* 21, 44; A Maurer, *From EMU to DEMU: The Democratic Legitimacy of the EU and the European Parliament* (Rome, Istituto affari internazionali, 2013) 14; W Wessels, et al, *Democratic Control in the Member States of the European Council and the Euro Zone Summits* (European Parliament, 2012) 29.

[6] A Herranz-Surrallés, 'The EU's Multilevel Parliamentary (Battle)Field: Inter-parliamentary Cooperation and Conflict in Foreign and Security Policy' (2014) 37 *West European Politics* 957.

[7] K Neunreither, 'The European Parliament and National Parliaments: Conflict or Cooperation?' (2005) 11 *Journal of Legislative Studies* 466.

[8] D Curtin, 'Challenging Executive Dominance in European Democracy' (2014) 77 *Modern Law Review* 1, 30.

[9] I Cooper, 'Parliamentary Oversight of the EU after the Crisis: On the Creation of the "Article 13" Interparliamentary Conference' (LUISS School of Government Working Papers, 2014) 2.

[10] For the preferences of national parliaments and European institutions on Article 13 TSCG and its implementation, ibid. with the most recent account; C Deubner, *The Difficult Role of Parliaments in the Reformed Governance of the Economic and Monetary Union* (Brussels, Foundation of European Progressive Studies, 2013); V Kreilinger, *The New Inter-parliamentary Conference on Economic and Financial Governance* (Notre Europe—Jacques Delors Institute, 2013); and Maurer, *From EMU to DEMU* (n 5).

France, Germany and Lithuania are analysed in more detail. Strong 'joint scrutiny' mechanisms are, for example, backed by the French Parliament, while the German Parliament prefers a weaker form of 'joint scrutiny'. This allows classifying parliaments according to three roles as *inward-looking*, *passively cooperative* or *actively networking* with respect to inter-parliamentary cooperation. Section V, finally, gives a summary of the findings of this chapter and an assessment of the prospects for inter-parliamentary cooperation in economic and financial governance.

II. COOPERATION BETWEEN THE EUROPEAN PARLIAMENT AND NATIONAL PARLIAMENTS IN THE TREATIES AND IN PRACTICE

According to Article 12 TEU national parliaments 'contribute actively to the good functioning of the Union ... by taking part in the inter-parliamentary cooperation between national Parliaments and with the European Parliament'.[11] The precise legal basis for inter-parliamentary cooperation can be found in Protocol No 1 on the Role of National Parliaments annexed to the EU treaties: 'the organisation and promotion of effective and regular inter-parliamentary cooperation within the Union shall be determined by the European Parliament and National Parliaments'.[12] Article 10 of Protocol No 1 specifies that a

> conference of Parliamentary Committees for Union Affairs ... shall ... promote the exchange of information and best practice between National Parliaments and the European Parliament, including their special committees. It may also organise inter-parliamentary conferences on specific topics ... Contributions from the conference shall not bind National Parliaments and shall not prejudge their positions.[13]

This provision of the Protocol recognises the Conference of Parliamentary Committees for Union Affairs of Parliaments of the EU (COSAC) which was established in 1989. Based on the COSAC model two new policy-specific inter-parliamentary conferences were created recently. On the one hand, the Inter-parliamentary Conference on Common Foreign Security Policy (CFSP) and Common Security and Defence Policy (CSDP) substituted the Assembly of the West European Union (WEU) in 2012. On the other hand, the need for better cooperation between national parliaments and the EP with respect to the EMU was acknowledged by the TSCG,[14] and it prompted the creation of an inter-parliamentary conference which had its first meeting in October 2013.

Article 13 TSCG is the product of the intergovernmental negotiations and has undergone significant changes during the negotiating process, revealing the difficulties met by the Member States in reaching an agreement on this point. The original objective of the treaty article was that national MPs meet regularly and

[11] Art 12 TEU.

[12] Art 9, Protocol No 1 on the Role of National Parliaments in the European Union annexed to the European Union Treaties.

[13] ibid Art 10.

[14] See above (n 1).

that this would happen in close association with the EP. Article 13 was completely revised twice and only the later drafts of the treaty drew a link to the existing inter-parliamentary structures.[15] Member States may have included the article in the treaty in order to facilitate the national ratification processes of the TSCG. The final wording of Article 13 agreed by the Contracting Parties is the following:

> As provided for in Title II of Protocol (No 1) on the role of national Parliaments in the European Union annexed to the European Union Treaties, the European Parliament and the national Parliaments of the Contracting Parties will together determine the organisation and promotion of a conference of representatives of the relevant committees of the European Parliament and representatives of the relevant committees of national Parliaments in order to discuss budgetary policies and other issues covered by this Treaty.[16]

In the national ratification processes of the TSCG and in discussions about how to achieve a 'genuine EMU' the question of the implementation of Article 13 TSCG emerged on the agenda and parliaments started to address the issue. Both chairpersons of European Affairs Committees and Speakers of Parliaments held informal ad hoc meetings in sub-groups and tried to coordinate their positions. After many actors had articulated their preferences, sometimes both individually and collectively, it was the 'Speakers' Conference' in April 2013 (the annual meeting of the Speakers of all EU parliaments) that agreed on a compromise about the organisation of the inter-parliamentary conference.[17] Thus the conclusions of the Speakers' Conference provided the basis for bringing Article 13 TSCG into practice in October 2013. Since then the inter-parliamentary conference has discussed whether it should adopt Rules of Procedure and possible provisions to be included into them: the Parliament of Lithuania presented a draft[18] which was not endorsed by the conference, the following Presidency (Greece) asked all parliaments for input, and at the September 2014 meeting (organised by the Italian Parliament) the internal organisation was an item on the agenda and discussed at the inter-parliamentary conference, but no agreement was reached and further discussions were postponed until 2015.

Many analysts have assessed inter-parliamentary cooperation as beneficial, both from a rationalist and a normative perspective: inter-parliamentary cooperation could reduce informational asymmetries, favour the exchange of specialised knowledge, facilitate policy formulation, and foster mutual understanding and a

[15] For a detailed discussion of the drafting of the TSCG, see V Kreilinger, *The Making of a New Treaty: Six Rounds of Political Bargaining* (Notre Europe—Jacques Delors Institute, 2012).

[16] See above (n 1).

[17] Conference of Speakers of European Union Parliaments, 'Presidency Conclusions—Nicosia, 21–23 April 2014' available at: www.ipex.eu/IPEXL-WEB/dossier/files/download/082dbcc53dbcb6ed013e3b68418b5327.do. For an analysis of the compromise, see Kreilinger, *The Making of a New Treaty* (n 15) 14.

[18] Parliament of Lithuania, 'Draft Rules of Procedure of the Interparliamentary Conference on Economic and Financial Governance of the European Union', 2013.

transnational public debate.[19] Inter-parliamentary cooperation could not only contribute to reducing the democratic deficit by giving a collective voice to parliaments, but the exchange of information and best practices for individual scrutiny could also lead to stronger parliamentary control of national governments and EU institutions. This would strengthen both elements of the dual legitimacy on which the political system of the EU relies—the democratic institutions of the Member States and the directly elected EP.[20] However, the TSCG and the Treaty establishing a European Stability Mechanism (ESM) do 'little or nothing to anchor new regulatory functions for the Union in democratic institutions'.[21]

At the same time, 'the intergovernmental logic brings with it an inter-parliamentary balancing':[22] the main theoretical rationale behind resorting to inter-parliamentary cooperation in economic and financial governance lies in the use of intergovernmental legal instruments in that area. More far-reaching concepts for multi-level parliamentarism insist that: 'The dominance of the member state governments in the European Council needs to be balanced with an equally strong voice of parliamentary representation.'[23] If Member States had not resorted to the intergovernmental or to the 'Union method',[24] economic and financial affairs would be governed by the Community method and the EP would be entirely responsible for democratic control.[25]

In practice, there are some challenges for inter-parliamentary cooperation.[26] The participation rates of national parliaments in such conferences illustrate the ambiguous interest of MPs in European affairs: COSAC meetings from 2009 to 2013 show a considerable variation across EU Member States and this assessment was confirmed for the inter-parliamentary conference on economic and

[19] See especially, Herranz-Surrallés, 'The EU's Multilevel Parliamentary (Battle)Field' (n 6) 2; A Benz, 'Linking Multiple Demoi: Inter-parliamentary Relations in the EU' (2011) 12 *Hagener Online-Beiträge zu den Europäischen Verfassungswissenschaften* 11; C Kraft-Kasack, 'Transnational Parliamentary Assemblies: A Remedy for the Democratic Deficit of International Governance?' (2008) 31 *West European Politics* 534; K Neunreither, 'The Democratic Deficit of the European Union: Towards Closer Cooperation between the European Parliament and the National Parliaments' (1994) 29 *Government and Opposition* 299.

[20] See, eg Neunreither, 'The Democratic Deficit' (n 19).

[21] M Dawson and F de Witte, 'Constitutional Balance in the EU after the Euro-Crisis' (2013) 76 *Modern Law Review* 817, 834.

[22] S Fabbrini, *Intergovermentalism and its Outcomes: The Implications of the Euro Crisis on the European Union* (LUISS School of Government Working Papers Series, 2013) 12.

[23] J Neyer, 'Justified Multi-level Parliamentarism: Situating National Parliaments in the European Polity' (2014) 20 *Journal of Legislative Studies* 125, 135.

[24] A Merkel, Speech at the opening ceremony of the 61st academic year of the College of Europe in Bruges on 2 November 2010.

[25] On the Community method, see for a summary, eg R Dehousse, *La méthode communautaire, système opérationnel "par défaut" de l'UE* (Notre Europe—Jacques Delors Institute, 2013).

[26] O Costa and M Latek 'Paradoxes and Limits of Interparliamentary Cooperation in the European Union' (2001) 23 *Journal of European Integration* 139; T Raunio, 'National Parliaments and European Integration: What we know and Agenda for Future Research' (2009) 15 *Journal of Legislative Studies* 317.

financial governance.[27] Thus relations between national parliaments have so far 'not develop[ed] into a balanced multilateral interplay including parliaments from all member states on the same footing'.[28]

In addition to that, two different concepts of inter-parliamentary cooperation coexist: the key question is whether there should be *centralised scrutiny* or *joint scrutiny*. 'Centralised scrutiny' means that inter-parliamentary cooperation is dominated by the EP, with only very limited input by national parliaments; the competing concept is inter-parliamentary cooperation as 'joint scrutiny' by national parliaments and the EP.[29]

These different concepts reflect disagreement about which functions an inter-parliamentary conference should fulfil. Disagreement typically centres on the actual purpose of inter-parliamentary cooperation: Should it decide? Should it control? Should it discuss? Moreover, it concerns basic issues such as the formal weight to be given to the two parliamentary levels: should the EP delegation have as many seats as each of the national parliaments or should it have more?[30]

The underlying explanation of the profound disagreements between national parliaments and the EP is a mismatch between the daily EU policy-making and formal treaty powers which lead to 'overlapping authority claims':[31] an incremental and informal empowerment of the EP, even in economic and financial governance, clashes with national parliaments and their constitutional role linked to intergovernmental treaties and their domestic role in controlling national governments. This prevents sharing the scrutiny tasks between national parliaments and the EP in EMU governance.[32]

III. INTER-PARLIAMENTARY COOPERATION AS *CENTRALISED SCRUTINY* DOMINATED BY THE EUROPEAN PARLIAMENT

The EP has traditionally been sceptical about enhancing the role of national parliaments, fearing that this might undermine its position.[33] In an own-initiative report on a genuine EMU, the EP stated in November 2012 that only itself, 'as parliamentary body at the Union level for a reinforced and democratic EMU

27 For data on COSAC: Kreilinger, *The New Inter-parliamentary Conference* (n 10) 5. For data on the first inter-parliamentary conference on economic and financial governance, V Kreilinger, 'Possibilities for Upgrading Inter-parliamentary Cooperation after the 2014 European Elections' (2014) 23 *Polish Quarterly of International Affairs* 57, 59.

28 Benz, 'Linking Multiple Demoi' (n 19) 11.

29 Cooper, 'Parliamentary Oversight of the EU' (n 9) 2.

30 Kreilinger, 'Possibilities for Upgrading Inter-parliamentary Cooperation' (n 27) 58.

31 Herranz-Surrallés (n 6) 15.

32 See Deubner, 'Stärkere Parlamente in der neuen WWU-Gouvernanz?' (n 5) 37.

33 See, eg B Crum and JE Fossum, 'Conclusion: Towards a Democratic Multilevel Parliamentary Field?' in B Crum and JE Fossum (eds), *Practices of Inter-parliamentary Coordination in International Politics the European Union and Beyond* (Colchester, ECPR Press, 2013) 255.

governance',[34] had full democratic legitimacy to exercise control in that area. The report, drafted by Marianne Thyssen MEP, described the possibility of creating a mixed parliamentary body as 'both ineffective and illegitimate':

> While reaffirming its intention to intensify the cooperation with national parliaments on the basis of Protocol No 1, [it] stresses that such a cooperation should not be seen as the creation of a new mixed parliamentary body which would be both ineffective and illegitimate on a democratic and constitutional point of view; [it also] stresses the full legitimacy of the European Parliament, as parliamentary body at the Union level for a reinforced and democratic EMU governance.[35]

In its blueprint for a deep and genuine EMU, also published in November 2012, the European Commission took a critical view on inter-parliamentary cooperation, too, and echoed the Parliament's view by stating:

> The role of national parliaments will always remain crucial in ensuring legitimacy of Member States' action ... Cooperation between the European Parliament and national parliaments is also valuable: it builds up mutual understanding and common ownership for EMU as a multilevel governance system ... Inter-parliamentary cooperation as such does not, however, ensure democratic legitimacy for EU decisions. That requires a parliamentary assembly representatively composed in which votes can be taken. The European Parliament, and only it, is that assembly for the EU and hence for the euro.[36]

The EU supranational institutions thus reject the view that cooperation between the EP and national parliaments may provide democratic legitimacy for EMU-related decisions. The final report 'towards a genuine Economic and Monetary Union' drafted by the President of the European Council puts the EP at the centre of ensuring democratic legitimacy and accountability. At the end of the process, the European Council conclusions of 13–14 December 2012 affirm that: 'The European Parliament and national parliaments will determine together the organisation and promotion of a conference of their representatives to discuss EMU related issues.'[37] This is exactly the wording of Article 13 TSCG as it had emerged in January 2012.[38]

The concept of inter-parliamentary cooperation as *centralised scrutiny* dominated by the EP has gained traction at the EU level. According to this reasoning *only* the EP is able 'to stress the points of convergence and the shared interests amongst the parliamentarians and citizens of different Member States, instead of aiming at achieving exclusively national interests'.[39] The President of the European

[34] European Parliament, Report with recommendations to the Commission on the report of the Presidents of the European Council, the European Commission, the European Central Bank and the Eurogroup 'Towards a genuine Economic and Monetary Union' (19 November 2012, 2012/2151(INI)) 19.

[35] ibid.

[36] European Commission, 'A blueprint for a deep and genuine economic and monetary union: Launching a European Debate', 28 November 2012, COM (2012) 777 final 35.

[37] European Council, Conclusions of 13–14 December (2012, EUCO 205/12).

[38] See Kreilinger (n 15).

[39] C Fasone, 'The struggle of the European Parliament to participate in the new Economic Governance' EUI Working Paper RSCAS 45/2012, 18.

affairs committee of the French Senate stressed that the EP 'has put pressure on other EU institutions to convince them that parliamentary oversight of the new governance is primarily ensured by itself'.[40] During the negotiations on the set-up of the inter-parliamentary conference on economic and financial governance, that are still not completed, the EP 'pursues the sometimes contradictory goals of keeping the conference weak, but at the same time maintaining [or securing] a privileged position for itself in the new structure'.[41]

In addition to that, in 2014 the EP has also considered a modification of its own internal organisation in order to respond to the needs of fiscal and economic policy coordination: possible options that have been discussed with respect to the structure and modalities for euro area governance within the EP include additional resources for euro area scrutiny within the existing economic and monetary affairs committee or a new parliamentary structure (an 'EMU subcommittee') entrusted with non-legislative scrutiny tasks.[42]

IV. INTER-PARLIAMENTARY COOPERATION AS *JOINT SCRUTINY* BY THE EUROPEAN PARLIAMENT AND NATIONAL PARLIAMENTS

A. The Argument for *Joint Scrutiny* in Financial and Economic Governance

The first report 'towards a genuine Economic and Monetary Union' in June 2012 floated the idea of 'joint [inter-parliamentary] decision-making',[43] but the later reports lowered the level of ambition and only called for an increase in 'the level of cooperation between national parliaments and the European Parliament'.[44] There are, however, many decisions concerning economic and fiscal policy coordination in the EU that are either taken in intergovernmental settings without proper control by parliament or build upon recommendations of the European Commission in the context of the European Semester that restrict the policy options that are available in terms of the budgetary and economic policy choices at the national level.[45] Or, in other words, 'the austerity drive, in particular through

[40] Sénat français, 'Compte rendu de la Commission des affaires européennes' (31 January 2013) available at: www.senat.fr/compte-rendu-commissions/20130128/europ.html. Translated by the author.

[41] Cooper (n 9) 2.

[42] S Bowles, 'Structure and modalities within the Parliament for euro area governance in the next legislature, Letter to Martin Schulz' (2014) available at: sylvie-goulard.eu/articles2014/Annex-3a-Chair-s-Announcements-ECON-structure.pdf.

[43] European Council President, 'Towards a Genuine Economic and Monetary Union' (26 June 2012) 6.

[44] European Council President, 'Towards a Genuine Economic and Monetary Union. Interim Report' (12 October 2012) 8.

[45] See, eg Chalmers, 'The European Redistributive State' (n 4); R Dehousse and L Boussaguet, 'L'impact de la crise sur la gouvernance européenne' (2014) n°149 Pouvoirs 7; FW Scharpf, 'Monetary Union, Fiscal Crisis and the Pre-emption of Democracy' (2011) 2 *Zeitschrift für Staats- und Europawissenschaften* 163.

the obligations provided for under the European Semester … sidelines national parliaments from the budgetary control that constitutes their most traditional and symbolic prerogative'.[46]

When fiscal and economic policies have become more closely coordinated at the European level, but continue to be national *policies* and not a common and single EU *policy*, parliamentary control in the EMU can neither be exercised solely by the EP, nor individually by each national parliament holding its government accountable. Parliaments in the EU 'are increasingly orientated to one another; each is becoming an intrinsic part of the others' operating environment'.[47] Thus *joint scrutiny* by the EP and national parliaments has been voiced as a solution,[48] because many experts fear that if the strongest national parliament(s) served as the benchmark for the individual scrutiny mechanisms to be adopted by other national parliaments, 'the EMU might become altogether ungovernable'.[49] A feasible solution is deeply informed oversight in an inter-parliamentary conference—linked to the European Semester, to European Council meetings (and the Euro summits at their margins) and to key Euro group meetings—with an awareness of the functioning of economic and financial governance and allowing for some room of manoeuvre for the executive(s).[50] Inter-parliamentary cooperation has the advantage of *combining* both parliamentary levels. If the German Finance Minister acts at the EU level in the Eurogroup or the Board of the European Stability Mechanism, he will obviously be under scrutiny of the Bundestag, but there could also be hearings by an inter-parliamentary body which would include MPs from other national parliaments as well as MEPs.

Some decisions in the EMU are taken without proper parliamentary control at any level (this concerns the ESM, the Eurogroup, European Council meetings or euro area summits, and the European Central Bank),[51] even though the heads of all these bodies appear before the EP, either in plenary or in the economic and monetary affairs committee.[52] An inter-parliamentary arena, where MPs and MEPs meet regularly, as a place for discussion and as a meeting point between

[46] Dawson and de Witte, 'Constitutional Balance in the EU' (n 21) 827.

[47] Crum and Fossum, 'Conclusion' (n 33) 252.

[48] Most recently the conclusions of the Speakers' Conference in Nicosia (April 2013) and the working paper issued after a meeting of a sub-group of speakers in Luxembourg (January 2013) make proposals that follow the idea of 'joint scrutiny'.

[49] For a summary of this view, not shared by the author himself, see Deubner, *The Difficult Role of Parliaments* (n 10) 35.

[50] See C Hefftler et al, *National Parliaments: Their Emerging Control over the European Council* (Notre Europe—Jacques Delors Institute, 2013) 12.

[51] The ESM treaty does not mention the EP and only mentions national parliaments in a commitment to provide them with the annual report of its board of auditors in Art 30 ESM (Dawson and de Witte (n 21) 833). See also Wessels et al, *Democratic Control* (n 5). For a more detailed account of the EMU institutional framework, see A De Streel, 'The Evolution of the EU Economic Governance since the Treaty of Maastricht: An Unfinished Task' (2013) 20 *Maastricht Journal of European and Comparative Law* 336, 353.

[52] Kreilinger (n 10) 14.

the democratically legitimised institutions of the EU level and the national level, could collectively fulfil this control function, even though the EP is apparently situated in 'a complex pattern of cooperation and competition with national parliaments'.[53] The possibilities at such a conference to discuss and to exchange best practices could also provide a remedy against the information asymmetry from which national parliaments suffer vis-à-vis their governments.[54] Such an inter-parliamentary conference, based on *joint scrutiny* and covering economic and financial governance 'could gradually develop into an arena for political competition where battles are fought about the direction of the Union's economic policy'.[55] Instead of separate and disconnected debates on economic policy, the inter-parliamentary conference could help to constitute a transnational debate and promote transnational interests, although in the case of other transnational assemblies their contribution to the democratic legitimation of decision-making beyond the state is only marginal.[56]

B. Ideal Types of Positions Towards Inter-Parliamentary Cooperation

National parliaments have consciously adopted different positions towards inter-parliamentary cooperation. Resulting from their institutional self-interest, they generally prefer *joint scrutiny* to *centralised scrutiny*, but their preferences for the precise organisation of this kind of inter-parliamentary cooperation differ. On the basis of different levels of activity, this chapter proposes to classify the attitudes of national parliaments towards inter-parliamentary cooperation into three different roles:[57] *(1) inward-looking parliaments* that rarely engage beyond the minimum requirements; *(2) passively cooperative parliaments* that participate in additional activities aimed at discussing inter-parliamentary cooperation; and *(3) actively networking parliaments* that try to build coalitions in order to bring inter-parliamentary cooperation forward.

[53] Crum and Fossum, *Conclusion* (n 33) 253. See also the previous Section III of this chapter for the EP.

[54] Curtin, 'Challenging Executive Dominance' (n 8) 29. See also Neunreither, 'The European Parliament and National Parliaments' (n 7).

[55] Kreilinger (n 10) 23.

[56] Kraft-Kasack, 'Transnational Parliamentary Assemblies' (n 19) 552.

[57] These roles do not substitute other classifications of parliamentary involvement in EU affairs. The roles are rooted in national parliamentary practices in each Member State and based on divergent visions of what function(s) a legislature should perform. This classification has been inspired by classifications for national parliaments in other domains, namely O Rozenberg and C Hefftler, 'Introduction' in Claudia Hefftler et al (eds), *Handbook of National Parliaments and the European Union* (Basingstoke, Palgrave Macmillan, 2015) and C Sprungk, 'A New Type of Representative Democracy? Reconsidering the Role of National Parliaments in the European Union' (2013) 35 *Journal of European Integration* 547, but the classification put forward in this chapter uses different categories and different distinctive features.

The three roles of national parliaments in inter-parliamentary cooperation are defined as follows:

(1) *Inward-looking parliaments* rarely engage in inter-parliamentary cooperation beyond the minimum requirements.[58] They put their priorities on the domestic arena. Such parliaments could be seen as 'gatekeepers'[59] that have the objective, for example, to prevent legislation at the national level rather than shape it at the European level or see themselves as a national 'public forum'.[60] They are not Europeanised in their attitude towards inter-parliamentary cooperation, but can be Europeanised in other activities related to EU affairs.

(2) *Passively cooperative parliaments* that participate in additional activities aimed at discussing inter-parliamentary cooperation dedicate some additional resources to cooperation with their fellow parliaments, but do not try to set the agenda. Only when it is necessary, do they articulate their preferences on the precise organisation of inter-parliamentary cooperation. They send delegations to inter-parliamentary conferences comprising MPs that represent government and opposition parties and both chambers, if applicable. These parliaments are Europeanised as passive 'European players',[61] so they could belong to this ideal type for general parliamentary involvement, but need not. Compared with parliaments that are inward-looking, they better understand the negotiation situation at the EU level.

(3) *Actively networking parliaments* try to build coalitions in order to influence the organisation of inter-parliamentary cooperation and have a network 'beyond their own domestic parliamentary arena'.[62] Such a parliament organises extraordinary meetings with like-minded parliaments; it performs a 'networking role'[63] with other parliaments (as well as supranational institutions) in an active way and could be seen as a 'European player'[64] in the domain of inter-parliamentary cooperation. In comparison with parliaments that are only passively cooperative, they are able to coordinate themselves more easily with their counterparts. Europeanisation has affected *actively networking* parliaments differently. They can be suspicious of giving a greater role to the EP[65] or including it in inter-parliamentary cooperation beyond the absolute minimum and could ultimately even imagine pursuing cooperation among national parliaments outside the EU treaties.[66]

[58] For this analysis, 'minimum requirements' means participation in the Inter-parliamentary conference on Economic and Financial Governance.

[59] Sprungk, 'A New Type of Representative Democracy?' (n 57).

[60] Rozenberg and Hefftler, 'Introduction' (n57) 33.

[61] ibid.

[62] Rozenberg and Hefftler, 'Introduction' (n 60) 34.

[63] Sprungk, 'A New Type of Representative Democracy?' (n 59) 551.

[64] Rozenberg and Hefftler, 'Introduction' (n 60) 34.

[65] T Winzen, C Roederer-Rynning and F Schimmelfennig, 'Parliamentary Co-evolution: National Parliamentary Reactions to the Empowerment of the European Parliament' (2015) 22 *Journal of European Public Policy* 75.

[66] For such a scenario, see Kreilinger (n 27) 67.

C. Examples of Positions of National Parliaments Towards Inter-Parliamentary Cooperation

In order to illustrate the different positions that national parliaments may have on inter-parliamentary cooperation, this sub-section considers in detail the stance adopted by the parliaments of Denmark, France, Germany and Lithuania during the negotiations on the inter-parliamentary conference for economic and financial governance. The activities and preferences of each parliament are analysed and subsequently classified into the categories above.

In the negotiations on the conference of Article 13 TSCG, the Danish Folketing, the French Assemblée Nationale, the German Bundestag and the Lithuanian Seimas have all played important roles and adopted strong and visible positions.[67] At the same time, the set of these four countries combines different degrees of parliamentary strength in EU affairs, big and small, old and new Member States and, as of 1 January 2015, three of these countries have the euro as their currency. This sub-section seeks to answer what their preferences have been and which roles these parliaments follow in their attitudes towards the inter-parliamentary conference in economic and financial governance.

1. *Denmark (Folketing)*

In Denmark, the national parliament is generally seen as the true source of legitimacy (compared to the EP): both its scrutiny system on EU legislation and the European affairs committee are very strong.[68]

The Danish Parliament has had a visible position in the discussions on the new inter-parliamentary conference based on Article 13 TSCG.[69] In November 2012 and in March 2013 the chair of the European affairs committee organised meetings with her counterparts. At their second meeting the chairpersons of European affairs committees from 15 Member States gathered in Copenhagen and declared their preference for 'establishing a small effective conference focused on substantial issues—to be held in the margins of the biannual COSAC-meetings'.[70] This could be interpreted as showing the institutional self-interest of European affairs committees to keep control over EMU issues and avoid empowering their fellow MPs who are most likely to come from budget, finance and economic committees in the case of the Article 13 TSCG inter-parliamentary conference, but it shows above all that the Folketing articulated its preferences and succeeded in building a large coalition.

[67] See Cooper (n 9) and Kreilinger (n 10).

[68] Winzen, Roederer-Rynning and Schimmelfennig, 'Parliamentary Co-evolution' (n 65) 9. See, generally T Raunio and S Hix, 'Backbenchers Learn to Fight Back: European Integration and Parliamentary Government' (2000) 23 *West European Politics* 142.

[69] The TSCG was signed and ratified by Denmark despite its opt-out from the euro.

[70] Chairpersons of European Affairs Committees, Joint letter to the Speakers' Conference (2013) available at: www.ipex.eu/IPEXL-WEB/dossier/files/download/082dbcc53dbcb6ed013e07d2d31930a6.do.

Hence the Danish Parliament has been an *actively networking parliament* in order to pursue its objectives, adopting a reluctant position towards an ambitious institutional design of the inter-parliamentary conference. In general, however, it is probably best classified as a *passively cooperative parliament* due to a lack of resources for cooperation,[71] and taking into account its only average participation rate in inter-parliamentary conferences.[72]

2. France (Assemblée Nationale)

The question of the role of the national parliaments in the EU has often been discussed in the French Assemblée Nationale.[73] This 'can … be understood as a consequence of the limited weight of the French Parliament within the domestic political system'[74] and allows some MPs to discretely articulate criticism about the EU. All political forces in France agree that the role of the national parliaments in the EU should be strengthened.

The French National Assembly was in favour of quickly establishing an inter-parliamentary conference and proposed following the model for CFSP and CSDP with six MPs per national parliament and 16 MEPs that would accompany and control the European Semester.[75] The Speakers of Parliaments of the six founding Member States[76] endorsed this idea at a meeting in Luxembourg in January 2013.[77] For euro area matters, the French would even like to establish (within that conference) a 'Joint Conference Committee' composed of six MPs per national parliament from Member States whose currency is the euro and 16 MEPs as full members.

The Assemblée Nationale has doubtlessly been an *actively networking* parliament that has tried to strengthen its own position against the government by exploiting the opportunities at the EU level to achieve this. It has had the clear objective to establish a strong inter-parliamentary body in order to give national parliaments a voice against intergovernmental, but also supranational, EU institutions. The positions are, however, far beyond the status-quo of inter-parliamentary cooperation and it has been difficult to find allies that share these bold objectives.

[71] C Hefftler, 'Inter-parliamentary Relations in the EU: What Drives National Parliaments' Participation in Cooperation beyond the Domestic Arena?' (UACES 44th Annual Conference, 2014) 10.

[72] See Kreilinger (n 10) 5 (reporting data on COSAC).

[73] See, eg O Rozenberg, 'Debating about Europe at the French National Assembly: The Failure of the Rhetoric of Unanimity' in C Wiesner, T Turkka and K Palonen (eds), *Parliament and Europe Rhetorical and Conceptual Studies on their Contemporary Connections* (Baden-Baden, Nomos, 2011).

[74] V Kreilinger, K Perepechay and O Rozenberg, 'France' in W Wessels et al (eds), *Democratic Control in the Member States of the European Council and the Euro zone summits Annex 2: In-depth reports on 12 Member States* (European Parliament, 2013).

[75] Assemblée nationale, 'Rapport d'information sur le projet de loi de ratification du Traité sur la stabilité, la coordination et la gouvernance au sein de l'Union économique et monétaire' (25 September 2012).

[76] Belgium, France, Germany, Italy, Luxembourg and the Netherlands.

[77] National Parliaments, 'Luxembourg Working Paper of 11 January 2013' available at: www.ipex.eu/IPEXL-WEB/dossier/files/download/082dbcc53b70d1c2013ccdb9a8692a61.do.

3. *Germany (Bundestag)*

While Germany and its parliament have always been among the most vocal supporters of the EP,[78] the Bundestag and Bundesrat were able to gain significant scrutiny powers with the treaty revisions of Maastricht (1993) and Lisbon (2009), mostly in reaction to decisions by the German Constitutional Court, which have significantly strengthened national scrutiny procedures.[79]

In the discussions around the inter-parliamentary conference of Article 13 TSCG, German MPs presented their ideas, but the Bundestag as a whole did not articulate an institutional position.[80] The German Parliament was present at the meeting in Luxembourg in January 2013 and thus endorsed the working paper. Only at a very late stage, in the run-up to the first meeting of the conference in Vilnius in October 2013, the German position was made clear: It would be 'premature' to seek the adoption of Rules of Procedure at that point, but the delegation welcomed the idea to discuss the aims and functions of the conference.[81] Although there is a strong participation in inter-parliamentary conferences and significant resources are available,[82] unlike the French Assemblé Nationale, the German Bundestag has not been interested in establishing an inter-parliamentary conference on economic affairs quickly and has insisted on limiting the conference to being an advisory body.[83]

As a consequence, the German Parliament was initially, until autumn 2013, an *inward-looking parliament*, before turning into a *passively cooperative parliament* which—despite having strong opinions on the subject—did not seek to build coalitions. This is rather surprising, because having in mind the pro-European stance of the German Parliament and its strong powers, one could have expected it to be a strong supporter of inter-parliamentary cooperation in economic and financial governance. But the passive attitude of the German Bundestag may be explained in light of the significant domestic powers of oversight in EU and EMU affairs it has acquired as a result of recent judgments of the German Constitutional Court.

4. *Lithuania (Seimas)*

The Lithuanian Parliament, as parliament of the country holding the rotating Council presidency in the second half of 2013, and selected to chair the first meeting of the Inter-parliamentary Conference on Economic and Financial Governance taking place in Vilnius in October 2013, was in a special situation.

[78] See Winzen, Roederer-Rynning and Schimmelfennig (n 65) 12.

[79] C Callies and T Beichelt, *Auf dem Weg zum Europäisierten Bundestag: Vom Zuschauer zum Akteur* (Gütersloh, Bertelsmann Stiftung, 2013).

[80] See Deubner (n 10) 48.

[81] Bundestag, 'Letter by the Head of the German delegation, Norbert Barthle' (2013) available at: http://renginiai.lrs.lt/renginiai/EventDocument/0f6147e3-6125-40b9-93d8-edc7c31e085f/Barthle_Lithuanian%20Presidency_EN_courtesy%20translation.pdf.

[82] Hefftler, 'Inter-parliamentary Relations' (n 71) 13.

[83] Bundestag, 'Letter by the President, Norbert Lammert' (2014) available at: www.ipex.eu/IPEXL-WEB/dossier/files/download/082dbcc5452b142001456a262f7335a9.do.

Although the time for preparing the first conference was limited, the Lithuanian Parliament prepared a draft of the Rules of Procedure:

> The Seimas had tentatively scheduled time during the Vilnius conference for the draft to be debated and, at the end, adopted. Some parliaments commended the efforts of the Seimas in preparing it, and a number of delegations (from Estonia, France, Poland and the UK) proposed amendments to the draft, on the presumption that this document would provide the basis for the debate in Vilnius.[84]

But the Bundestag and the EP succeeded in exerting pressure on the Lithuanian Parliament to remove the item from the agenda of the conference. The debate about how conclusions to be adopted at the end of the conference should be called and the way in which the Lithuanian Parliament managed to achieve its goals shows that it was able to use the prerogatives of the presidency.[85]

The Seimas has been *actively networking* in its Presidency function, but may have underestimated that some parliaments were just not interested in agreeing on Rules of Procedure at the first conference. It remains to be seen whether the Lithuanian Parliament will be an equally active European player after the semester during which it presided over inter-parliamentary cooperation: Even if the participation of the Lithuanian Parliament in COSAC is in line with that of other national parliaments,[86] it can be assumed that its resources are limited.

In summary, national parliaments showed different preferences on the precise organisation of the inter-parliamentary conference on economic governance foreseen by Article 13 TSCG. Most national parliaments prefer *joint scrutiny* to *centralised scrutiny*, due to their institutional self-interest. They have consciously adopted positions and articulated them to their peers. These positions are based on broader attitudes towards inter-parliamentary cooperation which can be classified according to three different roles (*inward-looking parliaments*, *passively cooperative parliaments*, *actively networking parliaments*): The Danish Folketing was *actively networking*, but might not always be able to pursue this strategy and more often acts as a *passively cooperative* body; the German Bundestag was *inward-looking*, but turned into a *passively cooperative* parliament; the French Assemblée Nationale was *actively networking*; and, finally, the Lithuanian Seimas took the privilege of its six-month presidency seriously and was *actively networking* during that period of time. The resources that are available in a national parliament seem to affect the extent of inter-parliamentary activities. Besides that, the motivation of the individual MP to participate is a factor that might also play an important role.[87] Parliamentarians have to juggle between commitments linked to (national) party, (local) constituency, the domestic political arena and international activities, like inter-parliamentary cooperation. Research has shown that the importance which

[84] Cooper (n 9) 20.

[85] See ibid.

[86] See Kreilinger (n 10) 5.

[87] See, eg C Deubner and V Kreilinger, *The Role and Place of Parliaments in a Genuine Economic and Monetary Union* (Notre Europe—Jacques Delors Institute, 2013).

individual MPs attribute to the EU for the success of their work has a significant effect on their activities to obtain EU-related information.[88]

Beyond the four national parliaments that were analysed here, a larger study gathering more data and covering more parliaments could provide additional insights. Many of the national parliaments that were not clearly articulating their positions, might in fact be *inward-looking* parliaments and constitute a silent group of national parliaments that carries the responsibility for the absence of a collective position related to inter-parliamentary cooperation.

V. CONCLUSION: PROSPECTS FOR THE RELATIONSHIP BETWEEN NATIONAL PARLIAMENTS AND THE EUROPEAN PARLIAMENT IN THE AREA OF FINANCIAL AND ECONOMIC GOVERNANCE

Article 13 TSCG foresaw the creation of an inter-parliamentary conference on budgetary policies and other issues covered by that treaty, but diverging preferences among national parliaments and reluctance from the EP concerning the internal organisation of the conference have so far prevented a smooth implementation of the provision. Deadlock, in particular, has emerged with regard to the adoption of the Rules of Procedure. Inter-parliamentary cooperation is not a new idea and the model of the CFSP/CSDP inter-parliamentary conference seems to be well-suited to the goal of having representatives from all major political parties and specialised MPs (like committee chairs) in each delegation.

Inter-parliamentary cooperation in economic and financial governance faces challenges because the relationship between the two parliamentary levels (*centralised scrutiny* or *joint scrutiny*) has not been clearly defined until now: 'centralised scrutiny' would mean that scrutiny is dominated by the EP, with only very limited input by national parliaments; whereas with 'joint scrutiny' national parliaments and the EP would cooperate more closely.[89] The EP and the other EU institutions prefer *centralised scrutiny* and many of their contributions in the negotiations on the implementation of Article 13 TSCG show that their objective has been to keep the inter-parliamentary conference, as an element of *joint scrutiny*, weak. Inter-parliamentary cooperation does, however, work more or less well in other policy areas: with a 'legal-constitutional status'[90] in the cases of the two other inter-parliamentary conferences, and without such a status in many ad-hoc inter-parliamentary meetings.[91] The explanation for the current deadlock seems to be the same as for the challenges which the inter-parliamentary conference on CFSP/CSDP had been facing: 'overlapping authority claims'.[92] But in the case of

[88] A Wonka, B Rittberger, 'The Ties that Bind? Intra-party Information Exchanges of German MPs in EU Multi-level Politics' (2014) 37 *West European Politics* 624.

[89] Cooper (n 9) 2.

[90] Cooper (n 9) 23.

[91] Kreilinger (n 10) 7.

[92] Herranz-Surrallés (n 6) 15.

CFSP/CSDP the changes had taken place step-by-step over a longer time period since the Maastricht Treaty (1993) than in the case of EMU where the real losses of sovereignty only took place with 'six-pack', TSCG and 'two-pack' (2011–2013). In CFSP/CSDP establishing an inter-parliamentary conference was debated in the 2000s; in economic and financial governance in 2013–14, only a few months after the changes had taken place.

This chapter has examined the preferences of the most important actors in the negotiations on the inter-parliamentary conference on economic and financial governance. Its two most vocal critics see a mixed parliamentary body as 'ineffective and illegitimate' (EP) or want to reduce it to an 'advisory role' (German Bundestag) Other national parliaments have been more active in inter-parliamentary cooperation and more supportive of the inter-parliamentary conference than the German parliament which was for a long time *inward-looking* and only became *passively cooperative* in late 2013. This chapter has also examined preferences and attitudes of the parliaments of Denmark, France and Lithuania in detail and classified their roles as alternating between *actively networking* and *passively cooperative* (Danish Folketing and Lithuanian Seimas) and *actively networking* (French Assemblée Nationale). Many other national parliaments which did not articulate their positions clearly, might be *inward-looking* parliaments with little interest in inter-parliamentary cooperation. In general, national parliaments prefer joint scrutiny to centralised scrutiny dominated by the EP, but have not been able to agree on a common position. The current deadlock means that much of the determination to establish some kind of powerful inter-parliamentary control has been lost. Thus one can say that parliaments have, once again, failed to be a collective actor at the EU level.[93]

The EU-related democratic deficit at the national level which was reduced in the 1990s when most national parliaments established institutions and mechanisms that forced governments to explain their actions and policies at the EU level,[94] seems to be much bigger in the case of fiscal and economic policy coordination than in EU affairs in general.[95] The Euro-crisis and the response to it have put national governments at the centre of EU policy making and parliamentary actors are standing at the sidelines. Thus it still seems possible that two parliamentary levels could work together against their declining influence, 'exert countervailing power',[96] 'discuss' matters of common interest and 'control' in areas with weak parliamentary scrutiny (but not 'decide'). The key activity of an inter-parliamentary conference lies in its capacity to scrutinise rather than in taking binding decisions: 'European decision-makers should be publicly heard, questioned and even

[93] Kreilinger (n 10) 17.

[94] Raunio and Hix, 'Backbenchers Learn to Fight Back' (n 68).

[95] See especially Chalmers (n 4); Dehousse and Boussaguet, R Dehousse and L Boussaguet, 'L'impact de la crise' (n 45); Scharpf, 'Monetary Union' (n 45).

[96] Curtin (n 8) 30.

criticised by the conference.'[97] If the Inter-parliamentary Conference on Economic and Financial Governance acquired decision-making power, this would significantly alter the institutional equilibrium. The 2014 Speakers' Conference stated that:

> Although the role, scope and title of the Conference are yet to be defined, it is clear at this point that the Conference can serve as a useful parliamentary forum to discuss and exchange ideas, information, and best practice. Speakers consider that the Conference could have its own Rules of Procedure and may adopt non-binding conclusions.[98]

To sum up, inter-parliamentary control would help reduce the existing weakness in democratic accountability and legitimacy linked to the genuine EMU in the making. The question 'What form of government for the EU and the Eurozone?' that this volume is asking, also raises the question about parliamentary control: 'whenever an issue concerns the currency, taxation or the welfare system, parliament must be brought into the debate in one way or another'.[99] National parliaments were seen as the 'losers or latecomers'[100] on their way to Europe. In the case of inter-parliamentary control of the EMU they still have to overcome some challenges that were outlined in this chapter and learn 'to fight back'[101] against the executives.

[97] V Kreilinger and O Rozenberg, 'The Inter-parliamentary Conference on Economic and Financial Governance' in House of Lords (ed), *The Role of National Parliaments in the European Union. Written Evidence* (2013), available at: www.parliament.uk/documents/lords-committees/eu-select/Role%20of%20national%20parliaments/nat-parl-evidence-volume.pdf, 118.

[98] Conference of Speakers of European Union Parliaments, 'Presidency Conclusions—Vilnius, 6–8 April 2014' available at: www.ipex.eu/IPEXL-WEB/dossier/files/download/082dbcc5452b1420014541dc98d61251.do.

[99] J Delors, *Rethinking the EMU and Making the Greater Europe Positive Again* (Notre Europe—Jacques Delors Institute, 2013) 4.

[100] A Maurer and W Wessels, *National Parliaments on Their Ways to Europe: Losers or Latecomers?* (Baden-Baden, Nomos, 2001).

[101] Raunio and Hix (n 68).

16

From Executive Federalism to Executive Government: Current Problems and Future Prospects in the Governance of EMU

FEDERICO FABBRINI

I. INTRODUCTION

IN HIS BOOK on *The Crisis of the European Union*, Jürgen Habermas articulated a sharp critique of the current form of governance of the European Union (EU), and made the compelling case in favour of the creation of a transnational democracy in the EU.[1] In particular, Habermas addressed his concerns to the mode of governance which prevailed in response to the euro crisis, and which he defined as a system of 'post-democratic executive federalism'.[2] Stressing the central role of the heads of states and government of the EU member states convened in the European Council and other intergovernmental settings, Habermas criticised 'this kind of executive federalism of a self-authorizing European Council'[3] and emphasised how this provided 'the template for a post-democratic exercise of political authority'.[4] The notion of executive federalism is multifaceted, and in the context of EU law it is often used to refer specifically to the execution of supranational law by the administrative branches of the EU member states.[5] In the broader federalism literature, however, the term identifies more generally 'the processes of intergovernmental negotiation that are dominated by the executives of the different governments within [a] federal system'.[6] From this point of view, the

[1] J Habermas, *The Crisis of the European Union* (Cambridge, Polity Press, 2012).
[2] ibid 12.
[3] ibid viii.
[4] ibid.
[5] See R Schütze, 'From Rome to Lisbon: "Executive Federalism" in the (New) European Union' (2010) 47 *Common Market Law Review* 1385.
[6] R Watts, 'Executive Federalism: A Comparative Analysis' Institute of Intergovernmental Relations—Queen's University, Kingston, Canada, Research Paper 26/1988, 3.

notion of executive federalism as used by Habermas aptly captures the reality of intergovernmental governance which became dominant in the EU since the eruption of the euro crisis to manage the European Economic and Monetary Union (EMU).

The purpose of this chapter is to analyse the emergence of executive federalism in the EMU, to identify the problems of this system of governance, and to discuss how several ongoing institutional developments and future treaty reforms may impact upon the current form of governance of the EU and the Eurozone. The chapter examines the growing importance of intergovernmental institutions in the governance of the EMU, describing the rise of the European Council as the new centre of EU politics and the creation of the Euro Summit as a new forum in which EU heads of state and government can take decisions on matters related to the Eurozone. It then evaluates the limits of this system of executive federalism, in particular focusing on the significant imbalances that it creates in the relationship between the EU member states—with the larger and wealthier states able to dominate the process to the detriment of smaller, and poorer ones. As the chapter reports, the problems of the current intergovernmental framework of EMU governance have been bemoaned by a growing chorus of academics—and increasingly also policy-makers have called for more legitimate and effective institutions to manage the EMU. Nevertheless, the EU constitutional architecture is subject to dynamic evolutions, and the effect on the form of governance of the EU and the Eurozone of several ongoing developments must be considered.

The chapter maps two recent institutional developments in the constitutional architecture of the EU and evaluates their potential effects on the current intergovernmental system of EMU governance. First, the chapter considers the recent efforts to increase the politicisation of the European Commission, notably by tying the selection of its President to the elections for the European Parliament. Here I emphasise how this process boosts the authority of the President of the European Commission vis-à-vis the other EU institutions, but I explain why this change will by itself hardly produce a shift of powers towards the European Commission, and an abridgement of the role of the European Council in the field of EMU. Second, the chapter considers the silent but incremental strengthening of the role of the President of the European Council (and of the Euro Summit). Here I underline how the semi-permanent President has been able to quickly consolidate itself as an indispensable actor in the functioning of the European Council (and the Euro Summit), but I also warn that only additional treaty reforms could make this institutional player a counter-weight to the EU heads of state and government, and notably the more powerful among them.

As the chapter claims, the system of executive federalism on which the governance of EMU has been premised thus far is unsatisfactory—and the ongoing institutional developments connected with the increasing politicisation of the President of the European Commission and the incremental strengthening of the President of the European Council (and Euro Summit) are not able to change the status quo. Nevertheless, the EU and the Eurozone are in need of a form of a strong, accountable government, which is able to address the political and economic challenges posed by increase interdependences, especially in EMU. The euro crisis and the political turmoil connected to it have made this need even more urgent. In the end, the chapter notices that only a new round of treaty reforms will be able to bring about a satisfactory institutional change in the constitutional architecture of EU and the Eurozone. Nevertheless, it concludes with a note of optimism, by mentioning the requirement of the Fiscal Compact that its contracting parties incorporate the substance of that treaty into the legal framework of the EU by 2018 at the latest.[7] As the chapter suggests, in fact, the obligation for the EU member states to domesticate the content of the Fiscal Compact in EU law offers a window of opportunity to replace executive federalism with a form of effective and legitimate executive government for our Union of states and citizens.

The chapter is structured as follows. Section II examines the rise of the European Council and the creation of the Euro Summit in the governance of EMU since the eruption of the euro crisis. Section III evaluates the problems of executive federalism in the EU and the Eurozone, in particular by emphasising the growing inequality between the EU member states, as evidenced both by the policies followed, and by the institutional architectures set-up, in response to the crisis. Section IV summarises the increasing calls from scholars and policy-makers in favour of reforming the current system of governance of the EU and the Eurozone. Sections V and VI then consider two recent institutional developments—namely the politicisation of the President of the European Commission, and the strengthening of the President of the European Council (and Euro Summit)—and discusses their prospects, as well as their limits, on the current intergovernmental system of EMU governance. Section VII, finally, concludes by acknowledging that only a constitutional reform will achieve a long-lasting effect on the governance of EMU, but explains how the Fiscal Compact creates a window of opportunity that should be used to establish a more effective and legitimate form of government for the EU and the Eurozone.

II. THE RISE OF THE EUROPEAN COUNCIL AND THE CREATION OF THE EURO SUMMIT

The latest round of constitutional reform in the EU—the Lisbon Treaty of 2009—introduced an important innovation in the institutional architecture of the EU, by giving formal recognition to the European Council.[8] Although the European Council had existed since 1974 as an informal gathering of the heads of state and government of the EU member states and the President of the European Commission,[9] and had played an important role at key moments of the history of

[7] Art 16 Fiscal Compact.

[8] See P de Schoutheete, 'The European Council' in J Peterson and M Shackleton (eds), *The Institutions of the European Union* (Oxford, Oxford University Press, 2012) 37.

[9] See Final Communiqué, Paris Summit, 9–10 December 1974.

European integration,[10] the role of this institution remained uncertain. Following the revisions of the Lisbon Treaty, Article 13 TEU explicitly recognised the European Council as an institution of the EU, and Article 15 TEU entrusted it with the task to 'provide the Union with the necessary impetus for its development and [to] define the general political directions and priorities thereof'. Moreover, Article 15 TEU clarified that the European Council 'shall not exercise legislative functions,' hence marking its difference from the Council (which instead is mainly—albeit not exclusively—involved in the business of law-making) and suggesting that the European Council vests executive powers. And it created the post of semi-permanent President of the European Council—a position which is incompatible with the 'hold[ing of] a national office'[11]—to ensure continuity in the work of the European Council and to steer the direction of the institution.[12]

According to the account of people involved in the negotiations, the Lisbon Treaty was not intended to alter the original EU institutional balance.[13] Nevertheless, at the same time as the Lisbon Treaty was entering into force, the euro crisis started to take its toll in the EU, with important effects also on the form of governance of the EU. Since the eruption of the crisis, in fact, the European Council has moved to the forefront of the EU system of governance, becoming the leading institution in managing and coordinating policy responses to the crisis.[14] As Uwe Puetter has explained, the European Council quickly emerged as the 'new center of EU politics', 'regularly deciding concrete policy issues in core domains of EU policymaking'.[15] In the field of EMU governance, in particular, the European Council acquired a growing importance in setting the economic agenda of the EU and its member states.[16] It designed the main legal and institutional measures aimed at tackling the crisis; and it promoted their adoption through the EU legislative process.[17] In fact, although Article 15(3) TEU foresaw that the European Council would meet at least twice a year, in reality, since the crisis' eruption, the European Council congressed as often as once a month, reflecting how intergovernmental decision-making became in practice 'the predominant strategy in day-to-day crisis management'.[18]

[10] See L van Middelar, *The Passage to Europe* (New Haven, Yale University Press, 2013).

[11] Art 15(6) TEU.

[12] See also B Crum, 'Accountability and the Personalisation of the European Council Presidency' (2009) 31 *European Integration* 685.

[13] See JC Piris, *The Treaty of Lisbon* (Cambridge, Cambridge University Press, 2010) 237 (explaining that the Treaty avoided making 'any single institution as politically too powerful'.)

[14] See Editorial Comments, 'An Ever Mighty European Council—Some Recent Institutional Developments' (2009) 46 *Common Market Law Review* 1383.

[15] U Puetter, 'The European Council—the New Center of EU Politics' Swedish Institute for European Policy Studies, Policy Analysis 16/2013, 2.

[16] See F Eggermont, *The Changing Role of the European Council in the Institutional Framework of the European Union* (Antwerp, Intersentia, 2012).

[17] See U Puetter, *The European Council and the Council: New Intergovernmentalism and Institutional Change* (Oxford, Oxford University Press, 2014) ch 3.

[18] D Smeets and M Zimmerman, 'Did the EU Summits Succeed in Convincing the Markets during the Recent Crisis?' (2013) 51 *Journal of Common Market Studies* 1158.

At the same time, despite the rising importance of the European Council in the management of the euro crisis, a new intergovernmental forum was created to debate the key issues specifically concerning the Eurozone: the Euro Summit. Although the ministers of finance of the Eurozone member states had been meeting in the Eurogroup since 1997,[19] in October 2008 the then French President, Sarkozy, took the initiative to establish an informal gathering of the heads of state and government of the Eurozone member states to discuss at the highest level matters related to EMU—and in October 2011 the heads of the Eurozone states adopted a statement giving a first structure to the Euro Summit.[20] This statement advanced 10 measures to improve the governance of the euro area, including the decision to hold regular Euro Summit meetings at least twice a year, to establish a post of permanent Euro Summit President and to coordinate the work of the Euro Summit with that of the Eurogroup, acting at a lower level in the composition of national ministers of finance. The legal nature of this statement was not clarified, and although part of its content was replicated in the European Council conclusions of October 2011,[21] it was uncertain whether it could be considered an international agreement concluded by the Eurozone member states.

Be that as it may, the Euro Summit was given an official legal recognition, albeit outside the framework of EU law, in the Fiscal Compact. Pursuant to Article 12(1) Fiscal Compact: 'The Heads of State or Government of the Contracting Parties whose currency is the euro shall meet informally in Euro Summit meetings, together with the President of the European Commission'. The President of the European Central Bank (ECB) shall be invited to take part in such meetings,[22] while the President of the European Parliament may be invited to be heard.[23] Moreover, the Fiscal Compact created to post of President of the Euro Summit, modelled out of that of President of the European Council, to 'ensure the preparation and continuity of Euro Summit meetings'.[24] And it required that, in order to provide a platform for coordinating action among the governments of the Eurozone member states:

> Euro Summit meetings shall take place when necessary, and at least twice a year, to discuss questions relating to the specific responsibilities which the Contracting Parties whose currency is the euro share with regard to the single currency, other issues concerning the governance of the euro area and the rules that apply to it, and strategic orientations for the conduct of economic policies to increase convergence in the euro area.[25]

The rise of the European Council and the creation of the Euro Summit produced important changes to the EU institutional system. Although according to Uwe Puetter

[19] See European Council Conclusions, 12–13 December 1997, as well as Protocol No 14 on the Eurogroup.

[20] Euro Summit Statement, 26 October 2011.

[21] European Council Conclusions, 23 October 2011, EUCO 52/11, 5.

[22] Art 12(1) Fiscal Compact.

[23] Art 12(5) Fiscal Compact.

[24] Art 12(4) Fiscal Compact.

[25] Art 12(2) Fiscal Compact.

the role of intergovernmental institutions—especially in the field of EMU—dates back to the Maastricht Treaty, and to the decision taken at that time to integrate new areas of core state sovereignty through intergovernmental policy coordination, rather than through the delegation of legislative authority to supranational bodies,[26] the Euro-crisis marked a clear shift of powers in the EU system of governance toward national chief executives.[27] Energised by the emergency posed by the euro crisis, the EU heads of state and governments congressed in the European Council and the Euro Summit took the lead in managing the EMU, marginalising the role of the European Parliament,[28] and directly setting the agenda of the other EU institutions: in fact, while the European Commission retained, and gained, important implementing powers, it mostly turned into an executor of the tasks assigned to it by the European Council.[29] While the role of the EU intergovernmental fora has been defended in light of the special legitimacy that EU heads of state and government enjoy within each member state,[30] however, the management of the EU and the Eurozone by this kind of collegiate executive has given rise to multiple concerns.

III. THE IMBALANCE BETWEEN THE STATES

The EU system of executive federalism, centred on the European Council, and now also the Euro Summit, has been the object of criticisms from various standpoints. While the system of intergovernmental governance of the EMU has been faulted for being too slow in taking decisions, and for producing deals which were not perceived as legitimate,[31] others have complained that the collective measures taken under the veil of secrecy by the executive branches of the EU member states congressed in the European Council and the Euro Summit have compromised the ability of the European or the national parliaments to ensure accountability, either severally or jointly.[32] In this chapter, however, I want to focus on another problem of intergovernmentalism in the EU and the Eurozone: namely its detrimental effects on the horizontal balance between the EU member states. As I detailed

[26] U Puetter, 'Europe's Deliberative Intergovernmentalism: The Role of the Council and the European Council in EU Economic Governance' (2012) 19 *Journal of European Public Policy* 161.

[27] See A Hinarejos, *The Euro Area Crisis in Constitutional Perspective* (Oxford, Oxford University Press, 2015) ch 6.

[28] See C Fasone, 'European Economic Governance and Parliamentary Representation: What Place for the European Parliament?' (2013) 20 *European Law Journal* 164.

[29] See European Parliament Research Service, 'European Council Conclusions: A Rolling Check-List of Commitments to Date' study, 7 October 2014, PE 536.359 (reporting lists of actions the European Council required other EU institutions to take).

[30] See N Sarkozy, Speech, Toulon, 1 December 2011, 9 (stating that: 'La crise a poussé les Chefs d'Etats et de gouvernements à assumer des responsabilités croissantes parce qu'au fond eux seuls disposaient de la légitimité démocratique qui leur permettait de décider'.).

[31] See, eg S Fabbrini, 'Intergovernmentalism and Its Limits: Assessing the European Union's Answer to the Euro Crisis' (2013) 46 *Comparative Political Studies* 1003.

[32] See, eg D Curtin, 'Challenging Executive Dominance in European Democracy' (2014) 77 *Modern Law Review* 1.

elsewhere,[33] the shift in power toward an intergovernmental institution such as the European Council, in the absence of adequate counterweights inherent in the involvement of supranational institutions such as the Commission and the European Parliament, resulted in a profound redefinition of the horizontal relations of power between the member states—with larger, economically stronger member states coming to dominate the EU policy-making process at the expense of smaller, financially weaker ones.

As Jonas Tallberg has explained, bargaining in intergovernmental fora such as the European Council is the result of several sources of power: states sources of power, institutional sources of power, and personal sources of power.[34] Although, formally speaking, all heads of states or governments enjoy equal status in the European Council—every EU member state having one representative which can authoritatively speak for its country—in reality 'differences between large and small Member States' shape power relations in the European Council.[35] In particular, aggregate states' sources of power play the most fundamental role in explaining negotiation in the European Council, with the result that large member states can dominate the process, although institutional and individual dimensions of powers can operate to mitigate this trend. Writing before the entry into force of the Lisbon Treaty, Jonas Tallberg thus concluded that:[T]he European Council offers more limited institutional protection to small and medium-sized Member States. The formal equality of the Member States, as expressed in the principle of unanimity [or consensus], is largely a procedural fiction, that helps to legitimise the outcomes of European Council bargaining.[36]

The experience of the management of the euro crisis by the European Council has empirically confirmed this analysis. As underlined both in scholarly research and public debate,[37] Germany and France, the two largest member states of the EU and the Eurozone, have acquired from 2010 to 2012 a predominant role in the decision-making process, reflected in the practice—proper of a *directoire*—of holding bilateral meetings before the European Council, resulting in decisions that would be later ratified by the European Council as a whole.[38] Since 2012, attempts have been made to expand this exclusive summitry system to include Italy and

[33] F Fabbrini, 'States Equality vs States Power: The Euro-Crisis, Inter-State Relations and the Paradox of Domination' (2015) 17 *Cambridge Yearbook of European Legal Studies* 1.

[34] J Tallberg, 'Bargaining Power in the European Council' (2008) 46 *Journal of Common Market Studies* 685.

[35] ibid 687.

[36] ibid 703.

[37] See, eg F de Witte and M Dawson 'Constitutional Balance in the EU after the Euro-crisis' (2013) 76 *Modern Law Review* 817 and P Legrain, Op-Ed, 'Eurozone Fiscal Colonialism' *The New York Times* (New York, 21 April 2014) (arguing that management of the euro crisis has created 'quasi-colonial relationship' between EU member states).

[38] See, eg Declaration by France and Germany at Deauville Summit, 18 October 2010 (requiring that budgetary surveillance and economic policy coordination procedures should be strengthened and accelerated) and European Council Conclusions, 28–29 October 2010, EUCO 25/1/10 (endorsing reform to strengthen budgetary constraints and enhance economic governance).

Spain, the third and fourth biggest economies of the Eurozone.[39] However, the political instability of Italy and the serious economic difficulties of Spain have hampered this attempt. In fact, because of the increasing economic problems of France too, the original *directoire* between France and Germany has been gradually replaced by a new equilibrium, in which Germany—the most populous and most prosperous member state of the EU and the Eurozone—has taken over as the hegemonic player in the European Council.[40] The requirements to constitutionalise budgetary constraints and to pursue a policy of fiscal consolidation—or austerity—as a way to respond to the euro crisis largely reflect the centrality of Germany within the EMU system of governance.[41]

Moreover, changes to the legal framework accomplished in response to the euro crisis have formally ratified the increasing inequality between the member states. As is well known, the European Council repeatedly decided to act outside the EU legal order to reform the architecture of EMU.[42] Yet, these intergovernmental agreements crystallised the reality of power asymmetries between the member states.[43] The Treaty on the European Stability Mechanism (ESM) is the epitome of this. The ESM is a permanent financial firewall to assist EU countries in fiscal distress, subject to conditionality.[44] Eurozone member states contribute to the ESM capital pro quota, based on their subscriptions to the ECB.[45] However, the ESM Treaty matches the asymmetry in financial contribution with an asymmetry in power—granting to the larger and more prosperous member states more power of decision-making vis-à-vis the smaller and poorer ones. To begin with, Article 48 ESM Treaty codified the rule that the Treaty 'shall enter into force on the date when instruments of ratification, approval or acceptance have been deposited by signatories whose initial subscription represent no less than 90 per cent of the total subscriptions set forth in Annex II'. This provision effectively granted to the four largest member states of the Eurozone—Germany, France, Italy and Spain—a veto right on the ability of the ESM to start operating, since each of them wield a quota in the ESM capital of more than 10 per cent. At the same time, it de facto rendered insignificant the ratification of the other (then) 13 smaller member states of the Eurozone, whose aggregate contribution to the ESM capital stock amount, in any case, to less than 10 per cent.

[39] See, eg Press Conference by Germany, France, Italy and Spain at Rome Summit, 22 June 2012 (agreeing to adopt measures in favour of growth) and European Council Conclusions, 28–29 June 2012, EUCO 76/12 (endorsing a compact for growth and jobs).

[40] See W Paterson, 'The Reluctant Hegemon? Germany Moves Center Stage in the European Union' (2011) 49 *Journal of Common Market Studies* 57.

[41] See Editorial, 'The Fiscal Compact and the European Constitutions: "Europe Speaking German"' (2012) 8 *European Constitutional Law Review* 1.

[42] See K Tuori and K Tuori, *The Eurozone Crisis: A Constitutional Analysis* (Cambridge, Cambridge University Press, 2014) ch 4.

[43] See further, F Fabbrini, 'States Equality vs States Power' (n 33) 13–20 (discussing also intergovernmental agreements on financial assistance and bank resolution).

[44] See Case C-370/12, *Pringle v Government of Ireland, Ireland and the Attorney General*, judgment of 27 November 2012, not yet reported.

[45] Annex I, ESM Treaty.

Moreover, the system of governance of the ESM entrenched even further the power of the larger Eurozone states. Pursuant to Article 4(3) ESM Treaty decisions by the Board of Governors of the ESM (the body grouping the Minister of Finances of the ESM parties) and the Board of Directors (the body grouping representatives of the ESM parties at a non-ministerial level) shall be adopted by unanimity. However:

> By way of derogation from paragraph 3, an emergency voting procedure shall be used where the Commission and the ECB both conclude that a failure to urgently adopt a decision to grant or implement financial assistance ... would threaten the economic and financial sustainability of the euro area. The adoption of a decision ... under that emergency procedure requires a qualified majority of 85% of the votes cast[46]

Since the votes are equal to the number of share allocated in the authorised capital stock,[47] decisions may be adopted even without the agreement of all the member states: yet, Germany, France, and Italy are endowed with a veto right, since no emergency decision can be taken against their will, each of them having a share of more than 15 per cent of the ESM capital.

The asymmetry of power between the Member States entrenched in the ESM contrasts with the attempts to strike a balance between states' power and states' equality achieved, for instance, in the design of the ECB.[48] Ironically, the ECB is largely credited for having played the most important role in responding to the euro crisis.[49] The EU intergovernmental institutions, instead, have lagged behind in their ability to successfully manage the interdependences of EMU.[50] Moreover, they have produced a major problem of inequality between the member states—as evident both in the decision-making process within the European Council (and the Euro Summit), and in the design of governance mechanisms outside the framework of EU law, such as the ESM. The rise of executive federalism, and the resulting shift 'from legislation to contract'[51] with the incremental use of intergovernmental agreements outside EU law, have produced a form of 'collective Bonapartism',[52] in which several member states, and lately especially Germany, based on their size or economic might, have been able to dominate the EU policy-making process to the detriment of the interests of smaller, economically weaker ones.

[46] Art 4(4) ESM Treaty.

[47] Art 4(7) ESM Treaty.

[48] See further, F Fabbrini, 'States Equality vs States Power' (n 33) 6–7.

[49] See M Draghi, Speech at the 'Global Investment' Conference, London, 26 July 2012 (stating that the ECB is ready to do 'whatever it takes' to save the euro), as well as ECB, Press Release, 'Technical Features of Outright Monetary Transaction', 6 September 2012.

[50] See S Fabbrini, 'Intergovernmentalism and Its Limits' (n 31) 1003.

[51] P Craig, 'Economic Governance and the Euro Crisis: Constitutional Architecture and Constitutional Implications' in F Fabbrini et al (eds), *The Constitutionalization of European Budgetary Constraints* (Oxford, Hart Publishing, 2014) 19, 29.

[52] H Brunkhorst, 'Collective Bonapartism—Democracy in the European Crisis' (2014) 15 *German Law Journal* 1177.

IV. THE NEED FOR EXECUTIVE GOVERNMENT

The problem of domination revealed by the law and practice of EMU intergovernmental governance strikes at the heart of the anti-hegemonic nature of the European integration project.[53] In fact, the EU system of executive federalism has produced a major challenge to the effectiveness and legitimacy of the EMU.[54] In this context, growing calls have been made in the public debate to reform the system of governance of the EU and the Eurozone, in order to increase its capacity to act effectively, and respond to legitimate popular concerns.[55] In a report written for the Constitutional Affairs Committee of the European Parliament, Miguel Maduro has emphasised how a genuine EMU requires a strong, responsible government.[56] As he put it, 'there is no self-government without government. Europe needs a strengthened political authority if it is to become a legitimate and accountable democratic authority'.[57] Two groups of German and French leading academics and public intellectuals—the Glienicker Group and Eiffel Group—have advanced arguments in favour of endowing the Eurozone with a stronger institutional foundation, through the adoption of a separate treaty establishing a Eurozone form of government, and have made a call for 'a European executive … capable of acting',[58] or an 'executive of the Euro Community',[59] legitimated through elections, and able to take binding decisions.

At the same time, growing awareness for the need to reform the form of government of the EU and the Eurozone has also emerged among top national and supranational policy-makers—although great uncertainty exists about how the EU and the Eurozone should move forward. In its inaugural report 'Towards a Genuine EMU' the President of the European Council acknowledged the need to 'strengthen[] democratic legitimacy and accountability' in the EMU,[60] and in its final report, it claimed that

> [T]he crisis has shown the need to strengthen not only the EMU's surveillance framework but also its ability to take rapid executive decisions to improve crisis management in bad times and economic policymaking in good times. Some intergovernmental

[53] See S Bunse and K Nicolaïdis, 'Large versus Small States: Anti-Hegemony and the Politics of Shared Leadership' in E Jones et al (eds), *The Oxford Handbook of the European Union* (Oxford, Oxford University Press, 2012) 249.

[54] See Habermas, *The Crisis of the European Union* (n 1).

[55] See, eg I Pernice et al, *A Democratic Solution to the Crisis: Reform Steps towards a Democratically Based Economic and Financial Constitution for Europe* (Baden-Baden, Nomos, 2012); M Monti and S Goulard, *De la démocratie en Europe. Voir plus loin* (Paris, Flammarion, 2012).

[56] M Maduro, 'A New Governance for the European Union and the Euro: Democracy and Justice', Report commissioned by the European Parliament Constitutional Affairs Committee, PE 462.484 (2012).

[57] ibid 27.

[58] Glienicker Group, 'Towards a Euro Union', October 2013, available at: www.glienickergruppe.eu/english.html.

[59] Eiffel Group, 'For a Euro Community', February 2014, available at: www.groupe-eiffel.eu/our-manifesto/.

[60] President of the European Council, Report 'Towards a Genuine EMU', 25 June 2012, 6.

> arrangements have been created as a result of the shortcomings of the previous architecture but these would ultimately need to be integrated into the legal framework of the [EU]. This is already foreseen under the [Fiscal Compact], and could be envisaged also for other cases. Reinforcing the capacity of the European level to take executive economic policy decisions for the EMU is essential.[61]

In addition, the European Commission has stressed the importance of improving the framework of EMU governance[62]—and the European Parliament has remarked how

> [A] substantial improvement of the democratic legitimacy and accountability at Union level of the EMU governance by an increased role of Parliament [is] an absolute necessity and a precondition for any further step toward a banking union, a fiscal union and an economic union.[63]

The EU heads of state and government congressed in the European Council have refrained from endorsing any blueprint of institutional reform that would reduce their collective authority. Nevertheless, individual voices have been raised in favour of a new settlement in the governance of the EU and the Eurozone. Hence, French President Hollande proposed the creation of an economic government for the Eurozone, built around a full-time President.[64] Italian Prime Minister Renzi called for an overhaul of EMU governance.[65] And the so-called Berlin Group, the Foreign Affairs Ministers of Austria, Belgium, Denmark, France, Italy, Germany, Luxembourg, the Netherlands, Poland, Portugal, and Spain, emphasised in its report on 'The Future of Europe' the need for 'a streamlined and efficient system for the separation of powers in Europe which has full democratic legitimacy. For some members of the Group, this could include … a directly elected Commission President who appoints the members of his "European Government" himself.'[66] At its October 2014 meeting, the Euro Summit tasked the President of the Commission jointly with the Presidents of the Euro Summit, ECB and Eurogroup to 'prepare next steps on better economic governance in the euro area' and to report back,[67] thus leaving open the door to the possibility of new constitutional reforms in the near future. In the meantime, however, two important institutional

[61] President of the European Council, Final Report 'Towards a Genuine EMU', 5 December 2012, 17.

[62] European Commission, Communication 'A Blueprint for a Deep and Genuine Economic and Monetary Union: Launching a European Debate', 28 November 2012, COM (2012) 777 final.

[63] European Parliament Resolution 'Towards a Genuine EMU', 20 November 2012, P7_TA (2012) 0430, para 9.

[64] See F Hollande, Speech, Paris, 16 May 2013, 6 (speaking of 'un gouvernement économique qui se réunirait, tous les mois, autour d'un véritable Président nommé pour une durée longue et qui serait affecté à cette seule tâche'.).

[65] See M Renzi, Speech, Strasbourg, 2 July 2014, as well as 'Europa: Un nuovo inizio. Programma della Presidenza Italiana del Consiglio dell'Unione Europea', July 2014, available at: www.governo.it/governoinforma/documenti/programma_semestre_europeo_ita.pdf.

[66] Final Report of the Future of Europe Group of the Foreign Ministers of Austria, Belgium, Denmark, France, Italy, Germany, Luxembourg, the Netherlands, Poland, Portugal and Spain, 17 September 2012, 8.

[67] Euro Summit Statement, 24 October 2014, para 2.

developments have been taking place in EU and the Eurozone, and their potential effects on the governance of EMU must be now considered.

V. THE POLITICISATION OF THE PRESIDENT OF THE EUROPEAN COMMISSION

A first development which has recently occurred in the system of governance of the EU is the politicisation of the President of the European Commission. Following a resolution of the European Parliament, at the May 2014 European Parliament elections EU political groups decided to bring forward lead candidates for the post of President of the European Commission, with a commitment that the *Sptizenkandidat* of the party winning a parliamentary majority would be appointed President of the European Commission.[68] On the basis of this procedure, in June 2014 the European Council nominated—albeit not without internal resistance—Jean-Claude Juncker, a former Prime Minister of Luxembourg who was the top candidate of the conservative European Peoples' Party (which came in as the party with a plurality of 29.4 per cent of the European Parliament's seats),[69] as President of the European Commission.[70] President Juncker was then confirmed in his post by a vote of the Parliament's plenary in July 2014,[71] and jointly with the national representatives in the Council, he drew a list of Commissioners, one per member state, who were vetted by the European Parliament through individual hearings and eventually confirmed as the College in October 2014.[72]

The efforts to connect the selection of the President of the European Commission to the elections for the European Parliament sought to increase the legitimacy of the European Commission, and at the same time to endow the Commission President with greater political clout.[73] Although strong disagreement exists on how to evaluate the process of politicisation of the European Commission,[74] it has been suggested that a Commission President backed by a strong parliamentary mandate could free the EU decision-making process from capture by the heads of

68 See European Parliament Resolution, 'On the Elections to the European Parliament in 2014', 22 November 2012, P7_TA(2012)0462, para 1.

69 See European Parliament, 'Result of the 2014 European Elections', available at: www.results-elections2014.eu/en/election-results-2014.html.

70 European Council Conclusions, 27 June 2014, EUCO 79/14, para 25 (proposing the appointment of Jean-Claude Juncker with 26 heads of state and government in favour, and 2 against).

71 European Parliament, Press Release, 'Parliament Elects Jean-Claude Juncker as Commission President', 15 July 2014 (reporting vote to elect Jean-Claude Juncker as Commission President with 422 votes in favour, 250 against, and 47 abstentions).

72 European Parliament, Press Release, 'Parliament Elects New European Commission', 22 October 2014 (reporting vote to approve the new College of Commissioners with 423 votes in favour, 209 against, and 67 abstentions).

73 See also the contribution of RD Kelemen, ch 11 in this volume.

74 Compare the contributions of C Antphöler and A Kocharov, chs 12 and 13 in this volume.

state and government congressed in the European Council.[75] If this was the case, the politicisation of the European Commission would represent a potential point of departure from the intergovernmental system of governance which has characterised the EU since the eruption of the crisis, in the direction of a parliamentary government for the EU.[76]

Nevertheless, there are obstacles that limit the capacity of the process of politicisation of the European Commission to bring about a fundamental institutional change in the system of governance of the EMU—absent a further revision of the EU constitutional framework. To begin with, the politicisation of the President of the European Commission clashes with the fact that the Commission itself is not a homogeneous political body with a clear-cut policy agenda—due to the influence that the 28 separate member states play in appointing the College of Commissioners, by common accord with the President.[77] Moreover, the current design of EMU challenges the ability of the Commission to take the lead in the policy-making process, notwithstanding the politicisation of its presidency.[78] First, since the Treaty of Maastricht the governance of EMU has been more about policy coordination, rather than legislation—where the power of the Commission is at its maximum; and second, the EU member states have created a web of administrative bodies for the governance of EMU, such as the Economic and Financial Committee, which run parallel to the Commission, and directly respond to the EU intergovernmental institutions. In this context, the European Council retains a privileged position in managing economic policies, and it will be difficult for the Commission to replace it as the authority in charge of setting the EMU agenda.

In fact, the European Council re-affirmed its centrality in defining the economic agenda of the EU even in the face of steps towards the parliamentarisation of the relationship between the European Parliament and the European Commission. In the same summit in which it decided to nominate Juncker as Commission President, the European Council unveiled a detailed programme which it tasked the new Commission to carry forward. In a document called 'Strategic Agenda for the Union in Times of Changes'[79] the European Council outlined the policy priority for the EU in the following five years and tasked the future European Commission to implement it.[80]

[75] See, eg M Kumm, 'What Kind of a Constitutional Crisis is Europe in and What Should be Done About it?' Wissenschaftszentrum Berlin für Sozialforschung (WZB) Discussion Paper No 801/2013, 19.

[76] See, eg S Hix, *What's Wrong with the European Union and How to Fix it?* (Cambridge, Polity Press, 2008) 162.

[77] See J Peterson, 'The College of Commissioners' in J Peterson and M Shackleton (eds), *The Institutions of the European Union* (Oxford, Oxford University Press, 2012) 96, 112.

[78] See Puetter, *The European Council and the Council* (n 17) 230.

[79] European Council Conclusions, 27 June 2014, EUCO 79/14, Annex 1.

[80] European Commission President Juncker himself took notice of this Strategic Agenda when delivering his speech in front of the European Parliament to obtain its vote of approval. See Jean-Claude Juncker, Speech 'A New Start for Europe: My Agenda for Jobs, Growth and Democratic Change', Strasbourg, 15 July 2014 (outlining his political agenda acknowledging that he will also 'draw on the "Strategic Agenda for the Union in Times of Change", as adopted by the European Council ... and on the orientations that will be given by the European Parliament in the months to come'.).

And in subsequent meetings the European Council has continued to set the economic direction of EMU. At the same time, it is quite significant that in unveiling its flagship initiative to create a €315 billion European Fund for Strategic Investments (EFSI) the new European Commission explicitly asked the European Council to endorse its initiative[81]—even though this was not formally necessary—confirming that the Commission itself believes that is the European Council which holds the keys for the adoption of any new major economic policy measure in the EU.[82] All this sheds some doubts on the potentials of the politicisation of the President of the European Commission to transform by itself the EMU system of governance.

VI. THE STRENGTHENING OF THE PRESIDENT OF THE EUROPEAN COUNCIL

A second development which has recently taken place in the system of governance of the EU and the Eurozone is the incremental strengthening of the President of the European Council (and of the Euro Summit). As mentioned in Section II, the Lisbon Treaty introduced the figure of semi-permanent President of the European Council, breaking with the tradition of having the European Council presidency rotate every six months between the member states as the presidency of the Council.[83] Yet, the Lisbon Treaty designed a fairly limited role for the President, and, rejecting the wish of President Giscard d'Estaing at the time of the European Convention, it entitled him to head only the European Council—and not the EU as such.[84] Moreover, according to Article 15 TEU, the President is to be elected by qualified majority by the heads of states and government congressed in the European Council, and can be removed by them according to the same procedure in the event of an impediment or a serious misconduct. Unlike institutions such as the Parliament,[85] or (generally) the Commission,[86] which are elected for a five-year term, the President remains in office for a term of two and a half years, renewable only once. And he is empowered to act more as a chairman of that institution rather than as an executive leader. These same features were reproduced by the Fiscal Compact in designing the presidency of the Euro Summit.[87]

[81] See European Commission, Communication 'An Investment Plan for Europe', 26 November 2014, COM(2014) 903 final, 6 (stating that '[t]he European Council is invited to endorse the setting up of the [EFSI]'), 13 (stating that '[t]he European Council is invited to endorse the overall approach'), 16 (stating that '[t]he Commission invites the European Council … to endorse the Plan with all its strands').

[82] See European Council Conclusions, 18 December 2014, EUCO 237/14, para 1 (endorsing the EFSI).

[83] See Art 16(9) TEU (setting rotating presidency for the Council).

[84] See further F Fabbrini, 'States Equality vs States Power' (n 33) 9.

[85] See Art 14(3) TEU (stating that '[t]he members of the European Parliament shall be elected for a term of five years').

[86] See Art 17(3) TEU (stating that '[t]he Commission's term of office shall be five years'). But see Art 17(8) TEU (stating that 'the European Parliament may vote a motion of censure to the Commission').

[87] Art 12 Fiscal Compact.

Nevertheless, the first President of the European Council, Herman van Rompuy—a former Prime Minister of Belgium, who was elected for two and a half years in November 2009,[88] and renewed for a second mandate in March 2012,[89]—made inroads into consolidating the position of the presidency, even beyond the letter of the treaties.[90] Otherwise, the heads of state and government of the Eurozone decide to elect Van Rompuy also as President of the Euro Summit in March 2012,[91] thus entrusting him an important institutional role in coordinating action between the Eurozone and the EU at large. As Henri de Waele and Hansko Broeksteeg have maintained, President Van Rompuy has 'succeeded in becoming an influential actor in his own right, through a dutiful exercise of his official powers, clever exploitation of some "grey zones", and tactful dealing with the Union's other institutional players'.[92] In particular, President Van Rompuy skillfully invested himself with important responsibilities in the governance of EMU, coordinating and steering the work of two task forces which prepared the road map of the legal and policy responses to the euro crisis by the EU institutions and the member states.[93]

The incremental strengthening of the position of the President of the European Council and the Euro Summit signals an interesting development within the form of government of the EU and the Eurozone, with possible implications on the equilibria within the EU intergovernmental institutions. In fact, at the handover ceremony with his successor—Donald Tusk, the former Prime Minister of Poland, who was elected in August 2014 as the second President of the European Council,[94] and, simultaneously, as President of the Euro Summit[95]—Van Rompuy affirmed that the 'President of the European Council represents the Union as a whole'.[96] Although technically this is incorrect, since as just said Article 15 TEU only vests in the President of the European Council the role of representing the European Council,[97] the statement signals a push towards a kind of presidentialisation of EU governance. Nevertheless, the prospects for such a development remain limited under the current constitutional arrangement. As Van Rompuy himself put it, the President of the European Council (and of the Euro Summit) enjoys very limited formal powers under the treaties, and his main task is to listen

[88] European Council, Press Release, 19 November 2009.

[89] European Council, Press Release, 1 March 2012, EUCO 37/12.

[90] See also the contribution of U Puetter, ch 14 in this volume.

[91] Euro area Heads of State and Government, Statement, 2 March 2012.

[92] H De Waele and H Broeksteeg, 'The Semi-Permanent European Council Presidency: Some Reflections on the Law and Early Practice' (2012) 49 *Common Market Law Review* 1039, 1070.

[93] See Report of the Task Force of the European Council, 'Strengthening Economic Governance in the EU', 21 October 2010, and President Final Report (n 61).

[94] European Council Conclusions, 30 August 2014, EUCO 163/14, para 2.

[95] Euro area Heads of State and Government, Statement, 30 August 2014.

[96] H Van Rompuy, Speech, Brussels, 1 December 2014, EUCO 257/14.

[97] See text accompanying n 84.

to the heads of states and government and to build trust between them.[98] In fact, the mode of election of the President makes him fundamentally dependent upon his peers within the European Council.[99]

Elsewhere I have advanced a comprehensive proposal on how to build upon the incremental expansion of the role of the President of the European Council and to reform the presidency by endowing it with the necessary power and legitimacy to take authoritative decisions for the EU as a whole.[100] As I have endeavored to explain, a President vested with adequate executive power, and elected through a popular democratic process (able to account for the asymmetries characterising a Union of states and citizens), would offer an adequate check to prevent the dynamics of inter-state domination that have been brought to the fore during the euro crisis. At the same time, an elected presidency could create a genuine forum for democratic competition and contestation on the agenda of the EU. The proposal to strengthen the role of the President of the European Council would be consistent with a logic of separation of powers in the EU, where the executive and the legislature act as separate institutions checking and balancing each other.[101] It goes without saying, however, that many challenges would surround such a blueprint for institutional reform—and ultimately a revision of the EU treaties would be warranted to this end.

VII. CONCLUSION: THE ROAD FORWARD

As this chapter has explained, since the eruption of the euro crisis, the EU heads of state and government congressed in the European Council, and the Euro Summit, have moved to the forefront of the system of governance of the EU and the Eurozone. Although the role of intergovernmental institutions in the governance of EMU found its roots in the Maastricht compromise, with the decision taken at that time to integrate areas of core state sovereignty but without delegating new powers to supranational authorities, the euro crisis and the responses to it proved to be a watershed in the institutional system of the EU and the Eurozone: the European Council, and now the Euro Summit, have emerged as the new centre of EU politics, sideling the other EU institutions, and centralising all key

[98] H Van Rompuy, 'Looking Back, Looking Forward' Speech at the Conference 'The State of the Union' Accademia dei Lincei, Rome, 7 November 2014 (stating that on the basis of the treaties 'the job description and formal competence of [the] President are rather vague, even meagre' and claiming that in his experience '[b]uilding trust is ... perhaps the most important task of a European Council President'.).

[99] See P Craig, *The Treaty of Lisbon* (Oxford, Oxford University Press, 2010) 117 (stating that the current 'appointment procedure for the Presidency of the European Council places the power firmly in the hands of that body'.).

[100] F Fabbrini, 'Austerity, the European Council and the Institutional Future of the EU: A Proposal to Strengthen the President of the European Council' (2015) 22 *Indiana Journal of Global Legal Studies* 29.

[101] See S Fabbrini, *Which European Union? Europe After the Euro-Crisis* (Cambridge, Cambridge University Press, 2015) ch 8.

policy decisions on how to tackle the euro crisis and put the EMU on a stronger footing. Nevertheless, the EU system of executive federalism has given rise to multiple problems of effectiveness and legitimacy. In particular, as this chapter has pointed out, an intergovernmental framework for decision-making has opened the door to dynamics of inter-state domination, with larger and more powerful EU member states able to impose their preferences, and entrench their strength, vis-à-vis smaller, economically weaker ones.

Growing awareness exists among top national and supranational policy-makers on the limitations of the current system of EMU governance—but much uncertainty persists on how the EU and the Eurozone should be reformed. At the same time, new institutional dynamics are taking place in the EU and the Eurozone, as a result of the growing politicisation of the presidency of the European Commission, and the incremental strengthening of the presidency of the European Council (and Euro Summit). But at the moment none of these dynamics seems to be able to bring about a real change to the existing EU intergovernmental system of governance. Yet the need for a more effective and legitimate executive government for the EU and the Eurozone is an issue that can no longer be postponed, given the rising levels of popular discontent, as evident by the surge of extreme, anti-system parties both in national and EU elections.[102] The EU and the Eurozone need strong, responsive institutions which can give voice to the peoples of our Union of states and citizens—because when voice is lacking, exit becomes the solution. This chapter has sought to identify possible scenarios in the reform of the EU institutional system. But it has acknowledged that any further step in this direction would imply a revision of the EU treaties—which is never an easy road.[103]

Nevertheless, there is some reason for optimism in looking ahead. The Fiscal Compact, in fact, includes a provision—inserted under the pressure of the delegates of the European Parliament (who joined the negotiations of the treaty as observers, despite not being involved in drafting it)[104]—which reads that:

> Within five years, at most, of the date of entry into force of this Treaty, on the basis of an assessment of the experience with its implementation, the necessary steps shall be taken, in accordance with the Treaty on the European Union and the Treaty on the Functioning of the European Union, with the aim of incorporating the substance of this Treaty into the legal framework of the European Union.[105]

The Fiscal Compact introduces an obligation for the EU member states that signed that treaty to find ways to bring back the content of the treaty into the law of the EU by 1 January 2018. Because of the nature of some of the legal innovations set

[102] See N Scicluna, 'Politicization without Democratization: How the Eurozone Crisis is Transforming EU Law and Politics' (2014) 12 *International Journal of Constitutional Law* 545.

[103] See Art 48 TEU (requiring unanimity to change the EU treaties).

[104] See European Parliament, Press Release, 'Fiscal Union: EP Representatives "Cautiously Optimistic"', 26 January 2012 (reporting role of European Parliament negotiators in influencing the drafting of the Fiscal Compact).

[105] Art 16 Fiscal Compact.

by the Fiscal Compact, this implies the necessity to amend the EU treaties—thus creating a window of opportunity for a comprehensive institutional reform of the EU.[106]

The European Parliament has '[i]nsist[ed] that the contracting parties fully respect their commitment to integrate, within five years at the latest, the [Fiscal Compact] into the EU treaties and ask[ed] for the remaining weaknesses of the Treaty of Lisbon to be tackled on this occasion'.[107] At the same time, German Chancellor Merkel has prominently argued in favour of a comprehensive constitutional revision of the EU treaties, vowing to put the Eurozone on more solid grounds and proposing new transfer of (surveillance) powers towards reformed EU authorities.[108] These high-level legal and political commitments towards treaty change open an important opportunity to deliberate anew about the EU institutional architecture—and possibly also to accomplish other needed reforms for EMU.[109] As Habermas has argued, it is time for the EU and the Eurozone to replace intergovernmental governance with a real form of transnational democracy.[110] Executive federalism must give way to executive government. Nevertheless, the important question, once more, remains 'whether societies of men are really capable or not, of establishing good government from reflection and choice, or whether they are forever destined to depend, for their political constitutions, on accident and force'.[111]

[106] See further F Fabbrini, 'Austerity' (n 100) 88 (discussing incentives for the EU member states in reforming the system of governance of the EU at the occasion of the domestication of the Fiscal Compact).

[107] See European Parliament Resolution 'On the European Council meeting of 30 January 2012', 2 February 2012, P7_TA(2012)0023, para 7.

[108] See A Merkel, Speech, Berlin, 18 December 2013 (stating inter alia that 'Wir müssen, wenn die vertraglichen Grundlagen nicht ausreichen, Verträge eben auch weiterentwickeln'.).

[109] See eg F Fabbrini, 'From Fiscal Constraints to Fiscal Capacity: The Future of EMU and its Challenges' in F Fabbrini et al (eds), *The Constitutionalization of European Budgetary Constraints* (Oxford, Hart Publishing, 2014) 399 (making the case for fiscal capacity in the EMU).

[110] Habermas, *The Crisis of the European Union* (n 1) 12.

[111] *The Federalist Papers* No 1 (Hamilton).

Index

www.ingramcontent.com/pod-product-compliance
Lightning Source LLC
LaVergne TN
LVHW052246200926
848481LV00002B/286
* 9 7 8 1 5 0 9 9 1 6 5 6 6 *